Philosophical Reasoning:
Critical Essays
by
Prof. N.G. Kulkarni

Philosophical Reasoning

Critical Essays on
Issues in Metaphysics, Language,
Logic, Ethics and Indian Philosophy

by
Prof. N.G. Kulkarni

Edited by
Geeta Ramana

Suryodaya Books

Cataloging in Publication Data – DK

[Courtesy: D.K. Agencies (P) Ltd. <docinfo@dkagencies.com>]

Kulkarni, N. G. (Narayan Govind), 1931-2011, **author**.
Philosophical reasoning : critical essays on issues in metaphysics, language, logic, ethics and Indian philosophy by Prof. N.G. Kulkarni / edited by Geeta Ramana.

pages cm
Includes bibliographical references (pages).

ISBN 13: 9788192570259

1. Metaphysics. 2. Language and languages – Philosophy. 3. Truth. 4. Logic. 5. Language and logic. 6. Philosophy, Indic. I. Ramana, Geeta, editor. II. Title.

DDC 110 23

ISBN 13: 978-81-925702-5-9
First published in India, 2015

Cover design by Prajakti Pai

Printed and published by:
Suryodaya Books
'*Suryodaya*', D-36A/1, Mohan Garden
Najafgarh Road, New Delhi – 110 059
Phone: (011) 2535 3435

Distributed by:
D.K. Printworld (P) Ltd.
Regd. Office: *Vedaśrī*, F-395, Sudarshan Park
(Metro Station: Ramesh Nagar), New Delhi – 110 015
Phones: (011) 2545 3975, 2546 6019; *Fax*: (011) 2546 5926
e-mail: indology@dkprintworld.com
Website: www.dkprintworld.com

Foreword

PROFESSOR N.G. Kulkarni was an important philosopher of contemporary India who made significant contributions to the tradition of analytical philosophy. For him philosophical analysis was not just an academic movement to be studied, but a way of thinking to be practised. He saw it as a methodological apparatus to be applied to any philosophical issue arising in Western or Indian contexts. Though Prof. Kulkarni was a man of reason, he might not have liked to call himself a rationalist in the popular sense of the term, as pointed out in the 'Introduction' to the section on 'Indian Philosophy', by Prof. Shubhada Joshi. Though he was a secular thinker and always disfavoured other-worldly metaphysics, he was not an extreme materialist. On the question of the existence of God, he was an agnostic, 'a timid fence sitter by definition', as he describes himself. However, his agnosticism was not a mark of timidity, but helped bolster his credentials as a philosopher. He preferred to 'sit on the fence' because he saw dangers on both the sides and correctly did not fall prey dogmatically to either the believer's or the disbeliever's side for any convenient or 'pragmatic' reason. To battle constantly with dogmas and remain in a state of enlightened ignorance and uncertainty require a different kind of courage which he had. In this sense he lived a life worthy of a philosopher.

Among the ancient Indian philosophical traditions, early Buddhism attracted him the most. Prof. Kulkarni was so fascinated by some of its insights that he praised the Buddha as *jagad-guru*. Yet he did not become a Buddhist, which makes him a true philosopher. He was fascinated by Russell, Wittgenstein, Dummett and many others, but refrained from becoming their camp-follower. He was always concerned centrally with the arguments, not the arguer.

He paid respect to all philosophers by critically analysing their arguments and hence though he honoured them all, he did not idolize any.

This collection contains a range of articles from highly technical ones such as those on many-valued logic, to the less technical but socially more relevant articles such as 'Freedom and Violence'. It contains a few articles giving a lucid exposition of the field of inquiry under consideration, for example, the article surveying 'Philosophical Analysis' and the one on the 'Definition, Nature and the Scope of Ethics'. But most of the other articles in this collection are argumentative, and not expository in character. In his argumentative writings he is not always a 'fence sitter'; in most cases he is a traveller, who takes his reader on an intellectual journey, to reach a destination through arguments and counter-arguments and also help the reader to look beyond the destination and enlarge one's own horizon. In some articles he takes the reader up to a dead end and indicates how the route does not lead to the destination and how one has to take some other route. Sometimes it is as if he were shepherding the reader safely through a jungle, battling the dangerous implications of theories behaving like beasts, or skirting the treacherous slopes of fallacies. In any case the reader finds the intellectual journey revealing as it enriches her knowledge about the philosophical geography of concepts.

Despite Prof. Kulkarni's sustained involvement in critical argumentation, he never resorted to negative polemics or *vitaṇḍā,* as his arguments always had a constructive character. He offered a critical examination of different views as a means of expressing his own philosophical standpoint or inclinations.

Prof. Kulkarni takes definite stands on different philosophical issues. Thus he argues that F.H. Bradley did not succeed in bringing out a paradox or contradiction in accepting relations. Against the coherence theory of truth he argues for the existence of belief-independent facts. He argues against the physicalism of Carnap and other positivists. But he does not adhere to Cartesian dualism or to Idealism. Here his position seems to be sympathetic to the Buddhist dualism of bodily and mental strands (*rūpa* and *nāma*). Sometimes he is ready to accept the causal dependence of mental phenomena on the brain, but he is critical of Searle's position that mental phenomena are just features of the brain. He is ready to accept the brain–mind identity theory in some form, but not in every form. For instance he does not accept Armstrong's view that the brain–mind identity can allow the logical possibility of a disembodied self. His position (to put it simplistically) appears to me to be a via media between Buddhism and Cārvāka.

He appreciates A.J. Ayer on the question of personal identity, which for him cannot be based either entirely or primarily on bodily continuity. He also raises doubts about memory as a criterion of personal identity and expresses dissatisfaction regarding the Buddhist conception of personal identity which reduces the self to a causal series of states of consciousness.

Prof. Kulkarni's writings contain his clear positions on major logical and epistemological issues. He criticizes for instance, the behaviouristic analysis of attitudinal propositions. On the question of the traditional definition of knowledge, he claims that Edmund Gettier's counter-examples do not make a serious threat to it, though the threat of infinite regress to the concept of empirical knowledge remains. On the question of truth he criticizes both 'sentences' and 'propositions' as valid candidates of the ascription of a truth-value and regards 'beliefs' to be the proper candidates, as also found in the early writings of Bertrand Russell and G.E. Moore. Moreover, he supports correspondence theory of truth as against other theories. Having explained and discussed three different forms of relativism, he argues for his rival view that there are belief-independent facts which we can ascertain by agreed procedures. To dispense with a world independent not only of our hopes and fears but also of our beliefs and disbeliefs is to invite disaster. He questions Putnam's proposal of constructing an alternative logic for Quantum Mechanics, which jettisons the distributive law. While discussing Dummett's theory of meaning, he also deals with the question of alternative logics and comments that they supplement, rather than supplant the simple and yet universally valid classical logic. In fact, he is critical of alternative logics in general. For him, to reject logical principles to solve problems such as future contingent statements and the indeterminacy principle is to go about ones business like the fictitious Chinaman described by Charles Lamb, who burnt down his house to roast his pig. Through some of his articles on morality he underlines the role of universalizability, impersonality and anti-authoritarianism in moral judgement and moral life.

Prof. Kulkarni was greatly fascinated by early Buddhism most, probably because of its analytical approach. One of the simplest but not easiest parts of the analytical method is separating issues, not mixing them up. What Prof. Kulkarni deeply appreciated in the Buddha was his separation of the existential problems of human life – those of human suffering and emancipation – from the metaphysical problems. The Buddha's attitude towards the so-called unanswerable questions (*avyākṛta-praśna*s) becomes his central analytical concern. Prof. Kulkarni maps the pragmatic as well as deeper theoretical grounds for the Buddha's silence on such questions. He also appreciates the Buddha's ethical approach. He finds in Buddhist ethics an egalitarian, liberal and non-authoritarian attitude. Prof. Kulkarni also has certain reservations about some Buddhist theories, such as those of momentariness and personal identity. He makes a short but striking comparison between the Buddhist path towards emancipation and Patañjali's Yoga. In the paper on the concept of *sthitaprajña*, titled, 'The Ideal of the Sthitaprajña: Some Platitudes and Some Paradoxes', Prof. Kulkarni gives an interpretation of the *Gītā*, centering on *karma-yoga*, which according to him can stand without metaphysical presuppositions of God and *karma* and is implicit in other forms of *yoga* as well. I have given above just some specimens of his views in a rather simplified form.

The interpretations and arguments Prof. Kulkarni proposes are definitely exciting, thorough and strong. They are based on his vast reading, analytical grasp and philosophical imagination. Nevertheless, it is possible that a critical reader may disagree with some of them. In fact, Prof. Kulkarni would have welcomed such disagreements. Just as he honoured philosophers by analysing and examining their arguments, the proper way of paying tribute to him would be to continue the debate over the issues discussed by him. Dr Geeta Ramana, his student and colleague, has done a good service to the cause of philosophy by compiling his papers and creating an opportunity for a meaningful critical engagement with the themes he has explored and the arguments he has advanced.

Pradeep P. Gokhale

Preface

NGK as Prof. N.G. Kulkarni was fondly known was a strong intellectual force in the academic circles of college and university life. He was a man of few words but clear opinions. Many will remember him as an energetic participant in the meetings of the Bombay Philosophical Society as well as a visiting faculty at the Department of Philosophy where he taught postgraduate students. Indeed faculty members too loved to attend his lectures and it is indeed my privilege, as a student of Prof. Kulkarni as well as faculty at the Department of Philosophy, University of Bombay, to be able to contribute to the preservation of decades of his reflections on philosophy.

Several papers of Prof. Kulkarni have been collated to present them under four themetic sections: Metaphysics; Logic, Truth and Language; Religion and Ethics; and Indian Philosophy. These reflect his journey from early to later interests, as Prof. Pradeep Gokhale has observed, and which I also adopt. I hope that the 'Introductions' before each section help in mapping important philosophical issues that continue to be of debatable interest in the diverse areas of academic philosophy.

Most of the writings in this collection are from his articles earlier published in philosophical journals and magazines, as well as papers presented in seminars and conferences.

Unfortunately one is not able to completely vouch for the exact edition or year of a particular reference, since Prof. Kulkarni continued his passion for philosophical reflection in the older, more orthodox fashion of thinking without paying too much attention to exact referencing details and concentrating more on content than form. I have however provided detailed information of sources as available on the internet, J.N. Library, University of Bombay and from his personal collection, for the benefit of readers and scholars who may retrace for more accurate references.

This book is also unusual in bringing out not only the thoughts of a sound academic philosopher who understood the demands of the contemporary socio-political world and the need for situating traditional ideas in them, but also the thinker as a person and a good honest man of integrity. Reminiscences by son, Sudhir Kulkarni and wife, Mrs N.G. Kulkarni, Dr S.K. Ookerjee, Prof. Rita Doctor, have made this a memorable edition for all those who respected and loved 'the teacher who taught without teaching'.

It has been a matter of serendipity to have discovered that the late Prof. S.K. Ookerjee had indeed penned his thoughts as soon as we requested him to contribute to this collection of essays. His observations truly offer an insightful glimpse into the nature of Prof. Kulkarni's very versatile mind.

The essays in this book are a good companion to understanding philosophy and philosophical reasoning. The diversity of topics reflects a multi-faceted mind capable of viewing the philosophical landscape, at times with an eagle eye, at times with an ant's firm and determined struggle to reach to an end, no matter how many detailed and elaborate steps it may take. If this edition helps readers understand the nature of philosophical problems then indeed our efforts shall have truly contributed in taking forward the legacy of Prof. Kulkarni and there can be no better tribute to this extraordinary teacher, philosopher and human being.

Geeta Ramana
Editor, Associate Professor,
Department of Philosophy,
University of Mumbai.

Contents

Abbreviations

CPR	*Critique of Pure Reason*, Kant
PI	*Philosophical Investigations*, Wittgenstein
Tractatus	*Tractatus-Logico-Philosophicus*, Wittgenstein
BG	*Bhagavad-Gītā*
SBE	Sacred Books of the East Series

Acknowledgement

WE acknowledge with gratitude the financial support provided by the University of Bombay. This tribute to Prof. N.G. Kulkarni is made possible primarily due to the enthusiastic and proactive support of Mrs N.G. (Vaidehi) Kulkarni whose initial contribution helped kick-start the process of collating this special edition. Many thanks to Mrs Shraddha Lad who volunteered and diligently typed the manuscript during her spare hours.

We are indebted to Prof. S.E. Bhelke, Prof. Pradeep Gokhale and Prof. Nirmalya N. Chatterjee for diligently proofreading the final manuscript, especially those that contained logical notations.

Heartfelt appreciation to Prof. Pradeep Gokhale for writing the Foreword and providing valuable suggestions that have enhanced the quality of editing this vast collection of articles.

Prof. Shubhada Joshi, Prof. Rita Doctor, Prof. S.K. Ookerjee, along with wife, Mrs Vaidehi N. Kulkarni and son, Sudhir Kulkarni have indeed enriched this volume by their reminiscences and insightful revelations. Special thanks to Prof. Shehernaz Nalwalla for generously contributing her expertise and recommending crucial inputs that have helped in maintaining a consistent and cohesive structure to this book. Finally, the Kulkarni family deserves all credit and merit for magnanimously sharing the poems penned by Prof. Kulkarni with the readers.

We are thankful to Prajakti Pai for an imaginative and creative cover design, symbolizing the abstract world of philosophy that is captured by the intellectual eye. We are also appreciative of the personal involvement of Mr Susheel Mittal and Mr Rajendra Agarwal of Suryodaya Books whose respect for academicians and scholars has enabled the publication of many a book on philosophy.

We are indeed deeply grateful to the following journals and institutions which had initially published Prof. N.G. Kulkarni's articles and have generously given consent to reprint them in this volume for the benefit of students and the larger academic community.

1. Somaiya Publications
2. Indian Philosophical Quarterly
3. Jadavpur Journal of Philosophy
4. The Radical Humanist
5. The Indian Council of Philosophical Research
6. Journal of the Indian Academy of Philosophy
7. Journal of the Philosophical Association (Now defunct)
8. The Philosophical Quarterly, Edinburgh
9. Datta Lakshmi Trust (Now defunct)

I would like to acknowledge the initiative, cooperation and support I received from the followings in bringing out this prestigious volume:

- Dr Subhashchandra E. Bhelke, Former (Retd.) Head of Department of Philosophy, University of Pune, Director, K.J. Somaiya Centre for Studies in Jainism, Mumbai.
- Prof. Nirmalya Chatterjee, Department of Philosophy, Rabindra Bharati University, Kolkata.
- Prof. Rita Doctor, Former (Retd.) Head of the Department of Philosophy, Ruia College, Mumbai, Counsellor, Institute of Chemical Technology (ICT), Mumbai.
- Dr Pradeep P. Gokhale, Dr B.R. Ambedkar Research Professor, Central University of Tibetan Studies, Sarnath (Varanasi).
- Dr Shubhada Joshi, Former Head of the Department of Philosophy, University of Mumbai.
- Mr Sudhir Kulkarni, Son of late Prof. N.G. Kulkarni.

- Mrs Vaidehi (*nee* Sulekha) Kulkarni, wife of late Prof. N.G. Kulkarni.
- Mrs. Shraddha Lad, Typist, Department of Philosophy, University of Mumbai.
- Prof. Shehernaz Nalwalla, Department of Philosophy, Vice-Principal, Wilson College, Mumbai.
- (Late) Prof. Sheriyar K. Ookerjee, Former Head of the Department of Philosophy, Wilson College, Mumbai.
- Prof. Srilakshmi Peddada, Adjunct Faculty, SVKM's Pravin Gandhi College of Law, Mumbai.

Geeta Ramana

A Brief Life Sketch

PROF. Narayan Govind Kulkarni was born on 12 March 1931 in the Bijapur district of Karnataka and had ancestral roots in Belgaum, a border town of Maharashtra and Karnataka. He was associated throughout his career with the University of Bombay (now Mumbai) from where he first graduated in Philosophy in 1952 followed by a postgraduate degree in Philosophy in 1954 for which he was awarded the Chancellor's Gold Medal.

He was awarded the British Council Bursary to Oxford in 1963 which gave him the opportunity to work with the famous philosopher A.J. Ayer, then Wykeham Professor of Logic at Oxford. In his tenure spanning over four decades, Prof. Kulkarni endeared himself to thousands of students of philosophy as he taught undergraduates and postgraduates progressively as Fellow and later as Senior Lecturer at the Wilson College (1952-60) and finally as Head of the Department of Philosophy at the K.J. Somaiya College of Arts and Commerce in Mumbai (1960-91).

Post his retirement in 1991, he continued to actively mentor postgraduate students at the Department of Philosophy, University of Bombay until 2003. Prof. NGK, as he was often addressed by his fellow colleagues and students, pursued his academic interests that culminated in publications in national and international journals as well as presentations at various academic fora. His research interest focused on early Buddhism, Western Epistemology, Meta-ethics and Analytical Philosophy.

With his command over the subject and impressive academic credentials, he was one of the country's leading experts for various UGC and ICPR seminars and workshops, and was invited by universities of Pune, Goa, Lucknow, Calcutta and Delhi. He was invited by the eminent scholar Prof. K.C. Bhattacharya to Indian Academy of Philosophy in 1969. He was Fellow and Visiting Professor under the UGC scheme for Advanced Studies at the Jadavpur University in 2002. In November 2010, still active at the age of 79 and as endearing to the philosophical community, Prof. Kulkarni was felicitated by the Maharashtra Tattvajnyan Parishad.

Prof. Kulkarni passed away in Pune on 10 February 2011 leaving a rich legacy of research publications and articles that focused on both the traditional and contemporary approaches to philosophy.

This book is an attempt to preserve for posterity the unique contributions of Prof. Kulkarni which we hope will inspire several generations of philosophy lovers.

> It is not cleverness or learning that makes the philosopher; it is a certain spirit; openness of mind, thoroughness of work, and hatred of superficiality.[1]

[1] Prof. S.K. Ookerjee wrote these memorable lines on a book gifted to Prof. Kulkarni on the occasion of his winning the Chancellor's Gold Medal in 1954.

Reminiscences

Prof. N.G. Kulkarni: The Man I Loved

Vaidehi Kulkarni

As a family we are proud to be closely related to an unusually bright and upright human being. His brilliance in academics and philosophy is better judged by subject experts. However, having heard unreserved and unstinting praise from subject experts, we conclude that he was amongst the very best in his profession. We were fortunate to experience, living in close proximity, his professional brilliance, which was only a reflection of an astute and analytical mind.

To have him as husband was indeed very fortunate. As a husband he was extremely tender-hearted, considerate and expressed his sentimental and romantic nature by composing a few poems that have been included in this volume. He saw to it that I was very happy and comfortable and did not allow whatever difficulties that came, to affect me. My parents and other relatives used to tell me that I must have had a mountain of good deeds to my credit from my previous births to have had such an extraordinarily loving husband. Indeed on the eve of my marriage to him, I saw in a dream, seven suns on the horizon of Bombay's Hanging Gardens. Also, significantly, just before he expired I saw a dream of the sun getting covered slowly but surely till it was completely eclipsed. He was indeed the sun of my life. Unfortunately, now, the sun has set. Time hasn't really healed my loss. I miss him, every moment of my life.

Prof. N.G. Kulkarni: My Father

Sudhir Kulkarni

My father was born in 1931 on 12 March to a school teacher in Bijapur, a small town in Karnataka. His family had ancestral roots in Belgaum and his early years were spent in an ordinary municipal school and in later years he almost paid for his own education by winning a number of scholarships. He came to Bombay in 1950 for higher studies and excelled by winning the Bombay University Chancellor's Gold Medal for Master of Arts (MA) in 1954 (amongst other prizes), beating even the better scoring Maths students to it. Even as an undergraduate he started teaching in Wilson College. He got married in 1957. It was a love-marriage with one of his students – my mother. In 1963-64, he was sent to Oxford, England by the British Council to learn under Prof. A.J. Ayer, the famous British philosopher. After a few years, he accepted a better offer by the Somaiyas that suited him financially since he had the responsibility of a big family on him. In order to send more money to his parents to support their big family in his native town, he lived simply (as was his nature), cut down on expenditure, made sacrifices like even walking from the railway station (Andheri) to our residence, 3-4 km away. He supported his family till they became financially independent. Though he cut down expenditure on himself and my mother, he never compromised on the basic needs of his children. Consequently, I had a splendid childhood. I still remember the absolutely delicious cheese toast and other sandwiches that he himself prepared and indulged us whenever we demanded them. I owe whatever good points that I have, to the morally correct, intellectually stimulating atmosphere created by my father and the emotionally secure affection of my mother.

There were so many deep phrases that he had coined like 'It is simpler to tell the truth', 'Honesty cannot be selective' and 'Nothing is more audible than a whisper'. As per the situation, he would come up with eloquent phrases. For instance, in my teenage I was so lackadaisical that he once remarked 'You are born out of place, out of time'. He then explained that I wasn't fit to be in a middle-class professor's home in present-day times but should have been born in earlier centuries to a nawāb or a king.

His English was highly outstanding. Once in my college days I and a friend disagreed about the exact meaning of a word. Finally I said that I would check with my father, who was the second best source that I knew. He then asked me who was the first and I said, 'the dictionary'. He was an agnostic. So he didn't believe in most of the traditions and rituals, though he was born to a highly orthodox and ritualistic mother. In spite of that, only because of the affection he had for his daughter-in-law (my wife Mrunal), he used to get flowers for her *pūjā* regularly and would sit through many religious functions only for her, though he did not in the least believe in them. He was extremely doting on his grandchildren, especially my first child Ishaan and composed a few poems on him.

Finally, not because he was my father, but I sincerely think that I have not met a more intelligent and mature person who also understood so well the nuances of the English language. The obituary we gave in the newspaper after him (reproduced in this book) tells it all. Though my father is no more, his mark is there – in some of the values that I feel strongly like integrity, self-respect and generosity. May his soul reach the exalted realms that it deserves.

The NGK: I Knew

Prof. Rita Doctor

The year was 1964. Though it was the beginning of the second term, we felt we were still new to the postgraduate class, interacting with students of other colleges, mentally trying to gauge their calibre and preparing a checklist of who would be the closest competitor! We were still trying to find our way through the maze of books and selected papers in the various journals – all recommended very enthusiastically by the faculty. Suddenly, a not-so-tall, slim man, dressed simply in a bush-coat, and a pair of trousers, walking at an unusually fast pace, entered the classroom; a multi-coloured cloth *jholī* hung from his shoulder. His opening remarks: 'Prof. Ms. Borde is not in good health, so I shall be taking you for Ross and Broad'.

My mind suddenly went back to the time (when still at the undergraduate level) I was first introduced to him at one of the Bombay Philosophical Society meetings (held at the Xaviers Institute of Education) by my professor, Ms. Rajam. 'Prof. Kulkarni has been a student of Wilson College', she said 'and later was on the staff. Now he heads the Department of Philosophy at Somaiya College.' He has been paid the highest compliment by his professor (Dr Lawande) who had publicly declared that 'the student has surpassed the teacher!' I had made a mental note of that and now sitting in the classroom, I knew what to expect! I was not wrong! Listening to his lectures was a treat! Be it Indian, Western, Classical, Modern, Postmodern, Logic, he knew it all! The names of reference books, sometimes the chapter numbers were rattled out as if they were written on the back of the palm!

The ideas came fast and so did the speech. One had to be completely alert to understand and comprehend all that was said, but the lectures made us think and prompted us to ask questions and he never got tired of answering them. Sometimes Socratic-like he would make provocative statements deliberately, so that discussions could take place. He had a very subtle sense of humour which would be missed if we were not alert enough! I always noticed that he never hurt or insulted a student even if the performance was mediocre. I have always appreciated that quality in him.

When I joined the teaching profession and needed a little guidance, he was one of the teachers (the others being Dr Ookerjee and Prof. Sinari) I would approach with the full confidence of getting the exact answers. Always open to listening to an alternate point of view and respecting it, was his strong point. Perhaps, the honourable exception was his strong objection to accepting Feminism as a part of philosophy! There he was merciless in his criticism.

An erudite scholar, affable, kind and approachable, it was his simplicity and forthright demeanour that endeared him to his students and colleagues alike. That is why we remember him with such affection!

For, to live in the minds of the students, is to be Alive – Always!

My Best Student

Prof. S.K. Ookerjee

N.G. Kulkarni was by far the brightest of the students I have taught. In fact, I would not hesitate to use the word 'brilliant' to describe his intellect.

During my long teaching career, I have had a handful of keen-witted students who grasped clearly the nature of philosophy and could argue philosophically, but Kulkarni was different from the very beginning, in that he came to the Bachelor of Arts (BA) philosophy class already equipped with quite an extensive acquaintance with philosophical literature. His special favourites at the time were Bertrand Russell and G.E. Moore (which he always pronounced to rhyme with 'boor'), and they remained so till the end. I found it difficult to understand how he could reconcile Russellian philosophy with a view that he expressed in perhaps the first paper he read at a college seminar, entitled 'Mystics: The Salt of the Earth'. Russell's *A Free Man's Worship* was a favourite book of his.

However, Kulkarni's achievement was not confined to his erudition. He could argue expertly and he was ever ready to challenge and combat what I said in my lectures. On one occasion, he and I had a bout about the Correspondence Theory of Truth, he arguing for it, and I, holding to the Comprehensive-Coherence Theory, very critical of it, while the other students in the class looked on not quite clear as to what was going on. I could never convince him that Coherence refers not only to a consistency between propositions but also between propositions and observed facts. Till the end, he maintained – as in his review of my book *Human Reason and Its Enemies* (perhaps the last piece he ever wrote) – that two consistently developed arguments could lead to contradictory conclusions, and that then the only way to decide between them would be to fall back on observation. I would respond that if two arguments reached opposite conclusions, we have to conclude that we have not so far yet reached the truth.

At times, however, he would hold on doggedly to his contention and keep repeating what he had said.

With Kulkarni in the class, always ready to pounce on the lecturer, I had to be extremely well prepared. In those days, Idealism was the accepted philosophy in the Wilson College Department of Philosophy, and F.H. Bradley was its patron saint. One day, Kulkarni shocked Dr Lawande (the head of the department) and me (his junior) by declaring that he totally rejected Bradley's philosophy and his key argument, the anti-relational argument. His critique of this argument was later published in the *Edinburgh Philosophical Quarterly* (1957). It provoked a response from A.C. Campbell, but I believe Campbell did not answer Kulkarni convincingly.

Although I remained a Bradleyian after Kulkarni's attack, it did make me more circumspect in my allegiance to that philosopher and certainly provided a certain ballast to my earlier enthusiasms. As he was far more familiar with recent philosophy than I was, with philosophers like Putnam and Davidson, I would consult him about their views and be guided by his knowledge.

Kulkarni was a simple and unassuming person, completely bereft of ostentation and pomposity. I always enjoyed his company immensely. He and his two very able co-students, Shirodkar and Tinaikar, would come to my house to discuss philosophy and also to listen to music (Adhik Shirodkar, became an eminent lawyer and S.S. Tinaikar later became Mumbai's Municipal Commissioner, entirely incorruptible and extremely firm). Kulkarni and I were often together at conferences and seminars. In 1971, we were both lecturing to the MA students at Margao, Goa. We had a great time. Kulkarni had never drunk any liquor and some of us convinced him that he could not come to Goa and not sip the famous *kājū* feni. Very reluctantly he agreed to taste it; he first sat on the bed, in case of any eventuality, and gingerly took a sip. He did not fancy it at all.

Kulkarni's almost childlike simplicity of nature sometimes made him reveal, rather embarrassingly, some of his very personal emotions. However, let nobody think that his friendly and ever-smiling exterior covered a weak spirit. There was a tough moral fibre underneath. He was outspoken and unafraid when required. When, for expressing certain opinions, I fell foul of the Principal of Wilson College and there was a possibility that I might be forced to resign, Kulkarni categorically told my colleagues in the department that if it came to that, they should all resign. And he would have done it. Similarly, he also annoyed the principal by expressing certain opinions at a staff meeting, with the result that the promise of a small raise in salary was withdrawn. Kulkarni said that if it was a question of speaking the truth vs. a salary increment, he knew what to choose. He left the college and became the Head of the Department of Philosophy at Somaiya College, serving there till he retired.

We got on very smoothly together, sharing knowledge, friendship and laughter. When the university started its Department of Philosophy in 1986, Kulkarni applied for the post of head. He was offered the second position, which he rejected, but he paid me a compliment by saying that had I been the head, he would have been willing to serve as my second.

I am very happy Prof. Kulkarni's writings are being published. I have listened, with profit, to Kulkarni reading many of these papers and I am quite sure that students of philosophy will find them of immense value. In fact, they have a value which extends beyond the university, to the wider reading public.

Poems Composed by Prof. N.G. Kulkarni

A Poem on His Wife (1)

My Thoughts of You

If my thoughts were birds,
I would send them through time and space,
To wing their way to your gentle heart,
And find in it their resting place.

If my thoughts had colour,
They would weave themselves into cloths,
To cover your queenly figure,
In the greenery of earth and the glory's of the sky.

If my thoughts were breezes,
They would bring you the scents of fields and oceans,
Play around your dear limbs with coolness,
And kiss them with the purest devotion.

If my thoughts were pictures,
They would steal under your eyelashes,
To dwell forever as living images
In the depths of your bright pupils.

If my thoughts had the power,
They would run as rain drops,
To cover the earth with grassy emerald,
For your white feet to walk on.

A Poem on His Wife (2)

A Prayer for Sulekha

Bright as a jewel, soft as a flower,
You walk through the world of chance and change,
Your hands and feet trace moving arcs;
And in the sweet gravity of the pensive hour,
You strike attitudes of unutterable grace.

I am at rest when you are near,
But when I contemplate the shifting world,
I am troubled and full of fear,
Then my agnostic is moved,
To a hesitant prayer;
May the sentinels of the eight quarters,
Guard my little Sulekha,
May she never feel the cruelties of heaven,
Or the mindless injustice of the human race
She should be wise, She should be brave,
Let dignity never depart from her gate,
And delight never leave her sweet face.

A Poem on His Grandson Ishaan (1)

Ishaan is today four,
May every year turn into a score,
And bring him hope and health,
Serene happiness surpassing wealth,
The great god who comes with calm seas,
Clear air and bright days, ever kind,
Grant him riches of the mind,
Greater than all gold and rubies.

13 September 1999

A Poem on His Grandson Ishaan (2)

On this sunny day in September,
Ishaan is six, frail as a flower,

Here's wishing him all that love desires,
Visible calm invisible power,
To shield him from all harm,
And take him from shadows into sunlight.

13 September 2001

In Memoriam

Once in a blue moon,
One amongst scores of thousands,
a person comes –
　So extraordinary,
　So compassionate,
　So brilliant,
　So pure,
　So solicitous,
　So full of goodness,
　So selfless. . . .
In other words – So great

In fond memory of the departed soul
from a very proud family – *February 2011*

I. Metaphysics

Introduction

Geeta Ramana

THE first three articles, 'Kant's Critique of Metaphysics', 'Bradley's Anti-relational Argument' and 'The Return of Coherence' draw on the difficulties of moving away from transcendence on the one hand and keeping a hold on the nature of internal relations that provide the grounds for a coherence theory of truth as well as an idealist metaphysics. Prof. Kulkarni deftly critiques this very assumption by bringing out the lacunae in Kant's antinomies as well as Bradley's argument based on the internality of relations.

He begins by sketching briefly Kant's critique of 'metaphysics' which cannot be separated from his critical philosophy. Interspersing the idea of the infinite in Indian philosophical literature, he lays bare the antinomy of time as having a beginning and an end; limited as well as endless. Kant, of course, refutes both the thesis as well as the antithesis and without a satisfactory definition of an infinite series. Prof. Kulkarni feels that he begs the question at issue. In discussing the strange idea that a series can have an end but no beginning, he describes this as a feeling of 'being tricked without knowing how'. We do not have the same feeling in contemplating a beginning but no end. And in a theistic context, though the conundrum continues, he sides with St. Aquinas (rather than Kant) in opting for a finite world on grounds of faith.

Arguments from natural theology are picked to show 'a logical lacuna' in Kant's account of the relation between the ontological and the cosmological arguments', treating them as it were, in isolation from those in the 'Metaphysics of Morals'. There is a need to reconcile 'God as a postulate of morality' and 'as a necessary condition for the existence of the world' and if the former holds good God need not be responsible for the existence of the world. One has therefore really not given any new anti-metaphysical argument and we have not really been able to mute the 'transcendental' voice.

Prof. Kulkarni's critique of Bradley's theory of internal relations is particularly sharp, not only because of an 'imprecise and inconsistent terminology' used by the latter, but more significantly because it does not contain any valid arguments. The analysis that 'all relations are self-contradictory' reveals the impossibility of such a situation (unless taken in the strictest logical sense of 'round squares'). There is an obvious circularity of moving from a non-relational absolute to the unreality of the relational structures, since one needs to prove inherent self-contradiction first to argue for the unreality of relations.

It is pointed that the unfortunate use of 'qualities' instead of 'qualified particulars' compounds the confusion that is made between 'distinction' and 'distinguishability'. One needs to distinguish, for example, between a quality and the particulars that manifest it. Prof. Kulkarni deflates Bradley's 'paradox of relations' argument showing that dependency of terms on relations does not lead to any vicious kind of regress and that dependency may be either in terms of causal or constitutive conditions. Thus a fundamental flaw in treating 'qualities' and 'relations' of the same order undermines the internality of relations and brings down Bradley's grand system of absolutism.

Prof. Kulkarni continues with his critique of the fundamental grounds for coherence and brings out the necessity for some form of experience in any justification for statements of truth, notwithstanding the demands of consistency and comprehensiveness. The relevance for belief – independent facts and unavoidability of transcendence in our conceptions of truth and knowledge – is a challenge and even without the need for system building, one can adjust to 'boundary conditions of experience' as Quine does. Amongst contemporary thoughts that question the scheme – content framework – Prof.

Kulkarni argues for the importance of the distinction between fact and belief, knowledge and reality.

The next two articles on 'Duality and Dualism' and 'Descartes' Philosophy of Mind: Its Contemporary Understanding' trace the philosophical problem of the mind–body relation starting from physicalist and identity theory and up to Searle's biological naturalism and Davidson's anomalous monism. The arguments throughout question the attempt to obliterate all phenomenological and thereby occurential accounts of experiences. It is pointed out that in fact even Dennet's philosophically heroic theory that converts all 'hard' problems of consciousness into 'soft' problems, needs to work out the 'dividing line' between the conscious and the preconscious in brain events. Further our judgements most often go far beyond the given. We still have no reasonable way of accounting for this purely on either physicalist or computational metaphors. Even Searle's brilliant thesis that takes the causal problem by its horns is deemed unsatisfactory as the problem of relating two distinct kinds of properties at the micro and macro levels remains, notwithstanding the observer-related dimension at the macro level. In a sub-section titled 'Beyond Behaviourism' Wittgenstein's arguments are analysed in great detail to show that 'they ultimately rest on a general scepticism concerning memory' and the motive in using ordinary language to recast or rather 'serve' ones philosophical purpose should be suspect.

Wittgenstein's notion of family resemblances is taken up next in 'Universals and Family Resemblance', Prof. Kulkarni remarks with insight that contrary to the general perception, Wittgenstein 'does not really leave everything as it is'. For example, the real problem with universals is not just the denial of essences over and above things being red nor the nominalist motivation in 'games have nothing in common except that they are called games'. Rather it is Wittgenstein's assertion that 'what different instances of a certain sort have in common is just their being instances of that sort'! This is an interesting observation that fits with Wittgenstein's distaste for engaging in any sort of theoretical tensions and investigating rather the fundamental source of philosophical 'puzzles'.

The problem with sense data that has occupied philosophers through centuries engages with Dr. Chubb's views on the same in the article, 'Are There Sense Data?'. In the process a very crucial and valuable point is made that one can present the problem with the relativity of perceptions without necessarily invoking either the notion of illusions or hallucinations. This means that 'one can introduce sense data without self contradiction and without errors of perception'. Now this is a remarkable move only because we cannot do away with perceptions nor negate their reality. We find Prof. Kulkarni's realist leanings in attempting to look at philosophical objects, in this case the humble tomato, as he puts it, 'in an extraordinary light'.

The final two articles of this section deal with one of the most discussed problems of personal identity in philosophical literature. Prof. Kulkarni, understandably, questions Strawson's traditional description of the mind–body problem as incoherent and points out that they are not self-contradictory, since we can and do discover and identify experiences. The underlying assumptions of both the Cartesian as well as the no-ownership theory depend on the sense of possession and this is the main point of Strawson's critique. Prof. Kulkarni feels that the Cartesian argument has not been addressed from the dualist standpoint. Merely asserting that one cannot ascribe experiences to oneself unless one can ascribe them to others begs the question at issue.

Strawson does provide an alternative to the mind–body problem; but does the main point of access to one's own experience and its implications get taken forward? Is Strawson's dogmatism in stating an inability to form any idea of oneself as a subject of experiences, true? Indeed, these are the questions that provoke Prof. Kulkarni to say finally that replacing the mind–body distinction with the distinction between *M* and *P* predicates does not really solve the problems of dualism.

In critically commenting on A.J. Ayer's arguments on personal identity Prof. Kulkarni endorses the importance of not only bodily criteria but also the need for 'the continuity of memory as a decisive criterion', given the various possibilities of dissociated consciousness and dilemmas related to multiple personalities.

We see that Prof. Kulkarni's strength is in analytically dissecting grounds of arguments, bringing out their implications and indirectly establishing the very views opposed by a particular philosopher.

1

Kant's Critique of Metaphysics*

> I have no wish to incur the reproach of picking petty quarrels with a genius to whom we must all look up with grateful awe.
>
> – Frege (In the course of expressing his disagreement with Kant on arithmetic but agreement on geometry)

I

KANT, like all great philosophers, has inspired divergent lines of philosophical development after his time. The most prominent (and the most unfortunate) was the idealism of Hegel. Then there were various moral theologies, attempts to found religion on morality – not to speak of attempt to found morality on religion. Then other pragmatic attempts like, the 'as if' philosophy which confined itself to the *Critique of Pure Reason*.** Pierce, we learn, read the *Critique of Pure Reason* everyday for two hours until he knew the whole of it by heart. Phenomenology and the various continental extravagances into which it entered as an element, owe something to him. His criticism of metaphysics received some attention after the positivist elimination of it and then he was bracketed with Hume, not just as his answerer, but as a fellow-worker who inaugurated a new enlightenment. If we confine our selves to the *Critique of Pure*

---

* Published in the special number (200 years of Kant), *Indian Philosophical Quarterly*, vol. XXXI, nos. 1-4, Journal of the Department of Philosophy, University of Pune, 2004.

** See Vaihinger Hans, The Philosophy of AS IF: A system of the theoretical, practical and religious fictions of mankind, Tr. by C.K. Ogden, Barnes and Noble, New York, 1968 (first published in English by Routledge and Kegan Paul, 1924).

Reason, the criticism amounts to total rejection. His general approach is not the same as Hume's whose dismissal of metaphysics is a remarkable anticipation of positivism of the Vienna circle albeit in a different terminology rooted in his 'psychological' method. But Kant's characterization of speculative metaphysics is no less severe. He writes:

> There is no polemic in the field of pure reason (speculative metaphysics). Both parties beat the air and wrestle with their own shadows, since they go beyond the limits of nature, where there is nothing that they can seize and hold with their dogmatic grasp. Fight as they may, the shadows which they cleave asunder grow together again forthwith, like the heroes of Valhalla to disport themselves anew in the bloodless contests.[1]

But the perception of him as a philosopher who provided a new and sound foundation for metaphysics, after decisively dismissing the delusions of 'transcendental metaphysics' was understandable, because that was precisely what he claimed to do. Not only are the negative conclusions of the *Critique of Pure Reason* supplemented by the positive ones of two later critiques but even in the first critique the noumenal order is accepted as an integral part of his critical philosophy. The use made of it is largely but not wholly negative. Kant is explicit that there can be no knowledge of noumena but only of phenomena. Absolute metaphysics is an attempt to gain a priori knowledge of noumena or things as they are in themselves, by using ideas of reason. By means of them it seeks to extend and complete our knowledge to reach the summit of it as it were. However, the proper use of the ideas of reason is regulative – to provide valuable guidelines to the investigation of phenomena.

Kant's rejection of 'transcendental metaphysics' is inextricably connected with the system of critical philosophy. Its architectonic is majestic in its sweep and the subtlety with which he elaborately works out intricate details of his arguments is impressive. An evaluation

---

1 Kant, *Critique of Pure Reason* (*CPR*), tr. J.M.D. Meiklejohn, Everyman's Library, 1972, 1991, p. 432.

of his critique of metaphysics, which he rejected with great patience and enormous subtlety, cannot be separated from an assessment of his critical philosophy. But an attempt should be made to single out, in general terms, some of his central ideas and their bearing on the metaphysical enterprise. For Kant all knowledge arises from the interaction of two distinct faculties – intuition (or sensibility) and thought or judgement. The former cannot be reduced to the latter as Leibnitz did when he regarded sense perception as confused thinking. Nor can the latter be reduced to the former as Hume seems to have done when he regarded thinking as the occurrence or arising of combinations and permutations of impressions and ideas (sensations and images) according to psychological law. The former is awareness of data or presentation. It is wholly receptive or passive. For knowledge to arise, the presentations must be regarded as representative of objects to which they are referred. The task of ordering and organizing the sense manifold is carried out in accordance with certain (a)priori concepts and principles which are innate to the human mind, in the sense that they are not abstracted from experience but are applied to it by the human mind. Without such ordering, object's cognition or knowledge is not possible. But even the awareness of presentations involves the forms of space and time which are a priori, that is, they are not abstracted from experience but are presupposed by it. They are indispensable forms of all presentations: 'time' of inner sense and 'space' of outer sense. But both the 'forms' of intuition and the 'categories' of the understanding are essentially principles of organization and give us the structure of a priori knowledge that we have in mathematics and physics. But if they are to give rise to knowledge, there must be presentation – the sense manifold, which arise in the human mind as a result of the action of the things-in-themselves. The 'forms' of intuition and the 'a priori concepts' of the understanding have application only to phenomena, that is presentations caused in our mind by things as they are or their appearances to us. If we try to extend them beyond the limits of possible experience and determine the nature of objectively existing reality by means of them, the result is intellectual disaster or transcendental illusion.

There are three bogus sciences to which this intellectually self-defeating attempt leads: rational psychology, rational cosmology and speculative metaphysics or natural theology. Of these the first is not of much contemporary interest. The other two deal with philosophical problems which have always been of interest not only to philosophers but to all reflective persons. Kant's treatment of them separates them more than they should be. For example, the cosmological argument for the existence of God and the fourth antimony discuss essentially the same problem. It is impossible in the course of an article to evaluate his critique of metaphysics without discussion of his project of critical philosophy and his peculiar brand of 'transcendental idealism'. I shall not, therefore, enter into such a discussion. That many lines of argumentation in the critique have been rendered untenable by subsequent developments in the field of knowledge is no surprise. The most serious is his dependence on the classification of proposition in traditional logic which is both confused and inadequate. Kant connects his categories and the (a)priori principle involving them, neatly (over neatly) with the heads and subdivision of this classification. The results are not happy and his claim to finality for the list of categories and related principles cannot be accepted. 'Transcendental Logic', the most important and difficult part of the critique, is most affected by this limitation in Kant's thinking. The 'Aesthetic' too contains arguments of uneven value and has been overtaken by developments in mathematics and physics. I shall not consider the implication of these developments for his philosophy even cursorily. Luckily many of the arguments of the dialectic stand on their own and can be considered on their merits.

The intellectual blind alleys into which we lead ourselves are not due to accidental errors or confusions which can be avoided with greater care. The tendency to overreach ourselves in using ideas of reason – which are not categories but arise from the attempt to extend the latter beyond the limits of possible experience – is built into the very structure of the human mind. Kant writes:

> There is therefore a natural and unavoidable dialectic of pure

> reason. Not that in which a bungler involves himself from want of requisite knowledge nor that which a sophist devises for the purpose of misleading us but that which is an inseparable adjunct of human reason.[2]

II

Though natural, and to persons of a certain temperament-irresistible, the attempt to acquire knowledge of reality by pure speculative reason is bound to result in worse than failure, viz., an intellectual impasse which manifests itself in the form of antinomies of reason. Kant sets forth elaborately, four antinomies – two mathematical and two dynamical. In each of them we are confronted with a choice between a thesis and an antithesis which are related to each other as contradictories; we must accept one of them and reject the other and yet both can be disproved, or proved indirectly through the refutation of the opposed statement. This is a pivotal part of the transcendental dialectic. Unless Kant's arguments or suitable reformulations of these can be sustained, the project to expose the transcendental illusion, once and for all, cannot be considered the last word on the subject as Kant apparently did. It is not my intention to discuss the antinomies at length. It is not necessary for my purpose nor am I equipped to do that (the best discussion of the topic I know of is in C.D. Broad's *Kant: An Introduction*).[3]

I shall select the first antinomy and argue that Kant's arguments are far from conclusive. The first antinomy concerns whether the world in space and time is finite or infinite (*śāśvata* or *aśāśvata* in Indian terminology). The thesis states: 'The world has a beginning in time and is also limited in regard to space'. The antithesis states: 'The world has no beginning in time and no limits in space but is, in relation to both time and space, infinite'. Kant adopts the procedure to *refuting both* the thesis and the antithesis and thus providing an *indirect proof of both* of them. In defence of the thesis Kant begins by

---

2 *CPR*, p. 210.

3 C.D. Broad, *Kant: An Introduction*, Cambridge University Press, 1978, pp. 210-75.

supposing that the world has no beginning in time. If so, its duration up to any given event in its history must have been infinite. This is impossible because, say the number of years that have elapsed before the year of Indian independence is a series that comes to an end, and is therefore finite. It has completed itself, as it were, and 'the infinity of a series consists in the fact that it can never be completed through successive synthesis'.

Kants 'subjective' definition of an infinite series is, doubtless, unhappy. A definition in purely logical and mathematical terms can be given which does not refer to any successive acts of synthesis either mental processes or mental processes accompanied by repeatable physical procedures. Possibly Kant imagined himself travelling backward in time and ticking off the years one by one, or completing the counting imaginatively. (Imagination plays a very important part in Kant's philosophy as a mediator between sensibility and understanding. A similarity to Hume, which is seldom noticed.) Either way the synthesis cannot be completed if time has no beginning. But Kant feels and argues, the series has been completed at the terminal point chosen by us (that the succession of phases in the history of the world continues after the selected point has no bearing on the argument). Hence the contradiction that an incompletable series has been completed.

There is something disturbing about this argument – a sense of being tricked without knowing how, as in the case of the ontological argument. Broad says that Kant here substitutes for the intrinsic synthesis which is uniquely characteristic of the temporal process, the extrinsic synthesis in terms of which his definition of the 'transcendental' conception of infinity is framed.[4] Russell makes perhaps the same point when, without referring to the direction or sense inherent in a time series, he simply says 'owing to the inveterate subjectivism of his mental habits he failed to notice that he had reversed the sense of the series by substituting backward synthesis for forward happening and thus he supposed that it was

---

4 Broad, op. cit., pp. 214-15.

necessary to identify the mental series which had no end with the physical series which had an end but no beginning.[5] This piece of philosophical psycho-analysis may be correct. But I think Kant was simply expressing a feeling of unease which many of us have in contemplating a progression which has an end but no beginning.

It is of some interest of notice that we don't have the same discomfort in contemplating a series that has a beginning but no end. Let us suppose that we are gifted with a body which is, like the soul in the *Bhagavad-Gītā*, immune to the destructive power of wind and water, fire and weapons. If there is no end to the temporal process, we shall never, travelling with the time arrow, complete the synthesis of the years that have to lapse in finite time. In other words, we feel no great difficulty in admitting that there is a first phase in the history of the world but no last phase. But a world process that has an end but no beginning seems incongruous, if not down right inconceivable. Kant seems to be expressing in a learned way this discomfort in contemplating a process that has an end (though a relative end point chosen by us, but no beginning). Our feelings of conceivability and inconceivability go with certain mental pictures we conjure up in contemplating these cosmic possibilities. They cannot be eliminated altogether though their inclusion may not be desirable in this context. Kant, I think is simply denying the conceivability of a history that has even a relative terminal point, but no beginning. He is asserting that infinite duration *cannot have lapsed* before a chosen temporal landmark. And yet, if time is infinite, this is precisely what has happened and will happen so far as the future phases in the history of the world are concerned. So, I think he is simply begging the question at issue.

In a formal way, the two suppositions can be stated in logical, mathematical terms, without any contradiction in either of them. To say that the world is finite in time is to say: choose any 'cut off' point you like and measure duration in any standard units, then no

[5] B. Russell, *Our Knowledge of the External world*, Open Court Publishing, 1914, p. 161.

more than *N* successive units of duration have lapsed before our 'starting point'. Similarly, with the same procedure, there is some number *N* (not necessarily the *N* representing past duration) such that no more than *N* successive units of duration will lapse after our chosen cut off point. To maintain that time is infinite is to say: with the same procedure outlined above, there is no number *N* such that it represents the upper limits of duration either backward or forward. Neither statement seems to be self-contradictory. But in this matter, as in some others of philosophical interest, philosophers have maintained that some suppositions, though not self-contradictory, are inconceivable or unintelligible where conceivability is not identical with our ability to picture or imagine the alleged state of affairs. That they do not always come down on the same side in a philosophical dispute is unfortunate, but it does not make the debate a delusion. In addition there is the bearing on these debates of the researchers into the nature of infinity and continuity by Cantor and his followers. These tend to show that what appears puzzling to the point of self-contradiction, to the common, non-mathematical man does not really involve a contradiction. The mathematics of infinite and continuous classes and series can be worked out consistently. The mathematical theories tend to help the advocates of infinitude of space and time because their position seems to be more paradoxical; but finitism in this matter, is not free from puzzles either. But a series of abstract entities like numbers is so unlike a spatial or temporal series of areas and durations that the analogy between them cannot be pressed beyond a point. Take, as an example, the series of rational fractions which ends with 1/1 but has no beginning. It has a last term but no first term. Can we use this example to show that though the world may have no first phase (or absolute beginning), a finite measure of time may have elapsed up to a given point in time?[6] or even to show that the world may have an absolute end without its having an absolute beginning because the series of rational fractions has no first term but has a last term? I think not, unless there are independent grounds for accepting such a supposition.

---

6 Broad, op. cit., pp. 216-17.

As for the other half of the antinomy Kant argues that to say that the world has a beginning implies that this beginning was preceded by empty time. But, he continues, there is nothing in any stretch of empty time to explain why the world should begin at that time rather than at any other. In the absence of any reason why it should begin at a given time, it cannot begin at any time and is hence without beginning. If the earlier argument against the everlastingness of the world is fallacious or inconclusive, then this argument strengthens the supposition of the infinitude of the world in time! But even without the appeal to Leibnitz's principle of sufficient reason, we can say that there is something very odd about the beginning of time. This seems like saying that there was a time when there was no time where this sounds like verbal jugglery. We can say that an absolute beginning to the world process presupposes empty time and the concept of empty time is not intelligible.

In a theistic context the difficulty becomes particularly acute – why did God create the world when he did rather than an earlier or later date? St. Augustine solved the problem by maintaining that the world and time were created together. A relative view of time is part of this view. Kant was an absolutist, no less than Newton. But, on the relative view, it is just a brute fact that there was a first event or a set of simultaneous first events not preceded by any previous processes. On the assumption of infinite time we never come across such an event or set of events however for back we may go in the history of the world. Both the alternatives are logically possible. St. Augustine makes finitism more plausible by obviating the need for empty time, but his view gives rise to certain paradoxes of its own. He will have to rule out as unintelligible certain questions which appear to be meaningful. For example, why is the world not older or younger than it is, whatever its age and however we may estimate it. Could we not be living in the $N + 1^{th}$ century or the $N - 1^{th}$ century instead of the Nth. Ultimately St. Augustine will have to say that the question of the age of the universe is meaningless, though particular events and processes can be dated and measured *within* the world. In the non-theistic context we shall have to say that the world emerges suddenly without any antecedent condition, a sort of creation without God!

The antinomy concerning extent in space need not be discussed at length. Against the infinity of the world in space, Kant says 'an infinite aggregate of actual things, cannot be viewed as a given whole, not consequently, as simultaneously given'. The world is therefore, as regards extension in space, not infinite.[7] If we go into the details, it becomes clear that Kant's argument rests upon the impossibility of completing the successive synthesis of the parts of an infinite world, in finite time. But he has already argued that clapsing of infinite duration is impossible. I have already argued that his arguments about time are inconclusive . . . Second, there seems to be a contradiction between this argument and the fourth metaphysical argument for his conception of space as an a priori intuition. 'Space is presented (represented?) as an infinite given magnitude.'[8] The matter need not be pursued further. I have said enough to show that Kant's arguments are at the least inconclusive. If so, one can consistently take either of the two positions. One of the two, the thesis or the antithesis is necessarily true. Or else we can say, both are logically consistent and neither is therefore necessarily true. St. Thomas Aquinas takes this view and opts for a finite world on grounds of faith. I would agree with him rather than Kant.

That Kant's arguments are, in many respects, blunted by advances in logic, mathematics and physics is undeniable, but even independently of them, his arguments are unacceptable, at least as they stand. In discussion of this topic, space and time are clubbed together and the same sort of attitude is taken to both, yet there is no a priori reason why we should do so. Finitism is much more plausible in the case of space than in the case of time. The reason is, as Kant among others has pointed out, space is a unity of coexisting parts, whereas time is essentially becoming and 'successively synthesizes itself'. That is why some philosophers and

---

[7] Kant, *CPR*, p. 261.

[8] Kant, *CPR*, p. 44.

mathematicians have maintained that there is no actually existing infinite and that all infinite results from addition of units in time. (This must be comforting to Kantians.) On the other hand, on the relative view, (finitude of) time is more plausible than that of space. Otherwise we have to agree with Aristotle that there is passage of time even if there is no other change.

III

In contrast to Kant's treatment of rational cosmology which is heavily dependent on the rest of his critical philosophy, his treatment of natural theology is autonomous. His criticisms of the traditional arguments for the existence of God are sharp and incisive, and have stood the test of time. These are so well known that it is not necessary to recapitulate them. As he points out, psychologically the argument from design (the physico-theological argument) occurs first to thinking persons, then the cosmological (first cause) argument and the ontological argument never, unless they have studied philosophy. Logically, the ontological argument is first and is presupposed by the cosmological and is a necessary supplement to the teleological, unless one is content with a very powerful cosmic architect or engineer. Kant was preceded by Gassendi whose objection to Descartes was the same as Kant's, viz., that existence is not a predicate in the logical sense. In our own day the analysis of the logical forms of different types of proposition and their unambiguous expression has reached a precision unknown to Kant. The contributions of Russell and Moore have exposed the fallacy in the argument decisively. But Kant made his point very clearly. Since existence is not a predicate like 'red', 'round', 'omnipotent', 'benevolence', it cannot be included in or excluded from any concept. Consequently all existential propositions are synthetic and neither self-evidently true nor self-evidently false. Terms like 'necessary being' are vacuous. The cosmological argument infers the existence of a necessary being from the existence of contingent beings. Its conclusion that a necessary being exists as the ground of contingent and conditioned existents is in a way less specific than that of the ontological argument – that the description 'the most perfect being' (*ens realissimum* of the scholastics) is necessarily, true of something. In other words there is a being whose essence necessarily implies its existence.

Kant finds here a nest of fallacies, the most important is that in the end, it falls back upon the ontological argument. He goes so far as to say that there is a 'stratagem by which it imposes upon us an old argument in a new dress and appeals to the agreement of two witnesses, the one with the credentials of pure reason and the other with those of empiricism, while in fact it is only the former who has changed his voice and dress for the purpose of passing himself off as an additional witness'.[9] Kant's rejection of the argument is justified but the relations between the two arguments are more complex. If the ontological argument is valid, then there can be no objection to the concept of necessary being postulated at the last step in the cosmological argument. Kant himself spends some logical ingenuity in showing that the *ens realissimum* of the former can be identified with the necessary being of the latter assuming their validity, which he rejects. But the cosmological argument can be accepted while rejecting the ontological argument. St. Aquinas did precisely that. His reason sounds curious to our ears, viz., that having no clear conception of his essence, we cannot deduce God's existence from his essence though God's essence is his existence.

> ... The proposition 'God exists' though of itself selfevident – since the subject and the predicate are identical for God is his essence . . . is never-the-less not self-evident to us because we do not know what the essence of God is.[10]

Of the five ways of St. Aquinas, three are versions of the cosmological argument taken over from Aristotle. It may be that this position is untenable in the final analysis. But if the concept of 'necessary being' is not empty or self-contradictory, such a position can be rendered

---

[9] Kant, *CPR*, p. 354.

[10] Aquinas Thomas, *Summa Theologica*, tr. Fathers of the English Dominican Province, Benziger Bros edn., 1947, I.2.ii, I.

consistent. In any case the claim of the ontological argument is much stronger – that we can frame a description, viz., that of 'the most perfect being' which is necessarily satisfied by an existent entity. This claim may be dismissed decisively as Kant does and yet it may be said there is an unconditioned being whose existence should be postulated as the ground of a contingent but causally connected series.

But they will fall together if the ground for rejecting the ontological argument is not restricted to a particular description – that of the most perfect being. However this notion may be further specified, but is applicable to any description whatever. The criticisms of Kant and subsequent philosophers clearly imply that whether a description or definition is instantiated is always contingent, to claim that there is or can be a description which is necessarily applicable is to utter meaningless verbiage or contradict oneself.

Many who believe in the existence of God would admit atheism is consistent. By the same token the believer, though wrong, is not contradicting himself. It can be that there is a being who possesses all perfections to the highest possible degree. But if there is, then his existence is contingent. If so he may not have existed. Now, we may ask what kind of a being is God whose existence is a matter of accident or chance. This last way of putting it may be objectionable for using words like 'accident', 'of chance' which have an emotive force not applicable here. Philosophically, all we want to convey is that the statement 'God exists' is neither necessary nor impossible. But nevertheless a sense of discomfort remains – a feeling of being let down by a contingent God. This feeling is at the back of J.N. Findlay's argument for the necessity of atheism, as also the attempt to revive the ontological argument by Malcolm and Hartshorne in the sixties of the twentieth century. They maintained that not 'existence' but 'necessary existence' is a perfection. But if 'existence' is not a predicate of perfection, J.N. Chubb in *Faith Possesses Understanding* tries to show what may be called the 'necessity of theism'. He defines God as the proper object of total self-surrender and only such object; and then argues that such an attitude is inconsistent with any doubt or conditionality. The fool who says in his heart 'there is no God' is better than the agnostic whose prayer is: O God, if there is a God, save my soul, if I have a soul. Chubb's argument is developed with great subtlety but I think it suffers from the same defect as the traditional formulations of the ontological argument.

But what is the bearing of the last paragraph on my criticism that there is a logical lacuna in Kant's account of the relation between the ontological and cosmological arguments. First of all it seems to me that philosophers like Aquinas are not wrong-headed. It is possible to reject the ontological argument and accept the cosmological, though in the end both may have to be consigned to the post-Kantian dustbin. Kant is too ready to think that once the ontological argument is disposed of, others will either fail or fall short of the ideal of religious devotion. But if Kantian and post-Kantian criticisms of the argument are accepted (and how can he reject them?) the existence of God, even if he exists, becomes contingent and considering the religious attitude at its most literal. We seem to be deprived of the very notion of a supreme being who is 'all in all" and a sort of atheism becomes necessary. Hence the attraction for some philosophers of reviving the ontological argument in some form. This suggests that notions like 'necessary being', 'ground of everything' and 'supreme being' have a significance analogous to, but not definable in purely logical and epistemological terms. Then all philosophers who are interested in religion may have to do their homework again. But even without this suggestion, which may let in irrationalism of all sorts – Kant with his over precise, pigeon-holding mind keeps the fourth antinomy and the cosmological argument more or less isolated from one another. He fails to realize that this has a bearing on his own moral theology and even the noumenal order which is integral to critical philosophy. Kant recognizes that if the improper use of reason generates antinomies and brings us to a standstill, reason is under an obligation to resolve these antinomies and clear the path for subsequent proper use of reason – 'pure practical reason' as it turns out.

Though I have discussed the first antinomy, in so far as it has a bearing on his criticism of a priori metaphysics – particularly Kant's 'rational cosmology', I shall not discuss the antinomies. To do so, with any degree of satisfactoriness, would require consideration of his theories of space and time and the role of categories in human knowledge. In short, it would necessitate evaluation of his 'mysterious meta-psychology' (Ryle's phrase). However, his general approach to the resolution of the antinomies is interesting. It is well known that he removes the apparent contradictions differently in the case of mathematical and dynamical antinomies. In the former case, both the thesis and the anti-thesis are false whereas in the case of the latter, both are true provided care is taken to distinguish between phenomena and noumena and interpret the two apparently contradictory propositions properly. His treatment of the third antinomy is a telling illustration of the latter method of resolution. One and the same phenomenon may be subject to two different types of causation – natural causation which connects phenomenon's with one another according to laws of nature. There is also what Kant calls causality through freedom, the power of initiating an action or a state spontaneously, without such an act initiating itself or being determined by any previous conditions according to laws of nature. Natural causation is applicable to all phenomena including voluntary human actions. The latter kind is applicable to me as a member of the noumenal order. In the first critique Kant claims to have proved the possibility of the idea of freedom. Its reality is proved by regarding it as a postulate of our moral experience which Kant regards as rational and objectively valid. For our purposes, the important point is that natural causation is applicable to nature regarded as a system of connected phenomena, whereas causality through freedom belongs to my noumenal, rational self. There is a great deal of intellectual tight-rope walking here which we need not discuss in detail. It has been suggested that Kant adopted this kind of solution to the third and fourth antinomies because he wanted to keep the door open for the reality of freedom and immortality and the existence of God in his later critique. The fourth antinomy regarding the existence of an absolutely necessary being is resolved by distinguishing between a cause within the phenomenal word (which can never be a self-explanatory being) and an intelligible cause or thing-in-itself which may be the cause of phenomena. In the second case, there is no infinite regress because noumena are not in space and time and hence it is enough if we take the first step and say that the phenomenal order as a whole is dependent asymmetrically on the noumenal order. It is better here to speak of the relation of ground and consequent rather than cause and effect; the category of causation is the relation of ground and consequent schematized through time.

Once again it is not possible to comment on the intricacies of this transcendental idealism. But we may note that neither Leibnitz nor Aristotle regarded God as the first, self-explanatory cause within the phenomenal world. The latter did not even regard God as the creator of the world. Whatever may be his difficulties in explaining the relation of God to the world, Leibnitz did not place God *within* the phenomenal world (we leave aside, for the time being, that space and time are, for him, not ultimately real). For him the existence even of an infinite series of contingent beings is not necessary and hence God is needed as the necessary being who is the ground of the series as a whole. The logical relation is exactly parallel to that of noumena and phenomena. The cosmological argument arises from a sense of wonder that there is a world at all and it can have non-theistic solutions. Heidegger concludes his *What Is Metaphysics*? with the comment 'why is there anything rather than nothing?'. Later and independently, Wittgenstein remarked: Not *how* the world is, is the mystical but *that* it is (*Tractatus* 6.44).

As regards moral theology or the *Metaphysics of Morals*, it is enough to remark that its arguments and conclusions are as controversial as those of 'Transcendental Metaphysics'. Just as Kant considers, more or less in isolation, cosmological antinomies and speculative theology, he does not consider the conclusions of the second critique in relation to his criticisms of speculative theology. Even if we grant that Kant establishes the existence of

God as a postulate of morality, has he shown that this ruler of the world is perfect in power, knowledge and goodness? Are not his criticisms of the physico-theological argument equally applicable here? It is enough if his God, who is responsible for the fulfilment of a necessary condition of the realization of the consummate good, is inconceivably more wise and powerful than the best of human beings. He need not even be responsible for the existence of the world. Kant hoped that his *Metaphysics of Morals* would replace the transcendental variety which he thought, he has destroyed for ever. The trouble is not that everyone does not agree with him. The trouble is that his arguments are of the same sort as those of older philosophers. Metaphysics is an attempt to jump out of our skins – an enterprise at once irresistible and impossible. Kant put us in human hide of double thickness and hoped that 'the still small voice' would lead us into the heart of things.

2

Bradley's Anti-relational Argument*

THE purpose of the present paper is a criticism of Bradley's well-known argument to prove that relations are unreal. I try to meet the difficulties raised by him against the reality of relations and argue that the mutual dependence of qualities and relations is not vicious and is, therefore, harmless. If successful, this attempt will only have proved that Bradley has given no valid reason for a very important conclusion which he held; it does not have the slightest tendency to disprove his conclusion or to prove that relations are real.

Bradley contends that relations are unreal because they are self-contradictory. It is clear, though he does not give a single illustration, that he is referring to such facts as 'Brutus killed Caesar', 'Blue is more like green than red', 'John loves Evelyn', or 'Bombay and Poona are a hundred and twenty miles apart'. I have deliberately given a mixed assortment of illustrations, for the contention is not that some kinds of relation are unreal, much less that this or that particular relation is unreal; any relation in virtue of its relational character is self-contradictory and therefore unreal. There is nothing in what Bradley says which would apply only to some sorts of relations but not to certain others. I shall call any relational fact a 'relational situation'. A relational situation is a complex whole consisting of the terms related, the relational bond and the peculiar mode of relatedness. If any one of these constituents in the complex be different, the total relational situation would be different. 'John loves Evelyn' is very different from 'Evelyn loves John' for though the relating bond and the related terms are the same the peculiar

* Published in *The Philosophical Quarterly*, Edinburgh University Press, 1957.

mode of relatedness is different. And it is very clear that 'John loves Evelyn' is different from 'George loves Evelyn' or 'Bob loves Betty'. Bradley maintains that relations are self-contradictory. One way of stating his position would be to say, 'A relational situation is inherently impossible'.

Now if any situation, fact or *state-of-affair*s is inherently impossible, then it cannot be realized and any proposition describing it and asserting its existence will be self-contradictory. It is inherently impossible that a given particular surface should be red and green all over and at the same time. It is inherently impossible that a geometrical figure which is a square should also be circular. And propositions describing these and such other situations and asserting their existence are self-contradictory. But none of the relational situations instanced above is inherently impossible and no sentence describing any of them and asserting its existence expresses a self-contradictory proposition. I hope it is as clear to the reader as it is to the author that the *state-of-affair*s described by 'John loves Evelyn' is very different from the impossible situation referred to by 'The cover of this book is red and green all over'. Countless relational situations of various kinds are realized but no inherently impossible situation is realized in any way. Men sometimes love and often hate, but who has seen a round square? Moreover, the distinction between the inherently impossible the self-contradictory and the inconceivable on the one hand, and the possible, the self-consistent and the conceivable on the other hand, *is applicable within the realm of relational situations and therefore cannot be applicable to it as a whole*. Just as the distinction between crossed and uncrossed cheque is applicable within the class of documents that are cheques and it is quite false to say that all cheques must be uncrossed. And it will be admitted that some relations are possible and some others impossible – a man cannot be older than his mother but he can be older than his aunt. So if some relational situations are possible and others internally inconsistent and therefore impossible, it follows, and follows necessarily, that any relational situation as such cannot be impossible.

At this stage, only two ways are open to those who still wish to maintain that relations are impossible. It may be that a situation, though prima facie self-consistent, is in reality internally inconsistent, and this may become evident on further reflection. I am told that quite a number of mathematicians tried to find a formula for squaring the circle, though square circles are part of the philosophical staple of illustrations of the impossible. The famous argument in the third chapter of *Appearance and Reality* aims at showing that, on reflection, a relational situation reveals contradictions. The alternative way out is to maintain that the words 'unreal' and 'self-contradictory' are used not in their ordinary sense but with a special significance by Bradley. This is in fact implied though never explicitly stated by the general philosophical position of Bradley, particularly his doctrines of a non-relational Absolute and immediate experience above the mediacy of thought.

As regards the second line of defence, I want to point out first of all that it cannot consistently be adopted by Bradley. His most important, if not his only ground for postulating a non-relational absolute, is that the relational scheme is infected with self-contradiction and unreality. So he cannot without circularity argue from the reality of a non-relational absolute to the unreality or limited reality of the relational scheme. Just as a theist who argues from the goodness of the world to the existence of a benevolent and powerful creator cannot, when confronted with the enormous evil in the world, escape by saying that if a God of love existed, all evil would be redeemed and would cease to be evil. Second, unless the relational scheme is proved to be inherently impossible or self-contradictory in the ordinary sense, the conclusion that it is unreal, or that the real is non-relational, cannot be justified. I may mean by 'self-contradictory' 'not fond of chocolates', but that does not prove that people who are not fond of chocolates are impossible and unreal. So the conclusion that 'relations are unreal' loses all its strikingness and nearly all its importance, unless the word 'self-contradictory' is used as it is used in the statements that round squares are self-contradictory.

Third, though it may be true that Bradley uses the word in other ways and with a special significance, it is also certainly true that he *uses it in the ordinary sense while elaborating the anti-relational argument*. His whole contention is that the acceptance of relations leads to the acceptance of two mutually contradictory propositions, and such an acceptance is self-contradictory in the ordinary sense. That he uses it differently in other places does not prove that he is not using it here in the usual way: not is it surprising, for a precise and consistent terminology is not among the merits of the author of *Appearance and Reality*. Finally, I do not think that anyone can escape by saying that relations have a limited reality and are less real than the absolutely real which is free from the maze of multiplicity and beyond the network of terms and relational ties. But as this would involve me in an elaborate discussion of categories, universals and existence, I shall say no more about it and the rest of this paper will be devoted to the anti-relational argument.

The essence of the argument is that relations presuppose qualities and qualities, relations. And yet, 'each can be something neither together with, nor apart from the other; and the vicious circle in which they turn is not the truth about reality'. Bradley first of all tries to prove that qualities depend on relations and that they are unintelligible either together with or apart from relations. 'Qualities', he says 'are nothing without relations', and a little later he says, 'you can never, we may argue, find qualities without relations. Whenever you take them so, they are made so and continue so by an operation which itself implies relation. Their plurality gets for us all its meaning through relations; and to suppose it otherwise in reality is wholly indefensible.'[1] The conclusion is vague and the argument obscure in the extreme. And the difficulties are not less when Bradley goes on to 'draw this out in greater detail'. 'Qualities are nothing without relations'. This may conceivably mean that whenever there is a quality its existence consists in that of a relation or a conjunction of relations. Some philosophers who have said,

---

[1] F.H. Bradley, *Appearance and Reality*, 2nd edn., Oxford University Press, 1897, pp. 21-22.

'matter is nothing apart from actual and possible sensations' have meant 'a material object *is* a series of actual and possible sensations related in a certain order and no more'. Or again some philosophers who have said, 'a substance is nothing apart from its qualities' have meant 'a substance is nothing but all qualities united in a certain way and is therefore resolvable into them without reminder'. And philosophers who have denied the self have identified it with the series of successive states of the self. 'The self' they have maintained, ' is nothing apart from its states'. Similarly, Bradley may be asserting that a quality is nothing apart from relations, in the sense that its very existence can be resolved into a relation or a set of relations. Or else he may be maintaining that a quality is dependent for its existence on a relation or relations without being resolvable into them. It would seem on the whole that he wishes to maintain the latter though the former is not altogether excluded in spite of the fact that in one place he clearly asserts its contrary.

Here Bradley is arguing that qualities without relations are impossible. A little later he argues that

> taken together with them they are equally unintelligible. They cannot in the first place be wholly resolved into (them) . . . to turn qualities in relation into more relations is impossible.[2]

It is perfectly clear from these statements that Bradley thinks it impossible to analyse a characterizing situation in terms of a relational situation without remainder. So when he says that qualities are nothing without relations he means to assert the dependence of qualities on relations. And the reasoning supposed to prove this dependence consists of two themes, leaving aside certain rejoinders to anticipated objections: (1) Whenever we find qualities, they are never without relations: '. . . they are made so, and continue so, by an operation which itself implies relation'.[3] This seems to imply that qualities are *causally dependent* on relations. (2) The very plurality of qualities implies relations.

---

[2] Bradley, op. cit., p. 25.

[3] Ibid., p. 22.

> The manyness of the qualities cannot, in short, be reconciled with their simplicity. Their plurality depends on relation and without that relation they are not distinct. But if not distinct, then not different and therefore not qualities.[4]

And the mixing up of these two very different considerations is, I submit, a confusion. For I take it that when Bradley wants to know how qualities can be made intelligible without relations, he *is not demanding a causal explanation of any given characterizing situation*. He is, and should be, engaged in the analysis of what may be called the 'logical structure' of characterizing and relational situations. And if his second argument mentioned above is sound, then the first is not only superfluous but its presence points to a confusion of purpose and, perhaps, to a failure to grasp the precise nature of the conclusion and the logical character of reasons relevant to its proof.

If one wants to disprove levitation the appeal is naturally to the causal laws of physics, and one may reasonably mention that even in situations where a body seemed to hang unsupported in the air, there were invisible tensions holding it in its exact place. If on the other hand, one wants to disprove the doctrine of transsubstantiation interpreted literally, then one should naturally say that even Christ's body is a body and that it cannot, as a whole, be present simultaneously in all the different places where the sacrament is taking place. Here it is not only unnecessary, but wrong to argue that if a body is at a given place at a given time, it cannot at the same time get to another place because it must travel the distance between the two places which, however, takes time. And one may not reasonably appeal to the fact that, if a loaf of bread is in Mrs. Brown's kitchen, then it has never been observed at the same time in the bakery or Mrs. Smith's kitchen.

It may be that by the sentence, 'Whenever you take them so, they are made so, and continue so by an operation which itself implies relation', Bradley is not asserting the causal dependence of a quality on relations; he may not be referring to such a fact as that the liquid

---

4 Bradley, op. cit., p. 24.

state of a piece of wax is due to its being sufficiently near a flame and to the causal relation between the wax and the flame. But that he does not think such considerations irrelevant to his conclusion is made clear by his mention in the preceding paragraph, of a 'considerable mass of evidence', 'furnished by psychology' which attempts to show how 'qualities are variable by changes of relation' and how 'the differences we perceive in many cases seem to have been created'.[5] Here he has in mind the variations in the perceived qualities of a physical object relative to variation in the percipient. Though he does not wish to lay weight on this evidence he clearly states that 'these considerations have an important bearing on our problem'. And in the following paragraph he points out that in the field of consciousness 'even when we abstract from the relations of identity and difference', we always find many qualities related together. This empirical appeal is accompanied by an attempt to refute a possible objection. The supposed objection is that there are certain undistinguished simple feelings and there may be a creature whose life consists of such simple unbroken feeling. Bradley admits the existence of such states without relations but wholly denies there the presence of qualities. This is very curious but the supporting argument is more curious still. He says:

> For if these felt aspects while merely felt, are to be called qualities proper, they are so only for the observation of an outside observer. And then for him they are given as aspects – that is together with relations.[6]

It seems to me impossible that there should be any feeling, however simple, which has no qualities present in it at all. There may of course be qualitatively undifferentiated states of mind with no external reference. But they must have at least one quality namely that in respect of which they are called feelings. Otherwise why call such a simple state of mind a feeling and not 'thingumabob'? And anyway, how could the observation of an outside observer create qualities

---

5 Bradley, op. cit., p. 21.

6 Ibid., p. 22.

where there are none? Either the 'felt aspects' in all their diversity were present in the feeling – *though not introspectively distinguished by the subject* – or if they were not, the outside observer is misobserving the diverse aspects together with the relations. And this is not the only appeal to observable matters of fact in support of what prima facie claims to be a self-evident proposition.

In the second paragraph after the one where the above-quoted lines occur Bradley again mentions a possible objection – which he says is hardly worth mentioning – 'that in perception one quality must be given first and before others, and therefore cannot be relative'. The answer he makes is that nothing 'is more natural than for qualities always to have come to us in some conjunction and never alone'. This is exactly like the man who supports the self-evident proposition that a body cannot occupy two places at once by an appeal to the loaf of bread in Mrs. Brown's kitchen which is not at the same time in the bakery. I want to insist on this point because it has an important bearing on the mutual dependence of qualities and relations and consequently on the alleged infinite regress involved in a relational situation. It may be that every characterizing situation (by 'characterizing situation', I conveniently refer to the fact that a given object has a given quality at a given time) is dependent on a network of causal relations which extends endlessly into the past. But there is nothing vicious in it, and this sort of dependence is intelligible.

But Bradley also maintains that a quality or a characterizing situation presupposes – apart from the causal relations which are responsible for its very existence – other relations which are logically involved in the very nature of a characterizing situation, his argument here, which is stated repeatedly and with vehemence is that, if there are many qualities, they are different from one another, and if they are different there are what he calls relations of distinction amongst them. I rest my argument upon this that

> if there are no differences, there are no qualities, since all must fall

> into one. But if there is any difference, then that implies a relation.[7]
>
> . . . and without that relation they are not distinct. But if not distinct, then not different and therefore not qualities.[8]

It is certainly true that if there are many different qualities then there must be relations of dissimilarity or what Bradley calls distinction amongst them. But why should there be many qualitites? It is logically possible that there should have been a single, simple, qualitatively uniform particular and that this should have been all that there was. I am not denying the fact, which is too obvious to be denied, that the actual world consists of qualitatively diverse particulars which are related by resemblance or difference. But here again the question is one of logical possibility, and not of fact. Bradley, however, here seems to answer that there must be many qualities which are distinct from one another; for if not distinct they will not be different, and if not different they fall into one, and hence there will be no qualities. It seems to me that the argument rests on elementary confusions. It is certainly true that if there are different qualities, *there will be and there must be* relations of dissimilarity or distinction amongst them. But it does not follow that if of a pair of dissimilar related qualities, one were absent, so that the relation of dissimilarity would be absent, the other term to the relation would cease to be the quality that it is. It is obvious, on the other hand, that relations of resemblance and difference rest on the intrinsic qualities of the terms related, so that as these qualities vary the relations also vary. It is true that if two terms have different qualities, this necessarily involves that they are dissimilar. But the dissimilarity is derived from the qualitative difference, not the difference from the dissimilarity.

So far, then, from the qualities presupposing the relations, the relations presuppose the qualities. There are of course qualities which presuppose the relations of distinction and resemblance. But these are not the original intrinsic qualities on which relations of

---

7 Bradley, op. cit., p. 25.

8 Ibid., p. 24.

resemblance and lack of resemblance depend. Take two coloured particulars *A* and *B*, one green and the other red. They are dissimilar in respect of colour and this relation of dissimilarity is logically dependent upon the two precise shades of colour that characterize them. But in virtue of this relationship between them *A* has the relational quality of 'being dissimilar to *B*' and *B* has the correlated relational quality of 'being dissimilar to A'. These depend on the relation of dissimilarity and are 'made' by it, if one may say so: but this is not true of the qualitative difference between red and green, which in fact 'makes' the relation of dissimilarity between the two coloured particulars. This distinction between relational qualities which are made by relations and intrinsic qualities which 'make' relations is very important and has a direct bearing on the supposed infinite regress involved in a relational situation.

Bradley's curious assumption that if there were not many qualities there would be no qualities, has for one of its sources, his unfortunate habit of speaking of qualities as though they could exist by themselves, and stands in various relations. It is, however, clear that it is not qualities by themselves but *qualified particulars* which are related. I am not assuming 'substances' in the traditional sense, but a quality must characterize some particular whether it is an event, a substance or a state of a substance. I, for one, cannot think of qualities floating about or of those 'bundles of qualities' which seem to be very fashionable in contemporary philosophy. Now if a number of particulars are all qualitatively uniform or characterized by the same quality, and to the same degree, then it will naturally be said that there is only one quality present in all of them, though the various particulars are all different from one another. This combined with Bradley's confused belief that a quality is made the particular quality that it is by its distinction from other, particular, different qualities, leads to the astounding conclusion that a single quality will be no quality at all. Surely a number of qualitatively uniform particulars, such as two billiard balls of the same size, shape and exactly the same shade of white, do not coalesce into a single billiard ball.

There is possibly also a third confusion namely between distinction and distinguishability. Two particulars may be distinct in the sense of being two different particulars, or even in the sense of being different in respect of some quality, without being distinguishable by us. We may confuse with one another two particulars which do not obviously differ, as sometimes we are unable to tell the one from the other of two identical twins or two proverbially similar peas. Two qualitatively uniform or exactly similar particulars may be indistinguishable, but for all that they will not lose their distinction. If so, they will not coalesce into one. Since Bradley does not distinguish between a quality and the particular or particulars manifesting it, it becomes easy to overlook this difference between distinctness and distinguishability. He is perhaps not guilty of this latter confusion, for it is rendered unnecessary by the former.

I am not in the least inclined to deny the general assertion that a characterizing situation involves a relational situation. I am only concerned to point out that Bradley has failed to distinguish the various kinds of dependence and interrelation between qualities and relations and has advanced confused arguments in support of his position. And this has led him to the mistaken view that the mutual dependence of qualities and relations is vicious. Even if two qualitatively uniform particulars remain distinct from one another, there will be the relation of resemblance between them. And even if the entire world consisted of a single, simple particular, it would not be devoid of relations altogether. It is very difficult to conceive a particular which has only one quality and no more. But if there were one, and if further, that constituted the entire world, there would be at least two relations. The quality characterizing this particular must be a determinate form of some determinable characteristic and the two would be related in the same way as are 'colour' and green. Second, the quality would inhere in or belong to the particular manifesting it. It is important to notice that these are purely 'formal' relations and Bradley does not seem to have thought of them in this connection. But they are relations nevertheless and conclusively prove that a characterizing situation involves a relational situation. But this sort of dependence as well as the others which were brought out while discussing qualitative differences, similarity and dissimilarity, and relational qualities are entirely intelligible and there is nothing vicious in them.

Having so far argued that qualities taken without relations have no intelligible meaning, Bradley proceeds to argue that taken together with them, they are equally unintelligible; for they

> cannot . . . be wholly resolved into the relations. You may argue indeed that without distinction, no difference is left; but for all that, differences will not disappear into the distinction. . . . Nothings cannot be related, and to turn qualities in relation into mere relations is impossible.[9]

But why should they be? *Why should qualities be turned into relations to be intelligible with them*? Such a resolution of qualities into relation is clearly impossible; impossible not only in the way it is impossible to bring down the moon to console the crying infant, or to transmute baser metals into gold, but impossible because of the unintelligible character of the demand itself. Though the sentences expressing the demand look meaningful, it is evident on reflection that they express nothing that can be understood.

Moreover, whenever we say that *A* implies *B* or entails *B* or necessarily involves *B*, so that *A* is unintelligible without *B*, all that we mean is that the combination of '*A*' with 'not *B*' is self-contradictory. We certainly do not mean that *A* can be resolved into or identified with *B*. Size necessarily involves shape, and shape involves size, and it is impossible to have a particular which has one of the two without the other. We can if we want, puzzle ourselves with an imaginary difficulty. 'Size', we may say, 'presupposes shape and is unintelligible without it. But unfortunately, it is equally unintelligible with it, for size cannot be resolved into shape.'

And it is clear that Bradley himself when arguing that qualities presuppose relations and are unintelligible without them, meant by

---

[9] Bradley, op. cit., p. 25.

this that the existence of qualities necessarily involves the existence of relations, a proposition which he attempted – successfully or unsuccessfully – to prove. He certainly made no attempt to show that qualities can be analysed into terms or relations and can be identified with them. And now, suddenly he shifts his ground and means by 'intelligible with relations', 'wholly resolvable into relations'. If 'qualities are unintelligible without relations' means 'qualities necessarily involves relations', so that to assert the existence of qualities and at the same time *deny* relations is self-contradictory, then the proposition expressed by 'qualities are unintelligible with relations' – if it is to be the contradictory of the first – should mean 'qualities necessarily exclude relations, so that to *assert* the existence of qualities and at the same time *assert* the existence of relations is self-contradictory'. *And unless the second is the contradictory of the first the dilemma does not arise.* For, the essential point of the argument is that if we accept qualities and relations, we shall be forced to accept two propositions *A* and *B*, each one of which is true and necessarily true, and both of which cannot be true together, as each is the contradictory of the other. *If, however, the two propositions are mutually contradictory then something is wrong, not with relations, but with Bradley's reasoning about them.* For we must be wrong in thinking that two mutually contradictory propositions are both self-evidently true. And it is important to notice that Bradley implies that both these propositions are self-evidently true. The supporting arguments are not premises from which these conclusions are deducted, but are meant to show that a denial of them leads to absurdities. At any rate the second proposition, that qualities are not intelligible with relations, is asserted on the ground that it is impossible to think of relations relating nothing, and that therefore there must be qualities that relate them; and the first proposition, that qualities are not intelligible without relations, on the ground that it is impossible for qualities to be many and different without at the same time being related as distinct entities and in virtue of their difference. So the two propositions are asserted to be either self-evident in themselves or to be necessarily implied by self-evident propositions. And if they are mutually contradictory, something in wrong either with the premise or the reasoning which results in these conclusions. As it is, we have clearly seen how the two propositions are not mutually contradictory because of Bradley's inconsistent use of the phrase 'intelligible with relations'.

After raising and accepting this imaginary puzzle Bradley goes on to assert that it gives rise to a 'diversity which falls inside each quality'. Qualities must be, for otherwise relations will relate nothings. And at the same time they must be related; otherwise qualities will not be qualities. So each quality has a 'double character as both supporting, and as being made, by the relation'. This double character breaks up a quality into two aspects; one which supports the relations of distinction and the other which results from it. And the same division will occur within each of these two aspects and again and again at every stage, without end. I have no doubt whatever that, here, as well as in some other connections, Bradley's mind is dominated by misleading physical models. But apart from that, his unfortunate habit of speaking of qualities, instead of qualified particulars, and his failure to distinguish intrinsic qualities from relational qualities give rise to this imaginary infinite regress. Since Bradley speaks of qualities, it is easy to see how he does not think of a particular which combines within its unity diverse aspects and must divide the quality into two aspects. *Since he does not distinguish between the intrinisic qualities which give rise to the relation of distinction and the relational qualities which result from the relation of distinction,* he speaks of one and the same quality breaking up into two qualities. Though with his confusions this way of speaking is natural and even inevitable, it is wholly indefensible and strictly speaking unintelligible. Reverting to one of our previous illustrations, take *A* and *B* which are red and green respectively. The red particular, *A* has many other qualities besides being red and one of them is 'being different from *B* which is green'. But this does not necessitate the breaking up of 'red' into one part which is distinct from 'green' and another which makes the first part distinct, though perhaps it is not itself distinct from 'green'.

One and the same particular has both these two distinct qualities and hence it is not necessary that a given, single quality should be divided into two, if such talk has any meaning at all. Second, it is not the same quality that supports, and is supported by, the relation of distinction. As we have already seen, it is the intrinsic qualities of 'red' and 'green' which give rise to distinction. If either *B* were red or *A* were green, then *A* and *B* would be similar instead of being dissimilar. So it is not dissimilarity that makes red and green red and green, but the difference between the two qualities gives rise to dissimilarity between any two particulars characterized by them. And the correlated relational qualities, 'being different from *A*' and 'being different from *B*', are distinct qualities, not identical with the qualities of 'red' and 'green' or with parts of these qualities.

Finally Bradley proposes to reach the same dilemma from the side of relations. He starts with the proposition that relations must have terms and only qualities can be the terms of a relation. So relations presuppose qualities, or else they will have to relate nothings, which is impossible. But he goes on to argue:

> But how the relation can stand to the qualities is, on the other side, unintelligible. If it is nothing to the qualities, then they are not related at all; and if so, as we saw, they have ceased to be qualities, and their relation is a nonentity. But if it is to be something to them, then clearly we now shall require a new connecting relation . . . and being something itself, if it does not itself bear a relation to the terms, in what intelligible way will it succeed in being anything to them? But here again we are hurried off into the eddy of a hopeless process, since we are forced to go on finding new relations without end. The links are united by a link, and this bond of union is a link which also has two ends; and these require each a fresh link to connect them with the old.[10]

The first criticism that I should like to make is that if a relation *R* holds between two terms, *A* and *B*, then it does not become a nonentity even if it does not bring about further changes in the terms related either causally or in other ways. This is not begging the

---

[10] Bradley, op. cit., p. 27.

issue between the advocates of 'internal relations' on the one hand, and those of 'external relations' on the other. I am neither denying nor asserting here that there are relations which do not affect their term in anyway besides that of merely relating them. If there are any such, they will not be nonentities; and if, on the other hand, all relations make a difference to their terms, the fact of any two terms being related is clearly different from the differences which arise in consequence of this relationship. So once a relation holds between two terms, there is no question of its turning into a nonentity.

Second, if the relation is to hold between its terms, it is not at all necessary that a fresh relation is required to relate the original relation to its terms.

(a) Bradley's statement that the original relation must itself bear a relation to the terms, in order to be something to them in any intelligible way, is itself unintelligible to me. *Either a certain relation holds between two particulars, or it does not; if it does not then the question of relating the relations does not arise; if it does then the terms are related and therefore do not require to be related anymore.*

(b) It is of course true that the relation may depend on other relations which hold either between the terms or between one or both of the two terms and other particulars. These, however, do not relate the original relation to its terms, but are its conditions, either causal or constitutive. If *A* is a niece to *B* then she must be daughter to a third someone, *C*, and *B* must be brother or sister to *C*. If *A* stands in the relation of being grateful to *B*, then *B* must, unless the feeling of gratitude is misplaced, stand in the relation of benefactor to *A*. So the relations, which are the constitutive conditions of a given relation *R* between *A* and *B*, do not relate *R* to *A* and *B*.

(c) Or again, the dependence may be causal, and the causal connections that bring into existence a certain situation may form an endless series. But this clearly is not vicious and indeed many philosophers have asserted that a beginning of time is inconceivable; if however there is a beginning of the world, then the chain causal connections can be traced back to the first cause or set of causes. Thus the litmus paper turning red in an acid solution comes to stand in the relation of similarity to all other red particulars at the time. And it may be, as some have said, that the present positions of the litmus paper and the acid into which it is dipped have behind them the entire history of the world and the endless revolutions of matter. But there is nothing vicious or unintelligible in it. *An infinite regress is vicious when, and only when in order to have the last term, we must have the first term; which, however, we cannot have because the series is endless.* If the series can conceivably have a first term of if we can have the last term, at any given time, without its being necessary to have a first term, then clearly in either case no vicious infinite regress arises.

(d) Again a relation may depend on some of the qualities of its terms and some of the qualities of the term may depend on the relations. This also is harmless if the qualities which depend on the relation are different from those on which the relation depends. I have already pointed out how relations of similarity and dissimilarity depend on the intrinsic qualities of the terms related, and how these relations in their turn give rise to correlated relational qualities of being mutually different. And sometimes both the qualities of the terms and the relation which they imply involve one another, because the nature of the system in which they are elements implies this mutual involvement. The positional qualities and the relations of distance between two physical things imply one another; they are also implied by the system of special relations in which they are elements.

Finally, there is strong reason to believe that Bradley's thinking is vitiated by misleading physical analogies. He talks as though a relation could become a term or a quality, so that, as we go down his infinite regress, we shall have more and more terms on our hands and a progressively increasing number of relations to relate them. There is a passage which is not quoted either by his admires or philosophical enemies, and I who belong to neither class quote it here:

> If you take the connection as a solid thing, you have got to show, and you cannot show, how the other solids are joined to it. And, if you take it as a kind of medium or unsubstantial atmosphere, it is a connection no longer.[11]

In talking of relations as though they could turn into terms – either qualities or solids – and in complaining against qualities that they cannot be wholly resolved into relations, Bradley is accepting and demanding the unintelligible, and therefore the impossible. He fails to realize that qualities and relations are not of the same order for either to be resolved into the other. He is like a man who strenuously tries to wear his coat on his legs and solemnly complains that it does not fit. No wonder it does not!

---

11 Bradley, op. cit., p. 28.

3

The Return of Coherence[1]

The truth is rarely pure and never simple
. . . Algernon in 'The Importance of Being Ernest'.[2]

BRITISH Idealism having been cast into the outer darkness by Moore and Russell for more than half a century is showing some signs of life. It would be inaccurate to speak of its revival. But some elements in it are, once again, in the centre of philosophical discussion. The coherence theory of truth and knowledge is undoubtedly the most important of them. The theory gives us the 'form' or 'structure' of the propositional systems we elaborate, as well as the world we hope to understand by means of them. The element, which gives the 'content' of British Absolutism and justifies the application of the term 'Idealism' to it, is not in favour at all. No eminent philosopher in the Anglo-American world would accept, in the words of Bradley, that 'Nature is a system of sentient experience'. Some form of scientific naturalism constitutes the orthodoxy, and coherence is called in to redress the errors and distortions of early analytical philosophy (atomism), positivism and its immediate successors. Questions about truth and knowledge form questions about meaning and so semantic consideration comes into play.

---

1 This article was presented at a seminar organized in honour of Dr S.K. Ookerjee on his completing 75 years. The felicitation was organized by the Department of Philosophy and the Bombay Philosophical Society in April 2000, at the Department of Philosophy, University of Bombay, India. Published later in *Philosophy and the Life World: Journal of Philosophy*, vol. 7 (2004-05), Vidyasagar University.

2 Oscar Wilde, *The Importance of Being Earnest* (Play), London: Dover Edition, 1990.

There is a movement away from atomism and towards a holistic theory of meaning. The philosophical tradition starting with British empiricism and culminating in the early theories of Russell and Wittgenstein is frowned upon. Coherence is made attractive by the difficulties of 'correspondence' which goes with empiricism and atomism, and the failure of various forms of foundationalism – the search for some basic, self-justified propositions which validate or lead to other propositions accepted as part of human knowledge.

The return to coherence appeared, rather early, in the philosophy of Rudolf Carnap. He regarded 'truth' as a syntactical predicate of systems of propositions, to bring in conformity to facts, as the criterion of truth requires comparison of sentences with a non-linguistic reality, which would be metaphysical. Later, when he was cured of his phobia for semantics by Alfred Tarski, he admitted 'truth' as a semantic predicate. But the choice of a system as true, from among the many alternative systems open to us, would be justified by pragmatic considerations. 'The ontological commitments of a system' would be guided by the convenience of the analyst concerned and not by metaphysical insights or speculations. Carnap never denied what would never have been admitted by Bradley – that it is possible to construct systems of propositions internally consistent and equally comprehensive, but mutually inconsistent. This is indeed a major difficulty of the coherence theory, and we have to consider whether the classical solution or the answers suggested by contemporary writers, particularly Keith Lehrer in his *Theory of Knowledge*,[3] are acceptable. He, as also Bonjour and Rorty, seem to think that once foundationalism is rejected, 'coherentism' – as they call it – is the only theory left in the field. All that remains is to work it out in detail and meet the standard objections.

The criticism of foundationalism plays a major part in paving the way for coherence. It is not necessary to devote much space to this criticism, partly because it is acceptable by and large and also because the ambiguities and defects in such criticism do not

---

[3] K. Leherer, *Theory of Knowledge*, UK: Routledge 1990.

affect the exposition of coherence in a new idiom. The difficulties of foundationalism present themselves under two heads: (1) the candidates for the role of basic, self-justified proposition, and (2) the relation between basic and non-basic propositions.

Philosophers now despair of finding propositions, which are at once self-evident and descriptive of the world – at any rate informative about it in any interesting way. Bradley seems to admit this indirectly when discussing the undesirability of mathematical propositions. Their certainty, he tells us, is due to their abstractness; what they gain in self-evidence they loose in richness of content. This is a weak and watery version of the contemporary common place view that all a priori propositions are vacuous. So leaving aside metaphysics in the grand style we may set before ourselves the modest task of organizing our knowledge of the external world. Here the basic propositions would be sense-datum statements – Carnap's protocol propositions – which merely record the immediate contents of sense experience. It has been argued that we can be mistaken even about these. But when objections are met and the method of introducing sense-data justified and carried to its logical conclusion, we seem to be left with a contemporary state of the subject, a statement about feeling 'somehow' rather than about being aware of something (in the world). The arguments in this regard may not be conclusive, but they are certainly forceful. Second, even if we are allowed a stock of suitable basic propositions, their relation to justified propositions presents difficulties. The task of translating physical object statements into logically equivalent sense-datum statements and at a later stage, statements about scientific entities into statements about physical objects has now been abandoned as hopeless. We shall have to have recourse to postulation and inference. This means controversy and more importantly, the certainty of our starting point is not transmitted to justified propositions.

In view of all this, fallible foundationalism may appear the more promising alternative. Here the strongest and the most plausible argument against granting a pre-eminent status to some commonsense propositions is that the sceptical argument questioning them is not self-contradictory or based upon an objectionable shift in the meaning of key epistemic expressions like 'certain' and justified' however unassailable they seem, and however much they go unchallenged in everyday life. This line of reflection is acceptable, but it is doubtful whether the consequences of its acceptance can be confined to fallible foundationalism. This brief exposition of the criticisms of foundationalism (and indirectly, realism) serves a purpose, for the most recent versions of the coherence theory are put forward because the alternatives to it are considered unsatisfactory. 'Coherentism', they seem to be saying, is our only hope.

What are the standard objections to the coherence theory, in any form? These are as follows: First, most advocates of the theory mix up the question of the definition or analysis of the concept of truth with the question of a general criterion or test for accepting the truth of any given proposition. Prof. Ookerjee has assured me that Bradley does not do so and Bradley has, indeed, declared more than once, that truth is agreement between our experience and reality; the more the former approached the later, the more truth it will have. Nevertheless it may be convenient to have the distinction more precisely stated. The truth of a proposition cannot be defined in terms of its coherence; it can only be defined in terms of truth. In the minimum or weaker sense, two propositions p and q are coherent if they are compatible, i.e. can be true together. In the stronger sense coherence is implication. That is, the truth of p is incompatible with the falsity of q. If the implication is both ways then neither can be true without the other being true. Classical coherence theory would exhibit our knowledge, ideally as a system in which every proposition implies every other. In practice, there will be sub-systems within our over-all system which are just compatible, and between which there is very little active commerce. But the intellectual journey is a striving, with varying degree of success, towards an all-inclusive, harmonious whole of experience.

Second, even as a test of truth, coherence will be effective only if at any given time there is one and only system which is more comprehensive than any competitor. When determining the fate of any given proposition *p*, we have to find out whether or not it coheres with the largest possible system of consistent propositions. Suppose there are two systems, *S*1 and *S*2, both of which are (i) internally consistent, (ii) equally inclusive but more inclusive than any alternative, and finally (iii) equally incompatible. In such a situation, coherence will break down as a criterion of truth. Classical advocates of the theory like Bradley insist that such a situation, if it arises, will be short-lived. Sooner or later, guided by the aspect of comprehensiveness, we shall find that one of our systems turns out to be more inclusive.

I am not sure this is always the case. Take Euclidean geometry and the two alternatives to it – elliptical and hyperbolic – which result from modifications of the parallels postulate. The alternatives are consistent if the Euclidean system is, and all are complete deductive systems developed with equal formal rigour. If we now ask – which of them is true of the actual world, that is whose postulates are satisfied by the structure of physical space? – The answer will be based on empirical considerations. The results of certain experiments – though not divorced from considerations of coherence – are of decisive importance. That they have gone in favour of elliptical geometry – as part of the general theory of relativity is not so important for our purpose as the *necessity of going beyond deductively closed systems*, to answer questions regarding the structure of the space–time world.

This consideration is reinforced by an argument intended to show that systematic coherence cannot be the sole test of truth. If a proposition say *p*, be accepted on the ground that it coherers with say *p*, *r*, etc. and these on the ground that they cohere with *s*, *t*, *v*, etc. clearly there will be an infinite regress, or else we shall have to turn round and justify the earlier ones. In spite of the use of temporal language – and of course there is temporal activity involved – the difficulty is purely logical. Both the regress and the circle can be easily avoided by breaking out of the confines of our propositional systems and appealing to facts of experience. Whether or not such a procedure leads to some form of foundationalism, it certainly leads to the abandonment of coherence as the sole criterion of a proposition or system of propositions.

Lehrer, while admitting that the difficulty must be met if the project of constructing coherence theory is to be carried out, seems to treat it as the difficulty of completing the process of justification – apparently endless – in a finite period of time. He writes: 'not all completely justified beliefs need to be justified by appeal to evidence'. Appealing to evidence is an activity or process that occurs over a time. Being completely justified in believing something is a state that exists at a time and need not result from the activity or process that occurs over a time. 'Being beautiful is a state that exists at a time and need not result from the activity or process of beautification.' A little later, he adds 'one may justify by appeal to evidence, but many beliefs are justified without such appeal just as one may beautify a nose by appeal to surgery but many noses are beautiful without such appeal'.[4] The argument is so perplexing that I prefer to think that I have failed to understand it. To say that 'a belief may be completely justified for a person because of some relation of the belief to a system to which it belongs' is intelligible and acceptable if it means that the system in question consists of the cognitive dispositions of the person which is not activated at the time that his 'belief that *p*' is said to be justified. If it means that there is such a system present to the mind of the observer *O* who pronounces on the cognitive claims of some other person *S*, then the contention is wide off the mark. If the claim that *p* by *S* is justified, then it must be related to some system of beliefs of *S* himself. But even if the dormant beliefs of *S* are added to the justificatory background, the problem is not solved. Then the question is, how they were justified when they were not acquired; nor is the difficulty removed if we all start with a stock of innate cognitive dispositions, for then the problem would be whether and how these are justified. The argument would be even more wide off the mark if the system

[4] Leherer, op. cit., p. 86.

in question is a possible system ready to be conceived and made operational on being justified in accepting that *p*. This is not like enjoying good health on account of the normal functioning of my liver which may go on even if I am not aware that I have liver.

Lehrer discusses the above difficulty in the context of what he calls 'explanatory' coherence. He refers to Carl Hempel's nomological–deductive model of explanation, where the proposition to be explained is deduced from certain observation statements ('boundary conditions') together with a statement of a relevant law. Our premises are both necessary and sufficient to ensure deduction. He rightly points out the notorious logical difficulty that almost any law can be used for the subsumption of the present case under it. But for our purpose the most serious difficulty is that a proposition deduced according to Hempel's model may not be explained by such deduction. He gives an example, which is certainly odd; but the oddity can be removed only by making explanation relative to what he wants to know. Thus our attempt to analyse knowledge in terms of explanatory coherence runs into a circle. I think the circle is only verbal and harmless. But it is not necessary to enter into details. The most amazing thing is that the difficulties he set out to rebut have nothing to do with the explanatory or any other form of coherence. That coherence is not an effective test when nothing answers to the description, 'the largest possible system of coherent propositions', and that every member of a system of consistent propositions cannot be justified by appeal to systematic coherence – these difficulties are left where they were before we set out on our intellectual journey.

The point, that the standard objections are not met by Lehrer, though he formulates them very clearly and fairly, comes out clearly when we consider the version of the coherence theory he considers satisfactory. He calls it undefeated personal justification, which is the same as complete justification. We begin with the acceptance system of a person at a time. That is, the system of all propositions accepted by a given person at a given time. We go through verific systems – systems to which a proposition under consideration is referred and in relation to which it is justified or validated. We finally arrive at an ultra system. The process is complex and so is the exposition (perhaps it could have been simpler if some of the twelve definitions were telescoped into others and the relativizing conditions were stated at the outset, so that each definition would have been easier on the eye and therefore on the mind).

Informally this is the gist of the process. We start, as noted above, with the acceptance systems of a person wherein at a given time, the inspiration that impels us in our search is the desire to accept truth and avoid error. We also reject or neutralize all competitors to the proposed statement. The resultant system is worthy of acceptance. Any new claim can be assessed by considering whether it or its negation coheres with our undefeated system. (In eliminating all false propositions and rejecting competitors, *we have settled that certain propositions are false before we arrive at our ultra system.* However, the apparent circle could only be apparent.)

But how do we eliminate the logical possibility of two alternative ultra systems with one of which a given statement is coherent, and the negation of the statement with the other undefeated system? It would be difficult to work out in detail such a situation in the case of singular judgements of perception. However, if the proposal being considered is a scientific hypothesis indirectly verified by experiment and which further is a member of a complex system of propositions, the dilemma can be very real. Lehrer says surprisingly little to show that coherence, as undefeated justification, can overcome the standard objections. First, we can easily preserve coherence by limiting our system. Second, we can suitably enlarge our system by offering new interpretation and reinterpretations and also by pleading illusion and hallucination in the case of troublesome perceptions. Bradley dismisses the first by saying that consistency without comprehensiveness is unstable and not worth having. He is right.

Of course, but theoretically we cannot lay down a limit beyond which such a procedure of immunizing ourselves against error is irrational. The two difficulties are connected. The first, unless it is just closing of eyes to 'inconvenient facts', leads to the second and finally results in the elaboration of an alternative system. Both concern the point at which our systems impinge on experience and this interface is of the greatest importance to a coherence theory.

Ordinarily we would say that we ascertain certain facts by experience and tailor our system to provide for their truth. A rigorous coherence theory cannot allow anything other than coherence as a criterion of acceptance. Lehrer writes:

> In fact we may easily supply an argument based on the isolation objection that can succeed against our theory.... To be personally justified all competitors in the justification game consists, apparently, in asserting firmly that the claimant is not isolated from the external world and that there is the appropriate truth connection between internal coherence and external reality.[5]

This is illustrated by a number of brief, endearing conversations. Apparently the sceptic wins if the last objection is not from any one cut off from the external world, and so our coherence theory yields the appropriate world. Lehrer writes:

> Personal justification of what we accept from perception, memory and introspection results from our accepting that these sources are trustworthy, and personal justification is transformed into undefeated justification and knowledge, when we are correct in accepting that these sources are trustworthy. The transformation argument meets the objection, appealing to sources of knowledge in the same way that it meets the isolation objection. Coherence transforms sources of information into sources of knowledge.[6]

It is easy to see how some form of foundationalism would overcome the difficulty by appealing to certain self-justified or basic propositions as the basis of the our system. But how is Lehrer's vindication of the coherence theory different from fallible foundationalism that starts with corrigible, basic propositions, which provide us with a reasonably firm basis?

---

5 Leherer, op. cit., pp. 143-45.

6 Ibid., p. 146.

His position is that the most obvious judgements of perception may be sceptically challenged without self-contradiction, and that their truth is based upon the reliability of our sources of information and our competence to make appropriate discrimination. I have no quarrel with this view. But two things may be noted. First, this type of acceptance of observer's competence and reliability of sources of information is not to adduce further propositions, which cohere with the proposition is correct. And *if the correspondence theory is correct in defining truth of a proposition*, then what we are asserting is that there is the existence of a certain state of affairs in the world of which our coherent experiences are an indication. Second, unless the evidence we have compels assent to the proposition being put forward, sceptical doubt cannot be ruled out of court here any more than in the case of fallible foundationalism.

The point of contact between experience and the world is so important that Laurence Bonjour provides for it by imposing an observation requirement and ruling that various beliefs that arise spontaneously in relation to stimuli are reliable and likely to be true.[7] This represents a concession to correspondence and abandonment of radical coherence. Lehrer rightly objects that it is not the spontaneity of a belief but its content that accounts for its justification. We may note that the same is true if we 'naturalize epistemology' (W.V.O. Quine's phrase) and lay down further requirement; for instance that our belief response must be reliable and caused in a regular casual way (Armstrong). It is easy to construct counter-examples, but the most important objection is from the point that our response *in fact* fulfils these or any other requirements. *We must know* that these requirements are met if our belief response is to constitute knowledge. So we have to appeal to knowledge of other propositions to justify our present claim to knowledge.

Prof. Ookerjee and many other philosophers would admit the need to go beyond a system of beliefs. But when we appeal to facts

---

7 L. Bonjour, *The Structure of Empirical Knowledge*, Harvard University Press, 1985, pp. 141-46.

of experience, so he would maintain, we still employ coherence and accept the statement that brings about the maximum coherence among our perceptual experiences. But here, I think, there is a shift in meaning from 'consistency among propositions' to 'conformity to facts of experience'. When we judge that the fingerprints on the murder-weapon are those of the accused, this will enter into the system of statements whose central proposition is the hypothesis that *A* committed the murder. Similarity, eye-witness accounts that *A* was present at a certain place on a certain occasion, report of ballistic experts, particulars entered in a sales register, etc. all enter into the prosecution story. But the experiences of the various persons concerned do not. Much less do the experiences and activities involved in establishing the competence and reliability of a witness. These are *tangential to our story, and not part of it* like evidential statements. These later, when based on sense perception, affirm the existence of certain state of affairs in the world. It is these congnitive claims that are elements of our system. In the simplest cases we seem to 'read off' facts in the world. Appeal to corroborative experience, intra-subjective as well as inter-subjective, is implicit in the acceptance. But even when explicitly brought into the picture, *they are not part of what we assert*.

This way of looking at the epistemic situation is based on a certain picture of the world, and on drawing, in a certain way, the categorical contours of physical objects, which are, overwhelmingly, the occupants of this world. We may modify this picture in various ways or challenge it altogether, but in making coherence the *sole criterion* of knowledge, we shall have to maintain that *we cannot and need not go beyond our propositional system*. If we achieve the maximum possible coherence in our system, it will approximate nearest to the world. Though coherence is the only way to achieve understanding of the world, the kind of approximation and the degree of it that we have attained, cannot be directly verified. The comparison of our system with facts totally independent of experience is impossible. Ookerjee is a blue-blooded Tory in philosophy. An intelligent and evolving Bradleyan, he holds with him that applying coherence thoroughly with a toe-hold in experience that reveals the broadest features of the world, we can construct a system that captures the general structure of reality.

Contemporary advocates of coherence, needless to say, have no such ambition and no sympathy for system building. Their desire is to delineate the contours of scientific discourse and trace significant movements within it. This can be done for any philosophically interesting area of language, like talk about minds, their activities, their relation(s) to the physical world, etc. The key to a proper understanding of meaning, truth and knowledge is 'holism' and the term occurs frequently in the discussion of the above themes. Quine stuck the keynote when he wrote in his now famous 'Two Dogma's of Empiricism':

> Our statements stand the trial of experience, not singly but as a body. The entire fabric of knowledge which is a man-made body of propositions has to be adjusted to boundary conditions of experience.[8]

We have a great deal of latitude in making these adjustments. Like Carnap, he would make the choice between alternative systems that are incompatible equal, pragmatic or even aesthetic in a broad sense. In him empiricism firmly controls relativism. But in some who followed, relativism overwhelms empiricism as when Nelson Goodman writes:

> . . . all we can learn about the world is contained in right versions of it; and while the underlying world, bereft of these need not be denied to those who love it, it is perhaps, on the whole, a world well-lost.[9]

This view is described, by Goodman as 'radical relativism . . . eventuating in irrealism', is motivated by aversion to realism with

---

8 W.V.O. Quine, 'Two Dogma's of Empiricism', in *Philosophical Review*, 1951, **60**(1): 20-43.

9 N. Goodman, *Ways of Worldmaking*, Indianapolis: Hacket Publishing, 1978, p. 4.

its represent atomism and talk of objective, independently existing reality. This apparently indefensible form of irrealism need not be considered in the context of coherentism because it is not a logical consequence of it. But the desire to all cognition – our descriptions with a reality independent of all cognition, our descriptions with facts neutral between them and therefore apparently not conceived or described in one way rather than another – is central to coherentism or holism.

Richard Rorty, for example, repudiates all such talks. But he accepts objectivity if it means inter-subjectivity. In fact, the latter is to be substituted for the former. Rorty thinks that those who talk of accurate representation of (mind) independent reality confuse two senses of words like 'reality', 'facts', etc. – the philosophical and the non-philosophical. In the latter sense

> to ask a witness if she has accurately represented a situation is to ask about her truthfulness and carefulness. When we say that good historians accurately represent what they find in archives, we mean they look hard for relevant documents, do not discard the documents tending to discredit (their) thesis, do not misleadingly quote passages out of context, tell the same story among themselves as they tell us and so on . . . (*it*) *is not to assume any thing about the events, nor about the truth conditions of statements* concerning such events, or about any other philosophical topic.[10]

The concluding sentence is particularly surprising because it is apparently a return to the harsh and literal application of the verification principle whereas Rorty characterizes positivism in its heyday to have been as intolerant and fanatical as any intellectual movement.

Hostility to independent facts has now assumed a strange form. By the time we have finished with representationism, we have arrived at the rejection of independent facts where 'facts' are understood in a sense that is ordinary, natural and taken for granted

---

10 R. Rorty, *Truth and Progress: Philosophical Papers*, vol. 3, Cambridge University Press, 1998, p. 73.

in all our discourse. Rorty correctly summarizes the qualifications of a good historian; but, still speaking non-philosophically, the qualifications are relevant because the person possessing them seeks to discover historical facts, as far as that is humanly possible. Surely all history is not concerned with archival material, even if our historian is, and takes herself to be concerned exclusively with documents. At some stage or other, there must be historians who soil their hands with excavations write down what they have witnessed, apply various, recognized procedures to determine the date of artefacts, etc. They are creating primary sources of historiography. Moreover, we can raise the question whether our historian is as impeccable as she claims to be. Perhaps, having become a social activist she is tampering with her material? Idealism is, sometimes, a powerful motive for falsification. Whether or not she is doing so is settled, not by what she says about herself, nor by what others say about her but by finding out as well as can be, what she has been doing. All this is elementary and may not logically imply any philosophical theory, either realistic representationism or pragmatic relativism – *but it does imply that there are belief-independent facts* which we can ascertain by agreed procedures. That the facts to be discovered are predominantly or even wholly linguistic does not make any difference to their independence. The process of ascertaining facts will involve the use of language and the conceptual scheme embedded in it. But the outcome of our procedure is decisively influenced by the non-linguistic component. Fact and belief, language and reality, scheme and content are inseparable but distinguishable.

It is not enough to tag on to 'a system of my choice' 'scientists of my culture circle accept it', and so on. It is vital to find out whether this is really so. Similarly, that there are alternative world-versions and that some of them conflict and that some thinkers, to whom I am sympathetic, accept one of them – all these have to be discovered.

Even if we supplement verbal behaviour with non-verbal patterns of behaviour, as Rorty tends to do, we have to find out whether they did occur, or are occurring, or will occur. Nor is it very paradoxical to imagine that there are facts, which nobody can now ascertain. Our ideal historian for example, may have found some secret papers and made momentous discoveries, but perished in a fire with all her papers. Nobody can now find out what they were. Rorty says that to retain the holism of idealists while junking their metaphysics, all that is necessary is to renounce the ambition of transcendence. But some degree of transcendence is built into our very conceptions of truth and knowledge, as in the above example. If coherentism is unable to accommodate it, it cannot claim to have disposed of ancient perplexities. To shock the intellectual bourgeois is a pleasant occupation, and may be profitable even to the shocker if he realizes fully the implications of what he is saying.

4

Dualism and Duality*

> To seek unity at the cost of truth is not the business of philosophy, however much it may have been the practice of philosophers to do so.[1]

In its modern form, the problem of the mind and body is a legacy of Rene Descartes. A dualism of the two substances, each with its distinctive essence and the two having nothing in common, is a corollary to his famous 'cogito'. But it would be wrong to suppose that he invented the problem. Some kind of distinction between the 'inner' and the 'outer' is found in every philosophy, indeed in any serious thinking about the world. The Buddhist conception of the human person as an aggregate of different strands, with no abiding soul underlying them, is at the opposite pole to Cartesian dualism. And yet among the elements that constitute human personality there is a distinction between the body (*rūpa*) and the mental strands (*nāma*). Buddhaghoṣa characterizes the latter as *arūpa* or formless. They are non-locatable but real and nameable constituents of a human being. Various philosophers who analyse or analyse away consciousness assure us that they are not denying the existence of mental processes. That is, of such things as seeing, hearing, remembering, feeling pain, thinking anxiously about tomorrow's weather, etc. These are not, however, what we or some philosophers take them to be. Our theorizing about them is defective and seriously

---

* Published in the *Jadavpur Journal of Philosophy*, vol. 14 nos. 1-2, 2002, pp. 5-24.

1 G.E. Moore, *Principia Ethica*, first published by Cambridge University Press, 1903, Dover Philosophical Classics, p. 222.

misleading. There is a real perplexity and the problem is to eliminate a difficulty or a tangle of difficulties.

I

The best point of departure for a contemporary discussion is the physicalism of Carnap and other positivists, set forth as part of their over-all view of philosophy in the twenties and thirties of the twentieth century. 'Reductive materialism', 'analytical behaviourism' are expressions that bring out its significance better. 'Physicalism', 'naturalism', 'materialism' widely vary in their usage and are somewhat ambiguous philosophically. The thesis is that mental processes *consist* in the occurrence of physical processes, more specifically in forms of bodily behaviour or brain events.

'Everything is matter in motion', is literally true though some forms of motion are chemical and electrical changes, which the older materialists could not have imagined. Put in the 'formal mode of speech' favoured by Carnap and other positivists, every psychological statement can be translated *logically* into a set of statements about actual and possible behaviour. The latter specify in principle, the meaning of the translated statements about mental occurrences.

When there is no one-to-one correspondence between observed behaviour and ascribed mental processes we fall back on events in the central nervous system. It is now generally agreed that the necessary and sufficient conditions of mental events and activities having a mental component are to be found in specifiable events in the brain. But considered as a thesis about the *meaning* of psychological statements physicalism is clearly unacceptable and is universally recognized to be so. The close and intimate relations between kinds of experience and patterns of bodily behaviour are contingent and empirically discovered. The truth of a physiological statement is, logically, neither necessary nor sufficient for the truth of a psychological statement. There is no need to argue this point in detail. But two points may be noted. Everyone would grant that a mental process may occur without recognizable specific bodily symptoms. Hypocrisy, politeness and stoic self-control are too common a feature of our social life to tempt us to deny this. The same set of facts would tend to show that a pattern of bodily symptoms may occur without the occurrence of a mental process correspondingly specific and generally associated with it. But it maybe argued, that though the occurrence of a mental process does not imply the occurrence of a specified pattern of bodily symptoms, it does imply the occurrence of *some form* of bodily behaviour or other. Conversely the occurrence of *some form of bodily behaviour* is a necessary condition of the occurrence of *any mental process*. This point is far more difficult to argue; but we may note that even if accepted it does not rule out the *logical possibility* of survival or reincarnation, which is perhaps the one thing the materialist would most like to do.

The identity theory gives up the translatability thesis but insists, nevertheless, that mental processes are identical with brain events. This amounts to an admission that as words are now used the meaning of a psychological statement is not given by a set of statements about bodily behaviour – including in the latter statements of neuro-physiology. But this brings me to my second point. It may be argued, and has been argued, that we could so alter our rules of usage that psychological statements are construed as statements about brain events. Further, this step may be recommended for philosophical and scientific purposes on the ground that it would make our usage more precise and accommodate the latest advancements in biology and physiology. The common analogy is with the Copernican revolution after which, talk about the movements of the sun is a concession to common usage recognized to be false and ruled out of court in physics and astronomy.

As for the identity theory itself, it is historically and logically the successor in the analytic tradition, to the physicalism of the positivists. While admitting and even emphasizing that the meaning of a psychological statement is not given by a set of statements about bodily behaviour, it maintains that a mental process referred to by such a statement is *in fact* identical with a particular brain event. There are no mental events over and above and besides, brain event, either in a different medium or made of a different stuff. It is thus a salvage operation – an attempt to nullify the consequences of the breakdown of the translations offered by physicalism. From another point of view it may be taken as starting with the traditional doctrine of psycho-physical parallelism and then knocking out (mentally of course), the series of mental events. An allegedly distinct mental event with its distinctively mental character is one with its neural correlate. The two events are one in somewhat the same way as Eliza, Elizabeth, Betsy and Bess are one in the nursery rhyme. (It will be remembered that they went to the woods and having found four eggs in a nest, ate one a piece and left three in the nest.)

There are many objections to the theory, some even suggest themselves. The basic difficulty is about the status of introspective reports about our own mental processes which the theory allows to be acceptable as far as they go. But it argues they don't go so far as to commit us to the acceptance of some form of dualism. They are, according to Jack Smart, vague and non-commital enough – to be compatible with the identification of the reported processes with events in the central nervous system. The subjective reports are accepted for practical purposes and presumably at the earlier stages of psychology and psychological physiology, for want of anything better. But as science advances, we can safely infer, they will be less and less useful, and perfected neuro physiology will render then otiose.

I have criticized the identity theory, including Donald Davidson's defence of 'anomalous monism' in detail, in a special issue of the *Indian Philosophical Quarterly* commemorating the fourth centenary of Descartes birth.[2] Rightly or wrongly I think that the comments are substantially valid. I shall not summarize, let alone repeat them. But as I remarked earlier, a central point in any

---

2 See article titled 'Descartes Philosophy of Mind: Its Contemporary Understanding' in this volume.

discussion of the theory is the logical and epistemological status of our introspective reports. These are detailed and specific enough to be useful in our social life. The crucial question is about the *content* of such statements. They are not in terms of neural and chemical categories which alone are used by physiology. What are they about then? To say that they are general and indefinite statements of which science offers more and precise formulations is not at all plausible. They involve totally different categories. The fact that we are unable to define a category precisely and a host of other technical terms does not affect the relevance of force of the objection.

Patients describe their pains, in some detail, to their doctor. We analyse and describe our feelings. We may declare that we have suddenly remembered some appointment to explain our leaving a room abruptly. All these are occurrential statements made in complete ignorance of neuro-physiology. We may accept that all the reported goings-on are completely determined by brain events or even that they are features of brain events. But they are features not described in chemical, electrical (and ultimately physical) terms. It is difficult even to imagine what it would be for the neuro-physiologist to observe them in the brains he is examining. Smart, Ullin Place and David Malet Armstrong refuse to admit that the events concerned have any features other than dynamic, electrical and chemical properties. Secondary qualities, for the sin of being integrally connected with perception and figuring in phenomenological language, must be condemned to nothingness!

II

Smart however throws out the suggestion that we can revise our language to render meaningful certain statements which at present are admittedly absurd. Statements such as, 'My thought about dinner is in the prefrontal lobe', 'This event in the visual area of my brain is confused', could be allowed in a revised language, the revision being motivated by advancements in science. Daniel Dennett and Richard Rorty have recently advanced views which can be regarded as an elaboration of this suggestion in a continuing development and defence of the Identity Theory. The basic move is simple, though the details of the debate about the mental and the physical between some of the most well-known contemporary philosophers have become labyrinthine. The suggestion is that we should regard our statements about thoughts, feeling, etc. in the same light as our statements about the sun – its rising and setting and its movements across the sky. After the Copernican revolution such talk is seen to be basically false and misleading but practically convenient and permissible once 'we see through it'. The Copernicans do not think it necessary to explain the fact of sun's motion. It is enough to explain why people indulged in such talk and continue to do so. Similarly it is enough to explain why people talk about inner, private, mental processes, not the processes themselves and their relation to the physical. It may be objected that our concern is with facts of sensory experience and that these are not obliterated by a change in our theoretical framework. Āryabhaṭṭa, who propounded the heliocentric theory long before Copernicus, explains our experience of the apparent motion of the sun by the analogy of a man sailing down the river in a boat who 'sees' the trees on the bank moving away up the river. Such common experiences of the relativity of motion have been noted and incorporated into the common sense picture of the world. The same common data – together with others are explained in one way by the Ptolemic theory and in a more acceptable and now well-established way by the Copernican theory. So the facts of experience cannot be rejected out of hand though their physical interpretation can be thrown overboard. To this, Rorty's response – on behalf of an imposing array of 'holistic' philosophers – is that there are no facts independent of theory. What we regard as facts depends on our theoretical framework in this field and ultimately on the entire fabric of acceptable statements, which constitute human knowledge. There are no 'absolute' facts, which rival theories seek to explain and which are the final arbiter of theories.

Since reports about experiences are taken to be about distinctively mental occurrences only because each one of us is alleged to have direct access to his own experiences – which he is denied in the case of others and which others are denied in his case – the primacy of the first person viewpoint and the consequent privacy of the inner world is a point of central importance in this discussion. Can each one of us take up a behaviourist stance towards his own experiences? Rorty quotes John Searle on this point from the latter's *intentionality*. Searle argues that no one who claims that 'mental states can be entirely defined in terms of their causal relations' has reached this view by a close scrutiny of the phenomena in question. No one ever considered his own terrible pain or his deepest worry and has concluded that they were just Turing machine states or that they could be entirely defined in terms of their causes and effects or that attributing such states to themselves was just a matter of taking a stance towards themselves. Rorty comments that 'for holists like Daniel Dennett suggesting that we can "scrutinize phenomena closely" is itself question-begging'. The phrase presupposes just the idea of intrinsic non-relational features that Dennett questions – the idea of features that were clearly and distinctly scrutable right up there on the screen of the Cartesian theatre before you ever learned to talk. It begs the question of whether the behaviour Searle describes is best explained by saying that such scrutiny in fact occurs or whether the appearance of scrutiny is as illusory as the appearance of phenomenology.

Both the objection and its rebuttal involve wider philosophical settings, and ultimately, all embracing philosophical perspectives. But if the debate is not to peter out into mutual accusations of misunderstandings and confusions, it should be possible to agree on some facts whose significance and incorporation into a wider contest is a matter of controversy. As pointed out in the course of my comments on the identity theory, we do accept as reports statements about such things as seeing, hearing, feeling pain, remembering intemperate exchanges with regret, anxiously awaiting the outcome of a major surgery, etc. When Wittgenstein deprives them of this status he is not elucidating ordinary usage but recasting it, relocating a set of usages on our linguistic map, to serve his own philosophical convenience. As we have noticed, the Copernican theory does not obliterate the facts of our experience as if the sun moved across the sky. Dennett and Rorty wave a philosophical wand which they hope will send them into the limbo of nothingness. They are also absent-minded about the daily acceptance in our social life of countless experiential reports.

Are we missing the point of the Copernican analogy that what needs to be explained is not solar motion – which is not there to be explained but people's belief concerning it? But is our belief that the sun seems to move across the sky, though it is the earth that is rotating on its axis, devoid of all intuitive elements? Do we not have visual experiences as if the sun were moving across the sky? When we say, 'The sun seems to move', the word 'seems' applies to physical motion not to our experience. Does not even the most normal perception contain a datum – a colour expanse, a sound, a feel, etc. – according to the sense-modality, which is interpreted in a certain way? To say that there is no phenomenology and it is enough to explain why there seems to be phenomenology, is on the face of it, an extraordinary statement. That fact and theory, data and their interpretation are inseparable may be granted. Data are data only in the context of a theory and facts come to us with layers of interpretation. But this does not mean that data cannot be distinguished from the interpretation put up on them in *a given situation*. To deny this is to maintain that all judgement is based upon or derived – though not always logically deduced – from other judgements or beliefs and thus invite an infinite regress. The regress can be brought out in another way. Phenomenological reports are attempts to describe what is given and suspend the belief or judgement, which we are inclined to base upon what is given. The distant mountain looks blue and smooth to me though I know it is variegated in colour and uneven in texture. If Dennett and Rorty are to be taken at their face value it does not really seems to me that there is a smooth, bluish roughly continuous expanse in my visual field. It only seems to me that it seems to me that I have such a visual experience. What does this seeming that it seems to me . . . consist in? Am I simply saying to myself that it seems to me that I have a describable visual datum? Such a view seems plainly false to me. But even if we accept this contention, the saying to oneself or declaring to others anything, involves auditory sensations and verbal imagery, which unenlightened persons like me are aware of. Or is it that we are not really aware of any such elements but it only seems to us that we are aware of such data? We are back again to square one and the horror begins again.

Take Dennett's attempt to show that there is no such thing as phenomenal consciousness. In his 'Quining Qualia'[3] he argues as follows: take Chase and Sanborn who both used to like the coffee served at Maxwell House but now dislike it. Chase says the taste has remained the same but he has become more sophisticated. Sanborn is equally certain that they no longer serve the kind of coffee they used to. The original taste was great according to him. This difference could be due to misremembering on the part of one or both of them, a change in their taste buds or some other physiological change, a change in their standards, etc. Thus there are many causes of disagreement between which only a neuro-physiologist examining their brains can decide. Phenomenal consciousness, if it exists, must be infallible or transparent. The example shows it is not. Therefore there is no such thing. The argument has been criticized on the ground that it assumes that memories of experiences must be infallible. However, the most ardent advocates of the transparency of consciousness have not claimed this but only that the occurrence and content of experiences are self-revealing when they occur. There is a problem here which can be debated at length. But a radical criticism is that Dennett's argument ascribes an undercurrent of experiences and mental states to Chase and Sanborn – their tastes (tastings) of coffee in the past and now, their memories of past 'feels' of coffee, etc. It is tedious to elaborate the point already made more that once that the dispute is not about the events that are taking place in the brains of the protagonists. Both they and Dennett describe the differences very well without any such knowledge and

---

3 D. Dennett, 'Quining Qualia', in *Consciousness in Contemporary Society*, ed. A.J. Marcel and E. Bisiach, Oxford: Clarendon Press, 1988.

speculate about its cause. The hypothetical neurophysiologist, by discovering the necessary and sufficient conditions of their mental states can at best settle their dispute. *But there would not be a dispute unless there were phenomenal states described without any knowledge of neurophysiology*. In denying incorrigible phenomenal states, Dennett is ascribing corrigible phenomenal states! He apparently knows very well what he is doing. His account in terms of Multiple Drafts model and hetero-phenomenology in his later work *Consciousness Explained* (1991) is hardly more illuminating. In the traditional account of perception there is something given to the observer which he confronts, as it were, and which he interprets or takes to be something. On some accounts, he takes the given as the sign of the presence of something physical. In the Multiple Drafts model the process is to be explained in terms of the working of a brain which themselves are elucidated by analogy with the workings of advanced computers. In our model, this single unified taking is broken up in cerebral space and real time, the judgement tasks are fragmented into many distributed moments of micro tasking. Since there is no place where it all comes together, no line the crossing of which is definitive of the end of preconscious processing and the beginning of conscious, many of the familiar philosophical assumptions about the denizens of human phenomenology turn out to be simply wrong.[4]

If all this is to have the beginnings of a satisfactory answer, its application to well-known problems in visual perception must be worked out in detail. There is no dividing line to be crossed between the conscious and the preconscious in brain events or in the steps in the execution of a programme by a computer. They are uniformly chemical–electrical or electrical in character and therefore all unconscious by their scientific description or all 'conscious' according to our model. But what is its moral for the problem of depth in visual perception, to take a well-known example? All persons who are sighted, experience depth in their visual field, though the images of all the objects in the visual

4 See, D. Dennett on 'Dennett', in *Cambridge Companion to Philosophy of Mind*, ed. Samuel Guttenplan, Basil Blackwell, 1994, p. 241.

field are flat and in the same plane on the retina. (This problem interested George Berkeley a great deal.) The Buddhist analogy of the rapidly rotating lighted end of an incense stick presenting a steady circle of illumination if the rotation is rapid enough, is a case where the stimuli are discontinuous but the awareness is of a sensibly continuous figure.[5] Whatever the explanation of these and many other phenomenological facts of this type in terms of brain mechanisms, it can't be denied that we are immediately aware of and do not infer a three-dimensional field in one case, and of sensible continuity in the other. We make all sorts of judgements on the basis of our presentations which go beyond them including the judgements that some presentations are misleading in some respect. How can the brain mechanisms concerned wipe out these distinctions?

III

Many long and intricate arguments have been offered by Paul Churchland for the elimination of distinctively mental occurrences. After all his labour of love, Dennett allows that our ordinary talk about human behaviour – condescendingly called Folk Psychology (FP) – can stand more or less as it is. Its descriptive and explanatory apparatus can function as usual for practical purposes. Churchland, on the other hand, wants neuroscience, with the help of computer science, to replace FP. When that day comes, sooner than many of us think, the false ontology of FP would vanish along with its present-day role in our life. Beliefs and desires, for example, are repeatedly declared to be like phlogiston, alchemic essences, and theoretical entities chimerical, in character. And this in spite of granting that neuro-science is unlikely to find sentences in the head! He speculates rather elaborately that one day we may communicate with one another without the mediatory role of sentences. It seems to me that the situations envisaged do not exclude sensory and

---

5 The same point is highlighted by the Gestalt psychologist Wertheimer when certain experiments that give rise to discontinuous exposures produce an experience of sensibly continuous motion.

reflective experiences. The best way to deal with such possibilities is for both sides to wait for thir realization. But in the meanwhile we have nothing better than 'sentence crunching' to put forward our view. Take, as a sample, Churchland's attempt to meet Thomas Nagel's arguments to show that brain events are not identical with mental states.

A typical argument by Nagel is the following:

1. My mental states are knowable by introspection.
2. Brain states are not knowable by introspection.
3. My mental states are not identical with brain states.

Churchland considers the second premises in this argument false. The same is true of arguments where more specific terms like 'temperature', 'tactile sensation' and 'mean kinetic energy' are used in premises. The reason for regarding 2 as false is that one and the same event can be both a mental state and a brain event. He writes:

> The trouble with such arguments as Nagel's is that the property ascribed by 1 and denied by 2 consists only in the subject item's being recognized, perceived or known as something under some specific description or other. Such apprehension is not a genuine feature of the subject fit for deriving identities. One and the same subject may be recognized under one description as 'qualia of mental states' and another equally accurate co-referential description of 'property of my brain state'.[6]

Nagel's argument could have been perhaps, put better. But the reply raises a number of points. It can be advanced validly by one who recognizes distinctively mental predicates though not mental processes or substances. But the audacity and charm of this position is precisely in the denial, which Churchland shares with Smart, Place and Armstrong, that brain events have characteristics over and above electrical–chemical and kinetic properties described by neural science. Churchland, in fact, is more emphatic in his denial when he dismisses beliefs, desires, sensations, etc. as constituting

---

6 P. Churchland, *A Neuro-Computational Perspective*, MIT Press, 1989, pp. 56-61.

the false ontology of FP. After some discussion he declares that (1) as far as qualia are concerned, machine states have them; and (2) as for intentional states, we do not have them any more than computers have true intentionality in Searle's sense![7]

We are not concerned at present with the tenability of these statements or the cogency of the reasoning that leads to them. But the crucial question is whether Churchland, who accepts them, can say that one and the same subject under one description may be recognized as 'qualia of mental states' and another co-referential description as 'property of my brain state'. Surely for him, and eliminativists like him, description in terms of qualia refers to postulated, chimerical entities of a false ontology. I have already maintained at some length that our phenomenological reports have an intuitive element, which cannot be analysed away. When it is argued that the apprehension of the brain event as an experience of qualia is not a genuine apprehension fit for deriving identities, one may grant that the feature specified by the introspective reports is not important for the purpose of scientific classification. The common man takes the whale to be a huge fish but zoologically it is not a fish at all. But the crucial question is whether the phenomenal description of the common subject, that is the brain event, is really applicable to it. If it is, the ontology of eliminativism is too narrow. If, on the other hand, the subject only appears to have a feature which it does not have, we introduce a dualism of subject and object and this very narrow version of physicalism goes overboard. Even for a person like Donald Davidson who accepts mental predicates, such an answer rests upon the rejection of the thesis of extensionality whose acceptance is necessary to every version of radical physicalism.[8]

I shall now make some brief comments on some very general

---

7 Churchland, op. cit., chapter 2, pp. 21-44.

8 I have argued elsewhere that Davidson's rejection of David Attfield's argument that his purely physical laws turn out to be psycho-physical, rests precisely upon a rejection of the thesis, which is anomalous in his case.

points I do not know why intrinsicality – having certain inherent characteristics not definable in terms of the causal relations a thing has or is supposed to have to other things – is denied of mental phenomena alone. Modest dualists like Nagel and Searle, we are told, will have to take refuge in such characteristics. There are however no such intrinsic non-relational, self-revealing characteristics. But the question of intrinsicality is a very broad logical-epistemological problem not confined to mental phenomena. It can be raised about admittedly physical phenomena or even logical and mathematical concepts (in this last case there is an easy solution). Moreover, in a given context a particular characteristic may be taken to be intrinsic though its presence may depend upon various causal and non-causal relations. A hue pervading a surface, say a specific shade of red, may be taken as intrinsic though it depends on the molecular structure and selective emission of certain radiations by the particular which has it; on the other hand, the effects it has on the various observers may be taken to be relational properties. Same is the case with ostensive definitions, the relation between evidence and conclusion (in contradistinction to restatement of evidence), the distinction between form and content, etc. There is a whole range of philosophical contrasts and dualities whose formal definition is fairly clear but whose application in a particular context needs qualifications and additional requirements which we can stipulate as we go along. So, unless the alleged mental phenomena are explained away with the help of brain events and computer programmes, the need for intrinsical characteristics does not reduce dualism to absurdity. Equally, rejection of realism with its impossible notion of correspondence between our thoughts and mind-independent reality does not imply rejection of dualism and acceptance of physicalism.

Once we give up the straightforward thesis of translatability or reduction of the mental to the physical we shall have to be content with factual identity. This factual identity underlies not only the early theories of Smart and Place but also the anomalous monism of Davidson, eliminativism and functionalism. Not only mental substances but also mental events and sometimes even mental predicates are abolished. Identity theorists allow, grudgingly, sensations and raw feels as occurrences, but they are identified with brain events. The rest of the mental apparatus, beliefs, desires, memories, perceptions, etc. are analysed in terms of dispositions to behave. Such analyses have never been carried out satisfactorily. When desires, for example, are analysed behaviouristically, perceptions are taken for granted as they are commonly understood; when perceptions, in their turn, are taken to be acquiring dispositions to behave, desires – normal desires are taken for granted. The thesis of extensionality, to give another notorious example, is required to deal with propositional attitudes. Unless it is true no form of physicalism is acceptable. But it has grave defects and we do not know how to patch it up to make it work in principle.

In the on-going discussion of the problem, a number of theories – identity theory, anomalous monism, functionalism and eliminativism – are considered alternatives to dualism with its irreducible, distinctively mental processes. But the variety of alternatives is only apparent. Once analytical behaviourism and dualism are rejected, the identity theory remains the only possible alternative, at any rate, at a basic taxonomical level. And further, if characteristically mental predicates are rejected, eliminativism results. In the most radical form of the identity theory, the brain events with which mental events are identified are not allowed to have any features other than dynamical, electrical and chemical properties. This is so in the early exposition of Smart and Place as also in the most elaborate version of it by Armstrong. What more can the eliminativist want or even assert as the content of his theory? Functionalism asserts that question of stuff or intrinsic character is irrelevant. What is essential when we deal with propositional attitudes is a certain structure or organizational economy which can be realized in a variety of material substrata. But structure, whatever its explanatory value, is the basis of functions or occurrences and the functions we want to elucidate are, in the case of humans, brain functions. To say that the mind is a structure irrespective of the material in which it is instantiated is understandable rhetoric. But if at least some psychological statements are taken episodically, the concerned mental occurrences have to be identified with brain events.

All these theories are monistic and the monism consists in accepting physical events and entitles as the sole furniture of the world. When even non-physical predicates are not allowed into our ontology, it is the ancient doctrine that 'everything is matter in motion'. If it is implausible and absurd to say, as Democritus did, that thought consists in the motions of dry, hot spherical atom, then it is equally absurd to say that it consists in an electrical event in the brain. In spite of being inspired by science and its spectacular advances the identity theory is a metaphysical speculative, unificatory theory.

IV

What about philosophers like Thomas Nagel who say that the gap between the physical and the mental, the objective and the subjective, is due to a deficiency in our conceptual equipment? We don't yet have the concepts needed to be able to offer the analytic statements needed by the identity theory of eliminativism. Albert Einstein effected a great unification by his equation $E = MC^2$. We don't have a grasp of the concepts needed to effect the identification of the mental with the physical. Searle at any rate is certain that there are irreducible mental events though they are features of the brain of the subject and caused by events in it. He calls this view biological naturalism, which it is claimed, reconciles materialism and dualism. The former is the view that the world consists entirely or physical phenomena and the latter claims that it contains irreducible mental phenomena. An important element in his view is the rejection of the thesis that 'the mind is a computer programme' and the mind is to the brain as the programme is to the hardware. Minds, in short, are computer programmes implemented in brains. This is called the thesis of strong Artificial Intelligence (strong AI for short) and is refuted in four simple steps.

1. Programmes are formal (syntactical)
2. Minds have contents (semantics)
3. Syntax is not sufficient for semantics
   (Therefore)
4. Programmes are not minds.[9]

1. Brains cause minds (mental processes constituting a mind are entirely caused by process in the brain).
2. Syntax is not sufficient for semantics.
3. Computer programmes are entirely defined by their syntactical structure.
4. Minds have mental content; specifically, they have semantic contents.

Conclusion 1: No computer programme by itself is sufficient to give a system a mind. Programmes in short are not minds and they are not by themselves sufficient for having minds.

Conclusion 2: The way that brain functions cause minds cannot be solely in virtue of running a computer programme.

To illustrate this reasoning, Searle uses the now famous Chinese-room argument designed as a thought experiment. Suppose there is a programme to enable a computer to respond with appropriate answers in Chinese by accessing its database whenever it is given questions in Chinese. The answers given by the computer can be as good as those of a native speaker of Chinese. Well imagine that you are locked in a room and in this are several baskets full of Chinese symbols. Imagine that you (like me) do not understand a word of Chinese, but that you are given a rulebook in English for manipulating these Chinese symbols. The rules specify manipulation of symbols purely formally, in terms of their syntax, not their semantics. So a rule might say, 'Take a "squiggle-squiggle" sign

[9] J. Searle, 'Searle', in *Cambridge Companion to Philosophy of Mind*, ed. Guttenplan, pp. 545-47; see also J. Searle, *Minds, Brains and Science: 1984 Reith Lectures*, Harvard University Press, 1986, Lecture II.

out of basket number one and put it next to "squoggle-squoggle" sign from basket number two'. Now suppose some other Chinese symbols are passed into the room and that you are given further rules for passing back Chinese symbols out of the room. Suppose that unknown to you, symbols passed into the room are called 'questions' and symbols you pass out of the room are called 'answers to questions'. If we further suppose that my answers would soon be as good as those of a person who knows Chinese, can we, on the basis of my performance, say that I have learnt Chinese? Hardly, if going through the appropriate programme is not enough to give you an understanding of Chinese, then it is not enough to give any other digital computer an understanding of Chinese (because) no digital computer by virtue of running a programme has anything that you don't have. The whole point of the parable is that understanding a language, or indeed having any mental states at all involves more than just having a bunch of symbols. It involves having an interpretation or meaning attached to those symbols. And a digital computer is defined in terms of its ability to implement programmes. And these programmes are purely formally specifiable, that is, they have no 'semantic content'.

The Chinese-room argument certainly achieves some thing. It shows that a digital computer has no understanding of the programme it implements, or rather, we need not ascribe to it understanding or any form of consciousness on the ground that it implements a programme that can be interpreted as answering questions in a certain field. As Searle points out, it simulates but does not duplicate intelligent bahaviour.[10] I agree that most of the replies to the argument are non-sequitur's. But that is not the end of the matter. The argument is essentially analogical. The man in the Chinese room, I think, takes the place of the Central Processing Unit (CPU) in a computer. If his formal manipulation is successful, without any understanding of Chinese such understanding is not present in the case of the computer either. More cautiously, we need

10 J. Searle, *Minds, Brains and Science: 1984 Reith Lectures*, Harvard University Press, 1986, pp. 28-56.

not ascribe understanding to it on the basis its processing activities. But the man in our example has, or goes through sensory experiences of discrimination and classification. Leaving aside his understanding of English (this, in the other case, is in the programmer not the computer), he actively discriminates between patterns of symbols and collocations of them. This is not a mean achievement and many human beings may fail to display the requisite skills (but this is not relevant to my argument). Are we ready to infer, positively, that this discrimination is present in the case of the computer, as we infer rightly, that the machine does not understand Chinese as a native speaker does? I agree that even the most perfect analogy should not be pressed beyond a point, and that the analogies are bound to have important dissimilarities. It may be said that the computer only goes through a sequence of states in a purely causal way involving no consciousness. Searle himself says:

> (I)n the sense in which human beings follow rules . . . in that sense computers don't follow rules at all. They only act in accord with certain formal procedures.[11]

I agree and feel no inclination to infer that the computer possesses sensory discrimination. But important issues are involved here.

We must distinguish two questions, one empirical and other conceptual. Does this system (organism, computer or robot) have or undergo characteristic experiences, say of seeing a yellowish, round, orange, or remembering the lines. 'I may cease to be before my pen has gleaned my teeming brain': This is an empirical question which we can answer on the basis of the similarity of a system and a specific state of it to ourselves and our relevant behaviour. There are no general rules for settling such cases. Second, what does it mean to say that this system is having or undergoing an experience or mental state? This is a question of logical analysis. It is difficult to answer it positively, but we can rule out answers in terms of bodily behaviour, dispositions to behave or brain event, at any rate in so far as these are described by the neuro-physiologist. In

---

[11] Searle, *Minds, Brains and Science*, p. 47.

short, we can rule out the deduction of the mental to the physical. But the philosophers who are starry-eyed about computers may be doing one of the two things when they claim that certain advanced computers think in the same way as humans do.

1. They may have persuaded themselves that there is nothing to human thinking apart from the occurrences of certain electrical events in the brain. They ascribe consciousness to computers in their physicalistic sense. I think that they are wrong but I cannot prove that they are.
2. They may reject the reduction of the mental of the physical, even to neuro-biological processes, as Searle does. They may think that when electrical events reach a certain level of complexity, conscious processes emerge and are associated with them causally. No doubt brain events are chemical–electrical and the brain functions as an integral part of an organism with complex body chemistry. But the body chemistry need not always be the basis of electrical activity. We can have sentience or consciousness based on 'reverberating electronic circuits'. If the latter are constructed in a computer without the bio-chemical basis it will be conscious in the same way as humans though this consciousness is irreducible to electrical activity. I am computer illiterate but I don't think any computers are conscious or that such computers will be constructed in the near future. The construction of conscious machines is most unlikely on the basis of our present knowledge of neurology, electronics, biochemistry, etc. But can we rule out the possibility a priori, as Searle seems to do.

A variety of intentional processes are 'caused by the brain and realized in the structure of brain'. Further, 'they are caused by biological systems while being at the same time realized in biological systems'. It is declared that conscious phenomena are all a part of our biological life history, along with growth, secretion of bile and digestion.[12]

---

[12] Searle, *Minds, Brains and Science*, pp. 24-34.

In his later contribution to Guttenplan's handbook he does admit that 'there is no logical on metaphysical obstacle to consciousness being caused in some other sorts of system whether natural or artificial'.[13] If so, lovers of computers may say that it has been or will be realized in some electronic systems. So, computational theory of the mind is not incoherent as Searle claims.[14] It is extremely implausible and the alleged proof of it, as shown by Searle, is lacking in logical rigour. But his own biological naturalism makes it easier for the second of the above alternatives to be maintained. If brain events completely cause mental events so that a world devoid of consciousness sees the emergence of it for the first time, then some of the embodiments of minds can be non-organic. After all, it is the electrical events in the brain, which are the necessary and sufficient conditions of conscious processes. The organism with its complex chemistry is, as it were, the infrastructure. To say that anything that caused minds would have the causal powers at least equivalent to those of the brain may be incontestable but not very helpful unless we specify in molecular, chemical and electrical terms what these powers are. To exclude computers as possible candidates we shall have to show that some complex chemical processes are necessary to the emergence of consciousness, not just incidental sustainers of the nervous system. As for biological naturalism, which is claimed to solve the above the problem of mind–body interaction, it is summed up in the two simple theses:

1. All mental phenomena are caused by process going on in the brain.
2. Mental phenomena are just features of the brain and perhaps of the rest of the nervous systems.

It is also said that minds are higher-level features of the brain, that mental processes are realized in the brain.[15]

The first of these statements is generally accepted though I

---

13 Searle, *Cambridge Companion to Philosophy of Mind*, p. 547.

14 Ibid., p. 548.

15 Ibid., p. 545.

would not agree that the complete causal determination of mental events by brain events is well established. The evidence we have is strongly suggestive of such a naturalistic conclusion but can be interpreted to give the mind more autonomy. But it is the second statement that is crucial to Searle's simple solution to the mind–body problem and is extremely controversial. What is meant by saying that mental phenomena are just features of the brain? Since they are irreducible to physical features and are private, how do they characterize the brain? 'There are exactly two sorts of processes that go on in the brain, first-person subjective consciousness and third person neuro-biological phenomena.'[16] Surely, conscious processes are not in the brain as bubbles are in a boiling kettle, or icing is on the cake. Is it more informative to say that consciousness is a feature of the brain than to assert that it is totally dependent on the brain?

Searle should say, as Davidson does, that some predicates are mental but they belong to physical entities. But Searle says spontaneously and repeatedly that mental processes are in the brain and are features of the brain. If there are 'irreducible' mental phenomena in the world, how can it be both that the world consists entirely of physical phenomena, that is, physical particulars, their properties and relations, and also that it contains subjective consciousness? The only way out is to make mental phenomena, characteristics of brain events. In other words, they are properties of physical events, not phenomena in their own right. This is our old friend epiphenomenalism however much we may try to avoid its paradoxes by asserting that intentional mental states are, in some situations, efficacious in bringing about bodily changes.

The same point can be made in another way. In his fourth lecture on the structure of action Searle speaks of the 'content' of an intentional state, this 'content' being the same as that of an action, realizing the intention. In his earlier work he traces parallels between intentional states and speech acts. I find the points made by him unexceptionable. But he uses keywords and phrases like 'content',

---

16 Ibid., p. 550.

'representation', 'mind to world fit' or 'word to world fit' which are clearly metaphorical. But their non-metaphorical interpretation is at the heart of the mind–body problem however irrelevant may be the ontological status of mental states to Searle delineation.

What then is the cash value of the statement that mental processes are realized in the structure of the brain or even that they are higher-level features of the brain? The existence of two equally real levels of the brain, one a macro-level mental processes and the other a micro level of neuronal processes is exactly analogous to the existence of two causally real levels of description of the hammer.[17] The solidity of the hammer, the liquidity of water are caused by the arrangement of molecules of which they are composed at the atomic and sub-atomic level. The macro properties are causally effective at the macro level. Similarly 'at the higher level of description, the intention to raise my arm causes the movement of the arm. But at the lower level of description a series of neuronal firings starts a chain of events that results in the contraction of the muscles'.[18]

Once again it is crucial to make up our mind whether there are mental processes, events in their own right as it were, or only mental properties of certain brain events. My overwhelming impression is that mental processes have a substantive and not an adjectival status. It is the second alternative that is suggested by repeated assertions that mental events are features of the brain. If the mind is adjectival then all causation is purely physical. This comes out very clearly when Searle explains how thought can give rise to actions. The answer is that thoughts are not ethereal and weightless. When you have a thought, brain activity is going on. Brain activity causes bodily movements by physiological causation. In other words, brain activity causes other neural events and finally muscular movements in its capacity as a physical process; only thoughts accompany and are a feature of, some brain events.

Second, the two-level causation referred to by Searle, is in the

---

[17] Searle, *Minds Brains and Science*, p. 21.

[18] Ibid.

physical world, a correlation between two 'standing states' not causation between occurrences. If we assume permanent atoms, we have at both the micro and macro levels, persistence of entities and the same entities. For contemporary physics the micro level is dynamic – one of continuous processes. If we like, we can analyse the stable macro state into a series of similar, continuous states, so that the two states are coordinate. In either case the analogy is not very helpful in understanding occurrent causation. Moreover the distinction between micro states and macro states with *supervenient* properties at the macro level is apparently observer relative. If we imagine all sentient beings with a capacity for sense perception and thought to be absent from the world, the distinction would vanish. Philosophers who have found the relation between the mind and the body more perplexing than the relation between digestion and the stomach deserved to be forgiven.[19] But how far the distinction will serve Searle's purpose when the micro level is purely physical and the macro level consists of mental processes is, I think a moot point. The distinction and its bearing on the mind–body problem requires to be thought out more carefully. My objection to saying that mental processes are features of brain activity remains.

---

19 When this paper was presented at a meeting at Jadavpur University, Prof. Soumitra Basu and Prof. T.K. Sarkar argued that the distinction between micro and macro levels of causation is not observer relative as mentioned in the concluding paragraph. The atomic and sub-atomic particles may so distribute themselves in space that one such pattern is a 'hammer' and an other a 'glass pane' and the former may 'crash into the latter'. Even in an observer-free world, a bit of some 'metal' may sink in 'water' but float on 'mercury'. These examples have convinced me that the distinction can be rendered independent of relation to any observer, though some elements in the distinction, for example, wetness of water, do refer to an observer with a specific sensory motor endowment.

5

Descartes' Philosophy of Mind: Its Contemporary Understanding*

Property was thus appalled
That the self was not the same
Single nature's double name
Neither two nor one was called

– Shakespeare, 'Phoenix and the Turtle'[1]

C.D. BROAD remarked while concluding his survey of Descartes' philosophy in *Ethics and History of Philosophy*[2] that his views on the relation of the mind and the body are 'clear and distinct but clearly odd and distinctly incredible'. The terms in which Descartes stated the problem almost ensured the impossibility of its resolution. The reasoning that culminates in the *cogito ergo sum* requires the total separation of the body from the mind. The two are regarded as separate substances each with its distinctive essence, their essential natures having nothing in common. We may, as good empiricists, give up the dualism of substances and substitute for it qualitative difference, difference in levels or even different ways of speaking. This approach apart from its inherent vagueness leaves a residue of dualism which makes some philosophers uncomfortable. For them the ideal solution would be physicalism. Since there is a

* Published in the *Indian Philosophical Quarterly*, vol. XXIII, nos. 1-2, 1996.

1 Shakespeare 'Phoenix and the Turtle' (1601), www.opensourceshakespeare.org

2 C.D. Broad, *Ethics and the History of Philosophy*, London: Routledge, 1952.

great deal of variation in terminology and scope for confusion, we shall take physicalism to stand for analytical behaviourism or the thesis that statements about mental processes can in principle be reformulated into logically equivalent statements about actual and possible behaviour. If the thesis can be successfully maintained a wholesale reduction of the mental to the material would be effected and perplexity about the mind–body problem, which has troubled philosophers since the time of Descartes, would vanish without a trace. But unfortunately the translatability thesis cannot be sustained. In the 1920s, and for sometime afterwards, it was maintained by logical positivists led by Carnap.[3] Other eminent philosophers in the English-speaking world, however either rejected it or came to abandon it. A.J. Ayer, for example, who accepted the thesis concerning other people's experiences when he first wrote 'Language Truth and Logic' very soon jettisoned it together with the asymmetry in meaning between first person and third person psychological statements which his position forced on him.

The near universal abandonment of the translatability thesis is understandable. It is not very difficult to see that the required equivalences between psychological statements on the one hand and behavioural statements on the other do not in fact hold. Mental processes are obviously related to bodily happenings in all sorts of ways. But the connections between the two are casual and contingent and are empirically discovered. This is especially true of the correlations between mental processes and brain events. (Sometimes a bodily component is analytically contained in the personal concept of 'laughing', 'sneezing', etc. But this does not invalidate the above statements.) There is no logical contradiction in admitting that a certain pattern of bodily behaviour occurs, and yet denying that the corresponding mental process occurs. The rejection of the translatability thesis does not mean the return of

---

[3] See Carnap's footnote to 'Psychology in Physical Language' in *Logical Positivism*, ed. by A.J. Ayer, The Free Press, 1959. In this he maintains that 'anger', 'desire', etc. are like the scientific concept of 'electron', postulated to explain observational data.

Cartesian dualism. Ryle does not offer precise definitions and logical translations but analyses mental concepts primarily in terms of dispositions to behaviour in specifiable contexts while offering ad hoc solutions to particular difficulties and threatening the dualist with the infinite regress – the old bugbear of philosophers. He leaves a considerable residue of inner processes, not analysed further in terms of behaviour. But his views are broadly physicalistic or naturalistic, though the success of his enterprise is hard to judge. This determination, not to allow the return of the Cartesian ego is not confined to Ryle and the positivists. It motivates philosophers of widely differing outlooks like A.J. Ayer, B.A.O. Williams and Derek Parfit (who are nearest to traditional philosophy) and the various advocates of the identity theory.

The Identity Theory

The most elaborate exposition of the theory is by D.M. Armstrong in his *A Materialist Theory of the Mind* who also refers to it by the alternative expression 'Central State Materialism'. But he shares with the early exponents – J.C.C. Smart, Herbert Feigl, U.T. Place – the basic approach as also the fundamental assumptions and methods by which the identification of mental processes with states of the brain can be rendered plausible. The identity theory accepts the lack of conceptual or logical connections between psychological and physical descriptions. But it attempts to salvage something for physicalism by substituting factual identity for logical or analytical identity. Borrowing Frege's well-known example Smart argues that mental process may be identical with corresponding brain events (commonly alleged to be their causes) in the same way as the morning star is identical with the evening star though the expressions 'morning star', 'evening star' are not synonymous.[4] An example that serves the theory even better is the identity of a lightning flash with a pattern of electrical discharge. Nobody

---

[4] J.J.C. Smart, 'Sensations and Brain processes', *Philosophical Review*, LXVII, 1959, included in *Body and Mind*, ed. G.N. Vesey, Allen and Unwin, 1964, p. 428.

nowadays would object to the identification on the ground that our perceptual reports of lightning are very different from the physicist's account of an electrical discharge.

An objection that almost springs to our mind is the undeniable fact that men could talk meaningfully and truly of their sensations, feelings, thoughts, memories, etc. long before the discovery of their neural correlates by physiology. Adapting a remark by John Locke we may say that God has not made men a two-legged creature with a bare capacity for sensations and leave it to neurophysiology to tell him what precisely they are. Even a neurophysiologist is not examining his own brain when talking about his mental processes. Does it not follow from all this that reports about sensations are not reports about brain events? The advocates of the theory think that the objection loses all its force once it is realized that they have given up the translatability thesis. When we report on experience of having an after-image, what we mean is not some statement of the form 'I have such and such a brain process'. But this does not show that what we report is not in fact a brain process. In general, we can have a contingently true statement of the type '*A* = *B*' and we can very well know that something is an *A* without knowing that it is a *B*?[5]

This answer is quite correct and plausible, as far as it goes, but it does not go far enough. A person can know of something say *X*, that *X* is *A* without knowing that *X* is *B*, when in fact *X* is *B*. But then there must be at least two different ways of 'locating', 'pinpointing' or identifying *X* via two different characteristics or aspects of *X*. And it can easily turn out that we know that *X* satisfied one of the descriptions without knowing that it satisfies the other. An ordinary citizen of Baghdad may have in fact met and talked to Harun-al-Rashid without knowing that the queer fellow he encountered was in reality the Caliph. Even if mental processes are identical with brain events they must have characteristics other than the electrical and chemical properties discovered by physiology. It does not

---

5 *Review*, LXVII, op. cit., pp. 428-29.

follow that the attributes noticed by the subject of experiences are irreducibly psychical attributes totally different from the attributes which figure in the physiological account. They could very well be other physical attributes. But it must be admitted that this is not a very appealing view to take. For, we shall have to postulate new forms of energy in the world and receptor cells in the organism to selectively respond to them, all unsuspected by contemporary science. Not a very tempting prospect for those who advocate the identity theory on the ground that it is the most simple, economical unified theory of the world in the light of knowledge provided by physics and physiology.

One element in the response to this difficulty is to regard reports of sensations and images by the subject to be vague, colourless and neutral, consistent with dualism as well as the identity theory. According to Smart the relation between introspective reports and those of the scientist are exemplified by the relation between the two statements:

1. Someone is coming through the garden.
2. The doctor is coming through the garden.

This general approach is shared by Armstrong who defines a mental state as a state of the person apt for bringing about a certain type of behaviour and also in certain cases a state apt for being brought about by a certain stimulus.[6] But is it true that our reports of sensations and feeling are so vague and non-committal as is made out? We do not always find it easy to describe our feelings because they change rapidly and also because their qualities cannot be categorized, checked and re-checked like those of a solid, stable material object in front of us. But for all that we do classify them, recognize them and compare them. There are the broad distinctions between different sense modalities and within each sense modality

---

[6] D.M. Armstrong, *A Materialist Theory of the Mind*, London: Routledge and Kegan Paul, 1968, p. 82. The first half of the definition clearly implies a rejection of epiphenomenalism. Indeed Armstrong argues that his theory is compatible with the logical possibility of survival.

there are qualitative distinctions such as the distinction between a bang, a buzz, a thud, a tinkle, a screech, a crash, etc. among sounds as heard. Older psychologists distinguished the simple constituents of a complex emotion (awe into fear and wonder) and distinguished between emotions and feelings. Patients describe their pains and aches to the doctor, indicating where they are felt, whether they are intermittent or continuous, the character they have, such as throbbing, burning, stabbing, etc. And of course great novelists describe the inner thoughts and feelings and changing moods of their characters, and with all respect to Ryle, with next to no indication of their behaviour. How could we do all this, unless the brain event which on this view are identical with our experience, at least have some irreducibly physical attributes of which we are introspectively aware and which are different from the attributes studied by neuro-physiology?

The second element in the attempt to avoid irreducibly mental qualities is to stretch the dispositional analysis of mental concepts to cover desire, memory and even perception and to accept their basic workability in spite of persistent and unresolved difficulties. Armstrong defines perception 'as nothing but the acquiring of true or false beliefs concerning the current states of the organism's body and its environment'.[7] A belief itself is to be understood in terms of selective and discriminative behaviour.[8] This still leaves a residue of 'raw feels' – sensations and feelings – whose occurrential character is hard to deny. These are to be specially accommodated by the identity theory. Take Smart's analysis of 'this is red' where what is 'given' may be a sensation or after-image, or better still, of 'I see a yellowish orange after-image'.[9] The analysis of the former is: a normal percipient would not easily pick this out of a clump of geranium petals though he would pick it out of lettuce leaves. The latter is analysed thus: 'There is *something* going on *which is like* what is going on when I have my eyes open, am awake, and there

[7] Armstrong, *A Materialist Theory of the Mind*, p. 209.

[8] Ibid., p. 340.

[9] Smart in *Body and Mind*, pp. 430-32.

is an orange illuminated in good light in front or me, that is, when I really see an orange.' (The italicized words are quasi-logical and topic neutral. Hence, we are told they are compatible with dualism and also the identity theory and its materialism.)

What are we to say of the argument? Assuming that the brain event when I see an orange is in fact similar to the pattern of brain excitation when I see an orange after-image, the fact remains that I am not aware of either of the two neural events. How then can I report that they are similar? Smart himself suggests that for his account to be successful, we should be able to report two processes as like one another without being able to specify in what respect they are alike. But surely the argument requires much more. It credits us with the feat of reporting two terms to be alike when we are not given either of them. Moreover the analyses are not just imprecise, as Smart admits, but more radically inadequate. Their acceptance would lead to the conclusion that the word 'red', for example, would not have the meaning it now has, if the world did not contain geraniums and lettuce leaves. The defect cannot be remedied by choosing different 'standard exemplars' for our definition; for the crucial error is to make the procedure for learning the meaning of an expression part of the meaning itself. To turn an account of our introspective reports of these experiences into non-commital reports of corresponding neural events, is really to put the cart before the horse.

It is said notably by Place that the language in which we describe our sensation, that is, the looks and feels, etc. of things, is a phenomenal language which is dependent upon public, physical language and is a modification of the latter in certain circumstances. We begin by learning to recognize the real properties of things in our environment. It is only later that

> we learn to describe our consciousness of them . . . in those cases where the appropriateness of his normal descriptive habits is in doubt, (the individual) learns to issue . . . protocols preceded by a qualificatory phrase like 'it appears', 'seems', 'looks', 'feels', etc.[10]

---

[10] Smart in *Body and Mind*, pp. 430-32.

Similarly, Smart speaks of the change from talking about the environment to talking about one's perceptual responses being a matter of inhibiting certain reactions because one has learnt that in the prevailing circumstances they are unlikely to provide a good indication of the state of the environment.[11] The upshot: there are no 'private' qualities inhering in mythological objects appearing on an internal television screen.

This answer raises many questions particularly in the context of the causal theory of perception.[12] As it stands it does nothing to remove the difficulty concerning explaining or 'locating' secondary qualities in the world of the physicalist's conception. On this view, the objects in the world including human brains are composed of the particles favoured by the latest theories of mathematical physics and possess only spatio-temporal, structural and dynamical properties with some chemical properties thrown in. The identity theory cannot dump perceived colour, etc. in the mind, not even as the internal accusatives of acts of sensing. (These latter would be simply electrical discharges in the brain even if admitted.) To accept a world of non-material, non-mental sense data would spoil the beautiful simplicity of its world picture. Neutral monism of course would water down its hearty and vigorous materialism and to regard colour, etc. as *appearances* to the observer of the 'real' properties would bring back dualism and the mind.

But even if we accept this account of sensations and after-images there are other kinds of mental processes such as thinking, remembering and experiencing various emotions talk about which can hardly be regarded as talk about the way things look, feel, sound, etc. Place frankly states, and Smart seems to suggest, that

---

11 Smart in *Body and Mind*, pp. 430-32.

12 Russell arrived at the causal theory of perception long before it was put forward as a solution to the mind–body problem. See 'Mind and Matter' in *Portraits from Memory and Other Essays* by Bertrand Russell, George Allen and Unwin, 1956; also see relevant chapters in *Analysis of Matter*, London: Kegan and Paul, 1927 and *Human Knowledge: Its Scope and Limits*, London: George Allen and Unwin, 1948.

these alleged mental acts can be analysed in terms of dispositions to behave, along the lines suggested by Ryle and Wittgenstein. Personally I think that this is an over optimistic assumption. Whatever may be the achievements of Ryle and Wittgenstein, I don't think they have succeeded in abolishing private mental process (in the case of Wittgenstein it is even doubtful whether he wanted to achieve this result). Remembering, experiencing anger, anxiety sorrow, etc. thinking about a problem and so on have as much an occurrential air – seem as much to be things that go on – as sensations and images. The fact that many mental predicates are often used dispositionally and have a 'behavioural' content does not lead to the conclusion that they are never used to refer to inner experiences or that this reference to inner experiences is not of primary importance in their use. So, unless the identity theory can provide an explanation that will cover all kinds of mental processes, its claim to have got rid of irreducibly psychical processes and attributes cannot be taken seriously.

It appears very strange that none of the advocates of the identity theory has bothered to ask himself whether mental processes can be identified with brain processes if what can be truly predicated of one of them cannot even be significantly predicated of the other. Broad pointed out more than nearly half a century ago that we cannot speak of a sensation as slow, circular or swift. But these can be predicted of brain events with perfect propriety. On the other hand, sensations and perceptions can be clear or confused but not brain events. Smart admits that so far no meaning has been given to such talk, but that we could do it if we wanted to by adopting a convention which would be an addition to and not a contravention of our existing linguistic rules.[13] A more subtle suggestion is that of Hilary Putnam that statements like 'a feeling of pain is identical with an excitation in the thalamus' can come to *acquire a meaning* by scientific advances and may even be regarded as true.[14] This will

---

[13] Smart in *Body and Mind,* p. 433.

[14] Hook Sydney (ed.), *Dimensions of Mind,* New York: New York University Press, 1960, pp. 155-57.

probably take place if physiology advances to a stage where it would be able (i) to derive from physical theory simple laws of common sense or 'mentalistic' psychology, and (ii) to make predictions which we are unable to make at present.

It is no objection to such a view that probably neuro-physiology would never reach this stage. Let us suppose that perfected neuro-physiology would one day be able to make predictions with the help of comprehensive theories, as accurate and detailed as those of physics today. Should we then be justified in saying that mental processes are brain events, just as we say today that 'light' is 'electro-magnetic radiation' or 'temperature' is the 'mean kinetic energy of a body'. Putnam thinks that in both the cases the justification for accepting an identity or rejecting it in favour of perfect correspondence applies with equal force. There is an important difference between the two cases. Even if one day neuro-physiology sets up detailed correlations between highly specific mental processes and equally specific brain events, it will have to rely upon the introspective reports by the subject of experience. *Otherwise it would have nothing to correlate with brain events.* The neurologist will have to apply the same stimuli to a number of subjects under controlled conditions and note that they report the same kind of experiences. The acceptance of the truth of these introspective reports is essential to the establishment of general principles of correlation between mental and neural events. Once our table of 'conversions' is available as a ready reckoner, we can 'read off' the experience of a subject by observing his brain state. But suppose that on a certain occasion the physiologist observes a brain state which he 'identifies' as a pain but the subject insists that he has no pain or that the physiologist 'observes' that the correlate of pain does not occur and yet the subject reports pain, what are we to do? If we are satisfied that he is neither lying nor has made a verbal mistake, we shall have to revise our tables and look for more exact correlations. We would be unwise to dismiss him as an ignorant person untrained in the techniques of science. (That way lies the road to a new scientific inquisition.) This is because the introspective reports provide not merely evidence for our correlation but also supply one of the terms to be correlated. Contrast this with what happens, say, in the case of the kinetic theory of heat. Our feelings of heat and cold may be the beginnings of our ideas of temperature – and within limits they provide rough indications of temperatures of bodies. But once it reaches a certain stage of sophistication, physics ignores them altogether and dismisses them with contempt when they conflict with its pointer-readings. Our feelings of warmth and cold are only 'appearances' – often misleading – of the real temperature of a body. Similar considerations apply to the identification of light with electromagnetic waves. The philosopher who tries to accommodate 'appearances' within the total scheme of things has a problem. The physicists, none. The subject has a veto here in neuro-psychology which he is denied in physics.

Another, perhaps even more important, difference between the identities effected by science and the identity proposed by our theory is that in the case of the former there is an already well-established criterion namely, spatio-temporal continuity in the case of objects of location in the same region at any given time in the case of events. In identifying mental processes with neural correlates which are normally regarded as their necessary and sufficient condition, location in the same region cannot be used as a criterion because, as noticed by us, mental processes have no spatial and extensible characteristics. If on grounds of economy and simplicity, we stipulate that mental events are where their causal determinants are, are we doing anything more than:

1. rejecting a subject of experiences in the manner of Hume, and
2. reviving the old theory of epiphenomenalism and dressing it up in new clothes?

Anomalous Monism: The Tortuous Path to Physicalism

The identity theory can be regarded in two ways. First of all, as an attempt to salvage a naturalistic view of the world from the breakdown of the translatability thesis. From another point of view it assumes, on reasonable scientific grounds, psychophysical parallelism. More specifically, perfect correlation and co-variation between mental events and brain events are taken for granted and then invariable concomitances are converted into identities for economy and unification. The two viewpoints are not incompatible. In Davidson's anomalous monism, the naturalistic motive is there, but it is essential to his argument for the identity theory, to deny the possibility of psycho-physical laws. It follows, unless one takes a non-human view of causation, that perfect correspondence between mental events and brain events is not possible either. Davidson's views are set forth in the essay on 'Mental Events'. This can be read with two others 'Psychology as Philosophy' and 'The Material Mind' which contain further comment and answers to objections. All these are also included in 'Actions and Events'.[15] This argument for anomalous monism depends on the following propositions. Davidson calls them assumptions, but they express very reasonable beliefs based on experience:

1. Mental events (singular, identifiable) are sometimes causes and effects of physical events.
2. Each true singular casual statement of this kind is backed by a strict causal law, i.e. if *m* and *p* are event-related as effect and cause, they belong to kinds of events connected by our law or they satisfy descriptions which instantiate a law.
3. Physical events are subject to law, and under physical theory constitute a closed system.

The domain of mental events does not constitute a closed system. With the help of these it is demonstrated that the connecting law mentioned in 2 cannot be psycho-physical. No such principle can be a strict law. Hence *m* and *p* in our symbolical illustration must fall under physical descriptions if they are to instantiate a strict law. Hence *m* too is a physical event. So, every mental event that is causally related to a physical event is a physical event.[16]

---

15 D. Davidson, *Essays on Actions and Events*, Oxford: Oxford University Press, 2001.

16 Ibid., pp. 223-25.

The reason why mental events (events answering to mentalist descriptions) cannot be governed by strict laws is that they cannot be pinpointed with accuracy.

> There is no assigning beliefs to a person one by one on the basis of his behaviour, his choices or other local signs no matter how plain and evident.[17]

Again,

> it is a feature of the mental that the attribution of mental phenomena must be responsible to the background of reasons, beliefs and intentions of the individual. There cannot be tight connections between the two if each is to retain its allegiance to its proper source of evidence.[18]

A.J. Ayer in his *Philosophy in the Twentieth Century* objects that if mental events cannot be pinpointed accurately enough to be related by a strict law, why should it be assumed that they can nevertheless be sufficiently accurately pinpointed to be the terms of causal relation.[19] The proper conclusion of Davidson's argument is either that mental events are not causally related at all or, that they do not need the backing of a strict law to be so related. The argument is even more inconclusive than Ayer takes it to be. He points out, in passing, that it does not follow from the argument either that events have no accurate mental descriptions or that the description is not known to the subject himself. In fact, Davidson ignores self-knowledge throughout his discussion. Towards the end of his 'Mental Events' he fleetingly refers to his saying 'nothing about the supposed privacy of the mental or the special authority an agent has with respect to his own propositional attitudes'.[20] His defence is that this appearance of novelty would fade if we were to investigate the grounds for accepting a scheme of translation. This presumbly is a scheme for

---

17 Davidson, op. cit., p. 221.

18 Ibid., p. 222.

19 A.J. Ayer, *Philosophy in the Twentieth Century*, London: Weidenfeld, 1982, p. 187.

20 Davidson, op. cit., p. 223.

the mutual translation of behavioural and psychological statements. But there is no such scheme which does not acknowledge and accept the authority of the agent. The extensive use of the method of 'verbal report' – a sanitized acceptance of introspective data – in correlating certain patterns of stimulation on the one hand and experience of sensations of colour or after-images on the other, is testimony that even most hardened behaviourist cannot dispense with the authority of the agent, at any rate, at the present state of our knowledge. A more recent example is Penfield's correlation between stimulation of different areas of the clinically exposed brain and the subject's reports of his experiences. Moreover, Davidson does not seem to realize that the dependence of psychological assertions on an indefinite background and their constant revisability does not mean that what is asserted is indefinite. Such assertions, both mental and physical, can be as definite as the situation permits. He seems to pass from indefiniteness of assertion to the assertion of the indefinite. If this is so there is no need to subsume mental events under physical descriptions to render them worthy of instantiating a strict law. We can of course be content with a law which is approximately true. One cannot be sure of having understood Davidson's contention correctly. There is an absence of illustrative examples throughout, except the rather unnecessary one of belief in life on Mars.

Davidson exaggerates the difference between his version of the identity theory wherein individual-dated unrepeatable events are identified one with another, and the more usual version where kinds of mental events are identified with kinds of brain events. The causal statements with which he starts are singular causal statements. But such statements are accepted as true only because we have evidence that there are general causal principles between kinds of events and believe that our particulars instantiate these kinds. His own stipulation, that our singular causal statements are backed by a strict causal law connecting kinds of events to which our cause and effect belong, admits this. There is thus no incompatibility between asserting identity between individual events and asserting it in the case of kinds of events. Indeed the former logically depend on the latter unless they are true fortuitously or as a result of lucky guesswork.

This comes out clearly in Davidson's reply to Attfield, appended to his 'Psychology as Philosophy'.[21] Attfield argues that anomalous monism is inconsistent and that it follows from the premises of Davidson that there are psycho-physical laws. Suppose the perception of a fly in Attfield's mind at *t*, is identical with the neurological change *p* at *t* in Attfield. Further, there is causal law that connects *p* with another physical event p_1 at t_1. Hence the law, that connects *p* (which is a perception) with p_1, is a psycho-physical law, Davidson accept the premises and rejects the conclusion. This is basically like arguing, Davidson comments, that from (i) Scott is the author of Waverly, (ii) Jones believes that the author of Waverly wrote Waverly, it follows that (iii) Jones believes that Scott wrote Waverly. The arguments fail because mutual substitutivity of co-referring singular terms (and also of equivalent functional expressions) breaks down in intensional contexts. This is an odd reply because it presupposes that the thesis of extensionality breaks down in intensional contexts, whereas physicalism, in any form, cannot be maintained unless the thesis is shown to be adequate. Davidson extends the point to non-extensional contexts, for causal laws connect events not extensionally but as described in one way or another. If every *p* is followed, after a suitable interval by p_1 and p_1 is in fact *I*, it does not follow that there is a law that connects *p* and *I*. Here *I* symbolizes some perception or intentional experience and *p*, p_1 and *I* correspond to *H*, *F* and *G* in Davidson's reply. But what about the relation between *p* and *I*? Unless the two are related by invariable or nearly invariable concomitance, the law connecting *p* and p_1 will be of no interest to psychology and cannot take the place of a psycho-physical law.

Beyond Behaviourism and Dualism

The relation of the mind to the body is one of the few philosophical problems directly tackled by Wittgenstein. Here, as elsewhere, his claim is that he does not offer any theories or explanations

---

[21] Davidson, op. cit., pp. 241-42.

but dispels doubts and confusions, by an unprejudiced survey of the working of our language. The problem, rather a tangle of related issues, is discussed as the problem of a correct analysis of our statements about persons and their experiences. In spite of his profession of neutrality, the main target of his hostile criticism is dualism of some sort – according to which statements about experience are about inner, conscious occurrences irreducible to observable bodily behaviour. The nerve-centre of his attack on such a view is that it involves a private language in which each subject – and he alone – can refer to his mental processes, and that such a language is logically impossible. If words for mental processes are endowed with meaning by ostensive definition of private object, they should never function as elements in our intersubjective communications, as they in fact do. But, if words like 'pain' and 'tooth ache' do not refer to and even cannot refer to subjective processes, are we not compelled to embrace the view that they are equivalent to descriptions about actual and possible behaviour? Wittgenstein and his defenders say 'no'. What are the motives and reasons for maintaining this apparently indefensible position?

It is of course possible to read undiluted behaviourism into some of the pronouncements of Wittgenstein. The famous 'Beetle in the box' leads up to the conclusion:

> If we construe the grammar of the expressions on the model of object and name, the object drops out of consideration as irrelevant.[22]

Even more emphatic and final is the statement from *Zettel*, 'joy designates nothing neither any inward not any outward thing'.[23] In spite of these and some other similar pronouncements, it would be wrong to regard Wittgenstein as a behaviourist. He clearly rejected the view that descriptions of behaviour logically entail the truth of experimental statements. Given this, to emphasize that 'an inner

---

[22] L. Wittgenstein, *Philosophical Investigations*, ed. G.E.M. Anscombe and R. Rhees, tr. G.E.M. Anscombe, Oxford: Blackwell, 1953, p. 293.

[23] L. Wittgenstein, *Zettel*, ed. G.E.M. Anscombe and G.H. von Wright, tr. G.E.M. Anscombe, Oxford: Blackwell, 1967, p. 487.

process stands in need of outward criteria' rather implies that the two are distinct. Nor is this merely a matter of inference. There are explicit rejections of behaviourism, in his 'notes on private experience and sense-data'. He raises the question: 'do you mean that you can define pain in terms of behaviour?' and answers: but is this what we do if we teach the child to use the expression 'have a tooth ache'. Did I define: 'Tooth ache is such and such a behaviour? This obviously contradicts the normal use of the word'. Again we have:

> But you will surely admit that there is a difference between pain-behaviour accompanied by pain and pain-behaviour without any pain? – Admit it. What greater difference could be there? And yet you again and again reach the conclusion that the sensation itself is a nothing – Not at all – It is not something but not a nothing either. The conclusion was that a nothing would serve as well as a something about which nothing could be said.[24]

It is not easy to decipher the significance of some of the above statements. But there is enough texual evidence to show that Wittgenstein was not and did not consider himself to be a behaviourist.

Anthony Kenny in his contribution to 'the private language argument' suggests that the behaviourist passages can be reconciled in the light of the attack on the primacy of ostensive definition in the earlier passages (27-35) of the *Philosophical Investigations*.[25] It is true that the full significance of Wittgenstein's comments can be appreciated only in the light of his attack on the equation of meaning and naming and the central role on this theory of ostensive definition in endowing signs with meaning. But, as the examples of colour and shape make clear, the criticism applies equally to ostensive definition of physical qualities and objects and not merely to mental processes and their qualities. Wittgenstein argues that the simple ceremony of pointing to something while uttering a word is not uniquely and unambiguously efficacious in determining the meaning of a sign.

---

24 Wittgenstein, *Philosophical Investigations*, p. 74.

25 Anthony Kenny, *Wittgenstein*, Cambridge, MA: Harvard University Press, 1973.

But he has no tendency to deny that our language contains names of physical objects and their qualities. On the contrary, one of the principal points made by him is that we misconstrue the grammer of our talk of experiences when we regard psychological words as standing for inner private, processes, thus assimilating this language game to the language game of describing the physical world.

The contradiction would, in a way, disappear if we take the view that Wittgenstein is not saying anything about psychological words which he would not have said about words referring to physical objects. This rather starting view is put forward by Peter Winch in his Introduction to the *Studies in the Philosophy of Wittgenstein* edited by him. He writes:

> And if we wanted to describe the language games in which we give names to material objects in the same sort of depth as Wittgenstein is here describing the language-games of talking about one's sensations, it would be equally important to insist that 'the object drops out of consideration as irrelevant'.

The reason for this is, of course, not that no object is involved in these language games, but rather because (to adapt a phrase used by Wittgenstein in a different connection) that part of the grammar of the expressions is clear enough. What we need to understand is the context of practices and interests which gives the purely formal conception of an object some definite sense in particular cases. For this reason it seems to me that it might be a symptom of confusion to insist too vehemently and for too long that 'pain' is not the name of an object. Of course, it would be equally confusing to insist too vehemently and for too long that 'pain' is the name of an object.[26] Unfortunately Winch does not tell us how long and how vehemently we should practise the two movements of this Hegelian process to attain philosophic wisdom.

How then are the ambiguities and vacillations, in our minds if not Wittgenstein's, to be removed, and a clear explanation offered

---

26 Peter Winch, *Studies in the Philosophy of Wittgenstein*, Routledge and Kegan Paul, 1969.

of how we can reject both behaviourism and Cartesian dualism? We may get some help if we leave aside, discussion of the impossibility of a private language, and the name–object relation, and turn to Wittgenstein's resolution of the doubt concerning other minds. The subjective, private, character of our experiences is but the obverse of the coin of which scepticism concerning other minds is the reverse. It is the lurking threat of solipsism that makes many philosophers turn away from dualism as from a blind alley. If it is true that each one of us has direct access only to ones own experiences, we are condemned to making precarious inferences about the contents of the minds of others. Such inferences are supposed to be justified by analogy between my behaviour and the behaviour of others. But analogical argument, in his context, is utterly inadequate if not radically defective. A necessary base for philosophical doubt as well as philosophical attempts at justification of belief in other minds is the contrast between the direct and certain knowledge I have of my own experiences and the indirect, problematic nature of my knowledge of the experiences of others. If we can get rid of this contrast we shall have demonstrated the emptiness of the sceptical position. Wittgenstein achieves this desirable result by the surprising method of maintaining that I cannot meaningfully be said to know, for example, that I have tooth ache.

> Other people cannot be said to learn of my sensations only from my behaviour, for I cannot be said to learn of them. I have them. The truth is it makes sense to say of other people that they doubt whether I am in pain; but not to say it of myself.[27]

There are several points of interest here. First of all there is the insistence that where doubt is senseless, affirmation of knowledge is equally senseless. This has continuity with Wittgenstein's insistence in the *Tractatus* that tautologies do not provide any knowledge but only facilitate the understanding of proofs. However, the statement 'I am in pain' is obviously not a tautology. Since the above is not a genuine declarative sentence according to Wittgenstein, prefixing it

---

[27] Wittgenstein, *Philosophical Investigations*, p. 246.

with 'I know' cannot result in a genuine proposition. Kenny thinks that the point made by Wittgenstein here is based on the picture theory of the *Tractatus*. He writes:

> A description must be independent of what it is to be compared with, if it is to be assessed as a correct or incorrect description.

'I am in pain' since it is an utterance which is a criterion for my conscious state, is not independent of it and so cannot be a description of it in the same way as 'there is a chair in the corner may be a description of it'. If this is the point being made it is of doubtful value. Wittgenstein grants that others can sensibly say of a person that he is in pain. 'He is in pain', said by others of a person *P* is made true or false by a certain state of affairs in the world. 'I am in pain' uttered by *P* of himself is made true or false by the same state of affairs, unless, on independent grounds we show that the latter utterance is non-declarative. It would be paradoxical to allow that a third person psychological statement is true and yet maintain that the corresponding first person statement is senseless. Moreover, if we grant as we all do, that when a man is in pain he cannot be mistaken. It does not follow that his declaration about his pain, when he makes one, is not independent of his being in pain. What makes the utterance true is not the fact of its being made but the fact which it asserts. The picture theory, like any version of the correspondence theory cannot demand more, and the logical demand central to it is fulfilled in the present case. In addition, he can lie about it, and it would be very strange to maintain that we can lie in a situation where we cannot tell the truth. According to Wittgenstein 'I know I am in pain' when I am in pain, expresses no empirical proposition but a proposition of grammar to the effect that doubt in such cases is non-sensical. In the notes he composed in the last eighteen months of his life and published under the title *On Certainty*, the same line of thinking is adopted about the certainties of commonsense on which Moore based his proof of the external world. He castigates Moore, not for maintaining that such propositions are true and certain but for declaring for example, 'I know this is a hand' in a situation where this is pointless and is in fact a misuse of the expression, 'I know'. If 'I know', etc. is conceived as a grammatical proposition it properly means that there is no such thing as a doubt in this case or the expression 'I don't know' make no sense in this case. And of course it follows from this that 'I know' makes no sense either.[28]

As an explication of the ordinary use of 'I know' and similar expressions, this may be largely acceptable. However, two points are perhaps worth making. First, it may be to make a grammatical point that I say I cannot be mistaken about my pain. But is it not legitimate to ask, 'why do we adopt this rule of grammar?'. Surely we do not issue a decree that doubt is impossible in the case of certain propositions, whereas it is permissible in others.There must be some differences in the circumstances in which different sorts of propositions and methods of their verification are accepted. Though we have some liberty in adopting alternative rules, the grammar we adopt reflects facts, especially certain broad features of the world. To explain certainty or lack of it, sense or nonsense, in terms of grammar, is a good first move but not a very satisfactory final move. Second, it is not very difficult to construct examples and not entirely imaginary either, where avowals about one's inner feelings are perfectly in order and serve a practical purpose. If a doctor who has failed to alleviate the pain of a patient doubts the correctness of his complaints, the patient may say, 'you can take it from me the pain has not lessened' or with exasperation 'I know my pain better than you'. Whether or not, it is natural to prefix 'I know' to such avowals is a point of minor significance. It is important to note that in the above example the patient may be wrong. He may be a hypochondriac who exaggerates his pains. I may be the best and final judge of whether I am in pain or not, but I may misdescribe what medical men call the 'modalities of the pain'. So, if it is the possibility of error that is needed to lend respectability

---

[28] L. Wittgenstein, *On Certainty*, ed. G.E.M. Anscombe and G.H. von Wright, tr. G.E.M. Anscombe and D. Paul, Oxford: Blackwell, 1969; also compare *The Blue and Brown Books*, 1958, Oxford: Blackwell, 1958 for an application of this approach at the other end to 'we cannot know when another is in pain'.

to such propositions, it is available and we may, with advance in neurology and biochemistry, even devise methods of detecting and discounting such errors.

If, at one end, Wittgenstein destroys the certainty of self-knowledge (rather shows it to be a phony certainty, not the kind we took it to be) equally at the other end, he dispels doubt by maintaining that scepticism concerning other minds expresses no genuine doubt. 'Just try in a real case to doubt someone else's fear or pain' he challenges us.[29] He grants of course that the behaviour criteria do not logically entail the occurrence of the mental process of which they are criteria. Since pain can exist without its normal expressions (they can be suppressed) and may be absent when the symptoms are present (these can be simulated or artificially induced) behaviour criteria are neither logically necessary nor logically sufficient. Nevertheless they are adequate and in normal cases lead to certainty.

> Am I less certain that this man is in pain than that twice two is four . . . does this show the former to be mathematical certainty? The kind of certainty is the kind of language game.[30]

If the sceptic persists and says that we have no right to be sure in this case, as the certainty involved is not logical or absolute certainty, Wittgenstein makes short work of him, 'but if you are certain isn't it that you are shutting eyes in the face of doubt? – they are shut'.[31] The precise import of these moves is not very obvious though the goal is evidently to cripple the sceptic at the starting point. Various interpretations have been offered by many including Reinhardt in the *Studies in the Philosophy of Wittgenstein* edited by Peter Winch.[32] But every suggested interpretation of what Wittgenstein is doing is

---

29 Wittgenstein, *Philosophical Investigations*, p. 303.

30 Ibid., part II.

31 Ibid.

32 L. Reinhardt, 'Wittgenstein and Strawson on Other Minds', in *Studies in the Philosophy of Wittgenstein*, ed. Peter Winch, Routledge and Kegan Paul, 1969.

accompanied by the qualification that if follows from his views, or is a part of it, without an explanation of what precisely his contention is, or of the central point of his remarks. We can however consider some of the possible interpretations:

1. Wittgenstein is suggesting that doubt is senseless unless there is specific ground for doubt. We can be and sometimes are mistaken about the inner processes of other persons. But so much is contained in our admission that behavioural criteria do not entail statements about mental processes. This does not legitimize idle, motiveless doubt. So in the absence of specific grounds for doubt the claim to knowledge is to be accepted, especially when the conditions in which inner processes are ascribed to others approach paradigm cases.
2. The above contention can easily develop into the view that doubt is possible and admissible in particular cases. But generalized doubt is not only pointless but also logically vicious. We can deny or doubt the truth of any particular description, but to maintain that we can do this in the case of all such statements is meaningless. To borrow an analogy from Ryle, it is as if, shaken by the discovery that many coins accepted as genuine by us are counterfeit, we were to conclude that all the currencies in the country are illegal. The point made by Wittgenstein is that the language game we play when we talk of persons and their experience has certain basic rules which constitute its framework. We cannot play the game and yet reject the framework. To do this would be to do something incomprehensible, though it may not be logically self-contradictory. Wittgenstein says repeatedly that there can be no justification for a language game as a whole. Particular moves within the framework can be criticized and accepted or rejected by reference to the rules of the game. We may change the rules of the game or even opt out of the game – though this is hardly conceivable in the case under discussion. But we cannot question the rules of the game, when engaged in playing it. Ultimately we can play and say that our language

game is part of a form of life which has to be accepted.

3. The outward criteria for inner processes do not logically entail the truth of psychological assertions. But for all that they are logically adequate. The natural expressions or symptoms of pain are not connected contingently with pain. They are part of the concept of pain. Totally unexpressed mental processes, like totally inaudible speech, are incomprehensible.

What makes the connection between mental processes and their concomitants more than contingent is the total setting – social and physical – in which the game is played, and also the nature of the game. Strawson, who takes this view of the relation between *M*-predicates and *P*-predicates in other ascriptions, gives the analogy of the relation between the description of the visual characteristics of a playing cards and their ranking in a game. From the description of the cards together with the rules of the game it follows that a king ranks above a queen and a queen above a knave of the same suit. But the rankings certainly do not follow from the physical character of the cards alone. This is a telling metaphor but it may not serve our present purpose very well. The rules of a card game are all conventional whereas laws connecting mental processes with their bodily accompaniments are natural and are discovered from experience, not laid down by us according to our purpose and convenience. It is possible to pursue this approach and seek other models and explanations. But the main thing is that further elaborations are needed and needed badly in this case and also in the case of the two earlier approaches. Like Wittgenstein's appeal to rules of grammar, this is a good beginning but hardly a comfortable resting point.

Has Wittgenstein succeeded in rejecting Cartesian dualism without, at the same time, embracing behaviourism? As understood by contemporary philosophers dualism involves not only immediacy and privacy of subjective experiences but also the assertion of the problematic character of other ascriptions which must rest on a precarious argument by analogy. If Wittgenstein's suggestion for resolving the problem of other minds is successful, or promising, to that extent, we have moved away from dualism. But if we reject behaviourism – whether analytical behaviourism of the type sponsored by Carnap or the more recent versions of the identity theory – then dualism of some kind becomes inevitable. In the old-fashioned metaphysical language we may say that the rejection of reductive materialism logically implies that there are mental processes qualitatively different from material processes and irreducible to them. It is a little difficult to understand why Wittgenstein insists that first-person psychological reports are not statements. Presumably words for sensation and feelings figuring in them do stand for inner processes. And if we grant as he does, that such a statement can be false even when in some cases the behaviour criteria are satisfied, it follows that their meaning is not given by descriptions of behaviour. If so, what do we gain by denying them a referential role in self-ascriptions? Dualism in this minimum interpretation is implied by the admissions which he makes and if the way out of scepticism suggested by him is acceptable there is no reason why a dualism should not accept it.

It is all very well for Wittgenstein to say,

> there is a kind of mental disease which looks for and finds what would be called a mental state from which all our acts spring as from a reservoir.[33]

He speaks in a similar vein in the *Philosophical Investigations*.[34] But we have mental pictures and myths not only in postulating mental processes, not given to us, but also in supposing that there is life on Mars or that there are things totally unperceived by us and so on. There is of course a kind of mentalism which he and Ryle successfully refute – namely the kind that regards mental events as taking place in a very thin supersensible medium. Spirit is only superfine gaseous matter. This is perhaps the natural, inevitable way of thinking of the common man. But it is not the view of Descartes, Plato or the Vedāntin.

---

33 Wittgenstein, *The Blue and Brown Books*, p. 143.

34 Wittgenstein, *Philosophical Investigations*, p. 308.

Agreeing with Ayer's criticism of the argument I further think that Wittgenstein's demonstration of the impossibility of a private language rests ultimately on general scepticism concerning memory. Second, contrary to his own prescription Wittgenstein is not describing ordinary language but recasting it, reinterpreting large segments of it to serve his philosophical purpose. Reforming our language, even for philosophical purposes, is not blameworthy in itself. 'Revisionist' is a term of abuse only in communist polemics and a philosopher need not be afraid of it. But we must be aware of what we are doing. And when we arrive at conclusions about the world on the basis of our examination of existing linguistic usage, we must be careful to avoid the pitfalls of this kind of a priori reasoning. There is, after all, an enormous ontological argument in reasoning that since our language is such and such, things cannot be or must be so and so.

Concluding Remarks

I have successively reviewed prominent attempts in the English-speaking world to get rid of Descartes' dualism and the philosophical burden imposed by it. We yield much, though not everything, in giving up reductionism or the translatability thesis. We can still banish Cartesian egos if we accept some version of the identity theory based on perfectly respectable, naturalistic speculation against an analytical background. But of the identity theory we can say that 'the more it changes, the more it remains the same' – utterly implausible. The perplexity of Descartes now takes on a more serious shape. We can still get rid of his immaterial substance, by maintaining as Strawson does, that a person is an indissoluble unity to whom both material and psychological predicates are equally applicable. To many this would seem to be a restatement of the problem rather than its resolution. So far as ordinary usages go some support the one-subject theory and some the two-subject theory. We can in fact, distinguish three classes of predicates: those that can be ascribed to the body such as height, weight and complexion, those that can be ascribed with varying degrees of naturalness to 'my mind' instead of 'me'. 'My mind was other where when the organ shook the air', 'To me alone there came a thought of grief', etc. Finally activities like walking, laughing, even pretending to laugh opening a door, etc. are best ascribed to a person regarded as a unity.

We may make the mind *existentially* dependent upon the body particularly the brain. The mind would then cease to be a substance losing its capacity for independent existence. We may avoid the worst excesses of epiphenomenalism by allowing a limited operational efficacy to mental processes once a stable well-organized series of them comes into existence as a result of the integral functioning of the brain. We cannot perhaps *define* personal identity in terms of bodily identity; but we can attempt to show – as many contemporary philosophers do – that there is no criterion of personal identity *internal to the experiences of a person*, and though such a criterion, for example memory, may be used for certain purpose, it is ultimately parasitic on bodily continuity. Ayer's attempt (which he gave up later) to reinstate the no-ownership theory and some of Strawson's arguments against the Cartesian ego depend on a failure to distinguish clearly between a procedure for identification and a principle of identity. It can be frankly acknowledged that we employ different criteria of personal identity on different occasions. They converge normally but can diverge in certain real as well as imaginary situations. Since personal continuity depends causally on bodily continuity, a person insisting on a subject for the sake of form can have one either in the person as a whole or in the brain.

In fact, the identity theory becomes far more plausible if, instead of identifying particular experiences with brain event, it identifies the mind with the brain. Armstrong does this, but to be plausible at all he must provide for the location of secondary qualities somewhere in the wide world and allow irreducibly psychical qualities, if not psychical processes. It comes as a surprise when he maintains that his central state materialism is compatible with the logical possibility of a disembodied mind.[35] According to him anyone envisaging such

---

35 Armstrong, op. cit., p. 91.

a possibility is conceiving the mind as a spiritual substance, and mental states as states of such a substance and not of the brain. Since the identity of the mind and the brain is only contingently true and spiritual substances are logically possible, we can cheerfully grant the logical possibility of a disembodied mind. This is perhaps to miss the point of the objections and put too much weight on the contingent truth of our equation. The objection is that the truth of the identity theory would make survival in a disembodied state or in association with some other material structure *logically impossible.* We start with an untutored conception of mental processes, based on introspection and independently of conflicting philosophies of mind. But if mental processes so conveived were identical with brain states, then the continuation of these would be *impossible*, when the brain is dissolved on death. *Ex hypothesi* survival is logically possible. Therefore the identity theory is not true. One can of course be wary of granting the *logical possibility* of survival, reincarnation, etc. Though such a possibility has been granted by many, including A.J. Ayer, it can be argued that what we are trying to envisage in such a case, when clearly stated will reveal some kind of incoherence if not logical contradictions. In any case survival is highly improbable on a naturalistic view.

Descartes was not only a person with a scientific outlook but was one of the inaugurators of it. If he were persuaded to throw away his religious piety as a burdensome baggage, perhaps he would have embraced some form of naturalism. In that case mental substances would go overboard but some in eradicable dualism of aspects, or qualities, would remain. The well-known phrase the 'ghost in the machine' which crystallizes the ridicule of Descartes in recent times does not seem to be justified. The ghost is there however much we may whistle to keep up our courage.

6

Universals and Family Resemblance[1]

In a well-known passage of the *Philosophical Investigations* (*PI*), Wittgenstein writes: 'Consider for example, the proceedings that we call "games". . . . What is common to them all? Don't say: there must be something or they would not be called "games"' – but look and see whether there is anything common to all. For if you look at them, you will not see something that is common to them all, but similarities, relationships and a whole series of them at that. To repeat: don't think but look! Look for example at board games, with their multifarious relationships. Now pass to cardgames; here you find many correspondences with the first group, but many common features drop out and others appear. When we pass next to ball games, much that is common is retained but much is lost. Are they all amusing? Compare chess with noughts and crosses. Or is there always winning and losing or competition between players? Think of patience. In ball games there is winning and losing, but when a child throws his ball at the wall and catches it again, these features have disappeared. Look at the part played by skill and luck, and at the difference between skill in chess and skill in tennis. Think now of games like ring-a-ring-a-roses; here is the element of amusement, but how many other characteristic features have disappeared! And we can go through the many, many, other groups of games, can see how similarities crop up and disappear. And the result of the examination is: we see a complicated network of similarities overlapping and criss-crossing: sometimes overall similarities, sometimes, similarities of detail (*PI*: 66). He adds: I can think of

---

[1] Presented at the 18th Session of the Indian Philosophical Association, 1968, Symposium.

no better expression to characterize these similarities than 'family resemblances' for the various resemblances between members of a family: build, features, colour of eyes, gait, temperament, etc. overlapp and criss-cross in the same way. And I shall say 'games' form a family (*PI*: 67).

The passages quoted quite clearly imply that the tendency to look for something common to all the entities which we commonly subsume under a general name is a mistaken tendency. The justification for applying a general term, we are inclined to think, must be the presence of a common property in the various things to which it is applied, whereas a survey of the things subsumed under a common name discloses that they form a group related by resemblances rather like the likenesses between the different members of a family. It would seem that in the historical controversy between realism and nominalism (or the philosophy of universals and the philosophy of resemblance, as they have been more recently called by Price),[2] Wittgenstein comes down on the side of the nominalist. Richard I. Aaron, in a note on an article by R. Bambrough on the subject published in the *Proceedings of the Aristotelian Society for 1960-61* observes that Wittgenstein has set forth a form of the resemblance theory in a forceful way.[3] In his opinion this restatement of the resemblance theory is not wholly new and what is more important, fails to meet the standard objections against it. Bambrough, on the other hand, claims that Wittgenstein has solved this ancient puzzle once and for all and that though he is easily mistaken for a nominalist, rejects both nominalism and realism. He can do this because he rejects a false assumption common to the contending theories.

I am not at all sure that what Bambrough claims to be the final solution to the problem of universals by Wittgenstein is either final

---

2 H.H. Price, *Thinking and Experience*, Harvard University Press, 1962.

3 See, R. Bambrough, 'Universals and Family Resemblances', *Proceedings of the Aristotelian Society*, 61, 1960-61, reprinted in *Wittgenstein: The Philosophical Investigations*, ed. George Pitcher, New York: Macmillan, 1966.

or Wittgenstein's. One thing is clear. Wittgenstein explicitly rejects the view that all things subsumed under a common term must have something in common. Equally, the basis for the application of the term, in his view, is the existence of similarities among the things to which the term is applied, sometimes specifiable and detailed similarities, sometimes over all similarities. Bambrough maintains that Wittgenstein rejected the nominalist view that games have nothing in common except that they are called games. (It may be noted that this is a picturesque and loose statement of nominalism. Stated more soberly it is the theory of resemblance which Wittgenstein seems to recommend.) What games have in common is that they are games, just as what all red things have in common is their being red. The realist comes to grief through seeking something common to red things *over and above their being red*. The nominalist rightly denies that there is any such common element and therefore wrongly concludes that the only thing common to them is their being called red. What they both overlook is the simple truth which Wittgenstein asserts, namely, that the different instances of a certain sort have in common is just their being instances of that sort. This is the objective justification for the use of the general term. The false assumption which the nominalist and the realist both make without being aware of it is that if the application of the general term is objectively justified, then the different instances to which the term is applied must have something in common over and above their being instances of the sort. Wittgenstein rejects this assumption and therefore rejects the realist's invention of an additional common entity, a transcendent or immanent or subsistent universal, as well as the nominalist's wrong-headed denial of an objective justification for the application of a general term. The rival theories spring from a common error and once this is exposed and rejected, it is easy to see how Wittgenstein can reject both, in so far as they are muddle-headed, and maintain what is valid in both the two theories, viz.: (1) there is an objective justification for our use of general terms, and (2) there is no transcendent or subsistent entity common to the different things to which a general term is applied.

As an exegesis on Wittgenstein I find all this profoundly puzzling and unsatisfactory. Wittgenstein does indeed demand in *The Blue and Brown Books* 'Could you tell me what is common between light red and dark red?'[4] and again in the *Philosophical Investigations* (p. 73) 'which shade is the sample in my mind of the colour green – the sample of what is common to all shades of green?' But I don't think he wants us to return in the first case the trivial, but according to Bambrough, enlightening answer: 'Nothing but their redness'. The context of the second quotation makes it clear that Wittgenstein's attacking the view that understanding the meaning of a general term consist in having in the mind a general representation – a 'generic image', as it was called in discussions of the subject in the 1920s – with an obvious reference to Galton's composite photograph.

After careful and repeated reading of the relevant passages (the most important being the series of connected passages from pp. 65-88) in the *Philosophical Investigations* and the brief discussion of the topic in the *Blue and Brown Books*, I find no trace of evidence either for Bambrough's diagnosis or for the solution which he offers on behalf of Wittgenstein. Moreover, it is extremely doubtful whether any philosopher worthy of discussion ever held that games, for example, should have in common something over and above their defining characteristic as games if their being grouped together is objectively justified. They feel dissatisfied with the correct but trivial statement that all games have nothing in common except their being games, because they regard the concept of games as a complex concept capable of analysis in terms of other concepts.

If Wittgenstein does not attempt to go beyond realism and nominalism in the manner indicated by Bambrough, what is the difference between his views and the philosophy of resemblance which, like the rival philosophy of universals, keeps on recurring in different forms throughout the history of philosophy? The

---

[4] L. Wittgenstein, *The Blue and Brown Books*, Oxford: Basil and Blackwell, 1958.

difference, I think, can be appreciated only when his views on family resemblances and the use of general terms are related to the general conception of language which permeates all that he has to say in the *Philosophical Investigations* (*PI*). Wittgenstein's remarks in this connection cannot be isolated from his discussion of such questions as, 'What is the essence of language?', 'What is it for a word to have meaning?', 'What is thought?', 'What is the nature of understanding?', etc. In fact, Wittgenstein launches into a discussion of games and family resemblances in order to remove the dissatisfaction which we may feel with his treatment of language. Why does he deal with the problem by means of illustrative language-games and the use of words in them (*PI* 65), instead of defining what is common to all the different uses of language or giving the general form of every proposition? Isn't he avoiding the crucial question? It is in answer to such complaints that Wittgenstein considers what is common to all the different activities to which we give the name 'games'. And conversely in considering the various objections against the doctrine of family resemblances and classification, he falls back in the final analysis, on his view of language, as an immensely complex structure of different linguistic activities or language games, related to one another in various ways, but with no one thing in common which makes them instances of language.

Thus the doctrine of family resemblances as the basis of our use of general terms stands or falls with a certain philosophy of language and meaning. Wittgenstein himself partly obscures the realization of this point, for while developing his view by answering possible objections as well as attacking alternative views, he operates at two different levels. At one level he is conducting a straightforward philosophical polemic, rebutting objections and raising difficulties for his opponents. Considered in this light, his arguments, though forceful and pertinent, are by no means conclusive. His criticism of 'imagism' – the view that to have a concept is to have a general picture or image of the things to which the concept is applicable, though decisive, are not startlingly new (*PI*: 72-74, 86, 139-42). And there are echoes of Berkeley when he says speaking of general samples or schematic representations: '. . . for a slip of pure green to be understood as a sample of all that is greenish and not as a sample of pure green – this in turn resides in the way the samples are unused' (*PI*: 73).

But at another level the purpose of his many and quickly changing illustrations, the conundrums he sets, and his stories of people behaving differently from ourselves either in a world oddly different from our own or in situation familiar to us – the purpose of all this is to free our minds from the obsession with a picture of what language is, or rather, ought to be, and how it should stand in relation to the world to which it refers. Wittgenstein wants us to look at the use of words as a *form of behaviour*, which, like other forms of behaviour, is to be understood in its physical and social setting and in relation to the ends it serves. Above everything, we should not look for a common pattern of relation in which every meaningful word stands to the things in the world. Second, he also wants to discount the view that the use of words, that is the intelligent use of them reflects an understanding of meaning and that it is these acts of understanding (mental processes) in which we grasp what is common to a number of things or a patterns of relation – that endow words with meaning. Wittgenstein was undoubtedly not a behaviourist and granted that the use of words may be accompanied by mental pictures and inner processes, such as 'a sense of illumination', 'a sense of atmosphere' that a word carries and so on. But equally undoubtedly he insisted that this is not always the case and that the absence of such inner accompaniments does not in any way render the use of a word unintelligent. Even if such processes sometimes occur, their occurrence has no bearing on the question whether a person has understood the meaning of a word. This is a question which is to be settled by observing whether he uses it in accordance with certain rules and the rules themselves, in the final analysis, are elicited from our actual behaviour and are shown by 'agreement in practice' (*PI*: 143 onwards). If we reject this conception of language and meaning – it is a sophisticated successor to the causal theory of meaning put forward by Richards and Ogden and espoused by Russell at one time – and insist that mental processes are not incidental accompaniments to the use of language but are integral to it, and that a world devoid of conscious processes is a world devoid of 'meaning', we shall have provided a totally different setting for the discussion of the entire range of philosophical problems.

I shall not enter into a discussion of these large themes. But if what I have said so far is correct, it essentially leads to two conclusions, which do not go well with a Wittgensteinian conception of philosophy. First, Wittgenstein's profession of neutrality in the battle between rival philosophical theories is not to be accepted at its face value. His philosophy does not leave everything as it is. Second, Wittgenstein's solutions to different philosophical problems are not piecemeal solutions to different perplexities, but form a system of interlocking and mutually supporting doctrines and attitudes as in the case of any great philosophical system.

7

Are There Sense Data?[1]

It would perhaps be conceded without much argument that the question, 'Are there sense data?' is more like the question 'Is space non-Euclidean?' than like the question 'Does Jupiter have moons?'. The former question arises and has to be settled within the context of complex theoretical system. Certain observation statements, regarding the measurements of angles formed by light rays from three stars constituting a triangle in space, are discrepant with well-known facts and accepted theories about propagation of light, gravitation, etc. taken in conjunction with certain a priori propositions about space and time which constitute the categorical framework of traditional physics. There are of course alternative ways of removing the discrepancy. In a somewhat similar way, there is a problem of perception and its relation to the external world because certain propositions regarding the nature of perception and of material objects, which we all accept or would like to accept, apparently require revision or partial abandonment in the light of facts concerning the relativity and systematic variability of our perceptions – facts summarized and exploited by the argument from illusion.

Hardly any philosopher would dispute that the following propositions are implicitly accepted by common sense and are an integral part of its general conception of material objects and our knowledge of them.

I. (a) Perception is acquaintance with or intuition of physical

---

[1] Published in the *Journal of the Philosophical Association*, vol. XIV, nos. 45-46, January–December, 1973.

objects (other words used by philosophers in this regard are 'prehension', 'apprehension', 'direct awareness', etc.).

(b) If *M* is the object of intuitive awareness on the part of a perceiver *O*, then from the proposition that '*O* intuits *M* as *C*', it following that '*M* is or has *C*' (*M* of course may have a characteristic *C* which *O* may not intuit or perceive).

(c) If C_1 and C_2 are incompatible characteristics, then if O_1 claims that '*M* is C_1' and O_2 that '*M* is C_2' then at least one of the two observers – O_1 and O_2 – cannot be intuiting *M*. (This follows from the definition of incompatible characteristics together with I(b).)

II. About the nature of material objects whose existence and nature are revealed to us in perception, the following propositions would unhesitatingly find acceptance by the plain man though they are not exhaustive of all that he believes about them.

(a) A physical object is a continuant which has both extension (size, shape, rest or motion, etc.) as well as extensive characteristics like colour and temperature.

(b) A physical object is public in that it is meaningful and it is in fact often true to say that two or more observers are perceiving the same part or side or surface of the same object.

(c) The characteristics of the physical object – some of them – are neutral between different modes of sensory awareness. For example, the size perceived by sight is the same as the size perceived by touch.

(d) It is meaningful to say that there is an object *M* which is not the object of acquaintance on the part of any observer whatever.

(e) The characteristics of a physical object – extensional and extensive – vary and change, but these changes are not in any way conditioned by facts concerning the position of an observer, the condition of his sense-organs of nervous system or the state of his mind or the fact that he perceives in some manner a given physical object at a given time.

(f) To this list we must add propositions concerning the formal structure of certain facts about a physical object, for example, that the colour and size of a physical object (its *real* colour and size, the colour and size that according to common sense, inhere in it independently of its being observed in any observer) are simple qualities and *not* relational properties. The colour and size of an object inhere in it dyadically, as Broad would put it. It would be both tedious and unnecessary to elaborate the argument from illusion and the perspectival and other systematic variations in perception on which the argument is based. But it is important to notice that the argument can be developed entirely on the basis of variations in perceptual consciousness, which is ordinarily regarded as veridical perception. True, errors in perception in the form of illusions and hallucinations are referred to in the exposition of the argument, but such a reference is not necessary. When from a series of continuously varying positions the rupee looks in different shapes – from circular to more and more eccentrically elliptical, there is no question of erroneous perception so long as we judge and believe that the rupee is circular. (Commonly we say that the rupee looks circular. It is only when we adopt the phenomenological approach to perceptual experience and attend to what is given to us as contrasted with what we judge to be the case that we say that the rupee looks elliptical, though in fact it is circular.) And these systematic perspectival variations in sensible size and shape are so far from being aberrations of perceptual experience that it would be difficult even to conceive visual perception without them.

When two 'normal' observers, under 'normal' conditions observe the same rupee from different positions and it appears circular to one of them and elliptical to another, both of them cannot be apprehending its real shape and at least one of them therefore cannot be intuiting the rupee perceptually. It is not necessary for the argument to maintain that the rupee is really circular and that the perception of it as circular is veridical and that all other perceptions are erroneous and that consequently in them the percipient is aware of a peculiar private entity – a sense datum, and not of the rupee – a public physical object. If the sense datum theory had argued in this fashion and proceeded on the basis of the internal or subjective indistinguishability of illusory and veridical perceptions, to maintain that in all perceptions the sensory core consist in the sensing of sense data different from physical objects, it would clearly be open to the charge of internal incoherence which Chubb levels against it. His contention that the theory cannot get started unless it assumes that in 'normal cases of perception we are directly aware of the existence of physical object',[2] and that the theory contradicts this unconscious assumption and refutes itself when it proceeds to the conclusion that in all perception we are directly aware of sense data and sense data alone – this contention would be perfectly justified.

But I have argued that the theory need not present the preliminary argument which leads up to the introduction of sense data with the uncritical innocence. Indeed the argument from illusion can confine its movement entirely within the circle of variable but perfectly normal and unmisleading perceptions of completely 'normal' percipients. The argument can be deployed in as similar unobjectionable way with respect to sensible colour, heat and cold, length and size, and so on. The argument would gain considerably in force and persuasive power if it is supplemented by a consideration of the correlations between different modes of sense perception of the same percipient. Certainly the argument as developed so far does not lead to the conclusion that *no perception* is a direct awareness of or confrontation with physical objects. But

---

[2] Most likely from J.N. Chubb, 'Propositions and Sense Data', in *Assertion and Fact: The Categories of Self-conscious Thinking*, Somaiya Publications, 1977.

from this point, the conclusion that when a number of observers are aware of the same surface of the same object at best only one of them can be apprehending it directly, the argument proceeds along well-known lines. It points out that the perception alleged to be revelatory of the real qualities of, say the rupee, is one of a continuous series of perceptions which vary gradually, that there is no abrupt transition from any of them to the next, no sudden change in quality when the authentic perception is reached. Further that all of them are internally, and in respect of their character as experiences, of the same kind and that causally too they are alike in that the immediately necessary and sufficient conditions of all of them are to be found in certain events in the percipient brain. None of these considerations is logically compelling and it would be consistent logically to maintain that a slight movement to the left or the right, a mere nod of the head can make the difference between a perception which is apprehensive, and a perception which is not, of the real qualities of the rupee. It may be arbitrary – as the advocates of the sense datum theory are fond of insisting – to accord a privileged place to one particular position, one particular angle of vision, one particular condition of illumination to the exclusion of an indefinite number of alternatives in each case. But then arbitrariness is not inconsistency and not half so serious. It is even possible to go so far with the argument and then refuse at the last stage to admit the existence of sense data as the objects of the intuitive element in perception by denying that perceptual experiences are intuitive or contain an intuitive element. This would in my opinion be a wide departure from common sense and include a denial of I(a) listed above. But the view of the idealists that nothing in our experience is pure datum, and the view of some of them that perception is judgement amount to such a denial.

Indeed it is possible to halt the progress towards the introduction of sense data much earlier by maintaining that in all the normal variable perception the percipient is directly aware of the rupee, the various sensible sizes, shapes and colours given to him being all appearances of the same object which he is intuiting all the time as he approaches it or goes round it. Chubb suggests such a view[3] and it is a possible view. But then we must recognize that we have abandoned I(b) listed above, unless indeed we have abandoned – without being clearly conscious of it – I(a) in the case of all perceptions but the one in which the rupee is sensibly circular, silvery-white and only so big as it is authorized to be. And to prevent the sense datum theory from turning the elliptical 'look' into an elliptical sense datum, we shall have to maintain that the something which is elliptical and confronts us in perception is only an appearance of the rupee and the relation between the rupee and its various sensible appearances (since it cannot be one of simple straightforward inherence) is *sui generis* and unanalysable (abandonment of II(f) and of some more common sense).

There are even more tempting alternatives to the introduction of sense data. In the course of his argument to show that different theories of perception are only alternative terminologies, A.J. Ayer suggests that we can even maintain that all our perceptions are veridical and yet avoid self-contradiction by stipulating, for example, that the penny changes from circular to elliptical in shape as the observer changes his position or that two observers are not seeing the same thing when one of them sees it as red and the other as green.[4] Certainly such a position avoids formal self-contradiction, but it involves the rejection of II(e) and II(c) and possibly of II(a). In any case it constitutes such a total departure from our ordinary conception of a material thing that it is difficult to see why anyone should think that all that is involved here is the adoption of a different terminology for describing the same incontrovertible facts. For this reason and also because I am in complete agreement with the substance of what Chubb says, I shall say nothing about the 'linguistic' version of the sense datum theory. And the alternative way of maintaining that all 'normal' perceptions at any rate are veridical, which clearly has the support and sympathy of Chubb

---

3 Most likely from Chubb, op. cit., 1977.

4 A.J. Ayer, *The Foundations of Empirical Knowledge*, London: Macmillan, 1940.

(though he does not make use of it in his refutation of the sense datum theory). If worked out fully, this would, I think, turn out to be only a little less fantastic. It clearly involves the abandonment of a number of propositions that fall under II(f) and also of II(c) and consequently leads to a breakdown of the correlations between perception of different senses – particularly touch and sight which are of crucial importance to our theoretical and practical dealings with physical objects.[5]

I have so far made an attempt to show that the argument from relativity of perceptions can be presented without any reference to illusions and hallucinations and without any tacit assumption that there is at least one perceptual situation in which we are directly aware of physical objects. The argument is but a preliminary to the introduction of sense data, and the various supplementary principles which are necessary if the theory is to prove its point, can all be denied without self-contradiction. But even though the introduction of sense data is not shown to be necessary, the theory is at any rate free of the fatal defect of internal incoherence.

But though the theory need not depend upon errors in perceptions for the introduction of sense data it does maintain that in all perceptions, veridical and illusory, there is a common incorrigible element of acquaintance which consists in the sensing of sense data. Chubb has many forceful and pertinent things to say about this lumping together of the illusory and the veridical. It is not my intention to dispute and reject all that he maintains in this connection. But I shall attempt to show briefly that this classing together of truth and error is not basically objectionable and that it does not lead to an obliteration of the distinction between the two – a distinction which must be preserved in any satisfactory philosophical theory.

If sense data can be introduced without self-contradiction and without relying upon errors of perception, then the complete subjective or

---

5 The stick 'half immersed in water', Chubb declares is bent to the eye though not to the touch, 'Propositions and Sense Data', op. cit.

internal similarity between a normal perception and a hallucination justifies us, so the theory could argue, in maintaining that there is not a radical difference in the type of objects intuited in them. The underlying assumptions are the principle of continuity and the proposition that if two experiences *qua* experience are indistinguishable then they cannot be experiences of objects of different types. Neither proposition is logically necessary, but they both appear plausible to me. We certainly cannot argue, as Chubb seems to, that since there was nothing to be seen, there was no seeing or direct awareness if anything. Certainly there was no physical object and consequently no visual experience of a physical object. But to conclude from this that there was no seeing at all, is to beg the question at issue. Any one who is convinced that there was 'seeing' is consistent in postulating an object for this seeing – an object which is different from a physical object. And if I have successfully shown that sense data can be introduced without relying upon the ordinary distinction between veridical perception and hallucinations and consequently without internal incoherence, then we cannot charge the theory with arbitrary invention of mysterious entities and the transformation of 'seeming to see a tomato' into 'seeing a seeming-tomato'. At any rate Chubb does not seem to be in the right when he argues that

> . . . if it is admitted that we can somehow make a distinction between perceptions which are veridical and perceptions which are delusive the argument breaks down, for it rests on the assumption that we cannot make this assumption.[6]

All that the theory maintains is that they are indistinguishable internally and *qua* experiences. We cannot tell them apart as we can a tomato from an apple and without reference to their relations to other experiences, or to something other than experiences. Nor does the theory lead logically to the conclusion 'that there is no distinction at all between so-called veridical perceptions and hallucinations'. If the sense data are introduced as elements in a representative or

---

6 Chhub, op. cit.

causal theory of perception then a veridical perception will differ from a delusion in the manner of its causation – by the fact that it is caused by a chain of events which terminates in a source external to the observer. If their introduction is part of a phenomenalistic programme, then a veridical sense datum is one of a family of actual and possible sense data related to them in certain definable ways and a delusive one is a 'wild' or isolated sense datum not related in this manner to other sense data. And these are perfectly legitimate and objective ways of re-drawing the ordinary distinction between the veridical and the delusive.

I am no defender of sense data nor an advocate of the sense datum theory. There are many weighty objections against it and it has its share of extravagance and paradox. My attempt has been the more modest one of showing that it is free from internal incoherence that it does not wipe out the distinction between truth and error, and finally that it is not gratuitous in so far as it attempts to deal with genuine difficulties systematically as do alternative theories about perception and its relation to the external world. The solution offered by the theory is within a certain philosophical framework and whether or not we find the theory plausible depends on how far we find this frame-work of conscious and unconscious assumptions congenial to us. Perhaps even more it depends on how far we are ready to tolerate those departures from common sense and the consequent extravagance and paradox which any alterative theory must involve. The tomato which Chubb holds in his philosophical palm is no ordinary thing – not the simple vegetable he swallows in his unphilosophical moments. It is a thing of unimaginable complexity with its infinite real shapes, colours and sizes projected through infinite pace! Why shouldn't it be? If we are not willing to introduce extraordinary entities we can make ordinary things a little extraordinary. Certainly we have the choice.

8

Strawson on 'Persons'[1]

In the chapter on 'Persons' in his book *Individuals*, P.F. Strawson launches a comprehensive attack on the entire nexus of the main problems connected with the relation of the mind to the body. In the course of a relatively brief essay, remarkable for compressed argumentation and analysis, he tackles the alleged duality of mind and body, the problem of personal identity, the problem of solipsism and its obverse – the problem of our knowledge of other minds – and claims to have provided a satisfactory solution to them all in respect of the essentials. He admits that the task of elucidating, in detail, the role of *P*-predicates as he calls them, that is, predicates which are ascribed only to persons, and how they play their peculiar role within our ordinary conceptual scheme still remains untackled. This is the real problem. But the bogus problems of traditional metaphysics – for so they turn out to be after Strawson's handling of them – arise from a failure to grasp the distinctive character of *P*-predicates and the (traditional) solutions suggested are internally incoherent. They involve, at once, a pretended acceptance of our ordinary conceptual scheme and a tacit rejection of some of its vital features. Indeed, without such incoherence, the problems themselves cannot be stated in their traditional formulations.

I

Strawson states the problem which is to be considered, in his own way. We ascribe to ourselves, things (that is predicates) of many different kinds – action, intentions, sensations, thoughts, height,

---

[1] Published earlier in the *Journal of the Indian Academy of Philosophy*, vol. VII, no. 2, 1968.

position, location, etc. Some of these such as location and height we ascribe to material objects. But others, such as sensations, feeling, etc. we should not dream of ascribing to material bodies. Now 'It can, and must seem to need some explanation that one's states of consciousness are ascribed to the very same thing to which physical characteristics, this physical situation is ascribed'.[2] We have here two related but distinct questions. First, 'why are one's states of consciousness ascribed to anything at all'? And second, 'why are they ascribed to the very same things as certain physical characteristics, a certain physical situation etc.'?[3] Predicates which we ascribe to ourselves as well as material bodies are called *M*-predicates and those which we ascribe only to ourselves *P*-predicates. So our problem, briefly stated is to account for the fact that *M* and *P*-predicates are ascribed to one and the same subject.

Two solutions – which Strawson considers and rejects as internally incoherent – the no-ownership theory, and the Cartesian theory of two subjects, both deny, each in its own way, the assumptions underlying the statement of the problem. The no-ownership theory – ascribed to Schlick and, with the usual ritual of hesitation to Wittgenstein, denies that mental states or conscious processes are ascribed at all to any subject except in a confused or metaphorical sense. According to this theory, mental states are not owned by any subject or pure ego underlying them. All my experiences are had by me only in the sense that they are all causally dependent on the state of a given identifiable body, that is my body. We may, if we like, say that they are all had by my body, that they belong to it. But this is misleading because experiences do not belong to my body in the way location, height, etc. do, but only in the sense that they are all causally conditioned by it. Strawson objects to this theory that it is incoherent in that 'one who holds it is forced to make use of that sense of possession of which he denies the existence, in presenting the case for his denial'.[4] According to

---

[2] P.F. Strawson, *Individuals*, London: Metheun, 1959, p. 89.

[3] Ibid., p. 90.

[4] Strawson, op. cit., p. 96.

the theory 'all my experiences are uniquely dependent on the state of a given body *B*'. In the above statement of the theory,

> any attempt to eliminate the 'my' or any expression with a similar possessive force, would yield something that was not a contingent fact at all . . . the theorist cannot consistently argue that 'all the experiences of person *P*' means the same thing as 'all experiences contingently dependent on a certain body *B*'; for then his proposition would not be contingent, as his theory requires, but analytic.[5]

Strawson is surely right to reject the no-ownership theory as formulated by him, for clearly the analysis it offers of personal identity or of the notion of experiences belonging to the same single self is quite inadequate. But he does not seem to be right in alleging that the theory is internally incoherent. It is true that 'all my experiences are dependent causally on my body' is a synthetic proposition. The causal relations between my body – particularly my brain – and my experiences are empirically discovered and I can identify my experiences without any precise knowledge of these relations. It is indeed arguable whether any meaning can be attached to the expression 'identifying my own experiences'. But there is no doubt that I can describe my sensations, thoughts, feelings, etc. and recall past experiences and in recollecting them 'claim' them as my own. And I can do this without knowing the precise causal relations between my experiences and my body. It is for this reason that the analysis it provides of the experiences of a single self is so patently inadequate. But an advocate of the no-ownership theory, since he analyses 'my experiences' to mean 'experiences dependent causally on my body', must hold that 'all my experiences are those that are causally determined by my body' is necessarily or analytically true. In fact, the clearest statement of the theory would be to say that this proposition is analytic. It is true the proposition would then amount to no more than the tautology that 'all experiences dependent on body *B* are experiences dependent on body *B*'. But this, so far

[5] Strawson, op. cit., p. 97.

from constituting an objection to the theory, is in fact a necessary consequence of its correctness. Strawson is surely wrong in thinking that the analyticity of the above proposition introduces an incoherence in the theory because the theory requires the proposition to be synthetic whereas the result of accepting its analysis would be to make it analytic. We may regard the proposition as synthetic – as we would all do perhaps, on reflection – and therefore reject the analysis offered by the theory. But the no-ownership theory is under no obligation to assert both that 'my experiences' means the same as 'experiences causally dependent on my body' and also that the proposition 'my experiences are dependent causally on my body' is synthetic.

The situation here is parallel to that which obtains in the case of Moore's refutation of the 'naturalistic fallacy'. As Prior has pointed out, Moore's arguments refute conclusively only those inconsistent naturalists, who, for example, analyse 'good' to mean the same as 'pleasant' and yet maintain that only 'pleasure is good' is a significant proposition. What Strawson does here is to accept the synthetic character of the proposition and combine this acceptance with the undoubted logical consequence of the no-ownership theory, viz., that the proposition in question is analytic and thus to point out an internal inconsistency within the theory. It is of some importance to notice this because he adopts the same strategy in his attempt to show that Cartesian dualism is not only unsatisfactory but self-contradictory and thus gives the impression of having discussed and rejected it on its own grounds, or at any rate, independently of the acceptance of his own central thesis.

II

If the no-ownership theory denies that mental states are ascribed to any subject, the Cartesian theory denies that they are ascribed to the same subject in the manner in which certain corporeal predicates are ascribed. According to this theory, *M*-predicates are ascribed to my body whereas *P*-predicates – or conscious state – are ascribed to a mental subject, a pure consciousness or ego. Against such a view, Strawson presents a complex chain of reasoning. He begins by saying that both the no-ownership theory and the Cartesian theory fail through not reckoning with all the facts. And here, he says, he has in mind, 'a very simple but central thought, viz., that it is a necessary condition of ascribing states of consciousness, experiences, to oneself, in the way one does, that one should also ascribe or be prepared to ascribe them to others who are not oneself'. Strawson explains that this means that ascribing phrases are used in just the same sense whether they are used to ascribe experiences to oneself or others. This gives no trouble to the non-philosopher but only to the philosopher who asks how the meaning could be the same when the method of verification was so different in the two cases or even when there was no question of a method of verification at all in one's own case.

We shall see later on that Strawson removes this difficulty by arguing that it is precisely this character which is definitive of *P*-predicates and their peculiar function. But, to continue the main argument, granted that one can ascribe experiences to oneself (only) if one can ascribe them to others, how is it that one can ascribe them to others? Now one thing is here certain: if others are thought of only as a set of Cartesian egos to which only private experiences can, in correct logical grammar, be ascribed, then this question is unanswerable and this problem insoluble.[6] For in that case one cannot identify the other subjects to whom one has to ascribe experiences in order to ascribe them to oneself. And one cannot identify other subjects only as subjects of experiences, possessors of states of consciousness.[7] Nor can the difficulty be avoided by adopting an indirect method and identifying a subject as 'the subject that stands to that body in the same special relation as I stand to this one' or in other words 'the subject of those experiences stand in the same unique causal relation to body *N* as my experiences stand to the body *M*'. But this is useless.

It requires me to have noted that my experiences stand in a special

[6] Strawson, op. cit., p. 100.

[7] Ibid.

> relation to body *M*: but it requires me to have noted this as a condition of being able to identify other subjects of experiences, i.e. as a condition of my having the idea of myself as a subject of experience, i.e. as a condition of thinking of any experiences as mine. . . .[8]

In such a situation, 'the most I may be allowed to have noted is that experiences, all experiences, stand in a special relation to body *M* and this is what makes it unique among bodies'.[9] Here, as in the case of the no-ownership theory, Strawson objects to the use made by the theory of the notion of 'my experiences' in explaining the notion of other subjects of experiences. 'What is the word 'my" doing in the preferred explanation?'[10] He demands, and adds that the explanation could not get on without it. And though the Cartesian must make use of this notion, he has no right to it, indeed he cannot form any idea of himself as a subject of experiences. For, unless he already knows how to ascribe, at least in some cases, states of consciousness to others, he cannot ascribe them in his own case. He cannot have any idea of his own case or any case.

And here it becomes clear that the indirect method of identifying other subjects of experiences is not open to the Cartesian only if it is true that I cannot form an idea of 'my experiences' unless I am already able to distinguish myself from other subjects of experiences, i.e. unless the Cartesian accepts Strawson's repeatedly proclaimed principle that I cannot ascribe experiences to myself unless I ascribe or am ready to ascribe them to others. And if this central thought which constitutes the nerve of Strawson's argument is rejected, the explanation offered is perfectly consistent, however implausible it may sound to Strawson or anyone else. It is only by foisting it on the Cartesian that Strawson is able to reject his account and demonstrate that sceptical doubt about other minds is internally incoherent. It would be relying on a total blindness to logical consistency on the part of the sceptic to expect him to argue analogically from his

8 Strawson, op. cit., p. 101.

9 Ibid.

10 Ibid.

own case to other subjects of experiences and yet at the same time to accept Strawson's dictum. On his own premises, he is consistent though not on Strawson's. Once again Strawson combines what is undoubtedly admitted as true by his opponent with what Strawson himself takes to be undoubtedly true and thus finds an internal inconsistency *within* the theory he is attempting to refute. The Cartesian may be wrong, but he has not been shown to be wrong on his own grounds. He would still be shown to be wrong if Strawson had given compelling or even highly persuasive reasons for accepting his fundamental dictum on which he relies so heavily throughout his argument. But even this seems to be doubtful. The chief difficulty for the Cartesian is supposed to be that on his account it is impossible to identify the subjects of experiences to whom states of consciousness are to be ascribed. All predication logically involves the identification of the subject and the possibility of distinguishing it from other subjects of the same type. And this cannot be done in the case of a set of Cartesian egos to whom only private experiences can be ascribed. There is no doubt that we cannot secure a direct reference to a subjects of experiences so conceived, but in so far as there is no difficulty in locating and identifying bodies, subjects of experiences could be related uniquely to different bodies which are identifiable. But, as we have seen Strawson denies the use of this mode of reference to the dualist by merely insisting upon his basic thesis that one cannot ascribe experiences to oneself unless one can ascribe them to others and thus begging the question at issue between himself and the Cartesian dualist.

Moreover, there is a further ambiguity in Strawson's formulation of the dualist's solution which may be of some importance. It is not clear whether in speaking of the 'unique causal relation in which my experiences stand to the body *M*', the notion of 'my experiences' and that of 'experiences standing in a unique causal relation to body *M*' are supposed to be the same (so that the second expression is only a paraphrase of the first) or the two are equivalent or finally, the two are independent so that the second characteristic in fact applies to the very series of experiences that constitute 'my experiences' –

whatever may be their defining characteristics as 'my experiences'. If the unique causal relation in which a set of experiences stands to a given body is taken as constitutive of their being the experiences of a given person, then the view becomes more or less identical with the no-ownership theory except that it maintains that such a series of experiences can be regarded as an independent logical subject. If we accept the view that the two expressions are logically equivalent without being synonymous, or alternatively, that the two notions are distinct (which is almost certainly Strawson's view considering his rejection of the no-ownership theory and his view that the causal relation between a given body and a given set of experiences are contingent) then the analogical argument to other subjects of experiences is not, in principle, vicious. For even if we grant the contention that I cannot form any idea of myself as a subject of experience unless I am already prepared to ascribe experiences to other subjects, I can still pass from a series of experience casually related to a given unique body to other series of experiences similarly related to other identifiable and similar bodies. In other words, I need not make use of the notion of 'my experiences' as distinct from the notion of 'experiences uniquely related causally to this body'.

Now, is Strawson right in his repeated insistence that I cannot form any idea of myself as a subject of experiences unless I am able or prepared to ascribe states of consciousness to other subjects? In other words, is Strawson's dictum which constitutes the nerve of his argument acceptable? It is true that if I have a notion of myself as a subject of experience, this notion implies logically a contrast between myself (as a subject) and other selves or persons. In ordinary language there would be no point in the use of the personal pronoun 'I' and its derivatives, unless I have occasion to refer to other persons by means of other personal pronouns or proper names or definite descriptions. But for the notion to be intelligible, the implied contrast or distinction between myself and other subjects of experiences need not be between myself and other actual subjects of experience. It is enough if I can conceive the possibility of other subjects of experience to whom under suitable circumstances, I am ready to ascribe state of consciousness.

The logical point behind Strawson's dictum is fully satisfied by the granting of such a possibility and does not necessitate that I should believe in the actual existence of other subjects of experience, much less that I should be right in such a belief. And unless such a strong interpretation is put upon Strawson's contention, the sceptical doubt regarding other minds cannot be dismissed as incoherent. The only sceptic whom Strawson can successfully refute by his argument is one who denies the very intelligibility or logical possibility of subjects of experience other than himself. So far as I know, nobody has ever maintained such an extreme form of scepticism.

Strawson is not unaware of this objection. He considers it briefly in a footnote on in his book, *Individuals*. But his treatment of it is rather cavalier. Having stated in his own way, the distinction between admitting the possibility of other subjects and admitting their actual existence, he proceeds to comment as follows:

> The shortest way with the objection is to admit it; (or at any rate to refrain from disputing it) for the lesser claim is all that the argument requires though it is slightly simpler to conduct it in terms of the larger claim.

Further he thinks it important to point out that we are concerned not with a single predicate or some group or other of predicates but with the whole of an enormous class of predicates such that applicability of these predicates or their negation defines a major or logical type or category of individuals. To insist at this level on the distinction between the lesser and the larger claim is to carry it over from a level where it is clearly correct to a level where it may appear idle or possibly senseless.

The main point here is a purely logical one: the idea of a predicate is correlative with that of a range of distinguishable individuals of which the predicate can be significantly, though not necessarily, truly affirmed. If this is the logical point behind the contention that one cannot ascribe experiences to oneself without ascribing them to others, then clearly it can only entail that if I ascribe experiences to myself I must grant the possibility of other subjects of experiences:

that is, it entails only what Strawson calls the lesser claim and not the larger claim that self-ascription of experiences implies the truth of actual other-ascriptions. And surely the distinction between the two is of great importance, because hardly any philosopher would deny the lesser claim, and the larger claim, which is denied by many, is alone sufficient to enable Strawson to achieve his ambitious programme of dissolving at one stroke scepticism and Cartesian dualism. What is involved is not merely a question of convenient exposition but one of validity of a logical inference of the modal type. Nor does it make any important logical difference that we are here concerned not with a single predicate or a small group of predicates but an enormous class of predicates whose application defines a logical type of particulars. If in the case of every single predicate or group of predicates all that we have to grant logically is the possibility of ascribing it to a whole range of distinguishable individuals before we can ascribe it to a given subject, the same would be true of our enormous category of predicates which simply comprises within itself all such predicates or groups of predicates. And if it is possible to deny without inconsistency that anyone of these predicates is truly applicable to others, then it is also possible to assert without inconsistency that none of them in fact applies truly to anyone other than myself. How the distinction between the possibility of true ascription and actual true ascription becomes idle or possibly senseless at this level is not at all clear. Perhaps it is idle only in the sense that a philosophical resolution of the solipsistic doubt is not necessary to convince the plain man of the existence of other persons; nor is it needed by philosophers themselves, who, after all, are plain men when they are not philosophizing. One cannot help wishing that Strawson had not chosen the shortest way with this objection and had made some attempt to show that the validity of his argument is not affected by the distinction which he admits but dismissed so lightly. In the absence of any such attempt, the central thesis which is vital to the entire structure of his argument and from which he draws consequences of the highest philosophical importance must be considered to stand on an unproved assumption at best, and his reasoning must appear to be a queer kind of cosmological argument from the existence of the finite to the existence of finite.

There are two other points worth noticing is Strawson's refutation of the Cartesian position. He not only assumes the truth of his basic principle, but also seems to assume that unless I already admit the existence of other subjects of experience I shall have to regard the experiences uniquely related causally to a certain body (i.e. my body) as all the experiences. He writes, 'the most I may be allowed to have noted is that experiences, all experiences, stand in a special relation to body *M* and this is what makes it unique among bodies'. Again he writes:

> if in identifying things to which conscious states are to be ascribed, private experiences are to be all one has to go on, then, just for the very same reason for which, there is, from one's own point of view, no question of telling that a private experience is one's own, there is also no question of telling that a private experience is another's. All private experiences, all states of consciousness will be mine, that is, no one's.[11]

It is easy enough to see the motive behind these rather strange statements but not the reason for them. Apparently, Strawson wants to disallow the very basis of an argument in which from certain given experiences related to body *M*, I can pass to other experiences related similarly to body *N*. He insists that no such distinction between 'certain given experiences' and 'certain other experiences' can be drawn because unless I am already in a position to ascribe experiences to others and thus distinguish myself as a subject of experience from other subjects of experience, all experiences will be mine and therefore, by a second application of his dictum, no one's. It seems to me that Strawson (apart from assuming the truth of his basic dictum) here assumes that the only experiences of which I can form any idea are the experiences felt by me though even these cannot be ascribed to any one – either myself or any other. I

---

[11] Strawson, op. cit., p. 100.

cannot form any idea of other experiences, for I am aware only of experiences connected with a given body *M*. In other words, the only experiences of which I can have any idea are those that I can refer to demonstratively, that is, refer to as 'this pain', etc. I am not sure that Strawson implies this. But how else are these statements to be interpreted? Unless he wants to maintain that I cannot even conceive experiences other than those to which I can refer demonstratively (or which are in some sense private to me) what significance is to be attached to his statement that just as 'there is no question of telling that a private experience is one's own, there is also no question of telling that a private experience is another's'. And in the statement – 'all private experiences, all states of consciousness will be mine, that is, no one's' – he clearly writes as if, in the situation that is being considered, there were no distinction between 'all private experiences' and 'all states of consciousness'. I see no reason why the Cartesian philosopher should suffer from this strange disability. And there is no reason whatever for accepting such a limitation in this case, because even if we grant the primitive character of the concept of a person and agree that we cannot ascribe experiences to ourselves without ascribing them to others, there must be some way and we must somehow learn to distinguish our experiences from those of others.

As Strawson himself points out, we do not ascribe experiences to ourselves on the basis of behaviour criteria whereas in the case of others we can ascribe them only on the basis of observed behaviour. Even if the behaviour criteria are considered logically adequate for ascribing some states of consciousness, we must somehow conceive of experiences which are not directly given to us and which we can only ascribe on the basis of behaviour to others though they can ascribe these to themselves without any such criteria. If we can form the conception of experiences outside the series of our own private experiences of which we are directly aware, and to which we can demonstratively refer, there is no reason why a Cartesian philosopher should not be able to do so without the benefit of our ordinary assumption or the assumption made by Strawson.

Second, the difficulties concerning the identification of other subjects of experiences – in so far as they do not centre round Strawson's basic dictum – are the same for him as for the Cartesian. On Strawson's view states of consciousness and *P*-predicates in general are ascribed to a person who is to be regarded logically as a primitive type of entity. That is to say, a person is not to be considered a compound of two entities – a body and a mind or ego – but a subject of a logically unique kind to which both corporeal characteristics and states of consciousness are properly ascribed. And he thinks that there is no difficulty in his case – as there is in the case of the Cartesian theory – of telling which subject a given experience or set of experiences belongs to. For, on his view, an experience is identified as the experiences of a given person and is hence logically untransferable to another person and, second, a person is not a private Cartesian ego and can be identified without any difficulty. But it is clear that a person is identifiable only because we can locate and identify his body and then ascribe to him certain states of consciousness on the strength of certain behaviour criteria. Strawson may object that to talk of bodies and bodily behaviour and states of consciousness distinct from them is to introduce a dualism which he has firmly and completely rejected. But this would be excessively pedantic or else disingenuous; for even if we speak of persons, it has to be admitted that a person can be identified by means of *M*-predicates and the *M*-predicates relevant to the identification of a person are of the same sort as are relevant to the identification of any physical object. Further, Strawson admits that we can ascribe *P*-predicates to others only on the basis of behaviour criteria which they themselves do not require in their own case though he adds that these criteria are in some cases logically adequate. Apart from this, I see no important difference between ascribing states of consciousness to a subject identified via *M*-predicates and on the basis of bodily behaviour and ascribing them in the traditional fashion analogically. That there is no important difference between the two comes out still more clearly if we consider a further objection which Strawson raises against Cartesian dualism. Apart from the difficulty of identifying the subject of ascription even indirectly, the dualist has an additional difficulty, namely, how to be certain that there is only one subject of experience connected with a unique body. 'What right have we', he asks, 'to speak of *the subject* implying uniqueness? Why should there not be any number of subjects of experiences, perhaps qualitatively indistinguishable, each subject and each set of experiences, standing in the same unique relation to body *N* (or to body *M*)? Uniqueness of the body does not guarantee uniqueness of the Cartesian soul.'[12] But how does Strawson propose to get over this difficulty in his own case? Once it is recognized that we identify a person as a subject who uniquely satisfies a set of *M*-predicates, what guarantee have we that the *P*-predicates ascribed on their basis apply to a single, unique set of experiences? We cannot surely plead that since we are speaking of the experiences of a given person – and not of a private ego – the difficulty does not arise. For unless we have already somehow excluded the possibility that the *P*-predicates ascribed in the way we have ascribed them may not refer to a unique set of experiences, the notion of a given person itself would be ambiguous. And if the two sets of experiences are assumed to be qualitatively indistinguishable then only an appeal to the principle of the identity of indiscernibles will save the situation. And this is open equally to the dualist. If on the other hand the experiences are qualitatively different, then methods similar to those adopted by psychiatrists to study co-consciousness and multiple personality can perhaps be used in this imaginary case too. But they are available or unavailable equally to Strawson and to the Cartesian philosopher.

III

Strawson's own positive thesis, that the concept of a person is primitive and that a person is not to be construed as a compound of two entities, namely, a mind and a body, flows partly out of his rejection of Cartesian dualism as internally incoherent. His elaboration of it is even briefer than his refutation of Cartesian

---

12 Strawson, op. cit., p. 101.

dualism and raises many issues which require independent, detailed discussion, of which perhaps the following are important:

1. Strawson insists that it is essential to and distinctive of *P*-predicates that they are self-ascribable without the use of any bodily behaviour criteria and other ascribable on such a basis. He maintains that these criteria must be logically adequate at least in the case of some *P*-predicates; otherwise the observed behaviour would be merely a sign of the presence of the ascribed state of consciousness and we shall be forced to use some kind of analogical argument from our own case and the door will be thrown wide open to scepticism. Hence he insists that there is no logical gap between the *P*-predicate which is ascribed and the bodily behaviour on the strength of which it is ascribed. The criteria are logically adequate or sufficient. Since Strawson would admit – though he does not state it explicitly – that other ascriptions can take place only on the basis of bodily behaviour, these criteria will be both necessary and sufficient. And yet he refuses to say that the relation between *P*-predicates and their criteria is analytic and that the meaning of *P*-predicates is given by the criteria of their application (that would be the thesis of physicalism). To do this – according to him – would be to forget that they have self-ascriptive uses in which these criteria are not necessary. But it is precisely this situation which many philosophers would take as constituting a problem rather than a solution. The relation between the two is neither inductive, nor analytic – and Strawson, of course, would not dream of accepting any synthetic a priori propositions. So it is difficult to see how exactly they are related. The analogy of the relation between the markings on a playing card and its value is so obviously different from the kind of situation being considered that it is doubtful whether it is very valuable. For one thing, the connection between the markings on a playing card and its value is conventional (not in the sense current in certain contemporary philosophical discussions but in the sense

the word naturally bears in common usage). Moreover, the statement that a certain card has a certain value or ranks above another in some game, is not the statement of a proposition at all. The attempt is to combine the sweetness of physicalism without its bitterness and it is not clear how this is to be achieved.

Strawson seems to keep on shifting between self-ascriptive and other-ascriptive uses to avoid both scepticism and physicalism. To insist that is how *P*-predicates are used and both these uses are equally proper is merely to state the difficulty rather than resolve it.

2. The few comments that Strawson does make to answer his query – 'How are *P*-predicates possible or, what is it in the natural facts that make the notion of a person intelligible?' do not seem to be particularly helpful. In order to do this he moves a certain class of *P*-predicates, those involving doing something such as going for a walk, writing a letter, etc. to a central position. These imply a characteristic pattern of behaviour without indicating a correspondingly specific or definite sensation or experience. Strawson thinks that here the resistance to regarding them as having the same meaning (in their first-person as well as third-person uses) is minimal. 'They release us', he remarks, 'from the idea that the only things we know without observation or inference or both are private experiences. We can know without telling by either of these means, about the present and future movement of a body.'[13]

   These considerations are supposed to remove the feeling of mystery that some of us may attach to the fact that we know without any observation or inference our own experiences by pointing out that we know in the same way our own bodily movements in the case of intentional action. Strawson clearly has in mind here the difference between our knowledge of our

---

13 Strawson, op. cit., p. 111.

own intentional actions and the predictions of our behaviour by others, which some philosophers have recently emphasized. But this does not give him what he wants. For when I know that I intend to go to Poona by a certain train tomorrow, I do not know that I shall be in the train tomorrow at a certain time or even that I shall leave my house to go to the railway station. One can conceive of a whole range of circumstances, from the stability of the earth through the regular running of railway trains to the integrity of my own nervous system, which may prevent my going to Poona. The realization of an intention in action requires the occurrence of a complex sequence of movements and we can logically eliminate one by one, the members of this series starting with the last and coming down to the very first step in the execution of the intention. Since the non-occurrence of these realizing movements is compatible with the truth of the statement that I intend to do something and that I know my own intention, it is clear that I cannot be said to know in such a case without observation and inference that I shall make such and such bodily movements. It is of course true that normally the various favourable conditions are present and I do confidently except that I shall do such and such a thing. But it is a tautology to say that if I intend to do *A* and do not subsequently change my mind, and the physical conditions necessary to the realization of *A* are fulfilled, I shall act in such and such away. Moreover, given the truth of the corresponding propositions, I know equally in the case of anyone else and with equal analytic certainty that he will behave in such and such a way.

3. Strawson insists that there is one and the same subject to which both *M*- and *P*-predicates are ascribed and he quotes some sentences to support his view that this is what we ordinarily do. There is no doubt that if ordinary usage were taken as a reliable guide in these matters, it would largely, perhaps overwhelmingly, support the single-subject view. But if we were made aware of the great differences in character between

what is ascribed by *M*-predicates and what is ascribed by *P*-predicates, we may be inclined to draw some distinction between the body and the mind and predicates appropriately ascribable to each of them.

Even ordinarily without any prompting from philosophers, sometimes we do speak of what goes in the mind as contrasted with the condition or the state of the body. It is not very difficult to give a series of graded examples where the contrast is drawn more and more explicitly and sharply, though perhaps, a total distinction between two different entities or subjects is seldom, if ever, made. So ordinary usage – to which great importance should be attached in the absence of any strong philosophical objections – is not completely undivided on this point. Replacing the distinction between mind and body by the distinction between *M*- and *P*-predicates does not dissolve dualism and the connected problems. *M*-predicates are ascribed both to persons and to physical objects, and *P*-predicates only to persons. These latter ascribe to a state of consciousness or this is part of what they ascribe. And we would not dream of ascribing these to material objects. I suppose the reason why we would not dream of ascribing them to material objects is that we do not ordinarily believe them to be capable of consciousness. Even if we agree that *M*- and *P*-predicates are ascribed to one and the same subject, we must admit that the former are ascribed in respect of certain features in which a person resembles a material body and the latter in respect of something in which he radically differs from material objects. This is really Descartes's distinction between thinking and extended substances, although there may be ground for rejecting in the precise form in which he stated it. But the radical difference in the character of what are ascribed by the two classes of predicates remains. And it is difficult to see how any theory can get rid of it without, in the process, hopelessly distorting or else completely ignoring the relevant facts.

9

A.J. Ayer on Personal Identity

THERE are three major discussions of the problem of personal identity in Ayer's writings. The first is in the chapter on 'Myself and Others' in the *Problem of Knowledge*.[1] The second is in the long essay on the concept of a person which is the title-piece of the collection of essays[2] in which it appears and, finally, the long section on personal identity in the *Origins of Pragmatism*[3] where starting with certain suggestions of William James, Ayer develops a theory which is as much his as James's. The general approach is Humean and the evil to be avoided is the admission of the soul as a substance in its own right. I shall not follow the chronological order in my exposition, but take the attempt to rehabilitate the no-ownership theory as my starting point, go on to a consideration of the attempt to base personal identity on memory and causation in the *Problem of Knowledge* and conclude with his most mature view of the subject in the *Origins of Pragmatism*.

The attempt to reinstate the no-ownership theory against Strawson's criticism of it reflects the materialistic approach to mind which has characterized many eminent English and American philosophers in the last quarter of the twentieth century. Very early in his philosophical development Ayer came to reject the thesis of physicalism, that statements about experiences are *logically* equivalent to statement about the bodily condition or behaviour of the person to whom they are ascribed. It may seem as if this implied the possibility of the occurrence of mental processes unrelated to

---

1 A.J. Ayer, *The Problem of Knowledge*, London: Macmillan, 1956.

2 A.J. Ayer, *The Concept of a Person and Other Essays*, London: Macmillan, 1963.

3 A.J. Ayer , *The Origins of Pragmatism*, London: Macmillan, 1968.

any physical body and we were forced back into the position of Descartes. Ayer argues that this is not so. He writes:

> . . . it does not follow that it is even logically possible for states of consciousness to exist independently of any physical body. The reason why it does not follow is that it may not make sense to talk of states of consciousness except as the experiences of some subject; and that it may well be that this conscious subject cannot be identified except by reference to his body.

Ayer continues, 'personal identity depends on the identity of the body and a person's ownership of states of consciousness consists in their standing in a special causal relation to the body by which he is identified. I am not maintaining of course that this is how one actually becomes aware of one's own experiences, but only that the fact that they are the experience of the person that one is, depends upon their being connected with this particular body'. Ayer attempts to rebut Strawson's charge that the theory is internally incoherent.[4] Briefly Strawson's argument is that the theory requires it to be contingent or synthetic that all my experiences are dependent on the state of my body, but at the same time, if the proffered analysis is correct, my experiences can only be identified as those dependent on this body and hence the proposition would be analytic. Ayer argues

> that these propositions can be reformulated in a way which shows that the contradiction does not arise. The contingent proposition is that if my body is in *such-and-such* a state then an experience of *such-and-such* a kind results. The analytic proposition is that if an experience is causally dependent in this way on the state of my body then it is mine. But now it is obvious that these propositions are distinct so that there is no inconsistency in holding that one is contingent and the other not.

A little later, he writes:

> We cannot ask which experiences are dependent on a body and are therefore to be assigned to such-and-such a person because this is to assume improperly that the experiences have

---

4 See Ayer, *The Concept of a Person and Other Essays.*

> been independently identified. The question we can ask is what experiences are dependent upon a particular body if this is just a way of asking what experiences the person identified by the body is having at the relevant time.

The next stage in the argument is a specification of the special causal relation of a set of experiences to a given body which on the theory constitutes the defining relation of their being the experiences of the same single self. Causal sufficiency would be too strong a requirement because it may be denied that experiences have sufficient conditions or that these are physical in character. We shall therefore have to maintain that an experience belongs to a given person in virtue of the fact that some state of the person's body is a necessary condition of its occurrence. To prevent this from being too weak we have to stipulate that the necessary condition in question will have to be an immediately necessary condition. For, the existence of my body presupposes the existence of the existence of the bodies of my ancestors and the detailed character of my experience depends partly on the behaviour of my fellowmen. These however provide conditions which are indirectly or mediately necessary for the occurrence and character of my experiences. The refinements of the theory, however, are not yet over. For Ayer is sufficiently impressed by well-attested cases of paranormal cognition to provide for the possibility of telepathy and extrasensory perception. We shall not enter into the details but the upshot of further emendations is that though certain stray experiences may have their necessary conditions outside my nervous system, it still remains true that 'no experience of mine shall have for an immediately necessary condition the state of any other body not my own'.

The central point of this theory is the contention that experiences can be individuated only by reference to the persons who have them and these in turn can only be identified by reference to their bodies. From these two propositions it follows that no experience of mine could have occurred unless my body has existed; more particularly it follows that the existence of my body will be implied by any statement in which an experience is attributed to me. But here I think it is important to distinguish between the *principle of identity* and *the procedure of identification* of a given object. It may be, and it is often the case, that the principle of individuation of *A* is distinct from the procedure for identifying *A* and that a description of this procedure is no part of the meaning of the statement that *A* is the same particular throughout a given stretch of time or that two characteristics or states belong to the same thing. This is quite obviously true of physical objects including human organisms. Passport offices and insurance companies rely upon identifying marks such as moles, birthmarks and combinations of them. Banks rely upon the distinctive features of handwriting for honouring cheques signed by their clients, assuming exceptional skill in forgery to be both rare and detectable. The most stringent of such tests is of course that of finger-printing, which is taken to be practically infallible. But none of these tests gives us the criterion of the identity of a given human organism – which is the occupation of a continuous path in the spatio-temporal order. If we observed a physical body unwinkingly from the moment of its inception to its present position in the space–time world, we would not need any subsidiary test of identification. In such a case the principle of identity and the procedure of identification would coalesce. Similar considerations apply to personal identity. We may grant that an experience can be individuated only by reference to the subject who has it. This means that experiences do not occur in isolation – in flashes and bangs of consciousness as it were – but only as members of fairly well-knit and continuous series. Other philosophers have made the same point essentially by saying that every experience must be the experience of some person or subject. This is by no means self-evident, but the realization of its negation is so hard to conceive, that we would be unwise to reject it off hand. We may further accept, what is again almost impossible to deny, that the only way of identifying persons is by reference to their bodies. But it does not follow that the criterion of the identity of a single self or subject of experiences is given by some specifiable relation of all his experiences to an identifiable physical organism.

These are of course difficulties here which do not arise in the case of physical objects; first of all, there is no difficulty in formulating a sufficiently precise criterion of individuation for physical objects including human organisms. Second the procedures of identification and criterion of identity are correlated empirically, and once the correlation is established, the former can do duty for the latter. Moreover, though the principle of individuality is in some sense a priori, and the subsidiary principles of identification empirical, they are coordinates in the sense of being both public and their fulfilment in any given case can be verified by suitable observations by anyone who is able to make them. In the case of self-identity there is great difficulty in specifying the relation which so unites experiences to one another that they are experiences of the same self. Moreover it seems hardly to make any sense for others to identify my experiences. This is not merely because, as Ayer correctly points out, there is no question of starting with a heap of experiences and distributing them by allocating each to its proper owner, but rather more fundamentally, because my experiences are not so given to others that they can refer to them demonstratively.

Even where it is a question of deciding what sort of experience I am having, when there is a certain event in my brain both the occurrence and character of the experience can be correlated with the brain event only on the basis of my report. If it does not make sense for others to identify my experiences, equally it does not make sense for me to identify my own experiences either, as it does not make sense for me to ask whether a given experience is my own. Ayer's attempt to tie the mind logically to the body must be considered unsuccessful. Interestingly, Strawson makes a basically similar attempt in a brief essay in *Freedom and Resentment*[5] without referring to Ayer's earlier essay and without showing any awareness of the rather surprising common ground between them in this regard. His main concern is to defend his one-subject theory against the two subjects theory of the Cartesians. The dualist divides personal

---

[5] Strawson, *Freedom and Resentment and Other Essays*, London: Metheun, 1974.

predicates into mental and physical and in some cases, splits up a complex predicate into a mental and a physical component. Even if he succeeds in this, Strawson argues he cannot ascribe them to two logically independent subjects because he *cannot identify* the subject of mental predicates by itself. He has to refer to a person locatable in the common public, world. The moral seems to be that the mind is logically inseparable from the body. I think the considerations urged by me against Ayer's theory, if valid are equally valid against the version of analytical materialism.

It is therefore not surprising that even philosophers who do not believe on causal grounds that minds can exist apart from the bodies to which they are attached have sought an internal criterion of personal identity, that is, a criterion that directly holds among experiences themselves and gives them an intimacy and warmth that cannot possibly hold between experiences of different selves. Causal relations are important and also the basis of the distinctive character of personal consciousness, but by themselves are not constitutive of personal identity. We can exclude the causal influences of one mind on another by restricting the relation to immediate or direct causation. But if we want to provide for direct transactions between experiences normally assigned to persons, at any rate as a bare possibility – we shall have to look for something more exclusive. Supplementing causation by similarity and gradualness of transitions, as Hume does, is not enough. It is logically possible that the streams of consciousness of two persons are qualitatively indistinguishable in certain stretches. In continuity of memory, we have the most promising candidate for our purpose. If we leave out habit, memory and remembering dates facts, etc. we are left with 'recollection', which operates within and not across streams of personal consciousness. Each one of us can remember – in this strict sense – only his own earlier experiences or objects, events and state of affairs perceived by him. James uses the word 'appropriation' for this and Ayer uses it throughout his discussion in *Origins of Pragmatism*. If selves are bundles of perceptions then they seem to mnemically insulated. Whenever we find it necessary, for any reasons, to go beyond bodily identity, to identify persons, it is easy to see that we bank upon continuity of memory as the decisive factor. This is so in the legal, psychiatric and other fields where questions concerning identity of persons have to be answered. Moreover stability and continuity of character of teleological unity which comes into reckoning as a third factor in such cases presupposes continuity of memory. The central difficulty, however, is that it is inadequate as the sole criterion and we have little hesitation on many occasions in ascribing certain earlier experiences to a person who is now unable to recollect them. This and other difficulties are discussed at some length in *Problem of Knowledge* but in the later discussion in *Origins of Pragmatism* though James's fancy word 'appropriation' (is) the same as recollection, they receive little attention. Rather it is acknowledged that appropriation supplemented by sensible compresence and sensible continuity is not enough and that a reference to the body is needed to incorporate certain experiences and segments of experiences into the psychical biography of the person to whom they are normally assigned. Since the basic problem is the same and also the general method of resolving it, we shall conflate the two discussions as we go along.

The following are the main difficulties in making memory the sole and sufficient basis of personal identity. It would be readily granted that each one of us has hundreds of experiences which he never appropriates or recollects later and which themselves are not recollections of earlier experiences. Some of these may have been intense and significant experiences when they occurred. I may correctly judge on the basis of my diary or the reliable testimony of others that I was in such and such a situation and must have undergone such and such experiences without being able to recollect them. We can stipulate that the required feature is not actual appropriation but that of being capable of being appropriated if suitable conditions are fulfilled. The fact that experiences long buried and apparently lost are recovered in dreams and under hypnosis with the aid of psychoanalysis and certain drugs, lends justification to our procedure. But if all the available methods of recovery fail, we shall have to lay down a priority that our requirement is fulfilled in every case. Apart from the dogmatism involved, we clearly reveal that continuity of memory is not a necessary condition for the correct allocation of experiences to person in the ordinary way. And such continuity is not sufficient either. I may 'recollect' experiences I never had as George IV presumably did when he talked about the glorious cavalry charge that he led at the Battle of Waterloo. It may seem, at first sight, that delusive memories should present no special difficulties for a particular theory of person identity just as perceptual errors are a common problem for alternative theories of perception. However, for anyone who relies entirely upon a criterion internal to experiences there is a serious trouble. We can minimize our difficulty by outlawing imaginary experiences but we cannot rule out the logical possibility that some other person was having at the time, and in the situation to which I refer, the kind of experience which I now recollect. It is interesting to notice that in both the types of situation, that is, a situation where memory is not necessary and situations where it is not sufficient, we fall back upon the body as a focal point of reference for the experiences of a person. The reason for believing that I must have had a certain kind of experience in the past is that, my body was present in a certain setting and exhibited characteristic patterns of behaviour which are normally expressive of such a state of mind. Equally the reason for believing that I could not have had a certain type of experience in the past is that the physical and physiological conditions, normally necessary for the occurrences of such experiences, did not obtain in relation to me.

In addition, there are other and in a way, more fundamental objections. If, experiences cannot be individuated except as the experiences of a person, then there would be a circularity – whether vicious or harmless – in analysing the unity of personal consciousness in terms of any relation binding experiences together specifically in the case of memory. Some philosophers would say that the very nature of a memory claim implies that a certain earlier experience belongs to the same 'I' which now has a recollective experience. Here again it is difficult to say whether the circle can be shown to be harmless, though I feel that the linguistic and quasi-linguistic considerations advanced by Ayer in *Problem of Knowledge* will not remove the difficulty.

Morever, in any analysis of self-identity in terms of memory some elements of experience enter into a personal stream, not because they are directly recollected but because they accompany other elements which are so recollected. But then, what is this relation of mutual accompaniment between two items of experience? It is their being elements in the same total state of mind. But this is another way of saying that they are experienced by the same person. That is, different items of 'sensible compresence' and 'sensible continuity' besides 'appropriation' are features needed for the analysis of personal identity. In his account of 'post-mortem' experiences, after declaring that he was inclined on account of them, to accept some form of dualism, Ayer goes on to express his disinclination to accept the soul as a substance and his belief that he had done his best in 'Origins of Pragmatism' to explain personal identity without appealing to a spiritual substance. I shall therefore consider briefly what we may consider to his most considered view of the subject.

James's 'sensible continuity' is the same as Hume's similarity. 'Within each personal consciousness thought is sensibly continuous'. He writes, 'that is to say, the changes in the quality of consciousness are never absolutely abrupt and where there is a time gap, the consciousness after it feels as if it belonged together with consciousness after it, as another part of the same self'. Whatever experiences are felt to be continuous are appropriated by a present identifying thought, and so are experiences remote in time, which are marked in its recollection with similar warmth and intimacy. 'Sensible compresence' is taken by James to be the relation which holds between contemporary experiences. To make the definition more adequate Ayer introduces the notions of 'indirect sensible continuity' and 'indirect appropriation'. The relation of indirect sensible continuity is that in which two experiences stand when they are not sensibly continuous with one another but are both members either of the same continuous chain or of different chains which are lined at one or more points by a relation of sensible compresence. For instance, in a case where E_1 and E_4 are not sensibly continuous, it may be that E_1 is sensibly continuous with E_2, E_2 with E_3 and E_3 with E_4; or it may happen that E_1 is sensibly continuous with E_2 and E_2 is sensibly compresent with E_3 and E_3 is sensibly continuous with E_4. In either case E_1 and E_4 stand to one another in the relation of indirect sensible continuity. Experiences related by direct or indirect sensible continuity or sensible compresence may be called neighbours. The notion of indirect appropriation can be explained thus. If *T* is an identifying thought which appropriates *E* across a time gap, it indirectly appropriates not only any neighbour of *E* but also any experience which *E* or any of its neighbours appropriates. Similar considerations apply to the appropriater. The appropriators of *T* gather together all the experience appropriated by *T*. It is easy to see that among the experiences indirectly appropriated by *T* there may be some which it directly appropriates. All such experience will be more strongly integrated into the personal stream of consciousness of a subject than others which are appropriated only indirectly. When two experiences stand to one another in the relation of sensible compresence or direct sensible continuity they cannot be related by indirect sensible continuity. Two experiences are said to be co-familiar if and only if either they are neighbours or one of them directly or indirectly appropriates the other. The self may now be defined as any class of experiences co-familiar with each other.

If we leave aside for a while the subtlety and complexities of the definition – it is clear that the chief end of our manoeuvres is to make good the deficiencies resulting from the erratic and uncertain working of memory and the resultant self-deprivation. However, there is a suggestion of circularity in the meaning of the phrases 'sensibly continuous', 'sensibly compresent'. What else could they mean but that one and the same person experiences together two items or that he passes without a break from one experience to another? Equally the prima facie circularity involved in analysing self-identity in terms of memory required to be handled. Ayer is too good a philosopher not be aware of them but he is too good an empiricist not to be hopeful of overcoming them. If the worst comes to the worst we may have to admit that Hume's dictum that all particular perception(s) are separate and isolable will have to be modified. We may have to admit that perceptions can occur only in series with a certain degree of coherence and that the occurrence of perception implies the occurrence of other perceptions though not the occurrence of some specific perception. In *Problem of Knowledge* he comes near to admitting this and in *Origins of Pragmatism* he expresses approval of James' contention that Hume created a problem for himself by separating perceptions and that 'perceptions themselves do the work for which philosophers have had recourse to a separate agency'.

But even if the theory escapes the charge of circularity it still has to meet the objection of being counter-intuitive. Under certain circumstances it may deprive me of experiences normally assigned to me and under others it may assign to me experiences normally assigned to others. For example, if loss of memory were to follow lapse of consciousness, we may have to conclude that the two series – one occurring before and the other after the gap – constitute separate selves. We may have segments of experiences during dreams or during brief intervals between two periods of sleep which are completely self-contained. Also, as in the case of the earlier and much simpler analysis, I may 'revive' and thus appropriate to myself either an unreal experience or an experience of the kind which did occur as part of another's personal stream. If selves are series of experiences there is no logical impossibility about some of them having common members. But the suggestion does produce acute discomfort. Ayer's strategy is to bring the body back into the picture and 'attach' experiences of persons to their respective bodies. But this time the link is provided not by psycho-physical causal relations but by kinaesthetic sensations which accompany other elements of experience belonging to a personal series. That a vast majority of our experiences are accompanied by a steady background of awareness of the body is undeniable. Even so these may be stragglers in dreams and trance-like states. The tactic here is to postulate that at least one member of such series is accompanied by bodily sensations whose locus is the body of the person concerned and then discipline these recalcitrant minorities to join the main stream. A similar course is to be followed in the case of unusually located organic sensations. Problems connected with dissociation of consciousness and multiple personalities are handled equally ingeniously while leaving it open for us to say that two independent selves may be attached to the same body. Equally, Ayer leaves it an open question whether the same person can be associated with different bodies. In all his philosophical writings on this problem Ayer has always admitted the logical possibility of the hypotheses of reincarnation and disembodied survival though he was more hesitant to admit the latter. If he could have his way to denying them he would have made life happier for himself.

Recently some philosophers, notably Bernard Williams, have attempted to reduce these admissions to absurdity and thus warn us against abandoning the security of the solid body science fiction about brain transplants and the facts concerning the mental consequences of the severance of the two cerebral hemispheres have been pressed into service in this context. Ayer makes only a brief reference to this area in his discussion of the vagaries of personal identity in the *Central Questions of Philosophy*.[6] Perhaps he thought that once the difficulties and ambiguities connected with self-identity in normal circumstances are sorted out, the abnormal cases – real and imaginary – could be accommodated more easily. He was as good a materialist as any in believing that it is causally unlikely, almost impossible, for the soul to survive the disintegration of the body. But as an analyst he was clear-headed enough to see that personal identity cannot be based either entirely or primarily on bodily continuity. In this I think he was right.

---

6 A.J. Ayer, *Central Questions of Philosophy*, London: Weisefeld, 1973.

II. Language, Truth and Logic

Introduction

S.E. Bhelke

THE rise of analytic philosophy was an important turning point for twentieth-century philosophy which had its roots in mathematical logic as well as developments in the empirical sciences. The claims made by the sciences are examined on empirical grounds and are objective and verifiable. The same procedure was followed in philosophy in order to establish empirical and verifiable claims that are communicable and intelligible to any person. Since metaphysics made claims that were neither intelligible nor communicable they were not accepted as part of legitimate philosophical discourse. A move was made to eliminate metaphysics. This was supported by the use of modern logic whose formal and abstract character helped in developing clarity and precision in philosophical discourse.

Since thought is intelligible through language, the clarity and precision of thought will also reflect in the clarity and precision of language. The use of language becomes a challenge to understand the meaning of a sentence with clarity and precision. This made Bertrand Russell advocate the position of logical atomism. *Principia Mathematica* was used as a model for logical and philosophical thinking. The milestones in this development were Russell's *On Denoting*, Moore's *Principia Ethica* and Wittgenstein's *Tractatus-Logico-Philosophicus*. This movement gave rise to analysis of language in the form of ordinary language philosophy and logical positivism influencing philosophical thinking all over the world.

In India these trends received a warm welcome. Scholars of Indian philosophy used this perspective and method to understand

and present Indian philosophy afresh. The study of this twentieth-century philosophy enriched the intellectual deliberations in India. The generation of scholars from the third and fourth decades of the twentieth century seriously studied the developments of twentieth-century philosophy and contributed to it vigorously by way of teaching and research. In this period, one of the prominent names that reflected serious scholarship was N.G. Kulkarni, whose contribution has been significantly valuable. In the present section of the book, a selection of his writings on this area of philosophy is presented.

The articles in this section, titled, 'Language, Truth and Logic', begin with the survey of analytic philosophy. It gives a clear and brief picture of the origin and development of twentieth-century philosophy in which philosophers like Russell, Moore, Wittgenstein, A.J. Ayer and philosophers of the Vienna circle contributed to the formulation of philosophical problems. Kulkarni discusses in detail the emergence of analytic philosophy against the background of idealism and discusses the problem of meaning as seen in Wittgenstein's *Tractatus* as well logical positivism and opines that the demarcation between atomism and positivism is 'uncertain and shifting'. This article ends with the contribution of ordinary language philosophy and the shift that is marked by a form of naturalism in philosophy towards the end of the twentieth century.

The next two articles by Russell deal with the problem of 'descriptions' and Strawson's criticism from the perspective of ordinary language. In this context Kulkarni, however, opines that Russell's attempt at developing an ideal language is actually revisionary. On the other hand, W.V.O. Quine's concern with the problem of 'referential opacity' is discussed with great clarity, albeit bringing out the difficulties in Quine's position, particularly with the notion of synonymy. The article 'In Defence of a Dogma' by Strawson and Grice attempts to reinstate the analytic–synthetic distinction that the logical positivists had held sacred.

Kulkarni analyses a very important traditional definiton of

knowledge in the article titled, 'Knowledge as Well-Grounded True Belief', discussing the differences between 'knowledge' and 'belief' as well as the famous counter-example by Gettier.

The problem of truth and its relation to certain logical and linguistic properties is addressed in the following article on 'Truth' which brings out in detail, the relation between truth-value and its relation to a proposition and belief. 'Meaning, Realism and Logic' discusses the problem of meaning with a focus on Dummett's observations on the 'grasping' of truth-conditions.

Kulkarni examines various forms of 'relativism' in the next article hinting quite clearly at its disastrous consequences. We see that the discussions on realism develop into discussions of relativism. The 'faces of relativism' are exposed in detail and Kulkarni takes up, in subsequent papers, discussions on modern logic which are rather technical. In spite of handling the technical discussions of modern mathematical logic, the reader feels as comfortable as he feels while reading the previous papers. He takes up the issue raised by Putnam in the article titled, 'Putnam's Proposal for Logical Form' which attempts to replace classical logic by quantum logic. This paper is followed by his reflections on three-valued logic where we see Kulkarni's independent thinking and significant insights into problems of higher logic. The paper on 'Alternative Logics', for example, illustrates the consequences of three-valued logic over two-valued logic.

All these papers of N.G. Kulkarni deal with technical problems in logic and language. Though the issues he takes up are rather tough in the field of philosophy, a reader can go through the articles with ease because he makes it simple to understand. It is a pleasure to read these papers, no less than a pleasure one gets in appreciating an art-form. The analysis he provides needs to be taken as a model for further studies in the area. Students as well as research scholars in philosophy are fortunate and will certainly profit from reading these papers carefully.

1

A Survey of Analytical Philosophy

ANALYTICAL philosophy had a quiet beginning at the turn of the century in the writing of Bertrand Russell and G.E. Moore at Cambridge. They both revolted against the tradition of British idealism which dominated, at the time, the English-speaking universities. Neither of them thought that he was replacing traditional philosophy by something novel and more fruitful. Russell indeed characterized the changing views he held at successive stages in his career by traditional labels 'realism', 'pluralism', 'logical atomism', 'neutral monism', etc. Moore never did so. Nevertheless he was much more traditional in his approach than was made out later. He never identified philosophy with analysis and thought of it as a necessary preliminary to whatever task it was that philosophers had set before themselves. It is difficult to remember today that when his *Refutation of Idealism* was published he was hailed as the founder of neo-realism (the older realism being that of Thomas Reid, the Scottish philosopher of common sense). As the philosophical scene changed Moore together with Wittgenstein became more influential than Russell who became increasingly hostile to 'ordinary language' philosophy.

Following Urmson in his *Philosophical Analysis*, we may distinguish three distinct stages, though overlapping, in the development of analytical philosophy: (i) logical atomism, (ii) logical positivism, and (iii) ordinary language philosophy or linguistic philosophy. However, even before the emergence of these successive periods, Russell and Moore produced a body of writings whose purpose was to introduce clarity and precision in the discussion of philosophical questions and make them more manageable.

Moore in particular spent a great deal of his time trying to clarify the statements made by other philosophers including his colleague Russell. Russell's own work during this period was predominantly in the field of foundations of mathematics. In collaboration with Whitehead he authored *Principia Mathematica* where the project of deriving pure mathematics from logic reaches its culmination and is set forth in details. This work is too technical for a layman to understand and evaluate. But it had a bearing on the general problems of philosophy which proved very important indeed. The symbolism and techniques of *Principia* provided a new arsenal to both logical atomism and logical positivism.

Logical atomism found its classic expression in Russell's lectures on the philosophy of logical atomism (1918) and the *Tractatus-Logico-Philosophicus* of Wittgenstein published in 1922. Of the two, Wittgenstein's version is more extreme and carries every trend to its logical conclusion; undeterred by the appearance of paradox and defiance of common sense. Russell's exposition contains many ideas he had derived from Wittgenstein when he has the latter's tutor at Cambridge. The philosophy may be characterized rather loosely, but fairly accurately, as the projection upon the world of the logic of *Principia*. It regards 'facts' not things or events as the basic constituents of the world. The reason is that our logical system starts with elementary propositions – i.e. propositions not composed of other propositions and not containing any logical constants. It sets forth the logical principles needed for deduction when various compounds of elementary propositions figure among our premises and conclusions. When we accept or reject any of the elementary propositions it must be in virtue of something in the world and not as a result of logical inference. So the world must be regarded as composed of atomic facts corresponding to true elementary propositions. The notion of a 'fact' is not defined; it is something in the world in virtue of which our propositions are true or false. Conversely a proposition is any sentence which is true or false. Wittgenstein begins his exposition with the declarations:

1. The world is all that is the case

i. The world is the totality of facts not of things.

ii. The world is determined by the facts and these being all the facts.

So we have on one side, as it were, a collection of atomic facts and on the other a system of elementary propositions which when true, 'mirror' the atomic facts. The elementary or atomic propositions are said to be logical pictures of atomic facts (or possible atomic facts). The atomic fact is a configuration of objects or simples which are the stuff of the world. The atomic proposition is composed of signs, simple signs. There is a one-to-one correlation between the objects and the signs, and the method of arrangement of the signs in the proposition reflects or corresponds to the manner of configuration of objects in the fact. This is the essence of logical picturing which consists in 'identity of structure' between the proposition and the fact that it pictures. No copying or qualitative similarity is needed, though Wittgenstein remarks that the picture and the pictured must have their 'form' in common (*Tractatus* 2.171).

Take for example, any dyadic or two-termed relation such as 'Othello loves Desdemona'. Schematically it can be represented by *aRb*, *a* and *b* representing the particulars or individuals and *R* the relation. The placement of *R* in relation to *a* and *b* shows the direction of the relation. In the above case the loving goes from Othello to Desdemona. The propositional sign as a whole pictures the configuration of objects in the fact. Wittgenstein thinks that all objects are of the some kind and joined together like links in a chain. Russell allows for a difference; the relation connecting the terms can be universal while the connected are particulars. Prof. Wisdom makes a parallel distinction between *components* which link together and *constituents* which are connected. For Wittgenstein's purposes things arranged in a certain way are better than sentences. Thus to take a whimsical example by Wisdom, if Wisdom is represented by a glass and Al Capone by a knife then placing the knife on the glass may picture the fact that Al Capone killed Wisdom and the glass on the knife the fact that Wisdom killed Al Capone.

Once atomic propositions are given they can be combined in various ways into conjunctions, disjunctions, implications, etc. and their mutual logical relations can be mapped and handled by very simple logical techniques. These various compound propositions are called truth-functions because the truth-value of the complex proposition as a whole is determined solely by the truth-values of the constituent propositions. Ideally, for atomism, every statement in our discourse is either elementary or can be shown to be a truth-function of elementary propositions. There are many types of proposition which cannot be fitted into this scheme and they have been listed by commentators and critics alike. One of the most important is the analysis of general propositions of the form (i) all *S* is *P*, and (ii) some *S* is *P* called universal and particular propositions respectively in traditional logic. The simplest of these are represented by quantified formulae of the type (i) $(x)\ Fx$, and (ii) $(\exists x)\ Fx$. Assuming a finite universe or universe of discourse the former can be analysed into a conjunction of elementary prepositions and the latter into a disjunction of them. But the logical equivalences do not hold unless we add that the individuals concerned (*a*, *b*, *c*, etc.) are all the individuals in the world. This means that the notion of universality has not been analysed away by our method but has to be reintroduced. Obviously the analysis does not hold in the case of *essentially open* classes unless we appeal to infinite conjunctions and disjunctions, i.e. conjunctions and disjunctions that cannot be completed.

This naturally brings in causal statements, statements of law and universal principles of every kind. Wittgenstein came to accept a view of causality like that of Hume independently. But even if statements of causation or of law in general are accepted as statements of uniformity (without bringing in the notion of necessity) our system is unable to accommodate them within a strictly atomic framework. To provide for general statements Russell accepted general facts. He also accepted negative facts after giving elaborate reasons to show that no alternative analysis is plausible. For Wittgenstein, however, all facts are atomic positive and mutually independent. 'A necessity for one thing to happen because another has happened does not exist. There is only logical necessity' (*Tractatus* 6.371). If a negation of the form *p* is true this is because there is no atomic fact to make *p* true.

Another serious problem is that of the so-called 'intentional functions'. Consider a statement of the type *S* believes that *p*. This is apparently complex and contains *p* as a constituent proposition. And yet the truth of the proposition as a whole is independent of the truth or falsity of *p*. The same result is obtained if we substitute for belief any propositional attitude like 'doubting', 'desiring' and 'wishing'. Wittgenstein's solution to this difficulty is not clear and authoritative commentators are not agreed what precisely it is. It is clear that he rejects a psychological subject and propositions as objects of contemplation. The rest is guesswork. Russell accepted at this time that judgement is a triadic relation where judging is directed to a complex of terms ordered in a certain way. Later attempts were made to translate intentional statements into extensional ones, notably by Carnap. Their success is dubious. The thesis of extensionality is vital to mathematical logic and the thesis of physicalism is that psychological statements are equivalent to statements about actual and possible behaviour. Russell definitely rejected the thesis years later in his *Inquiry into Meaning and Truth.*

One of the most important aspects of the atomism of the *Tractatus* is the notion that certain things can be shown but not said and the characterization of metaphysical propositions as nonsensical in the strict sense. What language has in common with the reality which it reflects cannot be expressed in the form of a proposition. An atomic proposition means the fact to which it refers in virtue of their identity in structure. But this identity shows itself similarly to maintain that every significant proposition is a truth-function (apart from tautologies and contradictions which are limiting cases) is to violate this basic tenet itself; and thus to try to express the inexpressible.

In other words, if logical atomism is true we cannot say that it is true. Wittgenstein drew the inevitable conclusion that his own propositions are nonsensical but added that they are 'elucidatory in character'. The aspiring philosopher 'must reject them as senseless, after he has climbed out through them, and over them. He must throw away the ladder after he has climbed on it' (*Tractatus* 6.54). Thus logical atomism becomes the metaphysics to end all metaphysics and its purest exponent a suicide bomber! But, as Russell pointed out in his introduction, Wittgenstein says a great deal about the unsayable. To escape from the ineffable he suggests a hierarchy of languages. We cannot talk about the structure of language *in that language*; but we can do so in a higher language with a structure of its own, and about this second language in the next higher type of language and so on without limit. Wittgenstein rejected this suggestion (Tarski's distinction between object-language and meta-language leads to a similar hierarchy). There is also no support in his writing for a suggestion made by some that the nonsense he talks in enunciating logical atomism is important illuminating nonsense whereas traditional metaphysics is pure nonsense, which serves only to create confusion.

Wittgenstein rejected metaphysical propositions as senseless. Its questions are like asking whether 'beauty is more or less identical than goodness'. The proper method of doing philosophy is not to enunciate theories of one's own but to point out to anyone who propounds them that he had failed to assign a clear meaning to some of his symbols and was therefore not enunciating any proposition at all. The only legitimate function of philosophy is the clarification of our thoughts and detection and exposure of nonsense whenever it occurs. The logical positivists gleefully accepted this rejection of metaphysics though they adopted a slightly different route to it. They also accepted the characterization of logic and pure mathematics as a series of tautologies lacking descriptive content.

Logical positivism or logical empiricism (as its advocates like to call it) grew up, as a movement around Morritz Schlick who was Professor of Philosophy at Vienna, in the mid-twenties of the twentieth century. He was joined by a number of mathematicians and scientists – Carnap, Neurath, Hempel, etc. – mostly refugees from Nazi persecution. They all had pronounced anti-metaphysical and pro-scientific attitude. The two pillars of positivism were (i) the verification theory, and (ii) the classification of all propositions into (a) empirical, and (b) analytic and the consequent rejection of synthetic-necessary propositions in every field of knowledge. The two tenets are complementary. As we have seen in discussing logical atomism if the elementary propositions of Wittgenstein are given content by making them reports of sense-experience the result is a version of empiricism. Logical positivism is empiricism carried to its logical conclusion and elaborated with the help of the powerful techniques of mathematical logic. A great deal of it is clearly foreshadowed in the philosophy of David Hume. The chief difference is that Hume supports his conclusions by appealing to the contents of the human mind whereas positivists employ logical analysis. This analysis is directed to language and different types of discourse in it. It therefore takes a linguistic form though it is a moot point how far the results of it are linguistic in a narrow sense.

A.J. Ayer's *Language Truth and Logic*[1] became the bible of positivism in the English-speaking world. The opening chapter sets the tone and tenor of the book. It is titled 'The Elimination of Metaphysics'. This elimination is effected wholesale by laying down the verification (or verifiability) principle as a criterion of meaningful discourse. It is stated thus by Ayer:

> A sentence is factually significant to any given person, if and only if, he knows how to verify the proposition it purports to express. That is if he knows what observation would lead him, under certain conditions to accept it as being true or reject it as being false.[2]

Schlick states it in the form of a simple slogan like declaration: The meaning of a statement is the method of its verification. The two formulations are not equivalent for there may be alternative procedures for verifying as we see in the example of an electrical

---

1 A.J. Ayer, *Language Truth and Logic*, London: Victor Gollancz, 1936.

2 Ibid., p. 35.

current running through a wire. In that case the observable state of affairs which are part of a particular procedure cannot be equated with the meaning of the verified statement. The verification required is not actual verification but possible verification or verification in principle. The former may not always be possible because of practical limitations. For example, statements about the other side of the moon could not be verified before the invention of space ships to travel around it. Second, to allow for the verification of laws of science and hypotheses which cannot be directly put to the test of observation we must provide for indirect verification. Third, since scientific laws and hypotheses cannot be conclusively verified we must distinguish between (a) weak, and (b) strong verification and allow that a scientific proposition confirmed or made probable by the results of observation is testable (Hempel's word) and therefore meaningful. Even after these obvious qualifications certain difficulties remain.

Let us begin by asking what is the logical status of the verification principle? Obviously it is not an empirical hypothesis to be tested by observation. Nor is it an analytic proposition in which case according to the positivists themselves it would be an empty tautology. It does not seem to explicate the meaning of the term 'meaningful' as commonly used. After some discussion Ayer said that it was a stipulation. But then it may be rhetorically asked, why should a metaphysician accept the stipulation? Ayer's retort was that unless they conformed to his requirement they could not be true or false and therefore cognitively meaningless.

A rather strict application of the verification principle leads to the implausible conclusion that propositions about the past are really about the observations we can make now or under certain conditions in the future, in support of them. To say that a great battle took place between the Marāṭhās and the Portuguese at the present site of the Pune University is to say either that I shall find such and such statements in standard works of history or that an archaeologist would find rusted weapons, skeletons, etc. if they dig to a certain depth on the site. It is even less possible to maintain that when we say of another person that he is angry, elated, or in pain, *what we mean* is that he is behaving in certain ways and would behave in certain ways if certain conditions were given. The difficulty here is compounded by the fact that I can make statements about my own experiences without the need for any verificatory evidence. Ayer who accepted both these corollaries from the verification principle in the first edition of *Language Truth and Logic,* later changed his mind and tried to show that propositions of the type, taken in the usual sense, can be supported by respectable inductive arguments. A great part of the difficulty can be removed by making verification not relative to a given person in specific situation but impersonal involving any suitable observer present in the relevant circumstances. This was Schlick's way of meeting the objection. But apart from leading us to other philosophical problems like those of personal identity distinction, between content and structure, etc. this brings us to the crux of the problem. If p is any proposition to be verified and $q, r, s \ldots$ are evidences for the truth of p, then however extensive our evidences may be it will *not logically entail the* truth of the conclusion. However, practically foolish and idle doubt may be, it is always possible to admit the truth of evidence and deny the truth of the conclusion. We may equate the meaning of proposition with its truth conditions. But then we shall have such trivial statements: 'It is raining means that it is raining'. We may add that generally we can find out whether it is raining or not.

We have to provide for indirect verification if scientific hypotheses are to count as meaningful under our criterion. Ayer stipulated that a statement S is indirectly verifiable if 'some experiential propositions can be deduced from it in conjunction with certain other premises, without being deducible from these other premises alone'. But Isiah Berlin pointed out that this would make any statement whatsoever meaningful. Suppose we argue

1. If the Absolute is lazy, this is white
2. The Absolute is lazy
3. (Therefore) This is white.

Here 3 follows from 1 and 2 but not from 2 alone, and 2 therefore is indirectly verifiable. Ayer responded by amending his definition and making it far more complex. But Alonzo Church constructed a very complicated counterexample to show that any *S* whatsoever is indirectly verifiable. Since then fitful attempts have been made to reformulate the criterion but with no satisfactory results. Substituting with the falsifiability criterion – which Karl Popper originally put forward to demarcate science from non-science, is not promising, for it too leads to unacceptable results if it is considered as a criterion of meaningfulness.

The denial of synthetic-necessary propositions serves the same purpose as the verification principle. It discredits the attempt to establish a priori conclusions about the world. It follows from the division of all propositions into two mutually exclusive and collectively exhaustive classes: (i) empirical, and (ii) analytic. This coincides with their classification into (i) contingent, and (ii) necessary, and also (i) a posteriori, and (ii) a priori. The three pairs of terms are not synonymous but they mark the same dichotomy and state complementary aspects of the two subdivisions of significant propositions. The positivists and their successors were helped in maintaining this view by the attempted reduction of pure mathematics to logic by Gottlob Frege and Bertrand Russell. If this view is accepted as it was very widely then, arithmetic does not consist in synthetic assertions but follows from certain definitions given in purely logical terms in accordance with purely logical principles. This reduction is faced with certain technical problems which necessitate extra-logical principles. But even if the project is not completely successful it can be argued that arithmetical propositions follow from certain definitions according to principles of logic, that is, they are analytic. The emergence of non-Euclidean geometries strongly suggests that systems of pure mathematics only deduce theorems from a given set of postulates. They assert conditional analytic propositions. If we ask what set of postulates is true, for example of physical space, the answer must be based on partly empirical grounds. Thus all necessity is dependent upon our linguistic rules and leads to tautologies with no descriptive content. No existential proposition as Hume had anticipated can be necessary. And the principles of logic themselves are dependent on very general topic-neutral (Strawson's phrase) linguistic conventions. This controversy is one of the liveliest in contemporary philosophy. It is not possible to cover the ground even sketchily. There has also been desultory debate about stray propositions, for example, about the transitive character of temporal succession, incompatibility of distinct shades of colour, etc. As is common in philosophical matters the controversy spills over into the field of ethical judgement, and aesthetic and religious statements. Armed with persuasive general arguments, positivists and their successors maintain that factual necessity is a myth. All propositions about what is not in the world are empirical and therefore contingent. The only thing left for the philosopher is to analyse our language and clarify the concepts embedded in it. Thus Wittgenstein's rejection of metaphysics as an independent inquiry, with its own specific problems and possible answers is rejected substantially on the same grounds but from a slightly different approach.

The line of demarcation between atomism and positivism is uncertain and shifting. Both of them practised linguistic analysis of a formal kind with the help of techniques of symbolic logic. Both of them pursued clarity through precise definitions, formalizing segments of our language by laying down postulates and developing a deductive system. The positivists indeed had the grand project of unifying all science by expressing all scientific propositions, including those of psychology and sociology in the language of mathematical physics. They thought they had the ground plan for this stupendous task. But the project fizzled out for various reasons. Analysis takes different forms according to the context and the purpose in hand. A very old form is to make explicit the meaning implicit in a usage. 'An oculist is an eye-doctor', 'a bachelor is an unmarried male', are examples. Such definitions are seldom of philosophical interest. When however in defining a term we amend and refine a usage we have an analysis of philosophical interest. Hume's definition of the cause of an event as its invariable antecedent spatio-temporally continuous with it, is an outstanding example. The former is called 'constructive' and the latter explicative by Carnap.

Another type is to bring out the real or logical form of a proposition, couched in a misleading grammatical form. 'Lions are real' can be restated as '$(\exists x)$ (x is a lion)' and brings out the distinction between subject predicate propositions and existential propositions, thus removing the misleading suggestion that led to the ontological argument. This may be called, following Wisdom, 'formal analysis' and the earlier two forms 'material analysis'. But the typically philosophical analysis is that of reductive analysis where we reformulate statements which are ostensibly about an entity *A* into statements about *B* and *C* related in a certain way. In such a case *A* is claimed to be reducible to *B* and *C*. The statement and set of statements which we claim to be equivalent to the original statement mentions only *B* and *C*, and not *A*. Thus *A* need not be assumed to be a real constituent of the world. Wisdom claims that this is a new-level analysis whose goal is to display the *ultimate* constituents of a fact. Formal and material analyses, on the other hand, are examples of same-level analysis. There are examples of analysis which are formal and at the same time new-level philosophical analysis. Russell's theory of descriptions as formulated by him and applied to statement like 'The king of France is bald' is a case of formal analysis. However, as applied to a statement about the golden mountain it can be formal and new-level. We cannot go into the details of Russell's theory but philosophically it is noteworthy that the phrase 'the king of France' does not occur in the three statements which he regards as equivalent to the original statement. In such a case we have provided a 'definition in use'. According to him we have not provided for say '*A*' an expression which can be substituted for it in every context as we can 'unmarried male' for 'bachelor' in any statement without affecting lists its truth-value. This sort of logical translation or reductive analysis practised extensively by atomists and positivists become a 'paradigm' of philosophy (Ramsey's praise of Russell's theory).

Statements about scientific entities were analysed in terms of behaviour of physical objects, those about physical objects in terms of sense data and statements about minds in terms of patterns of actual and possible behaviour. The objective was to remove the shadows of mysterious and doubtful entities from our philosophy until we are left only with elements given in our experience sense data, their qualities and relations. If we translate propositions about entity *A* – with which we feel uncomfortable into propositions about *B* and *C* which are transparent, then *A* can be said, in Russell's language, to be a logical construction of *B* and *C*. But it came to be realized that the required translations were not forthcoming. They failed in principle not on points of detail. The average man disappeared obligingly enough but physical objects refused to dissolve into families of sense data. Even more significant was the failure of physicalism; the attempt to translate psychological statements into equivalent statements about bodily behaviour – though Carnap stuck to it till the end – failed to win general acceptance. This was the cornerstone of the positivist attempt to effect the unity of science and the failure of physicalism threatened the return of the old tangle about mind–body dualism and with it the return of all the old problems of philosophy. Trouble was also brewing when some positivists, notably Carnap, refused to countenance semantic statements – statements about the relation of language to the word and seek refuge in a new version of the coherence theory of truth. This was retracted later; but the damage was done.

So after about a quarter century of dominance, 'positivism'gave place to 'ordinary language' philosophy or 'linguistic philosophy' in the narrow sense. The chief inspirations behind this movement were the later-philosophy of Wittgenstein and Moore's *A Defence of Common Sense* (1925). In an article with the above title Moore claimed that certain common sense propositions such as 'that is an ink-stand', 'my body has existed for several years on or near the surface of the earth', etc. to be *certainly* true and that he knew them. It is not for philosophy either to justify them or doubt their truth. What is doubtful is *the correct analysis of their meaning*. It would be wrong to say, according to Moore, that they are true on one interpretation of their meaning and false on another. Philosophers can propound alternative theories of the correct analysis of their meaning. Moore himself outlines in the above article some alternative views – naïve realism, causal theory, phenomenalism, etc., but was unable to make up his mind either then or later between them. What was Moore trying to achieve here? He introduces sense data more or less as Russell did, as objects of direct awareness in perceptual situation and further claims that he has certain knowledge of a physical object. How is the given sense datum related to the object not given in the same way, but known with certainty? That is the crux of the matter. Moore was not seeking constituents of matter even more ultimate than those given by physics such as electrons and protons. This is the suggestion of G.J. Warnock but it overlooks the fact that Moore is able to transform theories of perception into alternative theories of analysis of perceptual propositions only after introducing sense data by means of a philosophical argument. The gain seems to be that scepticism is ruled out at the starting point. Moore himself never claimed that propositions of other classes were known with equal certainty. But as Ayer points out, his argument can be easily extended to other classes. The discovery of the truth of a proposition – whether known certainly or not – is not the job of a philosopher. It is for the mathematician, geographer or botanist as the case may be. What then is left for the philosopher? The only answer seems to be that it is to analyse and clarify our knowledge.

Moore himself, as we mentioned at the outset, never identified philosophy with analysis though he practised it because he thought he was good at it. He claimed that analysis was by no means the only thing he had done (this is particularly true in the field of ethics). Moreover he pointed out, to know the correct analysis of a proposition is to know the structure of the fact described by it and thus to know something about the world. Nevertheless his *Defence of Common Sense* was taken by Malcolm and others to be the defence of ordinary language in which common-sense propositions are expressed.

The later-philosophy of Wittgenstein is the one which he taught to a small circle of disciples initially when he returned to Cambridge in the late thirties of the twentieth century. It was first made known to the world through the posthumous publication of *Philosophical Investigations* (later more was published of his earlier and later dictations and notes). This new approach is based upon a philosophy of language which is a total repudiation of his earlier view. In the *Tractatus* every meaningful sign denotes or names something in the world and every meaningful sentence describes an atomic fact. The rest is either operations on our sentences with the help of logic unless indeed we misuse language as in metaphysics. For this severe 'naming' theory of meaning Wittgenstein substitutes the 'use' theory of meaning. Our language performs a variety of functions depending on our purpose and the context in which we use it. There is no one common essence of language.

'Don't ask for the meaning, ask for the use.' Wittgenstein disabuses our mind of the notion that the use of a common term implies that the situations to which it is applied must have a common feature. But if we 'don't think but look' we shall find that our use is determined by 'family resemblances' which run criss-cross across the entire spectrum of situations. 'Games', for instance, is applied to various activities which have no one thing common; some of them have one thing in common and some other have another. Similarly the various language-games we play have nothing in common. They have to be understood in the concrete situation in which they are played out (a language-game is a set of integrated usages, some very simple, some highly complex). Wittgenstein argues that terms like 'simple', 'complex', 'elements', etc. have no one absolutely settled meaning. Their application varies from context to context. Ultimately language is part of human life and grows with it. It is flexible and though rule-governed can adapt itself to changing requirements. The rules can always be revised as needed and we have the freedom to change them as we like.

Philosophical perplexity arises when we forget this, tear words from their context and use them in a vacuum. We feel lost and do not 'know our way about'. Good philosophy consists in 'assembling reminders' to bring words back to their natural home to remove perplexity. It is to show the 'fly the way out of the fly bottle'. Again as in the *Tractatus*, but in a very different manner we propound no theories but illuminate our usage to remove empty puzzles. Philosophical problems are not solved but dissolved. This activity is like psycho-therapy. Hence the name therapeutic positivism is given to his philosophy.

The philosophy inspired by Wittgenstein and the later writing of Ryle and Austin gave rise to informal analyses whose purpose is to get a clear grasp of our language and through this the world in which and about which we employ it. Ethics was one of the fields where linguistic methods were employed extensively. Wittgenstein tackled apart from the problem of universals, the mind–body problem, personal identity and of course the relation of language to reality. The attempt always was to describe and never to explain, to remove bewilderment without propounding any theories of one's own. Wittgenstein was deliberately unsystematic and therefore his success is almost impossible to assess. Ryle and Austin though inspired by respect for ordinary usage bear only a family resemblance to Wittgenstein. They too practise informal elucidation. Both are methodical but Ryle is much more traditional in his methods of argument. His major contribution is to tackle mind–body dualism and the infinite regress, which he presses against his opponents, is a familiar weapon of metaphysicians. Austin is the most purely linguistic of the three. He engages in subtle minute dissection of ordinary usage. His main charge against old philosophers is that they substitute simple dichotomies like (a) voluntary–involuntary, (b) real–unreal, whereas ordinary language draws a number of distinct but related distinctions which he brings outwittily. He emphasized the non-descriptive uses of language and in his theory of speech-acts he classifies and systematizes uses of language. Again the success or failure of his attempt to effectively tackle traditional problems is hard to assess. But through all these developments spanning a century run these themes: (i) Philosophy is concerned with clarification not advancing theories of its own, (ii) It employs analysis which may take different forms, (iii) The philosopher is concerned with language though how the philosopher's concern with language differs from that of the philologist, lexicographer, etc. is not clear.

In the closing year of the twentieth century has seen a shift from analysis to constructive, unifying functions. There is a shift to some form of naturalism though not positivistic physicalism which is repudiated in discussing the mind–body problem. The attempt is to place the mind firmly in the world which is explored in the light of scientific knowledge. The same naturalistic perspective prevails in discussing personal identity. These are discussions by Dummett, Quine, Davidson, Goodman, etc. of the old problems of theory, meaning and epistemology. But they are methodical and employ formal logical techniques rather than linguistic ones.

2

Russell on the Problem of Universals

Russell's views on this age-old problem are set forth in the chapter on 'Universals' in *Problems of Philosophy*[1] and also very much more fully in the essay 'On the Relations of Universals and Particulars' in the Proceedings of the Aristotelian Society for 1911-12. In his later writings, the problem is discussed in scattered passages in *Inquiry into Meaning and Truth*[2] and *Human Knowledge: Its Scope and Limits*.[3] One may say that throughout his life Russell was something of a 'realist' concerning universals, though the realism of 'Inquiry' is more sophisticated than the simple straightforward realism of the *Problems of Philosophy*.

In the elaborate essay (reprinted in *Logic and Knowledge*)[4] Russell first addresses himself to the task of clarifying the distinction between universals and particulars. Many different criteria may be employed: (i) universals correspond to concepts, particulars to percepts; (ii) particulars are in space and time; and universals are either not in space and time or they are things that can exist in more than one place at the same time unlike particulars which can exist only in one place at a given time; and (iii) though these distinctions are legitimate, Russell thinks that a more fundamental distinction is provided in the context of logical predication. Particulars are terms

---

1 B. Russell, *Problems of Philosophy*, Williams and Norgate, 1912.

2 B. Russell, *An Inquiry into Meaning and Truth*, New York: Norton and Company, 1940.

3 B. Russell, *Human Knowledge: Its Scope and Limits*, London: George Allen and Unwin, 1948.

4 B. Russell, *Logic and Knowledge: Essays 1901-1950*, ed. Robert C. Marsh, London: George Allen and Unwin, 1956.

which can *only be subjects* in a proposition whereas universals are terms which may be either subjects or predicates.

Having clarified the distinction Russell proceeds to ask whether we can dispense with universals altogether and admit only particulars as was done by Berkeley and Hume. He answers this question in the negative. Even if nominalists dispense with universal qualities like 'white' and 'round', and turn the statement that '*x* is white' into the statements that '*x* is similar to or exactly like *y*' where *y* is a standard parch of white colour, we still have to accept 'similarity' or 'likeness' as a universal relation. There will be many similar patches of colour, cows, etc. all related by the same relation of 'likeness'. If the nominalist tries to escape this difficulty by arguing that these various relations are only similar, and not the same he will have to admit some standard relation of 'likeness' which these various relations resemble and the resemblance between them and the standard likeness will require a further standard of likeness and thus, there is an infinite regress. Moreover, the nominalist will have difficulty in choosing his standard instances or exemplars. He will discover that they can only be selected on the basis of 'community of predicates'. And if we are forced to admit the universal relation of 'similarity' why not admit other universals as well?

Having established that universals cannot be dispensed with, Russell goes on to consider whether we can eliminate particulars in favour of universals. This too he argues cannot be done. If particulars are dispensed with then a given object will be a complex of quality and what we normally regard as two distinct objects will have to differ in respect of some quality or other. But 'it is logically possible for precisely similar things to co-exist in two different places'. Either the two places themselves differ as particulars or on a relational view of space, the places are distinguished by a difference in the things which occupy them. But in the supposed case the things do not differ in quality and therefore must simply differ as particulars. We may sum up Russell's argument by saying that the reduction of things to bundles of qualities presupposes the principle of identity of indiscernibles and since this principle is not logically necessary the proposed reduction is not logically feasible. After this long and subtle discussion, Russell concludes that both universal and particulars are real, indispensable constituents of the real world.

By the time he came to write *Inquiry into Meaning and Truth*, Russell had come to believe in the identity of indiscernibles. He, therefore, modified his previous position to the extent of maintaining that particulars in space can be replaced by complexes of compresent qualities. Compresence is described as the sort of relation that holds between qualities which occur at the same time in the same total experience. Then a 'complete complex of compresence' is a group of qualities such that (i) all the members of it are compresent, and (ii) no member outside it is compresent with every member of group. Particulars or objects are simply complete complexes of compresence. That such a complex will not occur in two places at the same time, or will not recur in time is not logically self-evident. Russell takes the identity of indiscernibles to be an empirical generalization. His object in replacing things by such complexes is to eliminate the metaphysical 'substance' underlying qualities.

But Russell still argued that a minimum vocabulary to describe our experience will have to contain not only words for qualities but also relational words. Among relational words will be the word 'similar' or some synonym of it. A number of yellow patches for example are similar. That we require such a word to describe the world as experienced by us reveals not only something about the language we use but also about the structure of the world itself. This is the element of 'realism' that survives from *Problems of Philosophy*.

3

Russell's Theory of Descriptions

RUSSELL himself regarded his theory of descriptions as his greatest single contribution to philosophy. F.P. Ramsey called it 'the paradigm of philosophy' and his praise has been endorsed by G.E. Moore, Max Blackwell and many other philosophers. More recently the theory has come in for hostile criticism at the hands of linguistic philosophers particularly P.F. Strawson.

Russell's theory concerns the correct analysis of propositions containing denoting phrases such as 'a man', 'every man', 'an actor' and 'the queen of England'. Apparently such expressions are names or designations and statements containing them are about what these expressions stand for. But Russell's theory is that they do not really function as names and it is not necessary that they should denote anything to be significant. Since Russell equates meaning with naming he declares that such expressions are in themselves meaningless though they contribute to the meaning of the sentences in which they occur. And certainly statements such as 'The King of France is bald' are significant. How is this possible? Russell's answer is to analyse this and similar propositions in such a way that neither the descriptive phrases nor their synonyms occur in the analysis.

In the article 'On Denoting'[1] where the theory was first set forth Russell explains that in advancing the theory he wanted to solve three philosophical problems or perplexities.

1. First of all he wanted to avoid postulating subsistent entities corresponding to significant descriptions which fail to denote anything in the world. He had done this early in his career

---

[1] B. Russell, 'On Denoting', *Mind*, 1905.

following Meinong. If propositions such as 'The King of France is bald', 'The golden mountain is golden' are taken at their face value, that is, as *S–P* or Subject–Predicate propositions, then each of them says something truly or falsely about the subject denoted by the description. Therefore to be subject of predication 'the King of France', 'the golden mountain', etc. must be real in some sense though obviously they do not exist in the space–time world. Russell wanted to avoid the admission of 'subsistent' entities.

2. If 'The King of France is bald' is an elementary *S–P* proposition then either it or its negation, 'The King of France is not bald' must be true. And yet, if we go through the world we won't find the King of France either in the class of bald persons or in the class which excludes bald persons. We have to interpret such propositions in a manner that will preserve the law of excluded middle.

3. The third problem is to interpret statements in such a way that they are neither tautologously true nor tautologously false. Take 'Scot is the author of Waverly novels'. If 'author of Waverly novels' denotes and hence means the some as Scot then we are merely saying that Scot is Scot. If not, that is, if the two denoting expressions denote different objects then the statement is necessarily false. And yet the statement is significant. Russell's analysis of 'The King of France is bald' is as follows:

    1. $(\exists x)$ x is King of France
    2. (y) Ky is King of France, then y is identical with x.
    3. x is bald.

The three together are equivalent to the original statement, namely, 'The King of France is bald'. In general 'The thing that is *F* is *G*' is analysed into

1. $(\exists x)$ Fx . . . . (There is at least one x)
2. $\forall x\ \forall y\ \{(Fx \cdot Fy) \longrightarrow (x = y)\}$ . . . . (There is at most one x)

3. $\forall x\ (Fx \longrightarrow Gx)$ . . . . (Everything that is F is G).

'The King of France is not bald' can be interpreted in two ways depending on the scope of the sign of negation. If it extends to the entire formula, $\sim (\exists x)\ [Kx \cdot \{(y)\ Ky \supset (y = x)\} \cdot Bx]$, then the description has secondary occurrence. If on the other hand it is restricted, the predicative part, i.e. Bx, "$(\exists x)\ [Kx \cdot \{(y)\ Ky \supset (y = x)\} \cdot \sim Bx]$", then it has primary occurrence. More simply, there is primary occurrence if we are committed to the existence of King of France and secondary occurrence if there is no such commitment. If we take the formula as a whole and its negation (the case of secondary occurrence) then one of them must be true and the other false. Thus the law of excluded middle is preserved. If we consider the case of primary occurrence, then it is easy to see how both 'the King of France is bald' and 'the King of France is not bald' can be false when France has no King or more than one King. Since the denoting phrases vanish in our analysis and the proposition is seen to be a complex existential formula, there is no question of postulating entities to correspond to the subject terms in such propositions. Thus the Meinongean jungle is cut away at the roots.

The problem concerning significant identity statements is not solved so happily. It is rather bypassed in so far as our analysis contains no position in which a name occurs as a constituent. More important than these suggested solutions to their specific problems with which Russell started is the pervasive influence exercised by the theory on an entire generation of philosophers. It provides a model of logical analysis which while introducing no new type of entity yet clears away all subsistent objects suggested by misleading grammatical constructions. The tendency of the theory is to arrive at objects and their predicates at their lowest or most basic level. Hence its importance for logical atomism cannot be overemphasized. Wittgenstein accepted it enthusiastically and according to Miss Anscombe continued to accept it even during the later phase in his philosophy.

4

P.F. Strawson's Criticisms of Russell's Theory of Descriptions

In an article in *Mind* (1950)[1] Strawson criticizes Russell's views comprehensively. After explaining Russell's theory he makes a distinction between (i) sentences, (ii) the utterance of a sentence, and (iii) the use of a sentence. This is paralleled by the distinction between (i) an expression, (ii) the utterance of an expression, and (iii) the use of an expression. A sentence or an expression such as 'The King of France is bald' is a type or pattern of sounds or marks if the sentence is written down. In this sense the same sentence can be uttered or used by different persons or the same person at different times. Two utterances may have the same use or different uses. Broadly speaking the use as distinguished from mere utterance depends on the purpose of the speaker and the context of utterance. Two persons uttering 'The King of France is bald' make the same use if they express the same proposition. A person who uttered the sentence during the reign of Louis XIII would assert that Louis XIII was bald. The same sentence uttered by a person during the reign of Louis XIV would assert that Louis XIV was bald. These two are different uses. Anyone uttering it today would make an altogether different use of it, for example, as an illustration in a philosophical debate or an exercise in translation, etc. He *does not* today express any proposition that is true or false. Strawson's charge against Russell is that he has confused (i) and (iii). That is, sentence and the use of a sentence. Meaning and significance are predicated of sentences. Truth or falsity belong only to uses of sentences (perhaps we can

[1] The article is included in *Essays in Conceptual Analysis* ed. Flew, Macmillan, 1960.

add only to those uses in which a proposition is expressed). Strawson writes, 'generally as against Russell, I shall say this: meaning is a function of a sentence or an expression. Referring to truth or falsity are functions of the use of an expression'. Russell in his analysis proceeded as if anyone using the sentence 'The King of France is bald' were now asserting a false proposition. This is incorrect. The sentence is significant in the sense that it *can be used* to make a true or false assertion and not because every utterance or use of it is true or false. Russell, commenting on Strawson, remarks that all these distinctions are irrelevant to the main problem posed by definite descriptions. They are relevant only in dealing with the problem of reflexive or egocentric expression. If for 'the King of France' we substitute 'The prime between 24 and 28' or even 'the King of France in 1905', Strawson's entire argument, according to Russell, collapses.

Strawson however has other criticisms. He agrees with Russell that the sentence 'King of France is bald' is significant and also that it is true that there is in fact one and only one King of France and further he is bald. But Russell advances two false theses, namely: (1) any one now uttering it would be making a true or false assertion, and (2) that part of what he asserted would be that there was one and only one King of France. Anyone now uttering the sentence would probably make no assertion of at all. But suppose somebody today uttered it with a serious air as if he was making a statement, would we say 'That is false'? We would be inclined with some hesitation to say that the question of truth or falsity did not rise when we say in response 'There is no king of France'. We should certainly not say we were contradicting him or his sentence. In other words Strawson maintains that the statements 1 and 2 in Russell's analysis are presupposed by the sentence 'The King of France is bald' and if the latter sentence is true the presuppositions are also true. But if the presuppositions are false then our sentence has no truth-value, that is, it is neither true nor false. Strawson adopts this course because he considers that it is more in accordance with ordinary usage. Russell of course does not claim that he is correctly analysing descriptive phrases as they occur in everyday language but rather as they should be used in a model language for mathematics and science. But Russell did imply that the analysis could be applied to descriptions in ordinary language as his own examples about 'the King of France' and 'the author of Waverley novels' suggest. Russell maintains that ordinary language is not consistent and therefore he does not claim its sanction for his theory. But he gives an example to show that it is not with Strawson either, completely. Supposing there is a rule in a country that anyone holding public office should not think it false that 'the ruler of the world is benevolent'. An atheist who taking advantage of Strawson's theory argued that since there is no ruler of the world the proposition is not false and that he is entitled to hold public office, 'would be considered a pretty shifty character'. In fact, several years later in a brief essay in *Logico-Linguistic Papers*, Strawson admitted that *in some cases* a statement containing a definite description with no application is naturally regarded as false whereas in certain other cases the refusal to ascribe any truth-value appears more natural.

But Strawson still maintains that Russell went wrong in confusing (i) using an expression to make a unique reference with (ii) asserting that there is one and only one object of a certain kind. Russell thus 'progressively assimilates sentence containing uniquely referring expressions to uniquely existential sentences'. In other words he proceeds as if the propositions presupposed by a sentence containing definite description were explicitly *stated* as part of the sentence itself. This is no doubt a valid criticism from the point of view of ordinary usage. But Russell's theory is not just an explication of usage. It is revisionary and it could be claimed that the revision recommended by him is advantageous in scientific discourse.

5

Quine's Treatment of Propositional Attitudes

It was Russell who suggested in his *Inquiry Concerning Meaning and Truth,* the term 'propositional attitudes' to characterize such occurrence as believing, doubting, desiring and fearing. Statements about them, apart from their importance in psychology and philosophy of mind, raise pretty little problems in the field of philosophy of logic. Take statements like, 'Brown thinks it will rain tomorrow', 'Kepler believed that planetary orbits are elliptical' and 'John denies that he stole that money'. Apparently they are all complex statements containing as a constituent the clause following 'that' which can represent a statement by itself. And yet this subordinate statement does not figure as a truth-functional constituent of the containing statement. Taking '*S* believes that *p*' as the form of the most basic of such attitudinal propositions, we can easily see that the truth-value of *p* does not determine the truth-value of the complex statement. Not every statement believed by me is true nor do I believe every true statement. Similarly, for all false statements. Such statements are an apparent exception to the thesis of extensionality. This principle states that we can replace any statement by another of like truth-value, without affecting the truth-value of the complex in which it occurs; likewise designations with the same reference and propositional functions or predicates with the same extension are substitutable, one for another, without altering the truth-value of the statement containing them. All these three cases are neatly expressed by Quine in the phrase 'substitutivity of identity'. When this fails for designations and predicative expression relative to the statement in which they occur it produces acute discomfort not only for a philosopher with vested interests, but for all who combine good sense with insight into a simple and yet basic logical principle.

Even those who reject the definition of identity given by Whitehead and Russell will readily accept the following formula:

$$(x = y) \supset (fx \supset fy).$$

The principle is the basis of the most basic schema of inference involving the notion of identity. It is the converse of Leibnitz's doctrine of identity of indiscernibles and, in Quine's happy coinage, it states the 'indiscernibility of identicals'. And yet it breaks down in intentional and modal contexts. Consider the proposition (1) *Tom believes that Cicero denounced Catiline* to be true. Now it well known that (2) *Cicero is Tully* (Cicero = Tully). From (1) and (2) we ought to be able to deduce that (3) Tom believes that Tully denounced Catiline. But if Tom, like most of us here, is ignorant of the history of Latin literature he may either hesitate to accept or deny that Tully denounced Catiline. There is a parallel breakdown of the principle, when modal words are prefixed or suffixed to propositions. Consider the following three statements:

1. Necessarily, 12 is greater than 10.
2. The number of apostles = 12.
3. Necessarily, the number of apostles is > 10.

Quine is unperturbed by the difficulties in modal logic, for, having rejected the notion of analyticity or necessity in relation to propositions, he does not believe in the need for a modal logic to supplement or supplant the logic of *PM* (*Principia Mathematica*). But as he confesses, he cannot treat propositional attitudes so cavalierly. When, as a result of the attachment of modal or attitudinal words to a proposition the 'substitutivity of identity' breaks down there is 'referential opacity'. Quotation is another device that leads to the same logical consequence. The expression, 'believes that' in '*S* believes that *a R b*' prevents *a* from functioning referentially (or purely referentially). On the other hand, constructions which leave unchanged the referential force of expression occurring in the statements or terms to which they are applied, possess 'referential transparency' (the phrase is used by Whitehead and Russell in *Principia Mathematica*).

It may not be clear, at first sight, why Quine thinks that in such cases certain expressions which occupy a referential position in a statement standing by itself cease to do so when the statement in question is placed in a wider context. Now, the paradigm case of referential position is that of the subject term in a singular proposition. Whatever predicates are truly ascribable to the subject singled out by the subject term are so ascribable independently of our manner of reference to the subject. We may replace the term by any other designation or description, provided it has the same reference and the truth-value of the proposition will remain unaltered. If 'Cicero' in our example has a genuinely referential role and Tom's believes Cicero to be a denouncer of Catiline is a relational predicate true of him, then it should be true of him equally when he is referred to as 'Tully', just as 'being a Roman', 'being a great writer of Latin prose' and a host of other predicates is true of him independently of our choice of designations for him, in any of the statements we may make about him. A very simple, not to say simple-minded, answer would be that there are predicates – intentional and modal amongst them – which are asserted of an object not as such but according to our manner of conceiving it in a certain context. But to many this would be merely a restatement of the problem rather than a satisfactory solution to it. At the very least, they may feel, we should engage in a Kantian enterprise of asking and explaining how this is possible.

Quine is primarily concerned with the problem of referential opacity unlike Wittgenstein whose main concern was to defend his pronouncement that one propositional sign can occur in another only as a base for truth-functional operations (*Tractatus* 5.54). In the end, Quine's solution merges into Carnap's defence of the thesis of extensionality which, in its turn, can be regarded as an elaboration of a dark hint thrown out by Wittgenstein. Quine, no less than Carnap and Wittgenstein, rejects the surface suggestion of intentional statements, namely, that they state a dyadic relation between a subject on the one hand and a proposition which he contemplates and to which he directs a mental attitude. Propositions serve no useful purpose but only add to obscurity in the many roles in which they are cast by their sponsors – as meanings of sentences, as vehicles of truth and falsity, as the values over which the variable of the propositional calculus range and as objects of mental attitudes. The most telling consideration against them is not the charge of reification and acceptance of strange, subsistent entities but the absence of a criterion of identity. Quine's hostility to them is relentless and consistent. He is equally allergic to attributes, regarded as the designata of abstract nouns or meanings of predicative expressions. But his first step towards resolving our difficulty is to frame sentences containing expressions which name attributes. Instead of symbolizing 'Tom believes that Cicero denounced Catiline' by Tom believes (that Cicero denounced Catiline) where the bracketed that clause stands for a proposition as a unitary entity, we use '*YZ* (*Y* denounces *Z*)' for the dyadic relation of 'being denouncer of' and write the statement thus: Tom believes *Y* (*Y* denounced Catiline) of Cicero. We have here a triadic relation between believer (Tom), the dyadic predicate 'being denouncer of Catiline' and Cicero. The best way of reading it in ordinary English would be: Tom believes Cicero to have denounced Catiline ('by Tom Cicero is believed to have denounced Catiline' suggested by Davidson is unnatural but graphically displays the structure of the reformulated statement). We can make the belief in our illustration tetradic by making it relate Tom, Cicero and Catiline as denouncer and denounced, and the dyadic predicate '*Y Z*' (*Y* denounces *Z*). In *The Philosophy of Logic*, Quine even suggests treating 'believing *Fa*' as an attribute of the believer. As a final explanation we may identify this predicate with a neuro-chemical state of the believer, though this will hardly count as an *analysis* of belief. The syntactical possibilities are many and they can be ingeniously exploited with the help of techniques of mathematical logic. The upshot, in simple terms, is that instead of saying that *S* believes that *Fa*, we say that *S* believes *a* to have *F*, or *S* believes *F* of *a*.

The advantage is to revert to our main illustration, that we can say that Tom believes of Tully that he denounced Catiline even though Tom may be ignorant that Cicero = Tully. When the designations or singular terms are replaced by variables and quantifiers are used to bind them, complications arise. We may avoid all trouble by banning all quantification into intentional contexts (Quine is inclined to dismiss as nonsense the use of quantifiers across modal operators). But we cannot do this because the significance of a statement will vary depending on whether the quantifier is within the scope of the intentional expression or the other way round. But our endeavour is to prevent cross-reference from inside, an opaque construction to an indefinite singular term or a such-that clause outside it. So long as the statement following the that-cause is treated as a unitary object of the propositional attitude, belief will remain opaque. Hence the substitution of 'believes to' for 'believes that'. With care and skill the latter type of construction will keep belief transparent and preserve the substitutivity of identity.

At this stage it may be useful to pause and count our gains and losses. In reformulating intentional statements of ordinary discourse in this way we have no doubt saved the thesis of extensionality but our reformulations are not equivalent in meaning to the troublesome originals. This may leave Quine unfased who regards the notion of cognitive synonymy as dubious and incurably imprecise. But so long as we allow some weight to our intuitions of sameness of meaning in particular cases – as Quine himself declares he is ready to – this change in or loss of significance is not to be dismissed out of court. As Russell has pointed out we have here 'a complicated mixture of empirical and syntactical questions'. The preferred solution concentrates exclusively on syntactical aspects of the problem. We may say that Tom believes that Tully was Roman, as he believes that Cicero was Roman and the person whom he believes to be Roman is identical with Tully. But there is an important distortion of Tom's belief in the process of rendering it transparent. It is not merely that we fail to bring out the exact content of Tom's belief, and have to overlook his verbal disclaimers. We have to ignore the circumstance that the belief with which we credit Tom fails to affect his behaviour, particularly his reasoning and thinking about Roman history and Latin literature. Indeed it is even possible that information about Cicero/Tully may mislead him into making errors about Cicero. For Quine and others like him, who seek refuge in behaviourism to elucidate the concepts of meaning and belief this must be a serious matter. Meanwhile the empirical facts which are the source of our difficulty remain forgotten. These are that we talk about our beliefs and those of others, and that the correctness or incorrectness of the ascriptions of beliefs are independent of the correctness and incorrectness of the beliefs ascribed. If we take these psychological or behavioural if you like – facts at their face value, the syntactical saving of extensionality is of no great comfort.

But we have to take one more step – and a very crucial one – before the final solution is reached. The rephrasing of 'believing that' by 'believing to' has dispensed with propositions as objects of belief but has left us with attributes named by intensional abstractors like '*X* (*Fx*)' and '*XY* (*Rxy*)'. Intensions of every kind 'are creatures of darkness and I shall rejoice with the reader when they are exercised'. Instead of speaking of intensions supposedly named by certain expressions, we speak of these expressions themselves by enclosing them in quotes. Thus instead of saying, 1(a) 'I believe (Cicero denounced Catiline)' we say 1(b) 'T believes true Cicero denounced Catiline'. And 2(a) *T* believes *X* (*X* denounced Catiline) of Cicero, can change to 2(b) *T* believes '*X* denounced Catiline' of Cicero. Similarly 3(a) *T* believes *YZ* (*Y* denounced *Z*); Cicero and Catiline can be replaced by 3(b) *T* believes '"*Y* denounced *Z*" of Cicero and Catiline'.

Statements 2(b) and 3(b) could give rise to trouble if we use variables and quantifiers to bind them, for they contain constituent expressions which are in quotation marks. Even as it is, there is puzzlement about them. How can '*Y* denounced *Z*' which is the name of a linguistic expression, be believed of Cicero unless it is interpreted in the old intensional way? It looks as though when we switch to the formal mode of speech we have to take sentences as units for quotation.

Quine's semantical versions are modelled on Carnap's translations of intensional statements into extensional language except that Carnap uses expressions like 'say', 'utter', 'say to oneself' where Quine uses 'believes', 'believes true'. But subsequent discussion makes it clear that believing amounts to no more than uttering and writing sentences. Perhaps this was what Wittgenstein had in mind when he declares; 'But it is clear that "*A* believes that *p*" "*A* thinks *p*" are of the form "*P*" says "*p*"' (*Tractatus* 5.542). Some philosophers will feel dissatisfied with such linguistic formulations on the ground that belief is directed not to sentences but what they express. Such persons can say, if they like, '*A* believes the proposition meant by *p*'. But nothing is gained thereby. If propositions are accessible only through sentences, we can as well eliminate propositions and make do with sentences. But there are specific objections to this pattern of analysis highlighted by A. Church in 'Carnap's analysis of statements of assertion and belief'. The *S* quoted by us earlier in our analysis belongs to a particular language and the 'content' of the belief we are analysing is given or specified by the rules of that language. Exactly the same pattern of sounds or marks can express a different proposition in another actual or possible language. So our well-worn example will have to be stated thus: Tom believes true in English 'Cicero denounced Catiline' or Tom believes 'Cicero denounced Catiline' true in English. But this relativity to the English language is not present in the original – *Bt* (*Dc* · *Ct*). Suppose we translate the proposed analysans into German, then we can either leave the quoted sentence as it is in English or translate it into German. In the first case the German reader (ignorant of English) will have no information as to what it is that Tom believes. In the second case it becomes clear that our analysis aims at the common content of a number – an infinite number perhaps – of synonymous sentences. Moreover, it is not enough to utter a sentence or write it, for a person to believe its content. He must do so sincerely and in an affirmative frame of mind. It is also possible for a man to entertain unexpressed beliefs and it is even barely possible that he frames them without silent, internal, verbalization. Quine remarks that the first of these objections is far from conclusive on the ground that synonymy is an essentially imprecise notion.

Even apart from the problem of interlinguistic translations it is clear that the names of sentences formed by the device of quotation are peculiar. They are not mere designations such as we may set up by preparing a list of propositions/sentences and arbitrarily assigning a unique name for each unique sentence. Nor are they descriptive like 'pons asinorium' which is by designation equivalent to 'the fifth theorem of the first book of Euclid'. They are *expressions* of statements turned into *names of themselves*. If our interest were in words we would reproduce the exact words used by a person. The device of indirect quotation is suited for conveying the meaning expressed by a form of words without bothering about the originally used words. Even direct quotation can serve the same purpose. If we read the statement:

> Louis the XIV declared 'I am the state', unless we are greatly deficient in general knowledge we shall not suppose that the grand monarch uttered the English words reproduced in our statement. We shall rightly conclude that he used some French words conveying the same thought as the English sentence 'I am the state'.

As regards the other difficulties Quine does not condescend to deal with them, probably because they import into our discussion 'a pernicious mentalism'. Like many contemporary American philosophers he has a strong predilection for physicalism or behaviourism. He believes that the notions of 'meaning' and 'sameness of meaning' of expressions can be made as determinate as they can be only through behavioural criteria. The truth of the thesis of extensionality is necessary to the truth of linguistic physicalism of Carnap which is the expression in the formal mode of speech of the ancient materialistic doctrine – 'Everything is matter in motion'. The plausibility or otherwise of these larger viewpoints is beyond the scope of this brief paper. But some points may be made dogmatically. There is no logical connection between scientific naturalism and the attempt to analyse intentional concepts behaviouristically. Nor does the irreducibility of intentional concepts imply the existence of intentional entities. We should not embrace analytical behaviourism just because we want to puncture the pretensions of theological fanatics and priggish spiritualists. Second, in seeking behaviouristic explanations of mental phenomena we should not overlook the boringly familiar distinction between the meaning of an expression or the significance of a concept and the fulfilment of the conditions for its legitimate application. Finally it seems to me that in analysing belief in terms of behaviour patterns, we ascribe certain desires and wants to the subject and in attempting a behaviouristic analysis of desire we ascribe cognitions, sensations and beliefs to the subject. Even with these limitations, the behaviouristic analysis offered is far from satisfactory. The attempt to deal with both desires and beliefs simultaneously has not been made even perfunctorily either by Quine or anyone else.

6

In Defence of a Dogma by Strawson and Grice

I

STRAWSON and Grice[1] want to show that Quine's criticisms do not justify the rejection of the analytic–synthetic distinction. The distinction has cropped up at various times in the history of philosophy in various terminologies: (a) analytic–synthetic, (b) necessary contingent, and (c) truths of reason – truths of fact.

Though philosophical tradition by itself is unimpressive and strictly, unnecessary, the presumption is that there is some distinction which philosophers are attempting to express by these pairs of terms. But more importantly those who use the terms 'analytic–synthetic' do agree considerably in the application of the terms, i.e. in applying or withholding the terms in clear-cut cases. The usage is easily extended from cases where it was taught to new cases. In short the terms have a more or less *well-established philosophical use*.

> In general where a pair of terms in habitually and generally used in application to the same cases where these cases do not form a closed list, this is sufficient for saying that there are kinds of cases to which the terms apply.

II

Does Quine really hold the extreme thesis which his words suggest? His thesis is, perhaps, better represented as the thesis that the nature

---

1 Strawson and Grice, *Philosophical Review*, vol. 65, no. 2, 1956, pp. 141-58.

of the distinction and reasons for it are totally misunderstood by those who use the expressions (not the thesis that there is no difference marked by the expressions). Taking the reformulation to be correct his arguments could be answered in the following way. Quine shows that certain explanations (of the dichotomy) 'do not measure up to certain requirements of adequacy in philosophical clarification'. He admits to the analyticity group the notion of 'cognitive synonymy'. He allows that analyticity can be defined in terms of it. Unfortunately the former is as unclarified as the latter.

III

According to Strawson and Grice to say that *x* and *y* (E_1 or E_2) are cognitively synonymous is to say roughly that *x* and *y* have the same meaning or *x* means the same as *y*. Quine rightly points out that synonymy goes beyond coextensionality and is ready to admit that the latter notion is intelligible. *However the denial of synonymy is extremely paradoxical. The distinction between pairs of expression that are not synonymous and pairs that are, is not a philosophical one, but is made and used well enough ordinarily.* Quine's thesis involves the absurdity or paradox that it is senseless to make a statement of the form: *x* and *y* are coextensional but do not have the same meaning. If so the notion of correct translation from one language (*L*) to another *L* is also meaningless. (We may note that Strawson and Grice (a) tacitly appeal to 'pernicious mentalism' which Quine rules out of court; (b) they have a respect for ordinary usage which Quine does not share; and that (c) Quine maintains 'the radical indeterminacy of translation'.)

IV

(a) If sentence-synonymy is meaningless so is the notion of meaning. We could roughly define sentence-synonymy thus: 'Two sentences are synonymous if and only if a true answer to the question 'what does S_1 mean?' is also a true answer to the question 'what does S_2 mean?'

(b) There is a family of notions of which 'analytic' is one. Others are 'self-contradictory', 'necessary', 'true by definition', etc. Quine is demanding that a given member, say, 'analytic' be defined without reference to any other member of the family, and also that the explanation must be of the same general form as the rejected explanation (i.e. of the form '*A* is *BC*' or *B r C*). It is unreasonable to expect that the above type of explanation be generally available, if an expression is to make sense. There are many families of notions which are inter-definable, but not in the strict way. For example, 'morally wrong', 'blameworthy', 'breach of moral law', voluntary, etc.; another example: 'true', 'false', 'assertion', 'denial', 'judgement', 'proposition', etc.

V

An illustration of how one member of the analytic group, 'logically impossible' can be clarified informally is this. Take the two statements (1) My neighbour's three-year old child understands Russell's Theory of Types; (2) My neighbour's three-year old child is an adult. If we discuss the two with someone, we will begin by interpreting them in such a way that we can make sense of them and accept them, or reject them. *One may be forced to acknowledge* that (1) is literally true but not (2). In the latter case a point will be reached when we shall be forced to say that our interlocutor does not know the meaning of the expressions he uses. The ultimate distinction is between (i) not believing (while understanding), and (ii) not understanding what is being said. Strawson and Grice admit that *an analytic proposition can cease to be necessarily true but only if we change our usage* (Putnam holds the more radical thesis that *we can change our logic without changing usage* and thus render an *analytic proposition contingent*).

VI

Additional, *relatively minor* points:

1. Quine maintains that only in the case of stipulative definitions synonymy is clearly established. Strawson and Grice argue that this position is literally incoherent. The notion of

synonymy by stipulation is unintelligible unless the notion of "synonymy" is presupposed.

2. Quine expresses hesitation about whether some given proposition is analytic. For example, 'every green thing is extended'. Strawson and Grice suggest the culprit is not 'analytic'. It would be no better if we substituted 'true' for 'analytic'. In general hesitation arises because boundaries of application are not determined by usage in all directions.

7

Knowledge as Well-grounded True Belief (Backed by Good Reasons)

THE view that knowledge is analysable into well-grounded true belief or true belief backed by adequate reasons is a much discussed and vigorously defended thesis of contemporary philosophy. And yet as a proposal for defining knowledge it goes back to the time of Plato. In the *Theatetus* the third and last definition of knowledge discussed is that it is 'true opinion with explanation' ('logos' is the word used). The dialogue ends – as is usual with Plato – inconclusively after Socrates leads his interlocutors to admit that the suggested definition is unsatisfactory. The formulations in contemporary philosophical literature (Ayer, Chisholm, Armstrong) read like translations into current philosophical idiom of this old suggestion found wanting by Plato. But there is an important difference Plato's discussion makes it clear that he is concerned with knowledge in the sense of the ability to recognize or identify an individual. If I understand who Theatetus is then I must not only refer to him correctly by means of certain predicates characterizing him, but also be able to specify the ways in which he differs from others. This ability to indicate the differentia of the subject in question is taken to be the 'account' or 'explanation' which distinguishes knowledge from mere 'true opinion'. In recent accounts the knowledge sought to be defined is propositional knowledge. Knowledge that something is the case or is not the case. Second, the recent advocates of this definition of knowledge develop their theme in conscious opposition to the views of the Oxford philosopher Harold Arthur Prichard and his distinguished disciples like H.H. Price and W.D. Ross that knowing is a unique state of mind different in kind from believing and that the two are exclusive of one another. (Here too there is an echo of Plato who sharply distinguishes knowledge from opinion and assigns them to the exclusive spheres of the intelligible and the sensible.) The definition favoured by some contemporary philosophers quite clearly makes belief an element in knowledge which however goes beyond true belief.

We may take Ayer's lucid and persuasive discussion in the opening chapter of *The Problem of Knowledge* as a model of the definitionist thesis. Why do Prichard and his followers maintain that Knowledge and Belief are not only different but in a way opposed to one another? Their main argument is that what can be said truly of belief (and belief only) has to be necessarily denied of knowledge. If *p* is any proposition then to believe that *p* is compatible with the falsity of *p*. On the other hand, if I or any other subject knows that *p*, then *p* cannot be false. Hence the two are different in kind and exclude one another. We have belief in those spheres and only in those spheres where knowledge is not possible. Another consideration in favour of this view is that an analysis of knowledge in terms of justified belief leads to an infinite regress. If we accept or claim knowledge of *p* because of *q* which is the reason for *p* we can ask whether *q* itself is known. If it is, it will be because of a third proposition *r* which too has to be established independently. Thus there is an infinite regress. The thesis of Ayer and others is that knowledge does not exclude belief, but can in fact be defined in terms of belief or 'being certain that' plus certain conditions which must be fulfilled if the claim to know is justified. It can be urged against Prichard that there is no internal distinction between knowing and being certain that *p*. From the fact that a certain person is in a state of total conviction it does not follow that what he believes is true. This is because there is no state of mind of any person which entails that there is a certain kind of fact in the world. It is of course true that whenever I know that *p*, then *p* must be true. But this is a tautology and brings out a verbal or conceptual connection. We so used the word 'know' and related expressions that a claim to know that *p* is never admitted if it turns out that *p* is false. Nor do we admit the claim even when *p* is true, if the acceptance of *p* by a subject is the result of lucky guesswork or a happy coincidence. Accordingly, Ayer analyses knowing that *p* in terms of the following three conditions:

S Knows that $p^{=}$

(i) *p* is true.

(ii) *S* is certain or sure that *p*.

(iii) *S* has the right to be sure.

(R.M. Chisholm gives a similar analysis except that requirement (iii) is expressed thus: '*S* has adequate evidence for *p*'). It is easy to show that each of these conditions is necessary for knowledge. It would be self-contradictory to say that I know that *p* and yet *p* is false. Equally it would be absurd to say that I know *p* but I am not certain of it. The third condition is needed to exclude from knowledge those cases where a man happens to believe what is true without being in possession of any evidence to justify his belief or where what he takes to be adequate evidence has really no confirmatory value. Each of these conditions is necessary and it is hoped that taken together they are sufficient to mark off knowledge from mere belief.

The third requirement gives rise to difficulties and controversies. It is not easy to determine outside logic and pure mathematics whether or when we have the right to be sure. In the case of any empirical proposition commonly accepted as certain, there is a great deal of supporting sensory evidence. But this evidence is never conclusive. Should we therefore say that we cannot have any knowledge concerning matters of fact? Indeed philosophers like Descartes and Plato refused to grant the status of knowledge to perception on the ground that it is lacking in the sort of clarity and certainty present in the case of a priori propositions. Ayer himself maintains in the *Problem of Knowledge* that a physical-object statement should be treated as a hypothesis which is confirmed in varying degrees by the supporting sense datum statements. But however strong and extensive the sensory evidence, it will never logically entail the truth of the corresponding physical-object statement.

This feature of empirical knowledge is partly at the bottom of the problem raised Edmund L. Gettier in his brief but much discussed paper 'Is Justified True Belief, Knowledge?' first published in *Analysis* 1963 and included in *Knowledge and Belief* edited by A.P. Griffiths. Gettier argues that the three conditions listed by what we may call the classical analysis of knowledge are not adequate to define it. His method is to construct counter-examples where it is clear both (i) that the three requirements are met, and (ii) and yet the knowledge-claim is unjustified. Let us state one of the two examples in Gettier's own words:

> Let us suppose that Smith has strong evidence for the following propositions
>
> (f) Jones owns a Ford
>
> Smith's evidence might be that Jones has at all times in the past within Smith's memory owned a car and always a Ford and that Jones has just offered Smith a ride while driving a Ford. Let us imagine, now, that Smith has another friend Brown of whose whereabouts he is totally ignorant. Smith selects three place-names quite at random and constructs the following three propositions.
>
> (g) Either John owns a Ford or Brown is in Boston.
>
> (h) Either John owns a Ford or Brown is in Barcelona.
>
> (i) Either John owns a Ford or Brown is in Brest-Litovsk.

Each of these propositions is entailed by (f). Imagine that Smith realizes the entailment of each of these propositions he has constructed by (f) and proceeds to accept (g), (h) and (i) on the basis of (f). Smith has correctly inferred (g), (h) and (i) from a proposition for which he has strong evidence. Smith is therefore completely justified in believing each of these three propositions. Smith, of course, has no idea where Brown is.

But imagine now that two further conditions hold. First, Jones does not own a Ford but is at present driving a rented car. And second, by the sheerest coincidence, and entirely unknown to Smith the place mentioned in proposition (h) happens to be the place where Brown is. If these two conditions hold then Smith does not know that (h) is true even though (1) (h) is true, (2) Smith does believe that (h) is true, and (3) Smith justified in believing that (h) is true.

Gettier's article has given rise to a proliferating number of articles most of which aim at so reconstructing the classical empiricist definition as to meet his objection. Many have written of Gettier's fourth condition and different formulations of this fourth condition have been offered which added to the three usual conditions will give an acceptable analysis of knowledge. I must confess however that I fail to understand why so much noise has been made about this and other counter-examples. I shall not discuss in detail the various attempts to supply the deficiency in the classical definition. It should not be very difficult to see that any attempt to tighten up the condition is foredoomed to failure. The source of the trouble is the ever-present threat in all empirical knowledge of believing a false proposition on the basis of good evidence – evidence that would normally be considered sufficient justification for the accepted proposition. This threat is not removed by stipulating additional conditions. For whatever these conditions may be, we have to ascertain that these conditions are, in reality, fulfilled. That is, we have to *know* that these conditions are satisfied and not merely believe that they are on the strength of whatever evidence we may have examined. Nor will it suffice to raise the level of satisfactoriness of evidence. In Gettier's example Smith's evidence for believing that Jones owns a Ford would normally be considered overwhelming. But suppose we try to make it conclusive by adding that Smith checked the number on the licence plate and verified that a Ford car of the precise number was registered in Jones' name by the licensing authorities. Further Jones when questioned by Smith talked about the purchase of his new car discussing the price, the dealer, etc. Can we then say that Smith could not have gone wrong in believing that Jones now owns a Ford? Not quite; for Smith may have made an error in checking the entries in the register (for various reasons). Jones may be misleading Smith for his own reasons. He may have even arranged for false entries to be made in the register and so on and so on. In Gettier's example it is the 'justified' (it would be better to use the term 'well-supported') false belief which when disjoined with a proposition that happens to be true and for which Smith has no evidence that leads to the true conclusion (h). It is clear that the root cause of the trouble is the inconclusiveness from the logical point of view of sensory evidence for empirical propositions.

There are other cases such as those cited by Russell and Meinong where the trouble is the non-operation of certain causal factors that are normally operative and are considered necessary for the acquisition of knowledge. Russell cites the example of a man who looks at a non-functional clock at the exact moment when it is showing correct time and judges the time of day rightly but can hardly be said to know the time of the day.[1] Meinong imagines a person who lives in the vicinity of a garden where there is a harp made to whistle in the wind to keep the birds away. Suppose our man has grown hard of hearing with age but by a remarkable coincidence, has auditory hallucinations of the sound of the harp at the very moment when the sounds are to be actually heard. Here too we would refuse to say that the man had knowledge of the sounds of the harp. The examples of Russell and Meinong serve their purpose. But it would be wrong to attempt a *definition* of knowledge in terms of a causal relation between the belief situation and the situation known or claimed to be known. In his "Inquiry" Russell suggests that at the most primitive level, to say that an experience *E* is knowledge of an object *O*, is to say that *O* causes *E*. My knowledge that tea is hot is just the scalding of my tongue when I swallow it hurriedly. This approach is objectionable not only because it cannot cover knowledge of future events, as D.M. Armstrong suggests but also for a more fundamental reason. A part, and the most vital part of a knowledge-claim, is that there is a situation in the world which is as we believe it to be or as we experience it to be. And this harmony between the believed and the real character of *O* does not consist in the fact that our experience is caused by the object itself. And it

---

1 B. Russell, *Human Knowledge: Its Scope and Limits*, London: George Allen and Unwin, 1948.

is not necessary to construct cases where an experience caused by an object directly is not true of its real character however we may determine its real character. Perceptual errors are too common to require philosophical ingenuity to bring them to our notice.[2]

Armstrong, after rejecting the attempts to a causal analysis of knowledge, offers a reliability theory of knowledge. On this view non-inferential empirical knowledge is true reliable belief, the noetic response is like the reading of a good (reliable) thermometer whose reading (so long as it continues to be in good condition) corresponds to the environmental temperature. All we have to do is to specify to certain conditions which a perceiver has to satisfy to be a reliable observer. The filling in of this specification may vary from one type of perception to another and it is not the business of philosophy to list them. The general formula for direct knowledge of *p* is: (i) *p*, (ii) ($^{\exists H}$) [*Ha* there is a law-like connection in nature; {(x) If *Hx* then ($Bxp \supset p$)}].[3] Armstrong adds in addition to other explanatory remarks that the connection between the belief and the *state of affairs* is an ontological connection; however it is not a causal connection. The belief situation *Bap* does not bring about the *state of affairs* that makes *p* true. On the other hand, it is the *state of affairs* that brings about, frequently though not always, the belief-situation into existence. The attraction of such a theory for a determined behaviourist like

---

2 It is of course true that operation of causal regularities and our awareness of them is necessary for the ascertainment of truth and evaluation of truth-claims.

3 As Armstrong explains, *H* must be such that there is a real possibility of the situation covered by the law-like connection recurring; *x* ranges over beings capable of cognition and *B* is the belief operator. *A*'s non-inferential belief that *c* is *J* is a case of non-inferential knowledge if and only if:
($^{\exists H}$) [*Ha* and there is a law-like connection in nature; (*x*)(*y*) {if *Hx* the (if *BxJy*, then *Jy*}].
Further, *y* ranges over particulars and it is not the case that *BxJy* causes *Jy*. See, D.M. Armstrong, *Belief, Truth and Knowledge*, Cambridge University Press, 1973, p. 189.

Armstrong is understandable. But the theory is not at all plausible as an analysis of knowledge. We shall ignore the general difficulties in offering a behaviouristic analysis of belief. (In any case in this later work, Armstrong considerably waters down the physicalism of his *A Materialist Theory of the Mind* and writes freely of images, beliefs, mental attitudes, experiences.) It is a little surprising that he should think that when the causal condition is filled out with a reliability condition then the former becomes redundant and the reliability condition is sufficient by itself for giving an account of knowledge. It is true knowledge is not defined in terms of a causal relation between belief and the object of belief. But it is quietly taken for granted that when a subject fulfils certain specifications, then as a consequence of the operation of certain regularities in nature, his experiential response or belief response is such that the *state of affairs* believed in, prevails in the world. It is puzzling over what the non-causal ontological connection can be. Though Armstrong anticipates and tries to ward off a number of objections, some rather minor – he does not address himself to this central task of elucidating the nature of the connection symbolized by the implication sign between *p* and *Bap*. The belief does not cause or in any other way bring about the truth of the proposition believed. Is the theory anything more than suggesting without stating that a belief a subject of a specified sort (brought about as result of certain causal regularities) being reliable constitutes knowledge? If so this is no more than a combination of behaviouristically oriented pragmatism with causality which fails to elucidate the nature of knowledge. The general approach however can be shared by philosophers who are by no means behaviourists.

All those Indian philosophers who insist that cognition is valid when there is a subject–object contact without certain specifiable defects being present, take the same route. Such attempts fail to elucidate, let alone define the nature of knowledge, even when knowledge is confined to sense-perception. This for two reasons: First of all, even if the normal or non-defective conditions can be exhaustively listed, their 'normality' cannot be explained without circularity; 'normal conditions' being simply those conditions under which we assume that our perceptions reveal things as they are. No doubt, as well-settled earthlings we have excellent reasons for selecting these conditions and develop the notion of certain 'standard qualities' (Price's phrase) which we identify with the real qualities of objects. But if it is possible meaningfully to raise the question whether and when we are aware of objects *as they really are* this answer is not satisfactory at all. If however the conditions are listed in purely physical chemical and electrical terms, then there is no reason why all those perceptions and only those perceptions which occur under these conditions should represent or reveal objects as they are. Second all such accounts start from a set of beliefs about the external world which we take to constitute a body of shared, socialized, knowledge and hence beg the question at issue. They pretend to solve a problem which is already solved by our approach.

I do not therefore think there is any serious threat to the classical empiricist definition of knowledge from Gettier and if there is, the suggested solutions fail to remove the threat. However the threat of an infinite regressed mentioned by me at the outset remains. And this threat in its turn arises from the essentially inconclusive character of empirical knowledge. As we have seen, if to count as knowledge every true belief has to be supported by reasons, these reasons in their turn will have to be not only true but ascertained or known to be true, and for this we shall require still and more reasons and so on endlessly. Even if we are far more generous than Sir John Falstaff and reasons are as plentiful as black berries, we do not have an unlimited supply of them. In brief, our theory seems to say that in order to know p we have to know q and to know q, we have to know r and so on without end. This is no doubt an awkward consequence. But we should note that there is no circularity in the definition of knowledge. The knowledge of p is not defined in terms of the knowledge of q. But the definition has the awkward consequence that we are not in a position to know anything. A thorough-going relativist like Quine will accept this situation cheerfully, knowledge being for him, a system of statements fabricated by human beings, which they continuously modify to adapt it to the contours of their experience. Peirce tried to put a brave face on the difficulty by maintaining that it is not necessary for me to go on giving reasons forever; I can stop wherever I choose or wherever it is practically convenient. But as Ayer points out even if I do not have to *give* reasons endlessly, on this theory I have to *have them* and this seems impossible. Another way out of the impasse is to extend the coherence theory from the notion of truth to the notion of knowledge. A body of statements characterized by mutual support and corroboration can be taken as knowledge. This is not a definition of knowledge but a good pointer, perhaps the only available pointer that we have of knowledge.

But the most interesting response to the impasse is that of philosophers who restrict to the title of knowledge only to those cognitions which are as it were self-certifying. Plato and Descartes maintained that understanding and acceptance of a priori propositions is knowledge, the rest is belief, opinion or reasonable assurance and so on. This restriction is highly paradoxical in its consequences but I do not think it is due to any confusion. Ayer argues that philosophers, who maintain that only a priori propositions can be known, have confused two propositions.

1. It is necessary that what is known is true, $\blacksquare\,(Kp \supset Tp)$.
2. Whatever is known is necessarily true, $Kp \supset \blacksquare\, p$.

Rather, they have been persuaded rightly or wrongly, that evidence for a factual or empirical proposition can never be conclusive. Consequently it is not rational to be certain of them and in the absence of certainty no knowledge is possible. Cook Wilson, Prichard and their followers are a little more generous than Plato and Descartes. Price at any rate allows that in addition to apprehension of logical relations between propositions, we can know our own mental states in introspection and in a few favoured cases of recollection and sense data. Our knowledge of physical objects perceived by us is belief grounded in knowledge of sense data, the rest of our knowledge of the physical world is only reasonable assurance grounded in beliefs and other propositions of which we have only reasonable assurance. Lower still in the scale is taking for granted.

We can object that this is a gross violation of ordinary usage. Price is aware of it. He writes: 'Is the philosopher to use the word "know" in the strict and narrow sense in which Cook Wilson uses it? or shall he follow the more lax usage of ordinary speech and mean "the believing of some proposition which is reasonably certain"'? The second alternative would appear to be the more attractive. The less we depart from common usage, the less we shall mislead ourselves and our readers. But the trouble about it is that even the plain man would refuse to say 'I knew that he was at home yesterday but now it turns out that he was not' or 'in the middle ages men knew that the earth was flat but in fact it is not flat'. Thus common usage seems to be simply muddled on this point. Price could as well be Sophia's aunt scolding common sense for its slipshodness. Moreover, he underestimates the wilyness of the plain man. He would not say 'I knew that *p* but it turns out that *p* is false'. Rather. 'I thought I knew that *p* but now I realize that I did not really know that *p*'. In other words he would make a distinction between knowledge and knowledge-claims. He would say that the former is exempt from error but not the latter. I would agree with Price that knowledge unlike belief logically implies the truth of what is known. There may be linguistic and even epistemic propriety in claiming to know where certainty is not absolute (logical) but this does not in any way affect the logical connection between knowledge and truth. Second, those who oppose Plato and Price and others of that kind should go beyond a mere appeal to ordinary usage. They should point out – as Sophia's aunt does – the conceptual connections embedded in ordinary usage and consider how well established they are; whether any tightening or loosening of them is desirable in the light of certain broad features of our experience, or certain facts brought to light by science, etc. Moreover, we should not consider only the subtle and minute distinctions between different expressions but also certain unifying tendencies present in our language which are worth revealing and which it requires a little effort to notice. To concentrate on the first-person singular in the present tense is hardly the way to grasp the nature of speech and whatever it is that the study of language may reveal.

8

Truth:
Certain Logical and Linguistic Issues

Are you mad, are you mad? Is not the truth the truth?
– Falstaff (Shakespeare, Henry IV, Part 1, Act 2)

THOUGH it is common among philosophers to speak of the problem of truth there are, in fact, a number of distinct but related problems centring round the notion of truth. There is first of all the need for an analysis of the concept of truth. What is it that we say when we say of a statement that it is true? Alternatively what is it that makes any true statement true? Closely connected with the question of definition is the task of formulating the general criterion for distinguishing true propositions from false ones – if indeed there is a common single, criterion employed by us for different types of propositions. The two questions must be distinguished even if our answer to one of them has a bearing on our answer to the other; otherwise there will be needless confusion – us is evident from the writings of absolute idealists and certain pragmatists. Further assuming that truth is a property or a predicate, what are the subjects or bearers of truth and falsity? We ascribe truth and falsity to a number of things – propositions or judgements or statements, beliefs, sentences, even ideas – though this last ascription must be regarded as unhappy if ideas are taken to be concepts or general notions. All these ascriptions are, from the point of view of ordinary usage, quite proper. But the philosophers can legitimately ask:

> What are the final subjects of truth and falsity or what is it that can be said to be true or false in the primary sense – a sentence, a proposition or a belief?

A consideration of this problem involves naturally a discussion of meaning and reference, of the alleged existence of propositions as subsistent entities, of facts and their relation to propositions and leads from these have a tendency to get lost in the tangled thickets of the relation of the mind to the body.

None of these problems however need trouble us very long if we accept the non-predicativist theory of expressions like 'true' and 'false'. According to this view, first suggested by F.P. Ramsey,[1] these and cognate expressions do not stand for any attribute or predicate. They play no essential role in our language and whatever we say with their help can be said equally well without using them at all. More recently this redundancy theory of truth or the 'no-truth' theory, or the 'disappearance theory' of truth, as it has been called more picturesquely, has been elaborately defended by Ayer,[2] and Strawson[3] supplements the non-predicativist account with a brief discussion of the performatory functions of words like 'true' and 'false' without which the former would be inadequate and even misleading in its suggestions.

The main argument in support of the theory is that statements like 'It is true that moths fly by night' or, 'That the snow is white is true', have no more assertive content than the statements that result if we drop the prefixes and suffixes referring to truth-value, in these complex statements and assert the clauses by themselves. In general, if *p* is any statement then to assert '"*p* is true" is not to make any further assertion but simply to assert *p* itself. *p* and *p* is true' are logically equivalent and the equivalence is expressed by the simple formula: p is true $\equiv p$. That the right-hand side of the expression is simply an assertion of *p* shows that expressions like 'is true', 'it is true that', are eliminable from our discourse and consequently do

[1] F.P. Ramsey, 'Facts and Propositions', in *The Foundations of Mathematics and Other Logical Essays*, Routledge, 1931, pp. 142-43.

[2] A.J. Ayer, 'Truth', in *The Concept of a Person and Other Essays*, London: Macmillan, 1963, pp. 164-66.

[3] P.F. Strawson, 'Truth', in *Philosophy and Analysis*, ed. M. Macdonald, Oxford: Blackwell, 1954, pp. 260-77.

not stand for any genuine attribute. It is of some interest to note that Frege was aware of this equivalence and used it to establish that the truth-value of a proposition expressed by a declarative sentence is not its attribute. He exploits this consideration in support of his strange doctrine that the truth-value of a proposition is its reference so that every proposition can be regarded as a designation of 'the True' or 'the False': He writes,

> one indeed can say 'the thought that 5 is a prime number is true'. But close examination shows that nothing more has been said than in the simple sentence '5 is a prime number'. The truth-claim arises in each case from the form of the declarative sentence and when the latter lacks its usual force, for example in the mouth of an actor . . . the former contains only a thought and indeed the same thought as the simple sentence. It follows that the relation of the thought to 'the true' may not be compared with that of subject to predicate. . . . A truth-value cannot be part of a thought any more than, say, the sun can, for it is not a sense but an object.[4]

It is obvious that the non-predicativist theory relies heavily, if not exclusively, on assertion of truth in which the statement pronounced to be true is explicitly stated. In such cases it is undeniable that both the declaration of truth and the statement declared to be true are logically equivalent and that the more complex statement gives no more information than the simpler statement. Here the use of expressions like 'true' merely adds emphasis to what we say, like the formula 'verily' or 'verily, verily' which prophets and moralists are fond of prefixing to their pronouncements. Sometimes it serves to convey to our listeners that we are in earnest like placing a hand on our chest to accompany the spoken words. But there are cases where we may say, 'That is true', after a statement has been made by someone else. Here it does not sound very plausible to maintain that I am reasserting the statement to which I concede truth. At any rate,

---

4 G. Frege, 'Sense and Reference', in *Translations from the Philosophical Writings of Gottlob Frege*, tr. and ed. P. Geach and M. Black, Oxford: Basil Blackwell, 1960 (also in *Readings in Philosophical Analysis* ed. H. Feigl, Ridgeview Pub Co., 1982).

philosophers sensitive to the subtleties of ordinary usage must find such a position uncomfortable. Strawson in fact admits that there is a sense in which, in such a case, I am not asserting the statement I declare to be true anymore than I can be said to make an assertion when I answer a question put to me, with a 'yes'.[5] And yet there is another sense in which I can be said to be making a statement; in the first case I am agreeing with, endorsing, or underwriting the statement made by someone else (which amounts to a reassertion of it), and in the second case I can be correctly taken to have stated, by implication, the statement which is an affirmative answer to the question put to me. Agreeing with or confirming a statement, and answering a question are *practical* activities and the use of words like 'true' and 'false' is performatory in character. In saying, 'that is true', I am not stating anything, not even that I am confirming a statement but simply confirming it. Thus, though there is no difference in assertive content between *P* and '*P* is true', the latter serves certain purposes which are not served by the former. This explanation should remove, according to Strawson, the uneasiness some may feel when told that there is no difference between the two. There is a difference, but it does not consist in the fact that the more complex formula is a second-order statement about the simple first-order statement. The semantic theory realizing, rightly, that there is a difference between saying that a statement is true and just asserting it, wrongly maintains that the statement about truth-value is a meta-linguistic statement about the simple statement which is in object-language.

What are we to say about this further development and justification of the redundancy theory? It is undeniable that statements about truth-value serve many practical (i.e. non-descriptive) purposes. It can even be maintained that the performatory functions of words like 'true' and 'false' are their primary uses in ordinary language so that they often serve emotive and rhetorical purposes. But it does not follow that they do not also have a descriptive function. It may be said, as Strawson does

5 Strawson, op. cit., pp. 260-77.

more than once, that the traditional philosopher who treated truth as a property wrongly assumed that every adjective stands for a quality and that every sentence in the indicative mood expresses a proposition. Further, realizing that truth-value statements do not add any empirical information to what is already contained in the statements declared to be true, they embarked on a search for trans-empirical statements about supersensible properties and subsistent entities. But how is it to be established that every truly descriptive statement must be of the empirical type without begging the question at issue? Recognition of the equivalence between *P* and '*P* is true', even when combined with an elaboration of the stylistic and rhetorical functions of truth-value expressions, will not logically prove that truth is not a property and that attempts to analyse its nature constitute an illusory enterprise. Nor can we reasonably accuse the traditional philosopher of obstinately clinging to his prejudices and misconceptions unless our account of sentences containing truth-value expressions in the place of the predicate covers all types of such statements made in different contexts.

Truth and falsity are ascribed not only to statements asserted by us or by others in our presence, but also to a described statement or class of statements. How is our theory to be extended to them? Strawson considers certain examples of this kind including the statement expressed by the sentence 'what the policemen said is true'.[6] Instead of using this expression, Strawson writes, 'I might have repeated the policeman's story. In that case, I shall be said to have confirmed what the policeman said.' But he fails to see the oddity of confirmation, or repetition in which the statement confirmed is not reasserted either by me or anyone else. Nor is this all. There are cases where we may declare a statement to be true, which we are not even able to identify. I could very well have said: 'I don't remember now what the policemen said, but whatever it was, it was true'. Surely the word 'true' seems to have here a predicative or assertive role rather than a confirmatory role, especially if we remember that the above statement could have been made in a

6 Strawson, op. cit., pp. 271-72.

context where it serves no practical purpose. Ayer says that in such a case we are issuing, as it were, a blank cheque to someone whom we consider thoroughly reliable.[7] This is true. But then, to continue Ayer's metaphor, this is only because we are convinced that the person in question has enough cash-reserves in the form of true statements. It is neither straining ordinary usage, nor indulging in metaphysical talk, to say that whenever we confirm or certify the statements of others we have *discovered or found* out that certain statements made by them are true or that past experience *shows* that, in certain situations at least, they invariably tell the truth.

But an even more important point is that the example quoted above as well as another one discussed by Strawson ('All statements made in English are false.') refer to a closed class of statements whose members can be completely listed in principle. However far-fetched the notion of confirmation or reassertion may appear in this case we can at least suggest that an implicit or general confirmation is involved here. But even this suggestion is not available when truth is predicated of the members of an open class, where the expressions of generality are not just a device for a short-hand summary of particular cases. Consider the declaration of the Bellman in the 'Hunting of the Snark': 'What I say three times is true'.[8] It is not necessary to point out that 'what I say three times is true' is not equivalent to 'what I say three times' because the second quoted expression is not a statement at all. For the same reason it is obvious that this instance cannot be dealt with according to the schema suggested by Tarski in his semantic theory of truth. It would be nonsensical to say: '"What I say three times" is true what I say three times'. It would be wrong to dismiss this as a facetious example which causes amusement and a mild sense of shock, by its rejection of universally accepted criteria of confirmation. It should not be very difficult to give examples which pose the same difficulties as the Bellman's declaration, but are far from frivolous. Take the doctrine of

---

[7] Ayer, op. cit., p. 166.

[8] The Bellman in 'The Hunting of the Snark', *The Complete Illustrated Works of Lewis Carroll*, London: Chancellor Press, 1982, p. 734.

papal infallibility which may be expressed by the following sentence: 'whatever the Pope pronounces, ex-cathedra, on faith and morals is true'. Here again the word 'true' is ineliminable through simple re-assertion or along the lines indicated by Tarski. Profs. William and Martha Kneale have suggested, in their *Development of Logic*,[9] that the word 'true' can be eliminated from the above statement through suitable use of variables. A possible paraphrase of it would be: 'If any Pope, speaking of faith and morals ex-cathedra declares that *p*, then *p*.' Certainly the word 'true' does not appear in our reformulation but the elimination appears to be only nominal for two reasons. First of all, as it stands, the above formula does not express a proposition at all. We can take it as a statement only if we treat it, as in the case of the formulae of the propositional calculus, as a formula which is taken to be true for all values of the propositional variable contained in it. This means that the notion of truth is implicitly reintroduced. Further, within the restatement itself *p* in the consequent marks a place which when filled in with a suitable propositional expression amounts, not merely to the utterance, or repetition of a sentence but the affirmation of the *truth* of a proposition.

This last point brings us to a consideration of the utmost importance which, inexplicably, has been completely ignored by the exponents of the redundancy theory. Even if we admit that to state that any given proposition *p* is true is primarily or entirely to confirm it, or re-assert it, or certify it, or admit or confess it (if we enjoy that kind of thing we can get lost in tracing the nuances of difference among these different expressions) this will not advance the non-predicativist's cause if these various notions themselves involve the concept of truth. Assertion, for instance, is, as Chubb points out, putting forward a truth-claim.[10] It is to express one's belief that something is the case or that something is not the case. Merely to give utterance to a sentence is not to assert the proposition expressed by it. One may do this for illustrative purposes, or in

[9] W. Kneale and M. Kneale, *Development of Logic*, Oxford University Press, 1962, p. 585.

[10] J.N. Chubb, *Assertion and Fact*, Somaiya Publications, 1977, chap. X.

the course of storytelling, or else reporting what someone else has said in order either to endorse or reject the truth-claims made by him. Roughly speaking, to make an assertion is to employ a form of words, according to accepted rules of usage, to express what we believe to be true. And a belief or a sentence expressing it is true when it says, in Aristotle's famous and unexceptionable formula, 'Of what is, that it is, and of what is not, that it is not.'[11] Similarly to confirm or certify a statement made by another may be to offer a guarantee, but this guarantee is not of honesty or financial probity or solvency, but an acceptance and underwriting of a truth-claim made by him. A typical declaration that some proposition *P* is true is, to quote Chubb's metaphysical words,

> to raise our thinking, including the assertion which is called true, from the conscious to the self-conscious level . . . we say '"*p*" is true' rather than just '*p*' when our attention is drawn or a reference is made to a possible epistemological gap between what there is and what one who utters '*p*' says there is. '"*p*" is true' closes this gap and makes explicit the truth-claim which is implicit in "*p*".[12]

Not many philosophers today may like the heavy linguistic hammer brought to this task by Chubb but there is little doubt that he has hit his nail on the head (I have introduced the subtleties of single and double quote marks which Chubb neglects).

We may reinforce the criticism made so far and throw additional light on the question involved if we approach them tangentially and consider statements about consistency and inconsistency and mutual independence or entailment of propositions. If *p* and *q* are any two propositions we may say, as we often have to in our logic studies, that *p* and *q* are consistent; or that *p* and *q* are inconsistent. Quite clearly such statements are meta-assertions or assertions about assertions. A consistent non-predicativist will have to maintain that these too are performatory utterances whose purpose is to permit or

---

11 Aristotle (350 BCE), *Metaphysics*, Book IV, Part 7, tr. W.D. Ross, Internet Classic Archive, http://classics.mit.edu/index.html

12 Chubb, op. cit., p. 195.

forbid ourselves and others to assert *p* and *q* jointly. Similarly he will have to maintain that when we declare that *p* implies *q* we license people to proceed from the assertion of *p* to the assertion of *q*. That this is a logical corollary to the redundancy theory becomes obvious if we reflect that consistent propositions are propositions that can be true together, and two logically equivalent propositions are such that neither can be true when the other is false. Tarski's well-known definition of the relation of 'logical consequence' in terms of the notion of satisfiability of sentential functions refers implicitly to the notion of truth. If 'true' and 'false' are not predicative expressions, it follows that all those concepts which can only be defined in terms of the notions of truth and falsity too are non-predicative. And yet can anyone seriously maintain this position? Even if part of the task of the logician is to certify inference patterns which are acceptable and de-recognize others which are not acceptable, surely this activity rests on the recognition of certain logical relations between propositions or sets of propositions which hold objectively and independently of his certifying activity? Even conventionalists, like Strawson, who insist that logical rules arise from some very general and topic-neutral linguistic rules, must admit that these rules are very unlike the ordinary rules of say English or French grammar, and that they are indispensable to any system of symbolism by means of which it is possible to engage in intelligent communication. If this concession must be made by the conventionalist, then the notions of consistency, etc. together with the notion truth must be granted an objective basis.

How is the non-predicativist theory related to the semantic theory of truth? Tarski had two main purposes in elaborating his theory,[13] (1) to construct a definition which would state the necessary and sufficient conditions, in a formalized language, of the

---

[13] A. Tarski, 'The Concept of Truth in Formalized Languages', in *Logic, Semantics and Meta-mathematics: Papers from 1923 to 1938*, 1st edn. tr. J.H. Woodger, Oxford University Press, 1956, 1983, (also 'The Semantic Concept of Truth', in *Readings in Philosophical Analysis*, ed. H. Feigl and W. Sellars, New York: Appleton-century Craft, 1949).

application of 'true' to sentences in that language, and (2) to avoid the vicious circle and contradiction involved in the liar's paradox ('I am lying now') and certain other paradoxical statements. The second objective is attained by scrupulously observing the distinction between object-language and meta-language. *p* is true is a complex statement about *p* and the language in which it is expressed is meta-language in relation to the object-language in which *p* is expressed. A natural language like English contains sentences belonging to different language levels without any indication of the precise level to which a given sentence belongs. Once the distinction is enforced logical paradoxes of the type mentioned above disappear. So far as the first aim is concerned Tarski arrives at the disconcerting conclusion that ordinary language is so hopelessly ambiguous that no satisfactory definition of the concept of truth applicable to statements in it is possible. His own highly technical definition is applicable to formulae of the class-calculus, but it is possible to construct a definition along his lines for any limited fragment of a natural language.[14] As Tarski himself points out his definition leads, as a logical consequence, to such paradigm declarations as the following: '"Snow is white" is true (in English) *if and only if* snow is white.'

It is important to note that the above 'definition' cannot be generalized. For, if we write $(p)\ p \equiv p$, we shall not get the required universal definition. According to the conventions for the use of quotation marks the first occurrence of *p* in the above formula is a designation of the sixteenth letter of the English alphabet and we cannot say that *p* is true, any more than we can say that this tree is true. From our point of view the more important consideration is that in the paradigm instance the necessary and sufficient conditions for the truth of a mentioned sentence can be given by the use of the very same sentence. This means that so long as we only use sentences in our object language and refrain from talking about them, we need not use the word 'true' at all and yet say everything that we want

---

14 Black Max, "Linguistic Method in Philosophy", in *Language and Philosophy, Studies in Method*, Ithaca, NY: Cornell University Press.

to say about the world. This may be taken as implying the 'No-Truth' theory. Tarski himself claims the authority of Aristotle for his account and if we agree with him his theory would be a version of the correspondence theory. Many philosophers however would say that his theory is neutral in relation to the traditional theories for none of the advocates of the rival theories – correspondence, coherence, pragmatism – would deny the trivial statement that 'grass is green' is true if and only if grass is green.

If there is any substance in my criticisms then the non-predicativist has not established his thesis and there are good reasons for the commonsensical view that a truth-value statement says something about what is said to be true. But what is the subject of the predicate 'true'? Indeed it is the difficulty in finding a suitable bearer of the property of truth that may incline many persons towards the redundancy theory. In recent discussions truth has been ascribed to either sentences or propositions or indifferently to both. I shall argue briefly that neither alternative is very plausible and that it is best to ascribe truth to beliefs of mental states which include an element of belief or disbelief.

The ascription of truth to sentence is so implausible that no one would have indulged in such talk but for the supposition of some philosophers that this is the only way to avoid acceptance of propositions as subsistent entities.[15] The objections to propositions regarded as real entities are well known though we may admit that it is often necessary and convenient to speak of propositions and define a proposition as something which is expressed by a sentence or a set of sentences, and to which the various cognitive attitudes of belief, disbelief supposition, etc. can be directed. Apart from the unease we may feel in swallowing subsistent entities there are two serious difficulties in ascribing truth to propositions. If there are propositions distinct from both sentences and mental states directed to them then the world contains true and false propositions 'as it contains red and white roses'. It is then difficult to see why we should

[15] W.V.O. Quine, *Philosophy of Logic*, Harvard University Press, 1970, 1986, chap. I.

accept true propositions and reject false ones, unless we maintain, as Russell did at one time, that the preference for true propositions is a moral preference. Second, a false belief or judgement, on this view, consists in contemplating a false proposition and this is being aware of something real; whereas it seems obvious that a false belief is a belief about something *does not exist*. To these Quine adds the objection that there is no satisfactory criterion for the identity of a proposition.

But do sentences fare any better? In the context of ascription of truth and falsity, can we explain what we mean by 'the same sentence' without referring to the proposition they all express? Moreover if we cast sentences in the required role, we shall have to choose either sentence types or token-sentences. The main difficulty in ascribing truth to the former is that the same sentence may be true at one time and in one place and false at another time and in another place. This will be the case with all sentences containing tensed verbs and token-reflexives such as 'I am hungry' and 'It is raining'. We are therefore committed to reforming our language in such a way that personal pronouns, tenses and other token-reflexives are eliminated. We shall have to ascribe truth to what Quine calls 'eternal sentences'.[16] It is doubtful how far it is possible to reframe our sentences in the desired way. But even if this could be done our 'eternal sentences' will fail to express all the information expressed by ordinary language. For example, they will fail to indicate the absolute position in time of the speaker in relation to the events he is speaking about. On the other hand, if we ascribe truth to sentence-token then we cannot speak about their truth in the manner suggested by Tarski, for, being events, they cannot be designated with the help of quotation marks of any other device. Apart from this, it is difficult to see how a mere event like the production of certain sounds or the inscribing of certain marks can be true or false.

Since beliefs are the only possible candidate left in the field once proposition and sentences are eliminated, I plump for them. It

---

16 W.V.O. Quine, *Word and Object*, MIT Press, 1960, p. 193.

may be pointed out that the ascription of truth to belief is not only commonsensical but was done as a matter of course by Russell and Moore in their early writings. Propositions could be regarded as the content of a late-cut executed by a cricketer. Moreover our view introduces a certain duality between believing or mental processes involving belief on the one hand and what is believed or state of affairs in the world which is very handy in explaining error or falsehood. Perhaps without this duality, falsity cannot be explained at all. When Chubb speaks of an epistemological gap between what is and what we say there is, he is indirectly acknowledging this duality. It is therefore surprising that he should agree with the redundancy theory that the concept of truth is not a relational concept and that there is no need to find suitable bearers for the properties of truth and falsity.[17] I should maintain that being true is a relational property of a belief when it is related to the world in a certain way. This is a version of the correspondence theory which is exposed to notorious difficulties. I think all the well-known objections can be answered or else shown not to be relevant to the problem of *defining truth.* It is not possible to attempt this task in the present paper. But I must remark that I am totally unmoved by the jeers of philosophers who castigate the acceptance of 'ghostly' mental processes. Physicalists of all shapes have yet to offer a coherent let alone plausible analysis of statements about mental processes.

---

[17] Chubb, op. cit., p. 190.

9

Meaning, Realism and Logic

In the second half of the twentieth century linguistic studies have gradually come to the fore in the English-speaking philosophical world. Until now they occupy the energies of some of its leading lights almost entirely. Positivism and its successors, formal and informal analysis, have ceased to be fashionable. But they have left an enduring legacy. Dissection and exhibition of meanings of expressions and functions of language are valued for its own sake occasionally but often for the light it is supposed to throw on many intractable problems of philosophy. Distinguishing different meanings of expressions to avoid confusion in thinking has always been part of philosophy. But what is novel, though we have grown used to it, is debate about meaning of meaning and formulation of different theories about this all-absorbing theme. It is said that wrong philosophical theories like doctrines about real universals, non-natural qualities or even about inner mental processes distinct from patterns of behaviour, have their source in linguistic confusion due in turn to espousal of wrong theories about meaning of meaning.

Analysis of specific linguistic expressions to avoid confusion, equivocation, etc. has always been and will always remain an important part of philosophy. But the utility of having a correct theory of meaning of meaning is doubtful if only because theories in this field threaten to be as perennially controversial as traditional philosophical debates. Moreover, at this high level of generality we do not know how to choose between alternatives. Confronting a proposed analysis with a contrary instance should be decisive. But there are ways of dealing with apparent exceptions, which though high-handed sometimes, will technically save our proposal. Further, a disturbing feature of this situation is that choice of a particular theory points to, and is in turn influenced by a particular ontology, a particular view of what there is in the world.

It is therefore not every profitable to discuss various theories of meaning – the causal theory, use theory, denotative theory of Russell, the sense-reference duality of Frege. All of them with the possible exception of Frege, presuppose what they set out to explain. (This objection should be handled carefully. Otherwise every theory about the concepts of truth and meaning, since it claims to be true and a fortiori, meaningful, would be either circular or false.) For Frege the sense of an expression is something an attribute or set of attributes – the possession of which singles out an object for attention or locates a range of object for further consideration. The reference, on the other hand, is the object or range of objects so singled out. Every meaningful expression in language presents some thing for our attention and does so through its own mode of presentation. These views, which are nearest to common sense and most plausible, take on a distinct paradoxical character when Frege regards declarative sentences as the names of truth-values, i.e. either the true or the false conceived to be objects of a peculiar kind. On any view sentences expressing propositions should be meaningful in a way that is different from the way words and phrases which are parts of them are meaningful. Second, the meanings of statements or declarative sentences must in some sense, be derived from the meanings of their constituent expressions, though these latter themselves may derive their meaning from the relatively stable role they play in entire statements.

This involves, as Dummett points out in his *Seas of Language*, the rejection of both holistic and atomist theories of meaning and accepting a molecular theory. We are thus led to the acceptance of the sentence as the primary vehicle of meaning as of truth. I go along with him on these points and also in his view that the truth–condition theory of meaning is the most plausible. This originally propounded by Davidson is modelled on the T-schema of Tarski. The schema is essentially an equivalence between two sides. The

LHS ascribes truth to a quoted sentence and the RHS repeats the quoted sentence without any quotation marks, i.e. it uses it to derive a meaning sentence. We quote a given sentence in our LHS, use it in our RHS, and connect the two by the phrase 'means that' or an equivalent expression. As an illustration we have, 'Rome is the capital of Italy' means that Rome is the capital of Italy. We may, if we like, replace the RHS by an equivalent sentence, i.e. a correct translation of it into some foreign language. If to explain the meaning of a sentence is to explain what the speaker of a language grasps when he understands the meaning of a sentence, then our 'm-sentence' is not very satisfactory. The condition laid down is 'far too weak for own language and far too strong for a language we do not know'. One may know that a given 'm-sentence' is correct without knowing the meaning of the sentence being explained. However, since every other theory is open to equally grave objections, we may accept the truth-condition theory and see how it fares when applied to statements of certain classes.

Our theory requires that we can formulate a criterion for recognition by the speaker of the fulfilment of truth-conditions for a given statement. There may be no uniform or standard way of manifesting one's recognition; but to know the meaning of a statement is to recognize the truth of it when and only when the relevant truth conditions are fulfilled. To formulate our criterion in terms of actual knowledge would be far too restrictive. Our criterion has to be generalized to cover any cases which are, in practice or in principle, decidable. Dummett contends that natural language is full of statements which are not effectively decidable. These fall under the following categories:

1. Quantification over infinite domains.
2. Reference to regions of space and time inaccessible to us in principle.
3. Subjunctive conditionals.

For such conditions with a knowledge of what the truth conditions are. This is because we may never be in statements we cannot equate a capacity to recognize the satisfaction or non-satisfaction of truth – a position to say whether the truth conditions are fulfilled or not. Ascribing implicit knowledge of the condition to the speaker, Dummett argues, has no content because there is no practical ability to manifest it. If a person has knowledge of the meaning of a sentence *S*, he should be able to state its truth condition in a non-circular way.

The first of the three classes of problematic statements has a bearing on the foundations of mathematics and the demand of intuitions for constructive proofs. Their views apparently lead them to a revision of two-valued logic and the rejection of the law of excluded middle. They bare the transition from $\sim\sim p$ to p in some cases, and insist that no proposition of the type, $p \vee q$, may be set down as valid unless we are in a position to prove p or prove q, or can specify an effective procedure for doing so. I shall not discuss this any more for lack of effective knowledge. But I cannot help remarking that revision of logic may not be the best way to resolve difficulties in mathematics. Indeed there is some doubt whether Brouwer really denies the law of the excluded middle. The logical sign '$\neg$' comes nearest to the usual sign for negation but is not identical with it in meaning.[1] It has been suggested that Brouwer rejects the thesis: 'It is demonstrable that *p*, or it is demonstrable that it is not demonstrable that *p*', not the much simpler truth-functional formula which embodies the law of the excluded middle. I once compared the intuitionist, if he really demands rejection of some time-honoured logical principles, to Lamb's Chinaman who burnt down his house to roast his pig. The comparison still seems apt to me but I have already said too much for a person whose ignorance of higher mathematics is, by now, invincible.

The second class of undecidable statements refers to inaccessible regions of space and time and is of special relevance in defending formulations of the verification principle, but is of great interest even

[1] We assume that the late Prof. N.G. Kulkarni meant the sign that Brouwer used for negation.

otherwise. It is however the third class of subjunctive conditionals, which is particularly interesting. In solving the difficulties posed by them Dummett tentatively opts for a solution that rejects realism and the law of the excluded middle concerning them. He argues that semantic considerations may lead to a revision of two-valued classical logic and that the revision would be along lines suggested by intuitionism.

Consider the two statements:

1. "He is good at learning foreign languages".
2. "He is not good at learning foreign languages".

Let us call them *A* and ~*A* respectively. It is clear that to verify either of them we shall have to verify either of the two conditionals:

1. If he were to attempt to learn a foreign language he would do it quickly.
2. If he were to attempt to learn a foreign language he would not do it quickly.

The two have a common antecedent and contradictory consequents. They are of the form, $p \subset q$ and $p \subset \sim q$. It is not logically necessary that one of them should be true though we are inclined to assume that this must be so. Call the two conditionals *A* and ~*A* respectively. We are inclined to think that *A* v ~*A* should be true by the principle of bivalence, the principle that every proposition is determinably true or false. If for a given class of statements you reject bivalence you reject realism for that class; for in Dummett's view, realism concerning a given class of statements is just the view that each member of it is either determinately true of determinately false.

'He is good at learning foreign languages': if this is said of one who has had no contact with a foreign language, what are we to say of the matter? Quite clearly there is no evidence for the truth of either *A* or ~*A*, and consequently there can be no evidence to accept or reject *A* or ~*A*. There views are possible:

1. Unwilling to concede bare truth to either of the two counter-factual conditionals we may resolve the dilemma by denying

the principle of bivalence for them.

2. Second, we may postulate a specific physiological feature, say a particular brain structure, which is the basis of the ability when it exists and is absent when the ability is absent. Since the alleged brain structure either exists or does not exist, one of the two conditionals is true and the other is false.
3. The third view admits the absence of the all evidence for either *A* or ~*A* but insists that since one of them must be true by the law of the excluded middle, the corresponding conditionals are capable of truth-value. One of them must be barely true and the other barely false. We need not consider further the physiological or materialist view. Once we admit present ignorance, and the possibility of future verification is readily granted, by analogy with the verificatory procedures we now employ to investigate the brain, the rest is plain sailing and there is no difficulty in principle.

The third and first views present interesting problems. Dummett rejects the third ascription of bare truth to the conditionals after fairly full discussion, and opts positively but tentatively for the first-rejection of bivalence for statements of this class. An upholder of bivalence for the concerned class may say that in a way he is nor ascribing bare truth to such statements. Everyone grants that the categoricals which are the consequents of the two conditionals are verifiable. The truth of *A* follows from that of *A*, if *A* is true. Similarly, in the other case. This seems a futile contention and the thesis trivial. It is not disputed that we learn to ascribe abilities by observing the performance of a person, under certain conditions. If so, epistemically, the categoricals and the corresponding conditionals are on the same footing. It may be said that the overtly categorical statement does not reduce to the corresponding conditional and that the two differ in meaning. A man's ability to learn is a permanent but not directly observable state. This, Dummett contends, though not mere verbal jugglery, fails to offer a criterion for distinguishing cases where we can allow bare truth to a conditional, from cases where we have to admit that neither of two contrary-to-fact conditionals may be true. Appeal to 'a direct insight into counter-factual reality', Dummett contends, is empty.

The three views may be considered non-realistic, reductively realistic and naïvely realistic. Our explanation of meaning in terms of truth conditions will depend upon the view we take of a statement or class of statements in question. In the case of the second view reduction will take different forms according as we think that a logical translation of a reduced statement to a reducing, unproblematic, statement or a set of such statements is possible. But in any case a non-trivial answer is possible to the questions; 'What is the meaning of the sentence?'. If *S* is considered capable of a bare truth the corresponding m-sentence cannot but be trivial in form, and our explication of the meaning of *S*, non-explanatory.

Our model for a knowledge of *S* is the capacity to give a report of observation. The notion of an observation report is rather loose; but, according to Dummett, such a report must fulfil three conditions:

1. It must not rest on extraneous inference.
2. In every case where it is true it must be capable of being observed to be true.
3. The possibility of observing should not involve any procedure that will affect or transform the situation or object referred to.

The notion of a grasp of truth conditions, when the model for knowledge of truth conditions is the capacity to observe whether or not the sentence is true is problematic when applied to sentences not decidable in principle. In such a case we tend to appeal surreptitiously, sometimes explicitly, to mastery of observation sentences as a model for knowledge of truth conditions. The observations, which we imagine ourselves as making, are such that we are incapable of making them. We credit ourselves with capacities, which belong to beings with a different spatio-temporal perspective, or are gifted with observational and intellectual powers transcending our own. We try to convince ourselves that understanding undecidable statements is to grasp what it would be to be able to give observation reports of such statements. If we accept correspondence as a regulative ideal, viz., that there must be something in reality which makes a true sentence true then a second regulative principle follows, viz., that it must, in principle, be possible to know that a sentence is true, when it is true. This second principle depends for its application on how we construe the expression 'in principle possible'. A realist, however, ardent and generous he may be, will have to grant that if there is a sentence for which we have no conception of how it might be known to be true or false, then we have no grasp of its truth conditions. In crediting ourselves with additional powers by analogy with our actual powers we should not specify the former, so as to make them either trivial or superhuman ('direct insight into counter-factual reality', 'travelling by time machine' are examples).

The root cause of the difficulty is the assumption of realism which, according to Dummett's way of stating it, is application of the principle of bivalence to a given class of statements. It is because of the application of the principle that we are unable to equate knowledge of meaning of a statement with knowledge of grasp of its truth conditions. Such a knowledge attributed to a speaker of a language must be explicit knowledge, so that the truth conditions can be informatively stated. The accepted linguistic practice is to take the validity of the principles of two-valued logic for granted in delineating the semantics of undecidable statements. Classical logic depends upon the assumption that every statement has just one of the two determinate values, truth or falsity. Without abandoning bivalence we cannot construct a semantics for the class of un-decidable statements. It is probable though not certain that we have to acknowledge that classical logic does not apply to them, that some of its valid forms of argument may have to be revised or rejected. This, however, is no objection, according to Dummett, against a theory of meaning not on the basis of objectively determinate truth-values, but in terms of what is to count as proof. The standard explanations of the constants and axioms of intuitionist calculus are stated, not in terms of truth but in terms of proof. It is assumed that we can effectively recognize a proof. *pvq* is proved if and only if either there is a proof of p or there is a proof of q. If an actual proof is not available, there should be an effective procedure for construction a proof. For mathematics a statement is meaningful if a proof exists or can be constructed. Proof of a negative statement demonstrates the impossibility of finding a proof for that statement. For a meaningful statement either there is a proof or proof that it cannot be proved. The verbal intelligibility of a statement does not guarantee a decision procedure. The law of excluded middle is not universally valid. Our capacity to understand a statement consists not in finding a proof but in the ability to recognize one when found. Such a theory of meaning can be readily extended to non-mathematical cases. On extension the required notion is verification. Understanding a statement consists in a capacity to recognize whatever is counted as verifying it or establishing it as true. This does not mean that we necessarily have the means of verification at our disposal. The above comment is subject to two qualifications. First, we should recognize the interlocking character of the statements that constitute our knowledge, as Quine has emphasized. Second, in the case of empirical statements unlike in the case of mathematics, we should stipulate that understanding a statement is the twofold ability to recognize verification as well as falsification of it.

III

I have outlined some of the views of Dummett on the meaning of statements given in his two lengthy essays on 'what is a theory of meaning?'. I have left out much, but what I have selected for exposition is of fundamental importance. I hope the ramifying complexity and subtlety of the discussion are clearly brought out. I have four points to make, two relatively minor, and two others of greater interest.

1. First of all in the case of the counter-factual conditionals which, to a certain way of thinking, suggest a revision of classical logic, the conditionals are not interpreted truth-functionally. Otherwise, since the common antecedent is admittedly false,

both would be trivially true. Part of the difficulty may be due to the uncertainties in the interpretation of conditionals of everyday or even scientific discourse. We may refuse to assign any truth-value to them on some occasions. But this is not to assign them any intermediate value or any one of multiple values co-ordinate with truth-values. In this respect Lukasiewicz's three-valued logic is different from intuitionist logic. So far as the former is concerned the three numerical values represent certainly values which presuppose truth-values of classical logic. This is the suggestion of Profs. William and Martha Kneale and Mrs. Kneale in their monumental *Development of Logic* and I agree with them.

2. The two counter-factuals *A* and ~*A* have a resemblance to others which are not essentially unverifiable. If this is the case and if we further agree that this is a case of refusing to assign either of the two truth-values rather than that of assigning an alternative value, then their meaning should remain unaffected. It could very well be 'that we systematically misunderstand our language' and labour under the delusion that what is verbally intelligible is meaningful. This combined with the firm hold of classical logic may explain our resistance to a semantic based on many-valued logic. But a consideration in favour of classical logic is that many unverified propositions, singular conditional and so on, play a role in chains of reasoning which is unaffected by the fact that they are unverified. Even if some of them turn out to be essentially unverifiable, in some way, their role in reasoning would remain exactly the same, being dependent on their meanings apart from the significance of logical constants occurring in them.

3. Dummett argues that in intuitionist logic the meaning of logical operators is determined in terms of the role they play in a proof. He recognizes, almost immediately, that this does not mean that truth-values play no role in the construction of semantics. Proof procedures are inseparably connected with

the search for truth. Deduction is truth-preserving and in inductive reasoning we seek correspondence with reality and therefore truth as a regulative ideal. If this line of reasoning is followed up, we may come to the conclusion that alterative logics supplement, rather than supplant the simple and yet universally valid classical logic. From this point of view, the intuitionist logic may be regarded as a manual or handbook of logical principles which can be used in mathematical proofs of a constructive character without the fear of going astray. If some proof procedures are found opaque, give no real insight, we can abandon the law of excluded middle or the principle of double negation whenever they play a crucial role in the construction of such opaque proofs. This does not mean that the objectionable principles are any the less logical principles.

4. I have already argued that the counter-factual mentioned above, *A* and ~*A*, are of the same kind as others which are not essentially unverifiable. Dummett grants as much when he speaks of statements which are verbally intelligible but not really meaningful. Does this mean that he is using 'meaningful' in a technical and rather stricter sense somewhat like the positivist using 'nonsensical?'. There are of course cases of pure meaninglessness like collections of nonsense syllables or sentences containing Carnap's 'toovey' and 'teevey' applied to perceptible objects but bearing no discoverable relation to the experience of the speaker or hearer. But the more important point is that this stricter sense of 'meaningful' is dependent upon our ordinary, wider use of 'meaningful' which we understand intuitively, no doubt vaguely, even confusedly but not hopelessly so. If this is so, then confronted with statements which are essentially unverifiable, the realist doggedly insists that one or other of two such contradictory statements is true though we do not know which. Dummett thinks that the only alternative is to depart from classical logic and elaborate a semantics based upon many-valued logic. There is however another way out and that is, to say that our sentence do not

express propositions at all however much they seem to do so. It is a minor point that if there are declarative sentences to which it is proper to refuse any determinate truth-value even in themselves and without any relation to our knowledge, then the term 'proposition' has to be redefined. The trick is easily performed by saying that a proposition is any declarative sentence which is true or false or can be properly said to be neither. But it is more paradoxical and unsettling to say that they express no propositions and are therefore not proper candidates for assignment of truth-value, than to say that they are or express propositions to which an objective truth-value can be refused. Perhaps both the realist and the irrealist are seeking verbal formulations where each finds his own position least uncomfortable. In some situations the philosopher has to choose the kind and degree of discomfort he is ready to live with.

10

Three Faces of Relativism

How large unto the tiny fly
Must little things appear!
A rosebud like a feather bed
Its prickle like a spear . . .

. . .

A loaf of bread like a lofty hill
A wasp a cruel leopard;
And specks of salt as bright tosee
As lambkins to a shepherd

– 'The Fly' by Walter de la Mare[1]

laukikānām hi sādhūnāmarthamvāganuvartate ।
ṛṣīṇāmpunarādyṁnaṁvācamarthonudhāvati ।।

– Bhavabhūti[2]

The speech of worldly-wise sages conforms to the nature of things; but the world itself hastens after seers to verify their words.

RELATIVISM can have a quiet beginning as a corrective to naïve realism when we reflect on the variations in our perceptual experiences; when there is no ground for believing that there is a change in what is perceived. The maxim of Protagoras: 'Man is the measure of all things' is one of the earliest expressions of it. This physiological relativism – as we may term it – predates the rise of modern science. The argument from illusion rests on a range of facts which are quite well known, some of them being matters of everyday experience. But

[1] An English poet and novelist (1873-1956).

[2] Indian Sanskrit poet and playwright (eighth century CE).

they do not disturb our peace of mind. We have learnt to discount them and determine the 'real' size, shape, colour, etc. of objects in terms of certain standard or ideal conditions of observation. That the argument does not conclusively refute naïve realism may be granted. But the adjustments and qualifications, needed to save some articles of faith in the common-sense view of the world, would undoubtedly necessitate modifying or abandoning other equally important elements in it. Ayer in the brilliant opening chapter of *Foundations of Empirical Knowledge* is so busy defending the thesis that perception is a direct awareness of material objects, that he is unmindful of the transformation of the categorical contours of them as ordinarily understood. He is like a general who is desperately defending the front entrance to a building when the enemy has all but overrun the place through the back door.

This form of relativism is better termed physiological though idealist philosophers like Berkeley have argued that the immediate data of sense are in the mind, being causally dependent on the percipient. But as has been pointed out, particularly by Russell in the *Ultimate Constituents of Matter*, the dependence in question is rather upon our bodies than upon our minds. The perspectival variations in what is perceived are dependent on physical and physiological factors and can in fact be recorded by a camera or any recording instrument. In the lines quoted at the beginning, the poet's imagination roams freely to point a picture of the world as seen by the fly. But the scientific basis is surely the structure of the sense-organs and nervous system of the organism concerned. They determine in a way that is relative to the species, perceived size, shape, etc. For obvious reasons philosophers have concentrated on human perceivers though Protagoras refers, in passing, to perceptions of animals and madmen.

We may add to the argument from illusion (i) the account given by physics and physiology of the causation of our sensations, and (ii) the picture of the external world presented by mathematical physics which seems flatly to contradict the plain man's representation of it. The difficulties presented by these three lines of reflection can be tackled in different ways. They can be exploited to serve total scepticism concerning the existence of an external world. This however is more than can be claimed to be the logical outcome of these considerations. Scientific realism seems to be the best alternative to common sense, so long as we confine ourselves to perception in relation to the physical world. Idealism which dissolves the mighty framework of things in the contents of an infinite mind, or in a series of correlated and harmonious cognitions, remains a threat or an opportunity depending on one's philosophical taste. It would be tempting to disqualify the sceptic at the starting point. We can argue that the scientific and common-sense pictures of the world are complementary and, therefore, compatible; that total scepticism about the senses is incoherent because we cannot reject some perceptions as illusory unless some others are accepted and logically implied to be veridical. Both these views have been maintained by Ryle in his *Dilemmas* and by others, both before and after. But the attempts do not seem to be successful.

The minimum that relativism in this field will leave us with is a belief in matter as the cause of our sensations whose intrinsic nature is unknown to us and unascertainable by us. Sceptical arguments to show that even this is indefensible, always rely on some principle that must be, as pointed out by Moore, less certain than our belief in external objects. If we allow ourselves some further assumptions, we can claim some knowledge of the content and character of external objects. Such claim will be controversial because the principles assumed will never compel assent from every thinker. Scientific realism from the Lockean to its most modern versions remains a tenable theory, however untenable some of its details and however unconvincing some of its arguments. When philosophers argue that some feature of the world as experienced by us is an appearance and not a reality, they are worthy of attention. But I am inclined to think that just as there are limits to the liberties we can take with the world, there are limits to the tricks the world can play upon us.

The second form of relativism can be termed sociological–cultural. It is rooted in the findings of sociologists – particularly cultural anthropologists. Each culture is treated as an autonomous existence whose validity or acceptability is not to be questioned. Neither from within nor from without by those who do not share it. For, there are no cross-cultural objective standards by which we can condemn some and accept others. The standards of acceptability are set within cultural milieu for those who live within it. They can be applied to particular problems that arise within the cultural framework; but the framework itself cannot be overthrown by any neutral standards. We may opt out of it or in the historical course one framework may replace another. But there are no common standards of validity applicable to beliefs and attitudes independently of all cultural framework. This is very much like what Wittgenstein says about the autonomy of different language-games and the absence of overall rules applicable to all of them. The ultimate justification of the rules of any language-game is that 'this is how it is played, this is how we live!'. Indeed certain aspects of Wittgenstein's later philosophy may be aptly described as 'descriptive anthropology'. Some of the bolder practitioners of sociology of knowledge claim that their discipline should replace traditional epistemology.

I do not want to deny that there are valuable elements in this approach. This way of thinking may provide an antidote to hasty assumption of moral and intellectual superiority. It may also act as a check on excessive reformist zeal when such a check is needed. But it cannot replace the traditional search for objective moral and intellectual standards nor can it show that such a search is misguided. The desire to seek agreement with other human beings is an important, ineradicable, element in our mental and moral make-up. This tendency is carried to its limit in the conception of a disinterested observer surveying things exactly as they are, and the ideal of knowledge as pure contemplation, uncontaminated by any private, accidental factors. After all the sociologist of knowledge, perhaps un-intentionally, takes himself to be such a spectator who surveys different cultural patterns and describes their workings and elicits the norms and values of a culture from the practices of the members of a community. Second, different cultures will have not only each its distinctive norms but also certain common standards and methods of evaluation. To disentangle them may be difficult but to give up the search for them is an error; as much of an error as the imposition of common ideals on all communities and the outlawing of different theoretical and practical approaches to the world.

The third form of relativism that I shall consider is the latest and may roughly be characterized as epistemological–linguistic. It may owe its inspiration indirectly to Wittgenstein's remark:

> Here we see that the idea of 'agreement with reality' does not have any clear application.[3]

But its starting point is the simple and yet fundamental point that a scientific theory is underdetermined by observed facts which it seeks to explain. There is more in it than can be translated into its 'cash value' in the form of sensory experience. There is also the well-known fact that all the results of observation, available at anytime, can be organized and systematized in alternative ways between which the only ground for preference, sometimes, can be considerations of economy and elegance. This has led to the radical relativism of Quine and Goodman, the latter going to lengths which appear to be shocking. Quine points out that our empirical judgements are always embedded in theory. We can substitute one theory for another but we can never dispense with theory altogether. It is impossible to arrive at independent, theory-neutral facts and settle the fate of a theory by appeal to such facts. Add to this the fact, repeatedly emphasized by Quine, that we have the liberty to alter or abandon any statements. We like to make the totality of propositions fabricated by us and which we call science, conform to the boundary conditions of experience. In practice we follow the maxim of minimum mutilation but in principle, we can revise any propositions from the most elementary statements of history and geography to the most abstruse laws of mathematical physics, even the seemingly immutable principles of formal logic.

---

[3] L. Wittgenstein, *On Certainty*, ed. G.E.M. Anscombe and Von Wright, tr. Denis Paul and G.E.M. Anscombe, Basil Blackwell (1969-75).

Endorsing this position Goodman writes:

> We cannot test a version (of the world) by comparing it with a world undescribed . . . all we can learn about the world is already contained in right versions of it; and while the underlying world bereft of these need not be denied to those who love it, it is perhaps, on the whole, a world well lost.[4]

He describes his own position as 'a radical relativism under rigorous restraints that eventuates in something akin to irrealism'.[5] What would shock many people is Goodman's readiness to admit incompatible truths. Quine, clearly, is not prepared to go so far for he allows that when our system does not harmonize with certain experiential conditions some re-distribution of truth-values among the members of the system is required. The result of such a re-distribution must be a consistent system. Otherwise we could have admitted the new observation statements into our system without undertaking any revision; or we could have chosen the lazy way out by pleading illusion and hallucination. In principle, the alternative methods of revision are indefinitely many, but in practice, apart from logical consistency, pragmatic considerations govern our choice. But the one thing he and Goodman are not prepared to allow is that a theory can be accepted on the ground that it conforms to facts or describes them more adequately than its rivals. Facts, in short, have ceased to be sacred and along with them realism goes overboard – at any rate the cruder forms of it. And we are left with a combination of conventionalism and pragmatism.

What are we to say when confronted with this extreme form of relativism? It would be a mistake to dismiss this as an intellectual parlour game though it is difficult to determine how seriously some of its expressions are to be taken. So far, in the history of philosophy, relativism has led, through some tortuous reasoning, to idealism, or in a more straightforward way to scientific realism or else to agnosticism with varying degrees of completeness. The

---

[4] Nelson Goodman, *Ways of World Making*, Hackett, 1978, p. 4.

[5] Ibid., p. X.

most thoroughgoing form of the last type of theory conceives the world as something other than ourselves that causes our sensations and provides a mysterious setting for our activities. But a relativism that bypasses the real world and sees no need for it as the necessary stage of our activities including scientific system-building is not easy to comprehend.

In the more extreme version it does not seem to be defensible either. This version of relativism, like others, appeals to certain facts which are taken to be parts of a body of socialized knowledge. As in the case of physiological and cultural relativism this form too appeals to the existence of different versions of the world. The real world underlying them may be denied or ignored but not the existence of the alternative world-versions themselves. Even if we dismiss as 'pernicious mentalism' the reference to mental processes involved in building scientific theories as non-existent or irrelevant, the speech behaviour of humans remains as the minimum irreducible brute fact. We may regard men and women as rather complicated word-processors; but there they are undeniably – even if what they seek to characterize by their verbalizations – dismissed. Once we have this foothold we can extend our knowledge through logical analysis and causal reasoning. Even if this extension is not possible, the real world does not vanish – it coincides with ourselves. The alternative ways of world-making, like the different series of cognitions in Vijñānavāda, will be unrelated to one another or to anything outside them and independent of them. The earlier versions of relativism regarded the world as something other than ourselves whose intrinsic nature we are unable to comprehend or accurately determine. The latest, taken to its logical conclusion, identifies the world with ourselves and our apparently, autonomous linguistic activities.

Whatever plausibility this version of relativism possesses is due to two reasons: the first is the use of question-begging words in explaining the notion of truth. 'A version is taken to be true when it offends no *unyielding beliefs and some of its own precepts*.'[6]

---

[6] Goodman, op. cit., p. 17.

Or consider the statement quoted earlier '. . . Therefore all we learn about the world is contained in *right versions of it.*' We may well ask what the 'rightness' of a theory consists in. Apart from telling us that 'rightness' is not being used in a moral sense, Goodman recommends credibility and coherence as the tests of correctness. Second, in his attempt to reconcile incompatible truths Goodman seems to overlook important distinctions. Take the second of his illustrations:

(a) 'The King of Sparta has two votes'.

(b) 'The King of Sparta has only one vote'.

This pair of propositions is expanded to:

(a1) 'According to Herodotus the King of Sparta had two votes'.

(b1) 'According to Thucidydes the King of Sparta had only one vote'.

It is clear that (a) and (b) are different propositions from (a1) and (b1) which latter are not incompatible at all. We may disdain to appeal to objective facts to settle the fate of propositions (a) and (b), but can we not ask the question whether (a1) and (b1) are really true? Did the two Greek historians really make the statements ascribed to them? We can carry on with verbalizations – oral and written – as long as we like but either we face an infinite regress or else we break out of the prison of language we have built for ourselves. The difficulty is exactly parallel to that faced by Carnap when he declared that we accept one particular system of sentences among many alternatives available because 'scientists of our culture circle accept it'.

Such irrealism in not of purely historical interest – at any rate not yet. The motive underlying its adoption has been, and continues to be aversion to realism with its representationism, and talk of objective, independent reality for our cognitions to correspond to. Rorty, for example, repudiates all such talk and accepts objectivity only if it means inter-subjectivity. In fact, he substitutes the latter for the former. The situation is not better for the realist if he substitutes sentences for cognitions and speaks of the relation of language to non-linguistic facts. It is this hostility to representative realism which draws together Rorty, Putnam, Davidson, etc. Their agreements and differences are discussed from Rorty's point of view, in the first three essays published in Rorty's recent *Truth and Progress*. The complex and labyrinthine debate is growing tiresome to many who are not either the participants or those with ring-side seats in the elite universities. But two broad issues stand out in the debate between realism and relativism.

Throughout the exchanges cited above, realism is identified with representationism and consequently saddled with the 'copy theory of truth'. But there is a variety of direct realism found in the writings of S. Alexander and the early writings of Moore and Russell. In the Indian tradition it is represented by the Nyāya view that, under ideal conditions, perception is a kind of revelation as contrasted with the Sāṁkhya which makes the mechanism of perception representational. This kind of realism allocates all 'contents' of perceptual experience to the world and leaves the mind-organism if you like – a purely contemplative and selective role. The view has its share of difficulties; the most important being (i) that the ideal conditions cannot be specified without circularity or arbitrariness, and (ii) that the view is not easy to reconcile with the network of causal relations revealed by physics and physiology to be involved in the genesis of our sensory experience. But if the theory can be worked out consistently, it is to be preferred to any form of contemporary relativism.

Second, the hostility to independent facts sometimes assumes strange forms. Originally the target was the alleged comparison between theories or assertion on the one hand and language-independent facts on the other. (The realist position is at times made impossible and absurd by the insinuation that he needs to compare our descriptions with undescribed facts!) By the time we have finished with representationism we have arrived at a rejection of the existence of independent facts in a sense which is ordinary, natural and taken for granted as a truism. Rorty, for example, distinguishes between two senses of 'accurate representation' – the philosophical, which is objectionable and the non-philosophical. In the latter sense

> to ask a witness if she has accurately represented a situation is to ask about her truthfulness and carefulness. When we say that good historians accurately represent what they find in archives, we mean they look hard for relevant documents, do not discard the documents tending to discredit . . . (their) thesis, do not misleadingly quote passages out of context, tell the same story among themselves as they tell us, and so on . . . (it) is to assume that she behaves in the way in which good, honest, historians behave. *It is not to assume anything about the reality of past events, or about the truth-conditions of statements concerning such events or about any other philosophical topic.*[7]

The concluding sentence is particularly surprising because apparently it is a return to the harsh and literal application of the verification principle whereas Rorty characterizes positivism in its heyday to have been as intolerant and fanatical as any intellectual movement. The entire passage is loaded with evaluative words which correctly summarize the qualifications of a good historian but, still speaking non-philosophically the qualifications are relevant because the person possessing them seeks to discover historical facts as far as that is humanly possible. Surely *all history is not concerned with archival material* even if our historian is, and takes herself to be concerned exclusively with documents. At some stage or other there must be historians who soil their hands with excavations, write down what they have witnessed, apply various recognized procedures to determine the date of artefacts, etc. They are creating primary sources of historiography.

Moreover we can raise the question whether our historian is as impeccable as she claims to be, perhaps, having become a social activist, she is tempering with her material? Idealism is a powerful motive, sometimes, for falsification whether or not she is doing so is settled not by what she says about herself nor by what others

---

[7] R. Rorty, *Truth and Progress*, Cambridge University Press, 1998, p. 17.

say about her but by finding out as well as can be, what she has been doing. All this is elementary and may not logically imply any philosophical theory – either realistic representationism or pragmatic relativism but it *does imply* that there are belief – independent facts which we can ascertain by agreed procedures. That the facts to be discovered are predominantly or even wholly linguistic does not make any difference to their independence. This process of asserting facts or *state of affairs* that prevail in the world will involve the use of language and the conceptual scheme embedded in it. But the outcome of our procedure will be decisively influenced by the non-linguistic component. Fact and belief, language and reality, scheme and content may be inseparable but they are distinguishable. In general any attempt to justify our claims about the world will involve predictions. We shall agree not to interpose experience between language and the world. Speech behaviour is all. We shall accept what is hardly contestable that the pursuit of truth and the pursuit of best justified beliefs are indistinguishable in practice. But whether the patterns of linguistic behaviour which would confirm or disconfirm my claim have really occurred or I simply make a further claim that they have, is to be found out. Moreover, that is not the end. My peers and fellow citizens may express assent out of politeness, cynical boredom or to please me because I have the power of patronage. The 'significance' of their behaviour has to be assessed, which can be done behaviouristically and banishing philosophical doubt. Contemporary relativists write as if this process – with its appeal to 'independent facts' – is practically unimportant or philosophically insignificant. To shock the intellectual bourgeoisie is a pleasant occupation and may be profitable even to the shocker if he realizes fully the implications of what he is saying.

Alternative systems of propositions – if we want to say something about the world by means of them – are not purely verbal constructions. An element of creative imagination is involved in scientific theories but they all contain statements which purport to be records of observation. We may have a great deal of liberty in choosing them, or changing and chopping them. Even this liberty is more limited than Quine imagines. If we plead illusion and hallucination, without any of the usual grounds for such a plea being present, we shall be guilty of arbitrariness. Though not fatal like inconsistency, arbitrariness, practised on a scale and in the manner required to hold on to a theory 'no matter what', would be nearly as bad. Our world-versions are not island fortresses in a sea of experience (referring to experience as 'boundary conditions' encourages the dominance of the above picture). The living waters of experience constantly make their incursion into them. We may soothe ourselves with the reflection that we can dethrone our observations – statements any time we like. But once, relatively to a system they are assigned this status, they exercise a directive and sometimes decisive influence. I suspect that the class of experimental propositions – 'pointer readings' in Eddington's words – would be very nearly the same in different theories. 'All we learn about the world is contained in right versions of it', only because we have made room for it in our formulations.

In the verse from Bhavabhūti quoted at the beginning, the first line expresses common sense. The second, uncommon nonsense. Common sense can be ignored except when it is challenged. The relativists, when they claim that the world in so far as its existence is admitted will bend itself to fit into *any garments* of theories we tailor for it, are uttering uncommon nonsense. Because the nonsense is uncommon it is valuable; in curing us of addiction to crudely realistic pictures of the world, and in promoting flexibility in our thinking and a willingness to consider – within wide limits – any explanations, however far-fetched they may seem initially. But to dispense with a world independent not only of our hopes and fears but also of our beliefs and disbeliefs is to invite disaster. The world seems ready enough to give us a long rope but, in the end, unless we are careful, it will hang us.

11

Putnam's Proposal for Logical Reform*

IN this brief paper I shall consider a specific proposal by Putnam to replace classical logic by quantum logic. There are many puzzles and controversies in this highly esoteric branch of mathematical physics. There is the debate concerning deterministic vs. statistical laws. There are the mysteries concerning the behaviour of the electron as revealed, for example, by the phenomenon of 'superposition' which suggest that an electron has passed through both of two apertures when the experimental set-up makes it possible for it to pass through only one of them. Finally, there is the principle of indeterminacy. It is impossible to determine, by the most sophisticated methods, both the position and the momentum of electron with precision. The more accurate the value of one of the variables, the less accurate correspondingly, is the value of the other. The product of the two errors is constant and this suggests that the imprecision is not due to practical limitations but is, somehow, inherent in the situation.

Suppose p_1 is the ascertained position of an electron and m_1, m_2, are its possible momenta. The very fact of ascertaining the position makes it possible (theoretically) which one of the possible momenta the electron has. It is therefore true in Quantum Mechanics (using p_1 and m_1, m_2 symbolize the statement concerning the precise position and alternative momenta of the electron) that p_1 and also that m_1, v m_2; but it is not ascertainable either that $p_1 \cdot m_1$ or that $p_1 \cdot m_2$. Thus the distributive law has to be jettisoned. The difficulty can be tackled by advancing scientific theories of a highly general and speculative character; the principle of complementarity is one of them.

---

* Published in the *Indian Philosophical Quarterly*, vol. XXIV, nos. 2-3, 2002.

Putnam, however, prefers to remove the difficulties by adopting an alternative to classical logic. He explicitly compares this move to the adoption of elliptical geometry, in place of Euclidean, by Einstein to deal with light rays passing through powerful gravitational fields – such as the sun's. Putnam's proposal is not the first proposal of its kind nor is it the first attempt at reforming logic. Way back in the 1930s, Neumann and Birkhoff proposed a logic without the principle of excluded middle. Their logic was not three-valued nor was it truth-functional. When Lukasiewicz expounded, fairly systematically, his three-valued logic, Reichenbach proposed the adoption of such a logic for the purpose of dealing with microcosmic phenomena. Putnam himself, in an earlier essay on three-valued logic, approved of this suggestion. Later on, however, he came to feel that this would not accomplish the desired result. In an eassay entitled 'Is Logic Empirical?', first published in 1968 and reprinted in the first volume of his 'Philosophical Papers' under the title *The Logic of Quantum Mechanics* he argued for his proposal to reject the distributive principle at some length.

He assumes that scientific theories including quantum mechanical theories are to be understood 'realistically'. That is to say, they are not to be understood in purely operational or instrumental terms. Nor are we to have recourse to purely ad hoc hypotheses or metaphysical assumptions concerning the relation between the observer and the observed. In the above symbolic example the electron has some particular momentum, though we cannot specify whether it is m_1 or m_2. Neither the momentum nor the position of the electron is brought into being by our methods of measurement. So it is true that $m_1 \vee m_2$ just as much as it is true that p_1. But it is not true either that $p_1 \cdot m_1$ or that $p_1 \cdot m_2$. Why does Putnam deny the truth of these conjunctions instead of their knowability? The reason seems to be that having ascertained the truth p_1, I cannot ascertain the truth of either m_1 or m_2 so that if I knew either $p_1 \cdot m_1$ or $p_1 \cdot m_2$ I would know a logical contradiction. Let us grant that the impossibility of knowing both the position and the momentum of an electron is a theoretical impossibility and not merely the result of our ignorance. This theoretical impossibility can, in a loose sense, be termed logical. But surely, even if we equate truth with knowability – which can be done with some necessary qualifications – it does not follow that anyone who knew either of the two conjunctions would be knowing a logical contradiction. Knowing what is false is impossible conceptually, and since a logical contradiction is the paradigm of falsity, it is logically impossible to know a contradiction. But every impossibility of knowledge does not reduce to knowledge of impossibility, so that we cannot equate 'impossible to know that *p*' with 'knowing *p* which is impossible'. Since the realism adopted by Putnam implies that m_1 v m_2 is not only meaningful but true, and p_1 is known to be true, the conjuctions $p_1 \cdot m_1$ and $p_2 \cdot m_2$ *can neither of them be regarded a logically contradictory* though knowing either of them can be regarded as logically contradictory in some sense. Putnam thus seems to be mixing up truth-values with noetic or epistemic values. Once this is realized it can be shown that there is no need to discard the distributive principle to avoid a contradiction in Quantum Mechanics. Let us use *Kp* to symbolize 'it is known that *p*'. Then the situation in Quantum Mechanics is summarized by the following three formulae:

1. Kp_1
2. $K (m_1 \text{ v } m_2)$
3. $\sim K (p_1 \cdot m_1) \cdot \sim K (p_1 \cdot m_2)$

A possible derivation of a contradiction could run as follows:

4. $Kp_1 \cdot K (m_1 \text{v } m_2)$ . . . 1, 2. Conjunction.
5. $K [p_1 \cdot (m_1 \text{ v } m_2)]$ . . . 4, by acceptable thesis of modal logic.[1]
6. $K [p_1 \cdot m_1 \, v \, (p_1 \cdot m_2]$ . . . 4, distribution.
7. $K (p_1 \cdot m_1) \, v \, K(p_1 \cdot m_2)$ . . . 6, distribution of *K*-sign over disjuncts (?)
8. $\sim [\sim K (p_1 \cdot m_1). \sim K (p_1 . m_2)]$ . . . 7, De Morgan's.

Step 8 contradicts the premiss 3.

---

[1] We treat the *K*-sign as formally analogous to the sign for logical necessity.

The sixth step in the attempted derivation is clearly fallacious. Since the *K*-sign is formally analogous to the necessity sign in modal logic and the universal quantifier in elementary predicate calculus, we can bring home the fallaciousness of the above step by noticing that,

1. $(x)\ (Fx \vee Gx) = [(x)\ Fx \vee (x)\ Gx]$.
2. $N\ (pvq) = (Np \vee Nq)$ are obviously fallacious though the converse implications are valid.

On the other hand, if we insist that p_1 and $m_1 \vee m_2$ are both true and $p_1 \cdot m_1$ and $p_1 \cdot m_2$ are both false in quantum logic, though not in classical logic, it can be shown, I think, that a contradiction results. Putnam, throughout his discussion, gives the impression that it is sufficient to sacrifice the distributive principle to remove anomalies from Quantum Mechanics. At any rate he does not mention any other principle that has to be jettisoned. On the other hand, he insists that we can retain a number of laws of classical logic including the principles of excluded middle, double negation, simplification, conjunction and addition. He also adds $P. \sim P$ never holds even in quantum logic. We may set up the following simple derivation.

1.	p_1	Premiss
2.	$m_1 \vee m_2$	Premiss
3.	$\sim (p_1 \cdot m_1). \sim (p_1 \cdot m_2)$	Premiss
4.	$\sim (p_1 \cdot m_1)$	3, simplification
5.	$\sim p_1 \vee \sim m_1$	4, De Morgan
6.	$\sim\sim p_1$	1, D.N.
7.	$\sim m_1$	5, 6 disjunctive syllogism.

By similar steps, from the second conjunct in 3 we obtain

8.	$\sim m_2$	
9.	$\sim m_1 \cdot \sim m_2$	7, 8, conjunction.
10.	$\sim (m_1 \vee m_2)$	9, De Morgan's.

Step 10 contradicts premiss 2.

The only principles used in the derivation, not explicitly

accepted by Putnam in his writings, are De Morgan's law and the principle of the disjunctive syllogism. The former is a thesis in the three-valued logic of Lukasiewicz as also in Heyting's system of intuitionist logic. The principle of the disjunctive syllogism is not a law of Lukasiewicz's system. I do not know what Putnam's attitude would be on admitting them into his version of quantum logic. The principle of D.N. is a law in Lukasiewicz's system and I have used that half of the equivalence which is acceptable to Brouwer. He will have to reject at least one of them. And it is likely that once this is done other revisions may be required. The cost of reforming logic may be heavier than Putnam imagines.

In the essay referred to above, as also in *Two Dogmas Revisited*, Putnam insists that alternative logics are on par with alternative geometries. And yet there is a crucial difference. On a physical interpretation the three geometries result in incompatible theorems. Neither intuitionist logic nor the three-valued logic of Lukasiewicz contains a thesis incompatible with any of the principles of classical logic. So far as I know, no attempt has been made to develop such a logic. So far as the three-valued logic is concerned the best description of the situation is to say that under the rules governing logical constants, extended to cover the intermediate value, some of the principles of classical logic cease to be tautologies. But then there is ample reason to believe that. The numerical values of the system represent, not truth values but certainly values or noetic values. Moreover, if logic can be changed and chopped to suit a particular inquiry, there is no reason why different logics should not be employed in different fields. Logical principles will then exhibit local or geographical variations. Leaping electrons may defy the distributive law but an ambitious father who wants for his daughter, an Iyer who is either a well-placed civil servant or a green-card holder, will be perfectly content with some young man who is both an Iyer and a well-placed civil servant or else both an Iyer and a green-card holder. And rightly so; satisfaction of either of the two formulations will fulfil his heart's desire and neither will give him anything more than the other.

12

Are There Alternative Logics?*

> In logic there are no morals. Everyone is at liberty to build up his own logic, i.e. his own form of language as he wishes. All that is required of him is that if he wishes to discuss it, he must state his methods clearly and give syntactical rules instead of philosophical arguments.[1]
>
> Logic is the common ground on which the partisans of Hartley and of Reid of Locke and of Kant may meet and join hands.[2]

I

It is a measure of the transformation of the philosophical scene in our times that the question constituting the title of this paper would not have been raised before the twenties of the twentieth century, and even if raised, would have been answered with and unhesitating 'No'. How can we reason and argue with one another and attempt to convince one another, it may be asked, unless we have a common conception of what constitutes a valid argument and universally accepted canons to which we can appeal in evaluating arguments? If logic is a systematic investigation of the principles of reasoning whose validity is independent of varying topics of discussion, do we not destroy the very basis of rational debate if we allow that we

---

* Published in *Realism: Response and Reactions – Essays in Honour of P.K. Sen*, eds. Sandhya Basu and D.P. Chattopadhyaya, Madhabendra Nath Misra, Ranjan Mukhopadhyay, New Delhi: ICPR, 2000.

1 R. Carnap, *Logical Syntax of Language*, New York: Harcourt Brace, 1937, p. 17.

2 J.S. Mill, *A System of Logic*, London: Longman, Green and Co., 1843, section 17.

can choose between alternative logics to suit either our purposes or a special field of investigation in which we may be interested? And yet there are eminent mathematicians and logicians who have maintained precisely such a relativist view of logic; and some of them have made outstanding contributions to the areas of human knowledge which are paradigms of deductive excellence.

The main source of this change in attitude to logic is the general theory of a priori propositions which equates them with analytic propositions and explains their necessity as a product of linguistic rules. This conventionalist view has been inspired by Wittgenstein's characterization of logical and mathematical truths as tautologies devoid of any factual content. Surprisingly in the *Tractatus* Wittgenstein adopts an 'absolutist' view of logic though in his later philosophy he swung totally towards conventionalism. As evidence of the logical absolutism of the *Tractatus*, consider the well-known declaration: 'Logic is the investigation of all regularity; and outside logic all is accident'. Or 'Logical propositions describe the scaffolding of the world or rather they present it. They "treat" of nothing.'[3]

It is not necessary to go over the beaten track of the debate between conventionalists and their opponents. The arguments on both sides are familiar and the result seems to be a weary stalemate. But once we adopt the general view that certain allegedly synthetic and necessary propositions are vacuous tautologies it seems natural to extend it to logical principles. And yet this tactic of prescribing 'the mixture as before' encounters special difficulties in the case of logical truths. As Frege's definition of analytic truth specifies, and Ayer's explanation of their undeniability clearly implies, linguistic rules of our adoption are *only one base* of their necessary character; the other base being certain logical principles, particularly the law of non-contradiction. These principles cannot themselves be treated as analytic consequences of the adoption of certain rules for the

---

[3] L. Wittgenstein, *Tractatus Logico Philosophicus*, tr. P. Geach and M. Black, The Humanities Press, 1961, Proposition 6.12.

use of logical words, at any rate not in the same sense as in the case of non-logical words. It does not help much to add, as Strawson does, that these words are topic-neutral and occur pervasively in all types of discourse. Curiously this simple point is not appreciated sufficiently either by conventionalists or their opponents.

The logical fundamentalist, is for the most part, content to rely upon an argument which is the obverse of the just mentioned consideration. If logical principles are the consequence of linguistic rules, the derivation of the former from the latter involves logical principles which are not the products of our stipulations; otherwise, we are launched on an infinite regress. In general, anyone who sets forth certain premises and draws out their consequences, or following Carnap's advice specifies a language lays down its formation and transformation rules and proceeds to apply them, must conform to rules involving notions of implications, negation, generality, etc., and the need for such rules remains, however far we may proceed in making our stipulations, stipulations about these stipulations and so on. Quine, who in spite of his thoroughgoing relativism, sets forth this argument in 'Truth by Convention', tries to obviate the absolutism implicit in the argument by remarking that universal, non-conventional rules boil down, in the end, to generally accepted beliefs and practices or generally prevalent patterns of speech behaviours.[4]

This argument may be reinforced by pointing out that the validity or invalidity of an argument does not vary with the language in which it is expressed. As Quine notes in his *Philosophy of Logic*, logical rules do not take their colouring from the local features of diverse languages.[5] Even if logic is grammar, it is universal grammar to which all symbolisms whose goal is effective communication, must conform. With a few exceptions like Putnam, who maintains

---

4 W.V.O. Quine, 'Truth by Convention', in his *Ways of Paradox and Other Essays*, Cambridge, MA: Harvard University Press, 1976.

5 W.V.O. Quine, *Philosophy of Logic*, Engelwood Cliffs, NJ: Prentice-Hall, 1970.

not only that we can chop and change our logic to suit a particular field of investigation such as quantum mechanics but also that our choice is finally justified on empirical grounds, most conventionalist conform in practice, to the logic which according to Mill, is the common meeting ground of all thinkers. They are not in a hurry to bring the world down on their heads. Quine's discussion of 'deviant logics' is a particularly amusing instance. He combines revolutionary rhetoric with conservative practice thus adapting for philosophy of logic Disraeli's recipe for sound government.

Moreover his arguments are pretty mixed up. If, as he argues, convincingly, the deviant logician is faced with the predicament that 'when he tries to deny the doctrine he only changes the subject',[6] then there is no alternative to 'our' logic. It is worse than pointless to reject the adoption of a truth functional or non-truth functional three-valued logic to accommodate the puzzles of quantum mechanics on grounds of simplicity and convenience. The price is perhaps not quite prohibitive, but the returns had better be good, he remarks.[7] But what possible returns, even in an imaginary situation, can compensate for the disruption of classical logic? This is like a teetotaller refusing to drink a glass of wine on principle and then adding that the occasion is not grand enough or that the expected benefits paltry.

I do not find it particularly objectionable to say that the laws of logic are linguistic rules provided we recognize that they are non-arbitrary and that we don't make them, any more than we fabricate relations between numbers.[8] To regard them as essential principles underlying all symbolism is less misleading than to regard them, like Blanchard, as the most general laws of reality. The latter may suggest that they are of the same kind as the generalizations and theories of empirical sciences. The linguistic theory of necessary

---

6 Quine, *Philosophy of Logic*.

7 Ibid.

8 We may recollect Strawson's pronouncement that it is we, the makers of language, who make inconsistency possible.

truths goes with the view that these can be constituted and reconstituted by modifying our usage. It is this relativism which seems untenable in the case of logic. To focus concretely on some of the issues and arguments sketched above, I shall discuss at some length Lukasiewicz's three-valued logic.

II

It was in 1920 that Lukasiewicz, the polish logician attempted to construct a system of three-valued logic to solve the problem of future contingents raised by Aristotle in the 9th chapter of *On Interpretation*. Aristotle is here concerned with propositions about future events whose occurrence or outcome is not yet determined. He is convinced that there are such events for otherwise 'there would be no need to deliberate or take trouble, on the supposition that if we should adopt a certain result would follow, while if we did not, the result would not follow'. Since the truth or falsity of propositions is determined by their relation to facts, Aristotle argues, 'it is evident that when in future events there is a real alternative and potentiality in contrary directions the corresponding affirmation and denial have the same character'. While he admits that 'everything must either be or not be, be about to be or not to be' he also says, 'it is not necessary that of every affirmation and denial of opposed statements one should be true and the other false. For in the case of that which exists potentially but not actually the rule which applied to that which exists actually does not hold good.' At first sight it may appear that Aristotle here rejects the application of the law of excluded middle to future contingents. But his insistence that 'everything must either be or not be, be about to be or not to be', clearly implies that the law of excluded middle is applicable no less to future events than to past and present ones. Rather he seems to be rejecting the principle of bivalence – the principle that every statement is either true or false while retaining the law of excluded middle. To take his own example, though it is not already definitely true or definitely false that there will be a sea-battle tomorrow, nevertheless the entire disjunction 'either there will be a sea-battle tomorrow or there will not be a sea-battle tomorrow' is definitely true.

Prior summarizes his in *Formal Logic*[9] Ockham's fascinating discussion of neutral propositions, that is, propositions which are neither true nor false but indeterminate – in the context of divine omniscience. But it was only in comparatively recent times that Lukasiewicz has elaborated systematically a propositional logic which allows for the indeterminate propositions. Let p symbolize the assertion with respect to any such event that it will occur and $\sim p$ will be its denial. 'The statements under consideration' Lukasiewicz writes, 'are therefore neither true nor false and must have a third value different from **0** or the false and from **1** or the true. We indicate this by ½: it is the "possible" which goes as a third value with the false and the true. This is the train of thought which gave rise to the three-valued system of propositional logic.'[10]

If the variables of our system admit of three values then the familiar truth functions will have to be redefined or rather the old definitions to be extended to cover the cases where one or more of the variables take the intermediate value. This is done as follows:

i. $\sim p$ is true if and only if p is false and false if and only if p is true. Otherwise they both have the value ½.
ii. $(p \supset q)$ is false if and only if p is true and q is false. It is true if the antecedent is equal to or less than that of the consequent. In other cases it is equal to.
iii. A disjunction $p \vee q$ will have the same value as the disjuncts if these are uniform, otherwise the higher of the two values.
iv. A conjunction $p \cdot q$ is to have the same value as its conjuncts if their values are uniform, otherwise it has the lower of the two values.

It will be seen that the definitions are so doctored that if the arguments take either of the two extreme values, the values of the function are the same as those in the classical or two-valued

---

9 A.N. Prior, *Formal Logic*, part III, chap. 2, Oxford University Press, 1955, 1962, p. 241.

10 W.C. Kneale and M. Kneale, *Development of Logic*.

logic. The result may be summarized conveniently by means of the following matrices:

p	$\sim p$
1	0
½	½
0	1

$p \supset q$	1	½	0
1	1	½	0
½	1	1	½
0	1	1	1

$p \vee q$	1	½	0
1	1	1	1
½	1	½	½
0	1	½	0

$p \cdot q$	1	½	0
1	1	½	0
½	½	½	0
0	0	0	0

Lukasiewicz goes on to lay down general rules for defining 'negation' and 'implication' in any n-valued system.

I. $\sim p = 1 - p$.

II(a). $(p \supset q) = 1$ for $p \leq q$.

II(b). $(p \cdot q) = (1 - p) + q$ for $p > q$.

As may be expected, certain formulae which are tautological in two-valued system cease to be so in three-valued logic. One such is the law of excluded middle: $p \vee \sim p$ which, it is easy enough to see, takes the value ½ when p is ½ and consequently $\sim p$ too is equal to ½. In addition, following are some of the important theses of two-valued logic which cease to hold in the three-valued system.

1. $(\sim p \supset p) \supset p$
2. $(p \supset \sim p) \supset \sim p$
3. $[(p \supset q) \cdot \sim q] \supset \sim p$
4. $[(p \supset (q \supset r)] \equiv [(p \cdot q) \supset r)]$.

The last – the principle of exportation – is a rather surprising casualty. When p and q both take the value ½ and r is equal to zero, the RHS = ½ whereas the LHS = 1. And from the failure of this equivalence arises one of the oddities of the system – namely, that the principle of modus tollens (formula 3 above) is not a law though the principle of transposition, $(p \supset q) \supset (\sim q \supset \sim p)$ is. The two versions of the *reduction a absurdum* principle fail to come out true when p has the value ½. The third formula takes the value ½ when $p = 1$ and $q = ½$. In the system of intuitionist logic axiomatized by Heyting and approved by Brouwer as a manual of logical principles for mathematical reasoning too, $p \vee \sim p$ is neither an axiom nor a theorem. In Lukasiewicz's system the principle of double negation is a thesis but in Heyting's calculus $p \supset \sim\sim p$ is a thesis but the converse is not.

It is not necessary to carry any further this process of sorting out formulae which cease to be theses when we pass from two-valued to three-valued logic. Philosophically, the most important question is whether three-valued logic is, in any important sense, an alternative to classical logic. Prior writes,

> and should the view that there are neutral propositions be accepted, not only the law of excluded middle but the whole structure of two-valued propositional logic can be preserved by the understanding that the propositions substitutable for its variables are only those referring to matters of present, past or otherwise determinate fact.[11]

Prior does not express any opinion on whether there are adequate or even plausible reasons for accepting the view that there are neuter propositions. Rosser and Turquette in their course of an introductory dialogue in their book *Many-valued Logics* suggest that there are plausible examples of such propositions.[12] Only a dogmatic stipulation, they aver, will enable us to rule out a third and intermediate value for propositions. The spirit of scientific adventure however demands that we keep our minds open on this

---

11 Prior, *Formal Logic*, p. 250.

12 J.B. Rosser and A.R. Turquette, *Many-valued Logics*, Amsterdam: North Holland Publishers, 1952.

question. They argue and go on to address themselves to the task of sketching a formal framework for any many-valued logic. Their philosophical comments as also the remarks by Prior quoted earlier clearly imply that classical logic may not have that universality of application which has been claimed for it as a matter of course. If indeed there are areas where the principles of the *PM* (*Principia Mathematica*) system or that of Frege or Lukasiewicz's own version of classical logic have to be modified and other principles employed then three-valued logic or some system of many-valued logic is a genuine alternative to classical logic. But it is doubtful whether this is really the case.

III

To begin with we may approach this problem by considering the formal relations between classical logic and Lukasiewicz's proposed alternative. The three-valued system is a proper part of the two-valued system in the sense that every thesis of three-valued logic is also a thesis of two-valued logic; but there are formulae which are theses of classical logic but are not theses in the system of three-valued logic. Classical logic contains three-valued logic and it has been conjectured that an infinitely *many-valued* logic is related to three-valued logic in the same way.

Tarski has in fact demonstrated that there can be only one consistent and complete extension, namely the ordinary two-valued logic, for any formal system which employs the usual rules of substitution and detachment and contains the following theorems:

1. $p \supset \sim\sim p$.
2. $q \supset (p \supset q)$.
3. $\sim p \supset (p \supset q)$.
4. $p \supset [\sim q \supset \sim (p \supset q)]$.

And these formulae are theses not only in Lukasiewicz's system but also Heyting's system of intuitionist logic. Tarski's proof in outline is as follows: Employing the language of set theory and treating a deductive system as a set of sentences he defines (a) the set of consequences of any given set of sentences, (b) consistency of a set of sentences, and (c) completeness of a sentential set. The first major step in the proof is a theorem established by Lindenbaum, that every consistent deductive system can be extended to form a consistent and complete system. The next step is to show that for any given system *X*, there exists one and only one system *Y* which included *X* and is consistent and complete. And finally in a series of theorems with regard to alternative versions of the propositional calculus some of which employ only the sign of material implication, or both, negation and material implication, or the signs of conjunction and disjunction in addition to those of implication and negation, he shows that if any of these is enlarged to form a consistent and complete system the result is the classical propositional calculus.[13] It therefore appears in the words of W.C. Kneale and Martha Kneale,

> that even from a purely formal point of view the ordinary two-valued system has a unique status among deductive systems that can plausibly be called logic, since it contains all others as fragments of itself.[14]

If we turn to the nature of the intermediate truth-value symbolized by ½, Lukasiewicz suggests that it represents 'the possible' which goes as a third truth-value coordinate with truth and falsity. However it is very difficult to pin-point the precise sense in which he uses the word 'possible'. Quite obviously the word does not stand for purely logical modality. In this sense the statement that '*p* is possible' is implied by but does not imply the truth of *p* so that the statement '*p* is possible' can be regarded as true even when *p* is false. Lukasiewicz so understands 'possibility' that the possibility of *p* is incompatible with its falsity. Thus he is not using the words, 'possible', 'necessary', 'impossible', etc. in the same sense as C.I. Lewis in his system of strict implication. Adopting a suggestion

---

13 A. Tarski and J. Corcoran, *Logic, Semantics and Metamathematics: Papers from 1923 to 1938*, ed. Hackett, tr. J.H. Woodger, Oxford University Press, 1st edn., 1956, 1983, pp. 393-400.

14 W.C. Kneale and M. Kneale, *Development of Logic*, p. 575.

of his pupil Alfred Tarski, he defines possibility in the following way: $\Diamond p = (\sim p \supset p)$, where the diamond sign, following C.I. Lewis' notation, symbolizes 'it is possible that'. Using this definition and the sign for 'negation', 'necessity', 'impossibility' and 'contingency' are defined in the usual way and with satisfactory results. However a consequence of the definition is that '$\Diamond p$' comes out false when p is false. There is, no doubt, a usage of the word 'possible' in which a man cannot say for example that it is possible that his wife is at the theatre when he knows it for a fact that she is in the kitchen. For in this sense, what is possible is not merely that which is free from self-contradiction but that which is not known to be false. If so, given the usual definitions of modal concepts, the necessity in this context, means that which is known to be true, and the impossible, that which is known to be false. The contingent will be that which is neither known to be true nor known to be false. Thus the three numerical values represent noetic or knowledge-values or as suggested by W.C. Kneale and Martha Kneale[15] 'certainty values'. (Formally the two interpretations give the same results for knowledge is justified certainty.) The three-valued system could then be interpreted according to the table:

K = Known that. . . .

C = Certain that. . . .

$p = 1 = Kp$ or Cp

$p = \frac{1}{2} = \sim Kp \cdot \sim K \sim p$ or $\sim Cp \cdot \sim C \sim p]$

$p = 0 = K \sim p$ or $C \sim p$.

But on this interpretation, which seems to be the only plausible one in terms of propositions, the system *does not turn out* to be an alternative to classical logic. To quote to Kneales' once again. 'But so far from requiring us to abandon our ordinary two-valued logic this interpretation presupposes the ordinary distinctions of truth and falsity and the ordinary use of the word "not".' Applying the

15 W.C. Kneale and M. Kneale, *Development of Logic*, pp. 573-74.

device of the square of opposition we can exhibit the relations of the various expressions as follows:

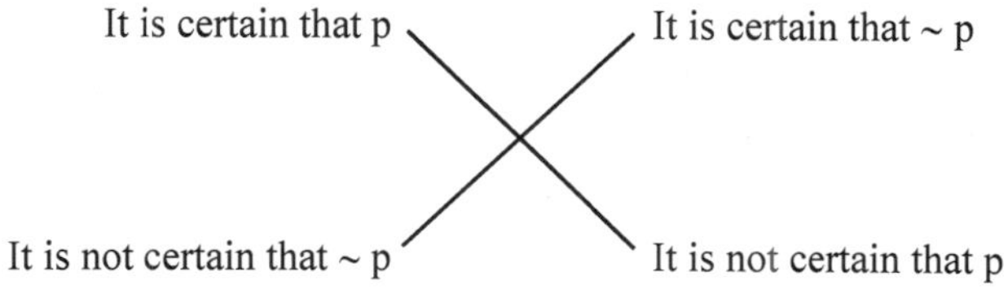

After explaining the formal relations between the various statements which are completely analogous to the relations between the *A, E, I, O* propositions of the traditional square of opposition, they comment,

> these relations are similar to those holding between the four modal expressions 'necessary', 'impossible', 'possible' and 'non-necessary'; and this is not surprising since 'certain' may be taken as an abbreviation for 'necessary in relation to what we know'. But what is logical here is the general notion of 'necessity' (or the notion of 'possibility' which may be taken instead as fundamental in the analysis), not the notion of knowledge and although pure modal functions cannot be defined by truth-tables like the functions of two-valued primary logic, they do not require a theory which is alternative to that of two-valued primary logic.[16]

While agreeing with this conclusion in the quoted passage, I would like to point out that even as expression of the theory of certainty values, the system seems to suffer from a grave defect. Though certainty-values are distinct from truth-values the two are interconnected and in certain procedures of reasoning they are brought together. If we look at the table for the implication given by Lukasiewicz we find that when $p = \frac{1}{2}$ and $q = 0$, $p \supset q = \frac{1}{2}$. That is to say, the system does not justify the rejection of a proposition on the ground that it leads to a false consequence. That is odd and appear to be contrary to certain well-entrenched and intuitively satisfactory methods of reasoning. Suppose p is a proposition which is not known to be true or false and is therefore 'possible'

16 W.C. Kneale and M. Kneale, *Development of Logic*, pp. 573-74.

in the sense defined by Lukasiewicz. Suppose further that p, either singly, or in conjunction with other true propositions, implies q in that sense of implication which we recognize intuitively in concrete instances of valid inference; then if q turns out to be false or is incompatible with a third proposition r which is known to be true, we would unhesitatingly reject p. In other words, we never allow that an implication with a false consequent can be other than false unless the antecedent itself is false. It may be argued that reasoning by *modus tollens* presupposes the principle of bivalence and that once the latter is abandoned we should not expect every rule to be authenticated in the same old way. This criticism may be considered as pinpointing – what is obvious in any case – that not all theses of two-valued logic survive in a two-valued system. It seems to me however that there is more to it than underlining the obvious. It is, of course, well known that all the truth functional signs defined in classic logic depart in meaning from their counterparts in ordinary language in varying degrees – the sign of implication more than others. But for all its paradoxical departures from ordinary usage, material implication taken in conjunction with other signs, preserves all the principles of reasoning, such as the transitivity of implication, *modus tollens*, etc., which we cannot help using in our reasoning.

Many persons find talk about alternative logics plausible and even attractive because of the development of alternative geometries. There is, however, a crucially important difference between the two cases. The two systems of non-Euclidean geometry were developed (in the second half of the nineteenth century) by modifying the parallels postulate in two conceivable ways when it was realized that the postulate was independent of the others. The modifications result in the development of two alternative systems whose theses are different from and incompatible with those of Euclid. (Indeed the earliest proofs of some of the theorems of non-Euclidean geometry were given by mathematicians who wanted to prove the parallels postulate by showing that its denial leads to absurdities). *It is not in this fashion that alternative logics have been developed or even an attempt made to develop them.* So much could have been gathered from the standard independence proofs for a system of the propositional calculus. The technique employed is that of interpretation or construction of models. Numerical interpretations are generally used. The elements of the system are taken to represent a group of numerical values. The constants of the system are specified by a scheme of interpretation. When the postulates are interpreted according to this scheme it turns out that all but one of them have a 'preferred' or 'distinguished' value – but this is not the case with the remaining postulate. It can also be shown that the rules of substitution and detachment, the permitted procedures of transformation, preserve the distinguished value of any formulae to which they may be applied. This is an effective demonstration of the non-derivability of a given postulate from the other. But it is important to notice that in constructing our models, it is necessary to use more than two numerical values so that the numbers 1, 0, etc. *do not stand for truth-values* and sometimes we admit more than one 'preferred' or 'distinguished' value. In short we do not combine the negation of one of the postulates with remaining to deduce theorems which are different from and inconsistent with the theses of classical logic. Since every one of our postulates is a tautology, the denial of any one of them is bound to result in contradiction.

It would seem then that there are no genuine alternatives to classical logic and the attempt to present the three-valued system as one is open to fatal objection. Advocates of its claims to be a rival to two-valued logic as a guide to reasoning (at any rate in certain fields) single out the law of excluded middle for rejection but they are too shy to point out that *the law of non-contradiction 'breaks down' in the system in exactly the same way and under the same truth conditions*. For some reason the principle appears to be more intimidating than the law of excluded middle. It is important to notice that in the alleged alternative system no less than in two-valued logic, to be a law is to take the preferred value 1 always. They cease to be tautologies under the rules of the extended definitions. Philosophers who are troubled by Aristotle's problem about future contingents or mathematicians like Brouwer who find certain methods of proof employed by Cantor objectionable and demand 'constructive' proofs must find other solutions to their worries. To reject logical principles to solve these problems or any others is to go about the business like the Lamb's Chinaman, who burnt down his house to roast his pig.

N.G. Kulkarni at Different Phases

CHANCELLOR'S GOLD MEDALISTS

Wilson College students have won the Chancellor's Gold Medal eleven times and we are proud to present here the photographs and brief records of the recent recipients.

Mr. N. G. KULKARNI
1954 — Philosophy

Mr. Kulkarni was also awarded the Bai Barkbai Popatlal Ghelabai Vallabh Vedanta Prize. Now a Lecturer in the Department of Philosophy, Wilson College, he shows the same lucidity of thinking and expression in his teaching as he did during his outstanding undergraduate and M.A. career.

fig. 1: The 1954 recipient of the coveted Chancellor's Gold Medal

fig. 2: A very young Kulkarni, in the august company of his teachers

fig. 3: With Professors: Mr and Mrs Borde & family, Rajam, Mrs Ookerjee, Karani

fig. 4: With Prof. Ookerjee and Prof. Lavande: the formidable trio of Wilson College, Philosophy Department

fig. 5a: 'YES I DO' says the couple with the blessings of the parents

fig. 5b: 'YES I DO' says the couple with the blessings of the parents

fig. 6: The family in full strength with the newly-wedded couple

fig. 7: A romantic farewell by wife before departure to Oxford

fig. 8: Trying out the snowballing effect!

fig. 9: The Perfect Couple: Looking at the world with tinted glasses

fig. 10: Stalwarts of the philosophy fraternity at Chubb's Study Circle, captured in a happy mood

fig. 11: Greeting Dr Chubb on his birthday around 1991

fig. 12: Prof. N.G. Kulkarni inaugurating the Philosophy Association at the Ramniranjan Jhunjhunwala College, and being felicitated by the Principal G.D. Joshi in the year 1991-92

fig. 13: A doting grandfather

III. Ethics and Religion

Introduction

Rita Doctor

LISTENING to Prof. N.G. Kulkarni's lectures at the MA class had left all of us enthralled. Whether it was Indian/Western/Classical or Contemporary philosophy, words just kept flowing out of his mouth (hardly having notes or books for reference). And we often used to wonder 'how one small head could carry all he knew!' Later, listening to him at various seminars and the Bombay Philosophical Society sessions was a veritable treat and, today, I feel honoured that I am able to contribute in a very small way to the compilation of this book.

The introductory chapter in this section begins with the article, 'Definition, Nature and Scope of Ethics', which could be read very profitably even by a layperson. The distinction between positive and normative ethics is explained in simple language and a brief reference is made to philosophical ethics which deals with the meaning of ethical terms, the significance of moral judgements and their relation to other types of judgements.

The second chapter on 'Objectivity in Ethical Judgements' begins with the question whether moral judgements could be called judgements at all. Prof. Kulkarni then goes on to discuss the pros and cons of naturalistic and non-naturalistic views; why the objectivist is in a slightly stronger position, and that in matters of moral dispute the views of the 'morally sensitive' are more to be relied on than those of the 'insensitive'. Those interested in Contemporary Philosophy should find this chapter useful.

The third chapter 'The Place of Reason in Morality' is a 'must read' for both the beginner and the keen student of philosophy, since it considers seriously the issue of scepticism about value judgements in general and moral judgements in particular. In this context Prof. Kulkarni works out some of the principles underlying the objective and rational character of moral judgements.

The fourth chapter 'Freedom and Violence' is an extremely readable chapter and should appeal to anyone with an analytic mind. After defining the two terms – 'Freedom' and 'Violence' – Prof. Kulkarni makes a few pertinent suggestions: (a) We need to explore alternatives to violence, (b) it is not advisable to use evil to bring about a good, and (c) force should never degenerate into mindless violence. The last chapter 'Setting Terms to God' discusses the traditional answers to the problem of evil and the references are to both Indian and Western philosophers. Prof. Kulkarni was fond of describing himself as an 'agnostic', a 'timid fence-sitter' – that was often reflected in his lectures and also comes out clearly in this chapter. He badly wanted 'some faint glimmer of a special awakening', so that the whole world would have taken on a 'different colouring', but sadly, that did not happen.

Unfortunately, that is the inevitable fate of the atheist and the agnostic!

1

Definition, Nature and Scope of Ethics

THE starting point of ethics or moral philosophy are judgements that we pass on human conduct in everyday life concerning right and wrong, good and evil. We pronounce that certain types of action are right and certain other types of action are wrong. For example, telling the truth is right, but cruelty is wrong. Apart from the keywords 'right', 'wrong', 'good' and 'evil' other terms like 'duty', 'obligation', 'ought', etc. also figure in such judgements. Usually these judgements are passed with uncritical confidence. We accept the standards of right and wrong prevalent in our community and apply them to familiar situations. But sometimes the situation is unusual and calls for reflection. There may be situations where we cannot tell the truth without endangering the life of an innocent person or keep a promise without neglecting a suffering person who needs our help. Whenever there is such a conflict of duties we begin to wonder which moral rule we should follow. Another source of moral reflection is the fact that the moral codes of even civilized communities differ on certain points. Islam permits polygamy in certain circumstances but Christianity insists upon monogamy at all times. We may then wonder which type of marriage is the ideal or the right type of marriage. When we engage in reflection to resolve our moral dilemmas, we are but a short step away from moral philosophy. The moral philosopher, unlike the ordinary man who wants to solve his particular problems, aims at discovering the general principles underlying our moral judgements.

Moral philosophy may therefore be defined as an attempt to reflect upon our moral judgements in order to arrive at a system of clear and consistent rules or principles of conduct. It aims at removing the difficulties and apparent inconsistencies in our moral thinking. It raises questions concerning the meaning of terms like 'right', 'wrong', 'good', 'evil', etc. as used in the moral context. It also discusses whether all our particular moral rules can be derived from a common universal standard or whether we have to accept a plurality of moral rules. If the latter, how are we to resolve the problem of conflicting moral rules? Again what is the object of moral judgement – act, motive, intention or consequences? The answers to these and other fundamental questions are not independent of one another but form a system of interlocking doctrines.

It is also common to define ethics as 'the normative science of the conduct of human beings living in societies'. The term 'conduct' here refers not to all actions but to voluntary actions involving a choice. Purely physiological actions like blood circulation or reflex actions like the knee-jerk do not come within the scope of the moral judgement. Simple instinctive actions, though voluntary in principle, are not judged morally. Conduct therefore is the sum total of actions involving a choice that can be criticized, praised or blamed.

Ethics is said to be normative because its principles formulate certain 'norms' or 'standards' or 'ideals' referring to which human conduct can be assessed or evaluated. Moral laws do not describe how men actually behave but rather how they ought to behave it they want to lead the good life. Apart from ethics, logic and aesthetics too are normative sciences, the former deals with principles of valid thinking and the latter with standards of beauty and ugliness. A normative science is contrasted with a positive science like physics, psychology or sociology, which deals with phenomena as they occur in the world. Every positive science aims at description and causal explanation. It gathers facts by observation and experiment, classifies them and finally attempts to explain them with the help of generalization and theories. It is not concerned with judging or evaluating facts. Psychology for example deals with human conduct. But the psychologist *qua* psychologist does not concern himself with whether the conduct described by him is morally good or bad.

But the two types of science are related to one another. Ethics cannot ignore what psychology tells us about desire, voluntary decision, character, etc. We cannot pass judgement on conduct without understanding its nature and the various factors involved in it. It is a matter of common experience that our moral judgement may be revised if our appreciation of the facts of a case is changed. Equally, a sociologist or psychologist cannot ignore men's moral beliefs and ideals in describing human behaviour for these are among the factors that determine human behaviour.

Positive Ethics, Normative Ethics, Philosophical Ethics

The central part of ethics is normative in character. It is an attempt to formulate a set of consistent norms or ideals of human conduct. But there can also be a positive science of ethics. We can survey the moral beliefs and practices of different communities trace their development and finally try to correlate changing moral beliefs and practices with economic, geographical, biological and other factors. Such an inquiry deals with the facts of moral experience and behaviour in a purely descriptive fashion. It does not deal with the problem of, which of these moral principles is rationally justified or worthy of acceptance. Hobhouse's 'Morals in evolution' is a classic example of such a study.

Normative ethics of course is the attempt to formulate clearly rationally acceptable principles of conduct. It does not merely state or describe moral standards. It tries to determine whether a set of moral principles is valid and therefore acceptable. Finally there is philosophical or metaphysical ethics. According to traditional philosophers this inquiry deals with the question of the final justification of moral principles. It deals with the place of moral principles in the total scheme of Reality. It also critically considers the presuppositions of morality and tries to discover how far they are valid. For example, moral judgements on conduct presuppose that the moral agent is free to choose between right and wrong. Philosophical ethics discusses whether and in what sense, this freedom is a fact.

Many contemporary philosophers however take a different view of philosophical ethics. According to them it is a conceptual inquiry which analyses the meaning of ethical terms and their interrelations. It deals with the nature or significance of moral judgement and how moral judgements are related to other types of judgement. Such an inquiry answers neither factual nor normative questions. Its aim is "the elucidation (clarification) of the logic of moral discourse".

2

Objectivity in Ethical Judgements

AMONG contemporary philosophers of analysis in the English-speaking world it is now orthodox to maintain that moral judgements are not, in the logical sense, judgements at all. They are not propositions capable of truth or falsity in the ordinary sense. They are not descriptions either of natural or of non-natural qualities of actions, experiences and states of affairs mentioned in them. Moral discourse, we are told, is part of practical discourse and ethical sentences perform a variety of practical functions such as expressing and evoking attitudes, commending, advising, evaluating, commanding and so on. This new subjectivism has developed partly as a reaction to the non-naturalism of writers like Moore, Ross and Broad which it finds unsatisfactory, and partly out of a new interest in the non-cognitive or emotive functions of language. Non-descriptivism in ethics can take various forms. There is the analysis of ethical judgements in terms of expression of attitudes originally put forward by Ayer and Stevenson. (This attitudinarian analysis has been developed and defended with characteristic patience and subtlety by Price in his *Gifford Lectures on Belief*.) Second, there is the imperative or injunctional analysis developed by R. Carnap and R.M. Hare. In addition there are the not easily classifiable contributions by Toulmin and Nowell-Smith, the latter suggesting a 'multi-track' analysis of ethical judgements. In this brief paper I cannot deal with even the essentials of these different forms of non-descriptivism much less can I discuss, even cursorily, all the important issues raised in one of the liveliest branches of contemporary philosophy. I propose to do two things first. I shall try to show that the arguments put forward by non-cognitivists against non-naturalism (or intuitionism as it is rather misleadingly called) are not so strong as might appear at first sight. Second, I shall try to bring out certain strong points of the objectivist which tend to be ignored.

We will confine our discussion to the analysis of sentences expressing judgement of intrinsic goodness such as '*X* is good' or judgements of intrinsic-rightness (if there are any such) such as '*A* is right'. If we reject naturalistic analyses of such judgements and of the meaning of the predicates figuring in them, and yet maintain that they express assertions we seem to be committed to the following propositions:

1. The predicate terms in these judgements stand for unique non-empirical properties termed by Moore 'non-natural'.
2. The subject terms, of course, stand for experiences, or actions, etc. which are desirable in empirical or natural terms. Now it is very implausible to maintain that such judgements are inductive generalizations. Therefore if they are assertions at all, they express necessary and synthetic connections between certain good-making or right-making characteristics on the one hand and moral goodness or rightness on the other.
3. As a consequences of 1 and 2 we have to appeal to intuition to deduct the presence of non-natural qualities and also to perceive the necessary connection between certain empirical properties and the rightness or goodness which is supervenient upon them.

   Now many contemporary philosophers find these epistemological requirements impossible to accept, if not unintelligible. Synthetic necessary propositions in particular evoke contemptuous dismissal. Apart from these considerations, it is desirable to avoid postulating qualities and connections of a wholly new kind which are not supported by our experience in other fields. To this general principle of philosophical parsimony there can be no objections in principle. However, if the correct analysis of moral judgements is controversial, and if further we find that an objectivist analysis of them does most justice to our moral experience, then to object to non-empirical concepts and synthetic necessary connections on the ground that our *non-moral* experience provides no examples of them, is not very pertinent. The question – begging character of this procedure – comes out clearly in S. Toulmin's argument in *The Place of Reason in Ethics*. Toulmin classifies all properties into (i) simple, (ii) complex, and (iii) causal properties. He then argues in detail that 'goodness' does not fit into any of these categories and concludes that, there cannot be a property of the sort alleged by Moore. Since the three classes of qualities are all derived from the field of empirical experience the argument can hardly be regarded as conclusive.

Perhaps the strongest argument against non-naturalism is that, in the end, it is defective in the same way as naturalism. The latter is unacceptable because it turns ethical statements into purely factual or theoretical statements and thus deprives them of their peculiarly ethical force. Let us grant that there are unique properties such as 'goodness', 'rightness' and 'obligatoriness' and that certain actions and experiences are characterized by these qualities. But why should I perform an action just because it has the quality of rightness, even if this quality be of the non-natural kind? Why should the possession by certain state of affairs of these peculiar qualities have any practical or ethical significance any more than our knowledge about remote galaxies. If the real point behind Moore's refutation of Naturalism is the Humean principle that an 'ought' sentence cannot be derived from a set of 'is' sentences then isn't non-naturalism reduced to doing precisely this in the end? I do not want to underrate the force of this argument. I only want to remark that Hume's principle cannot be accepted without qualification. On any view which provides for reasons in support of our moral altitudes, judgements or principles, some kind of transition from factual premises to moral conclusion is inevitable. When asked why an action is right or obligatory we may answer that it is an action which is the fulfilment of a voluntary commitment or that it is an action which relieves human misery. The reasons cited will all be of the empirical, fact-stating type and are generally taken to support our moral conclusions. Some kind of connection between the two must be accepted by all who engage in justification of moral judgements. The weakness of the objectivist perhaps is that he makes it one of logical entailment.

If the point behind this argument is psychological rather than logical, so that the judgement that '*A* is right' is supposed always to provide some motive for doing *A*, then again the objectivist and the subjectivist are in the same position. In most ordinary people there is a desire to do what they consider to be right or what is recommended to them as morally right, by persons whom they respect. The objectivist does not deny this fact, indeed he need not deny the importance of the many related practical functions performed by ethical judgement. On the other hand, the subjectivist cannot create such a tendency if it does not exist. It may perhaps be objected that this is to miss the point that the objectivist analysis *cannot* provide for the action guiding character of moral judgement whereas the subjectivist analysis does so, by recognizing, that moral utterances are, 'from the start practical'. So far as the alleged strength of subjectivism is concerned, I may remark that unless moral utterances are reduced to *mere* injunctions, or expressions of approval there must be some distinction between I(a) 'Do *A*' and (b) 'You ought to do *A*', and II(a) '*A* is approved' and (b) '*A* ought to be approved'. Even if we use the utterances containing the moral words from the pairs given above, there is no *logical reason* why the person addressed should set himself to doing or approving *A*.

The alleged difficulty for the objectivist can be best brought out by considering the relation between the judgement '*A* is right' and the feeling of approval which this judgement arouses . . . almost invariably. Similarly the judgement that '*A* is wrong' invariably evokes a reaction against doing it. C.D. Broad, having noted the above facts, proceeds to comment as follows:[1]

---

1 See his reply to Frankena in *Philosophy of C.D. Broad*, ed. P.A. Schilpp, Tudor Publishing for Library of Living Philosopher, 1959.

> one will have to hold either (a) that the psychological proposition in question is an empirical generalization or (b) that it is a necessary synthetic proposition. The former alternative is implausible and the latter is to be avoided if possible. Now on some forms of the non-predicativist theory, the proposition would be analytic and that would certainly be a point in favour of such forms as the non-predicativist theory. We can estimate the force of this difficulty by considering a parallel difficulty about judgement of truth and their relation to belief. We certainly have an invariable tendency to reject or disbelieve what we judge to be false. Is the psychological connection in this case contingent and empirically discovered? Or is it a synthetic and necessary connection? If there are certain 'emotive' theories of truth which make the connection analytic, shall we opt for some form of non-predicativism concerning truth which analyses truth in terms of approval and acceptance of beliefs?

Sometimes, subjectivists allege that the moral experience of good men and women who habitually do what is right and can give good relevant reasons for their decisions and actions, does not support objectivism or even that it goes against it. Toulmin in his *Place of Reason in Ethics* asks one such hypothetical good person, whether in making his decision, he is guided by the intuition of non-natural qualities. Toulmin is confident that his good men contemptuously reject any such suggestion. Strawson in an article on 'Ethical Intuitionism'[2] makes substantially the same point. A number of persons may all agree in their judgements that certain actions are morally right. Now if we ask some of them whether, when they apply the word 'right', they have the experience of intuiting the non-natural quality of rightness they would probably reply that they have no such experience. From this we conclude either that the word 'right' is used in different senses by the persons concerned or else that intuitionism misrepresents our moral experience. Since the former alternative is impossible to accept we must conclude that intuitionism has gone astray in its analysis of moral judgement. I shall not say anything about the attempt to use a rigged up opinion

---

[2] *Philosophy* (Journal) January 1949.

poll (and an imaginary one at that) against a philosophical opponent. But it must be pointed out that the appeal to plain good men and women is both proper and decisive when we want to settle the fate of a normative theory or a value-judgement within the field of ethics. But if our purpose is to choose between meta-ethical theories concerning the character of moral discourse and its relation to other types of discourse such an appeal is of dubious value unless the good men and women are trained in philosophy.

H.H. Price, who could hardly be accused of being a positivistic or linguistic philosopher, writes,

> the notion of a moral fact is rather a strange one. It is not easy to see what kind of a fact it could be, or in what sense it could be a fact at all. The view that rightness and wrongness are properties which actions have is a strange one. It is still odder, perhaps to say that obligatoriness is a property which some actions have, and that you are ascribing this property to an action (or rather, to a possible action?) when you tell me that I ought to do it.[3]

Even those who are firmly convinced that there is some rational basis for our moral judgement, must be experiencing 'naturalistic' moods when non-natural qualities seem to dissolve into thin air and vanish from the world altogether. And yet, non-naturalism assigns a place to reason in our moral life in a perfectly straight-forward sense. Moral judgements express beliefs which can be true or false and can be supported by relevant and correct reasons. It is true that our basic value-judgements, i.e. judgements that certain things are intrinsically valuable and certain actions intrinsically more right or morally fitting, cannot be derived from any premises nor can they be established in any way that will satisfy a person who chooses to question them. But this would be the case on *any analysis* of moral judgements and it would be wrong to use this difficulty to cause discomfort to the objectivist as some non-cognitivists have tried to do. Equally the difficulties presented by conflicting duties cannot

---

[3] H.H. Price, *Belief*, Muirhead Library of Philosophy, George Allen & Unwin, 1969, p. 378.

be resolved neatly by any one who is not prepared to admit that they can be derived from a single general principle such as that of hedonistic utilitarianism. The differences between teleologists and deontologists cut across the dividing lines between rival meta-ethical theories and assume slightly different forms.

Though the practical difficulties concerning our basic value judgements are the same for the rival moral philosophers, the objectivist seems to be in a better position in accounting for our conviction that in matters of moral dispute the views of 'morally sensitive' and disinterested persons are right or correct than those of the insensitive. On the subjectivist view, the use of words like 'correct' and right' in this context is merely an endorsement by us of the attitude of one of the parties to the dispute. Is this all that we do when we say that the way of life advocated by a Buddha or Jesus is better than that advocated by a thug? Hume who anticipated the emotivist or non-propositional analysis of ethical judgements frankly declared 'It is not contrary to reason to prefer the destruction of the whole world to the scratching of my finger' (*Treatise* II.iii.3). Contemporary moralists shrink from this conclusion and try to make room for reasons, some of them even going so far as to re-introduce analogues of truth and falsity in our moral judgements. But how can we speak of truth and falsity of utterances which express no beliefs? And how can a statement or set of statements function as a reason for declaration which expresses nothing that can be true or false? It seems as if 'ethics without propositions' (a phrase coined by W.H.F. Barnes) must necessarily be ethics without reasons. Many contemporary subjectivists have made a strenuous attempt to account for the difference between moral 'attitudes' and others which express non-moral tastes and preferences; but it cannot be said that they carry conviction.

The first strong point of the objectivist then is the seriousness with which we argue about our moral differences and the conviction we feel that even when we are unable to persuade one another, some important or substantial difference still persists. We may continue our efforts by non-argumentative methods. For example, we may try to induce an attitude of sympathetic imagination in our opponents taking the help of great poets and novelists. But whether we succeed or not, we never quite give up the hope of agreement. It has been noted often that our moral judgements are always implicitly universal and that when we adopt a certain attitude towards an action we desire and expect others to share our attitude. As Findlay puts it in his 'Morality by Convention',[4] we are ready to subject our moral judgement to the test of 'social attrition'. But he goes wrong in thinking that when our expectation that others would agree with us is belied, we regard our own judgement as false. I would rather say that the very fact that we seek agreement and in the end the agreement of all reflective persons is an indication that some thing impersonal like truth or falsity is at stake.

Findlay of course makes it clear that the agreement we seek is not necessarily with our immediate contemporaries but with the 'great company of reflective persons wherever they may be situated in space and time'. But he fails to notice that sometimes a man is to be quite alone in the face of opposition by the whole world. Most people, not 'heaven-born prophets', would do well to avoid such an opposition, if we can manage it. But, the right, or even the duty to stick to our moral convictions, is not the prerogative of a Buddha or Jesus. Thus while we are ready to consult others, revise our opinions in the light of the advice given by disinterested and sympathetic persons, we are equally prepared, after an attempt to eliminate all bias and selfishness from our judgement, to stick to it. Our moral life then combines these paradoxical but not inconsistent tendencies: the tendency to seek agreement or conformity and the tendency to exercise our individual judgement. Both these are brought out by *Taittirīya Upaniṣad*. In cases when we are in doubt concerning conduct, the Upaniṣad asks us to 'seek the company of learned persons competent to judge, devoted, not harsh lovers of virtue and behave as they may behave in such a situation'. But a little earlier a teacher tells his pupils, 'Those things among us which are

---

4 *See* 'Morality by Convention' in *Mind* (Journal), 1944, vol. 53, no. 210.

good deeds should be revered by you and no others', thus giving the pupil the right to judge even the conduct of his teacher. This is particularly pleasing because the Indian tradition[5] is so heavily conformist.

Not only do we seek agreement, and try to compose our differences in as disinterested a manner as is humanly possible, but we also recognize that certain methods are out of place in achieving moral persuasion. Any agreement secured by use of force is, by definition, not moral. Torture is equally to be condemned as the use of subterfuge and deception to secure agreement. Even more important is our feeling that certain possible methods which involve neither violence nor deception should be ruled out of court in moral matters. If a scientist could invent a belief-inducing drug, we should certainly condemn its use in bringing about moral agreement; and the method of hypnotic suggestion which is already available to us, is no better. Thus, it is not merely the fact that our moral judgements are expressed in the indicative, but the whole weight of the procedures outlined above suggests that they have a claim to objective validity. Perhaps when Moore and other objectivists speak of non-natural qualities, they are projecting these procedures on the world. If so we may not accept their statements as literally true. But in substance they are right. We constantly speak and behave as if moral judgements involved something impersonal, independent of our individual emotions and preferences.

---

[5] *yānianavadyānikarmāṇitānisevitavyāni, noitarāni. yāniasmākamsu-caritānitānitvayāupasyāni, vr̥ttavicikitsavāsyāt, ye tatrabrahmanāḥ-sammarśinaḥ, yuktaḥāyuktaḥalūkṣādharmakāmāḥsyuḥ, yathāteta-travarterantathāvarthethāḥ* । Those actions which are irreproachable should be performed and no others. . . . Now if you have any doubt concerning an act or concerning your conduct; if there are brāhmaṇas present who are competent, experienced, independent, gentle (not harsh) lovers of virtue as they may behave in such a situation so should you behave in such a situation. – *Taittirīya Upaniṣad* I.ii

3

The Place of Reason in Morality

SCEPTICISM about moral judgements, and value judgements in general, seems to come naturally to thoughtful persons when they become aware of persistent moral differences and the difficulties in resolving them. Unresolved doubt easily culminates in subjectivism with its corollary that reason has no place in morality except in (i) applying accepted standards to particular situations, (ii) adapting means to chosen ends, and (iii) modifying moral attitudes of ourselves and also of others by resolving differences concerning matters of fact. Those who want a more vital role for reason in our moral life insist that reason is and ought to be more than a 'slave to the passions', that it can have a say in choosing ends, in determining criteria of right and wrong.

If we take the cognitivist or the non-naturalist view of moral judgements it is easy to see the place of reason in our moral life. Whatever may be the distinctive character of ethical judgements, they would be subject to the polarity of true/false and hence objective and rational. On the other hand, if we agree with Hume and the contemporary emotivists that there is no question of truth and falsity here it seems as if we would be constrained to agree with him further that 'it is not contrary to reason for me to prefer the destruction of the whole world to the scratching of my finger' (*Treatise* II.iii.3).

I do not want to go into the details of the subjective/ objective controversy in the context of contemporary meta-ethical theories. The arguments on both sides have been presented repeatedly and at great length. But it may be worthwhile to point out that the arguments against 'ethical intuitionism' are inconclusive in somewhat the same way as scepticism concerning the senses fails to refute naïve realism. Second, some of the difficulties urged against the cognitivist have to be faced by the non-cognitivist too though in a modified form. But it must be admitted that there is an air of implausibility about non-naturalism which strikes even a philosopher like H.H. Price who is neither a positivist nor a linguistic philosopher.

But can we give up 'objectivism' and yet maintain the rational character of moral judgements and arguments? This is an intermediate position which has its peculiar attractions and equally peculiar difficulties. S.E. Toulmin, for example, maintains that moral judgements are objective in the sense that we can support them with reasons and can discriminate between good reasons and bad reasons. The attempt is to combine 'ethics without propositions' with 'ethics with reasons'. To the question 'what is the relation between moral judgement and the supporting reasons?', the only answer is that it is neither inductive nor deductive but of the peculiar kind involved in moral reasoning or evaluative reasoning in general. Any such intermediate theory must either (i) sever the connection between truth and falsity on the one hand and statement expressing belief, or (ii) sever the connection between truth and falsity and rational support. Neither course is attractive in view of the firm connections between the notions of 'belief', 'truth' and 'reasons', though the second appears to be more defensible and may even claim the support of ordinary usage.

If we support the objective from the truth and falsity or rational from objective we can bring out the rational character of moral judgements by highlighting certain features of our moral life and moral reflection.

Moral evaluations, unless they are regarded as mere expressions of tastes and preferences, have a built-in generality. This is not merely because they are criteria-based and supervenient on the acceptance of certain factual propositions. They are totally resistant to variations in space and time. In this respect they are like scientific laws which are unaffected by mere differences in location and dating.

1. We seek agreement with others in our moral attitudes and evaluations. This involves 'universalizability' of our moral principles but goes beyond that. Even a morally repugnant creed like that of the Nazi's can be universalized. What is involved is disinterestedness and a sort of impersonality which is exemplified at its best, in the lives of great saints of all religions.
2. We take our moral differences seriously and are ready to subject them to what Findlay calls 'social attrition'. We not only tolerate but welcome criticism.
3. Not all methods of composing moral differences are acceptable. Deception and torture are as out of place as in a scientific discussion. Even methods not involving force or fraud such as the use of drugs or hypnosis are ruled out if our goal is moral agreement.
4. This impersonality goes with deep personal commitment. Our inability to persuade others does not mean that we decide to conform to the consensus of our contemporaries. The quotation from *Taittirīya* brings out both these features of our moral life that the tendency to seek agreement and the tendency to exercise individual judgement and stand firm on our convictions, if necessary. Authoritarianism is inconsistent with true morality. It is the whole weight of the features and procedures outlined above and not just the fact that moral judgements are expressed in the indicative, that supports the 'objective' or rational character of moral judgements. When Moore and other objectivists speak of non-natural qualities they project these procedures on the world. If so they are misleading and literally wrong, but basically right in suggesting that something impersonal and analogous to truth is involved in our moral life.

4

Freedom and Violence

THE more the freedom, the less the violence and conversely, the more the violence the less the freedom. It is nice to begin with the statement of an exception-less principle, whereas in social inquiries exceptions are the rule. Every general statement has to be immediately qualified to be worth serious consideration. But the non-controversial character of our maxim is purchased at a price. It is general enough to command universal acceptance but permits internal difference regarding the nature of freedom and the nature of violence – 'true freedom' and 'true violence – if you like. Of the two, the concept of violence is much less contentious than that of freedom. The most blatant forms of coercion involve the use of force, or very effective threats of use of force to compel a man to do what someone else wants him to do. Here the person compelled is reduced to a mere instrument of the purpose of others. He can truly say, 'Not I but the evil outside me acts through me'. But there are other cases of loss of freedom through coercion which are more subtle. We may remember the statement of the apothecary in the most famous play of adolescent love: 'Not my will, but my poverty consents'.These other cases can be grouped around the paradigm of the use of physical force which represents total loss of freedom. The different typical cases which move away from free action and progressively nearer to coercion form a fascinating study in the field of moral psychology. Such reflections will lead us to actions which are, in the words of Aristotle, 'voluntary in principle, but involuntary in fact'. The doer deserves 'pardon, pity or praise'. Borderline cases present difficulties, as borderline cases always will and we may agree to disagree or make ad hoc decisions on the cases in question.

All injustice is a form of violence. Formal freedoms guaranteed by a liberal democracy will remain empty and ineffective in a society deeply divided by economic and social disparities. The early decades of industrialization in England – the bleak age – provide examples of human suffering including child labour, which seem shocking even in India of today where there are pockets of such suffering not well concealed from our view. Even more shocking is the fact that this mass of human misery should have been defended in the name of freedom, the sanctity of the family and the laws of nature and of God. All these rationalizations show that violence is easy to defend and the defences sound very plausible, especially if we are not at the receiving end. The commonest form of justification of human suffering and the use of force consists in arguing that they are inevitable or practically necessary. The paradigm of justifications is expressed in the platitudes – 'You can't make an omelette without breaking an egg', 'Into each life some rain must fall', etc. Uttered with an air of assurance and apparent profundity they generally put an end to discussion. But really, they should be a starting point. Except in the case of an individual or a small number of known persons we cannot visualize the consequences of coercive or violent action with any degree of confidence. And when the breaking of an egg takes the form of imprisoning hundreds and torturing and killing thousands or even hundreds of thousands, such justifications are no more than empty rhetoric designed to put our conscience to sleep and inflate our egos into believing that we are agents of a great political, social or religious transformation. If the violence is linked to an ideology, fascism, communism, Islam and nowadays, Hindutva. No matter what ideology it is – it is harder for us to resist its lure. The epigram of Friedrich Engels, 'Force is the midwife of progress', crystallizes the crusaders' zeal to transform the world. Paradoxically even the ideal of liberty is used to defend the enslavement of a people and the use of war to extend the area of freedom. Two World Wars were fought to make the world safe for democracy and nearly a hundred years later, we are still busy promoting the same ideal by the same methods.

All this shows the need for a clear, dispassionate, thinking about social affairs. To do so one must rise above the accidents of one's birth and cultivate the attitude of 'the impartial spectator within our bosom' (Adam Smith's phrase). This is difficult and often painful. Spinoza declared, 'I shall regard human actions and desires exactly as if I were dealing with lines, planes and bodies'. This may be an impossible ideal – though Spinoza attained it as nearly as a human being can. The trouble with us is that the ideal is not even acknowledged to be relevant. Raucous and even abusive advocacy is the norm. The search for facts is guided by polemical needs. Inconvenient facts are ignored or suppressed. In the worst possible cases 'evidence' is fabricated. Diversionary tactics are employed by raising issues and facts discreditable to one's opponent though they have no bearing on the subject under discussion. There is nothing new in these methods, but the pervasive influence of mass media especially television combined with the spread of literacy has endowed them with great power beyond the dreams of demagogues even fifty years ago. When Hitler wanted to rouse the German people to a pitch of righteous fury he had nothing better than mass meetings and radio broadcasts at his disposal. The mass meetings continue but the thousands who switch on the same television programme at the same time constitute a kind of a mass meeting. The result is a heightened awareness of real or imaginary grievances and intensification and exaltation of emotions and a readiness to support policies and programmes, which if discussed in the cold light of reason, are seen to be unworthy of our devotion. All this creates an intellectual and moral climate in which periodical outbursts of violence are an ever-present possibility, predictably realized from time to time, though the times and places of their occurrence are not always predictable.

The loss of freedom for the ordinary citizen is there for all to see. In such a general climate of insecurity and fear the actual use of violence is not necessary. The fact that it can be used is enough to deprive one of free speech and action. What Hobbes says of the state of nature is equally true here:

> Foul weather lieth not in a shower or two of rain but in an inclination thereto of many days together. So the nature of war consisteth not in actual fighting but in the known disposition thereto during all the time there is no assurance to the contrary?

It is this climate of fear and insecurity which curtails our freedom in India today, though the apparatus of democracy functions reasonably effluently – periodical elections which are free and fair by and large, free press and an independent judiciary. It is often said that civil society must provide a suitable milieu for freedom to survive and flourish. Our media are full of discussions of particular evils – corruption in ruling circles, administrative lapses, electoral malpractices, etc. Such discussions sometimes threaten to become a substitute for concrete remedial action. But when we come to social and political activism, violence must be firmly ruled out so long as other means are available. The excuse invariably offered by those who destroy public property, hold up traffic and kill and maim selectively or indiscriminately is that only such behaviour makes the concerned authority sit up and take notice. There is some truth in this, but such justification of violence is both dangerous and counter-productive. Violence invites counter-violence which in its turn provokes still more violence from the original protestors, and so the oscillations go on. By conveniently choosing a particular point in this spiral – an optional starting point – analogous to an optional stopping point in statistical investigations, we can always point an accusing finger at our opponents and say, 'I am doing this now because he did the same or worse earlier'. All such rationalizations must be resisted and the fallacies involved in such arguments pointed out in concrete detail. This must be done not only in the case of those whom we dislike but also in the case of those whom we like and who have a genuine grievance to redress and a worthy cause to promote.

I do not know whether the use of violence is ever justified in the social field. In the rarest of rare cases, to borrow a phrase from our Supreme Court, it may be. I want to make a few points briefly on this theme. (1) The alternatives to violence should be sincerely explored to their limit. (2) We should never do evil so that good may come out of it. We should reluctantly accept some evil to avoid for greater evil. (3) And finally the use of force should be controlled and limited to the purpose in hand so that it does not degenerate into mindless revenge. This is the most difficult of all requirements of justified use of violence. When we use force we are embarked on a slippery path moving from evil to greater evil with no end in sight. Apparently we cannot curtail the freedom of our opponents without curtailing our own.

I said at the outset that the concept of freedom offers far-greater difficulty than the concept of violence. It is difficult to pretend when indulging in violence, that it is true non-violence. But the denial of freedom can be construed as true freedom. Hence Rousseau's picturesque phrase 'forcing people to be free'. Any number of idealistically inclined philosophers have said 'Freedom is rational self-determination' or 'Freedom is obedience to the Law, not arbitrary behaviour' or more grandly, 'True freedom consists in living in harmony with the nature of things'. This way of speaking has more support in ordinary usage than I thought once. It also represents a very important strand in our moral thinking. Whether it solves the problem of free will must remain an open question. But it has the awkward consequence that only the good man is free. Even this slightly paradoxical conclusion is suggested by a great deal in our moral thought. We speak for example of a man being a slave to his passion when he is in the grip of an unbreakable, vicious habit. When a passing impulse sweeps a man off his feet we say his action is 'out of character', and he himself on regaining his balance, may say, 'I was not myself'. But nevertheless there is a sense in which both the good man and the bad man are free. Moral agents are free to choose between right and wrong. When a man is blamed morally we clearly imply that he could have acted otherwise. He could have left undone what he in fact did and could have done instead what he did not do. The crux of the matter is to give a clear and acceptable interpretation of the phrase 'he could have acted otherwise'. In particular, we have to decide whether any interpretation we give involves absence of causal determination and further whether moral responsibility requires such absence. In short we have to decide whether contra-causal freedom is necessary to save moral responsibility. This freedom of indifference is often dismissed contemptuously for involving a real contingency or chance in the course of events. William James calls it the dilemma of determinism; and he alone among other great philosophers, sees nothing objectionable in accepting chance.

I shall leave alone the sleeping demon of determinism. For my purpose I have taken what J.L. Mackie calls the 'straight rule of responsibility'. A man is responsible for all his intentional actions and only for them. Complications arise because an action or intention can be brought 'under different descriptions'. These can be resolved easily once questions of psychological fact are settled, which is not always as easy thing. We also need the distinction between ignorance of fact and ignorance of law, the latter being no excuse legally but morally it may be. Once we sharpen our definition it provides a basis for legal accountability; and in a civilized society this approaches and nearly coincides with moral responsibility. The degree to which this happens may be regarded as the index of the moral health of a community. Freedom, in this sense is the absence of restraint within the legal framework of a society and it is the freedom of indifference. It is important to realize that freedom of choice is morally neutral though it is the basis of much moral good and a necessary condition of any creative life. Freedom has its risks and dangers that are absent from a regimented society. These must be accepted by anyone who values an open liberal society. A good reason for skirting the issue of freedom vs. determinism is that our answer to it has no bearing on our discussion of conditions that must be fulfilled if the citizens of a democracy are to enjoy the freedoms guaranteed by their constitution. We should have economic and social justice to provide substance and reality to formal freedoms. But formal freedoms in the forms of fundamental rights are not mere, empty shells. Communists dismiss them as bourgeois rights. But the history of communist dictatorships all over the world shows that those who sacrifice liberty for bread often end up by losing both. How to ensure that formal freedoms become a living reality without the use of violence is the problem for many of us in Asia and Africa. I think that, on the whole, the attempts to combine capitalist democracy with social welfare have succeeded better than attempts to develop communism with a human face. But neither path can be regarded as a heaven-sent guide, in spite of the recent collapse of communism.

It will be seen that our subject can be discussed at different levels. But primarily it is a problem of political and social organization. The attempt is to establish and strengthen a state that promotes basic freedoms. This cannot be done without a supportive social environment with a certain culture. Non-violence is a key element in this culture. Violence indeed is the antithesis of freedom even when used justifiably. I have argued very unoriginally that without economic security constitutionally guaranteed rights become empty words. You may say, as often as you like, that a duchess and a shop assistant are equal before the law; but if the shop assistant has no means to approach a court, she can only quail before the majesty of the law. Glaring social inequalities with disabilities attached to birth have the same effect of abridging and sometimes totally negating legal rights. And often social injustice goes with economic deprivation. So ensuring social and economic justice must be part of the ideal of freedom. How to do so without sacrificing legal rights is the million dollar question. Respect for the laws is the basis of any civilized life. Hence the absence of restraint which is the essence of freedom is within the framework of law. It takes centuries to build a society in which habitual obedience to the law is taken for granted even when such obedience is inconvenient to oneself. But it takes a couple of decades to destroy or bring into disrepute such a culture.

In the long run, if not immediately, habits of clear, dispassionate thinking play an effective role in bringing about the kind of society we have in mind. These again have to be cultivated over centuries and can easily be dissipated and rendered ineffective by sharp, violent polarizations within a community. Historically speaking every society has not valued them. Even today every country does not tolerate, let along promote them. After all, if we have a monopoly of truth and are the sole agents of God on earth why is any other view needed? The dissenter is either stupid or dishonest and deserves to be either silenced or eliminated. If such an outlook is widespread it will soon put an end to meaningful debates and all creative free inquiry except, perhaps, in the purely physical sciences. We must learn to allow the presentation and dissemination of views with which we disagree. We may even consider these views perverse and dangerous. But so long as hatred and violence are not preached or implied, such a view must be opposed intellectually and not with the coercive machinery of the state.

In India it is often said that certain views or representations hurt the sentiments of a section of the community. However, we must all learn to be hurt in this way, without calling for the blood of those who have offended us. It is the price we pay for living in an open society. We cannot deny our opponents the freedoms we claim for ourselves. I do not want to deny that some state prohibitions and bans may be necessary, if there is an imminent danger of public disorder. The judgement that this is so in a particular case has necessarily to be left to those who are in power. It is obvious that their judgement is inspired by political expediency and the desire to avoid trouble in the immediate future. We may try to minimize this danger by appointing an expert committee whose opinion carries weight without having a binding character. But such a body can be packed with 'our people' who are pliable. In the end lovers of liberty will have to work hard to preserve their freedom. Whenever a legal ban is being considered the pleas for tolerance and preserving the decencies of debate should grow louder and be genuinely non-partisan. There is no reason why the state too should not take part in this process of educating the public. This is a tall order but I see no alternative to it. No mechanism or law or institutional arrangement will work unless we are committed to a certain way of life and are ready to actively labour for it. It is of importance to notice that this task of promoting the free circulation of ideas is in no way concerned with the distinction between the majority and the minority. Bigotry is bigotry is bigotry. If we cannot defend a view on the ground that it is the view of the majority, we should not defend it on the ground that it represents an effort to maintain ethnic identity, or that criticism of it hurts the sentiments of the minority, or some such slogan which masks our opportunism or cowardice or both. In his *On Liberty* J.S. Mill has a heartwarming passage where he says that even if all mankind minus one were of one view, and he of another, they have no more moral right to force their view on him than he would have if he had the power. Brave words, though hard to translate into action. But I think it is equally a part of the liberal outlook that we cannot claim exemption from criticism and corrective action for an opinion or policy on the ground that it is held by (one man or) a minority, whichever way the minority may be defined.

5

Setting Terms to God

Thou are indeed just, Lord, if I contend
With thee; but sir, so what I plead is just.
Why do sinners' ways prosper? and why must
Disappointment all I endeavour end?
– Manley Gerard Hopkins[1] (1844-89)

THE just man's complaint against the world and God who made it has figured prominently in debates concerning the problem of evil. But it is by no means the only component of the problem. We can however easily understand why it looms so large in our consciousness when we think of evil. As St. Thomas Aquinas points out 'Nothing seems to be more repugnant to divine providence in human affairs than the affliction of the innocent'. The complaint has been voiced again and again in human history and in all the leading religious traditions. The Psalmist noted that the wicked flourish like the green bay tree while the good suffer. Draupadī in the Vanaparva blames Yudhiṣṭhira bitterly for his constant harping on *dharma* and delivers a tirade against providence and concludes that either there is no *Īśvara* or else he is blind. (In this she made a tactical mistake. Yudhiṣṭhira reproaches her for daring to question the existence of God. That would lead to anarchy, he says and encourage men to behave like beasts. Draupadī, since she was not really ready to deny the existence of God or his perfection beats a tame retreat.) In the 'Book of Job', which is the classic exposition of the perplexity in the Judaic–Christian traditions, Job's lamentations are pointed but God's answer delivered from a whirlwind, though it silences Job, is not clear in respect of its philosophic import. There is no point

---

1 Manley Gerard Hopkins, *Poems*, London: Humphrey Milford, 1918.

in multiplying these examples but it is of some importance to note that the complaints emanate not only from agnostics and godless philosophers but also from devout believers and even some of the great saints themselves.

But aside from the apparent indifference of the course of natural events to moral distinctions there is a vast amount of suffering and confusion, pain, destruction and death. Indeed there are times when the malevolence of man combined with the mindless cruelties of nature makes the world a place of pure horror to contemplate. Beginners in philosophy know that various solutions are possible and have been developed by different philosophers. There is the Absolutist–Pantheist solution which denies reality to evil. A metaphysical dualism which ascribes all the good in the world to God and evil to some other source – either an active principle of evil or a passive principle which resists good. Ditheism is routinely ascribed by Western textbooks to Zarathustra – but the prophet's position seems to have been far more subtle. A typically twentieth-century solution is to offer a finite God – and limit God's omnipotence in one way or another – as is done by Rashdall and S. Alexander and perhaps even William James. Finally the theistic position, which while insisting on the reality of evil and the perfection of the Supreme Being who is the sole ground of the world, tries to 'justify God's ways to man' by showing that the evil in the world is subordinate to and serves as an instrument for the realization of greater and higher good. There is no point in traversing this well-trodden ground. I shall consider three approaches to the problem which partly cut across the distinction between absolution, theism, ditheism, etc. The first two are metaphysical, the third largely coincides with classical theodicy derived from Leibnitz and may be called the causal theory of justification of evil.

The first metaphysical theory is the denial of reality to evil by Advaitins, Spinoza and Absolutists. This may take the form of moral positivism: 'Nothing is good or bad in itself but we apply these terms egocentrically to things according to their effects on us'. Spinoza is the most clear-headed and consistent exponent of this view. Christopher Isherwood, after raising the problem of the origin of ignorance and evil and noting that 'slightly different' answers have been given by the prophets, writes: The question 'why does God permit evil?' is to a Vedāntin as meaningless as the question 'why does God permit good?'. 'The fire burns one man and warms another and is neither kind nor cruel.' Other formulations of this viewpoint are 'evil is good in the wrong place', 'evil is misperceived good' or 'there is no evil from the absolute point of view'. To soften the sense of shock that is produced by this last formulation, Absolutists hurry forward with the qualification; 'but of course it exists in the phenomenal world, *it is* a fact of experience'. In refutation of this paradoxical view the following dilemma is offered to its proponents: 'Either there is evil in the world or nothing is itself evil. But to misperceive what is not evil as evil is itself an evil. So in any case evil is real.' But there is I think a more fundamental criticism. Whenever we say, 'there is something which is such and such', or 'such and such exists or is real', we cannot modify or cancel the import of such statements by a denial of reality at some other level or from some other point of view. There are no degrees of reality as there are degrees of temperature or duration or wealth or wisdom measured by some standard procedure. Nor are there any levels of reality as there are levels of development where the higher includes and surpasses the lower. Nor are there types of reality as there are types of incommensurable entities (sound and colours for instance). Philosophers, who have spoken of Reality or 'higher reality' as contrasted with mere existence, have always employed as a criterion of higher or highest reality, some feature or perfection which some, or someone existent possesses but not the others. For example, '*Brahman* alone is real because it is eternal and self-contained whereas *prapañca* is not'. Such formulations clearly betray an intuitive grasp of common or core meaning of existence-affirmations which is univocal, regardless of variations in the nature of entities whose existence is affirmed. Or else denial of reality to an existent may be a rhetorical way of stating an evaluation, viz. that the thing in question fails to measure up to certain standards of excellence. A mother irritated by unfilial behaviour may say, 'you are not *really my daughter*; I bought you for three bushels of corn'.

Moreover once we admit the existence of evils as facts of experience, it is impossible by subsequent evaluation to wipe them out. People who live in terror and die in pain or break down under the load of unbearable grief or anxiety have gone through experience where the distinction between 'is' and 'seems' is not applicable. Even though an analysis of their causes and later effects by others or by the subject himself reveals some relieving features and desirable consequences, they remain in themselves indelible black spots on the face of the universe.

The second metaphysical approach is not so paradoxical as the absolutist. On this view evil, though real is not some-thing positive in itself. It has a secondary parasitic existence in the absence of some corresponding good. St. Thomas Aquinas writes, 'evil cannot be known simply as evil for its core is hollow and can be neither recognized nor defined, save by the surrounding good'.[2] Again '. . . evil denotes the lack of good . . . not every absence of good is an evil . . . . but what is evil is privation; in this sense blindness means the privation of sight'.[3] Blindness seems to be a favourite example of St. Thomas. Though he distinguishes between natural and moral evil, and cites wrong-doing and the penalty imposed on the criminal as instances of the latter, the discussion is largely of evil as defect or deprivation in general. Also, in spite of the play of St. Thomas's luminous mind the discussion is obscure on certain points on account of his reliance on Aristotelian and scholastic maxims concerning causality in relation to actuality–potentiality and form and matter. Contemporary writers who have to explain the doctrine directly without recourse to these maxims like Fr. Copelston have to walk the tightrope between denying evil positive being and denying its existence altogether. To those who lack Aquinas's theological

---

2 T. Aquinas, *Summa Theologica,* Christian Classics, 1981, la, xiv, 10 ad-4.

3 Ibid., la, vi, viii, 3.

motivations the doctrine appears to be 'mere quibbling' as Hospers puts it in his bulky textbook. Without going so far we may remark (i) that it is not always plausible to maintain that every evil is a deprivation – being blown up in an accident for example or being orphaned, in the case of children whose parents die in natural or man-made calamities, (ii) even if every evil can be exhibited as a deprivation, the absence of a corresponding good is not the sole being of any evil but at best its necessary condition. The hardship and suffering consequent on some privation cannot themselves be regarded as further privations. St. Thomas and others like him have recourse to the doctrine to maintain that God does not choose *evil as such* directly. He chooses to impart his goodness to creatures and they receive it to the extent their creaturely limitations permit. The limitations inherent in their specific natures make evil a possibility. St. Thomas adds that God has to permit certain evils so that certain other goods may exist.

Finally what I have called the causal theory is the doctrine of theodicy derived from Leibnitz in its modern form. On this view God could have made a world entirely free from the evils we experience. But it would have been a world containing lesser amount of good and also a world devoid of good of a higher sort. The present world is the best possible because the evil in it enhances and enriches the good in it. It is not necessary to go into the detailed articulation of this theory. The key elements are: (1) The distinction between natural and moral evil; the former being the by-product of the autonomous working of nature, the latter is sin or morally wrong choices by man with all their ramifications for the agent and the community at large. (2) God is directly responsible for natural evil for he is the author of nature and the laws governing it. Man with his free will is responsible for moral evil.

The anti-theistic view is that God could have avoided both and should have done so. The theist admits that God could have prevented natural evil but only by constantly interfering with the operation of natural laws when and only when the consequences would have been harmful to man. But this would have meant an unstable world where no one could be sure whether certain consequences would follow certain actions and occurrences. So the suffering caused by natural calamities is the necessary price we have to pay for a settled social life on this planet. This argument has convinced many and has been carried over into the discussion of moral evil, to answer the question – 'Why does not God interfere with the wicked when their actions cause great harm to tens of thousands of innocent men and women?'. But it is totally fallacious. In the circumstances envisaged it *is not necessary* for God to suspend the laws of nature; it is enough if he alters by an act of his omnipotent will the position and disposition of certain portions of matter. Surely he can prevent flooding of inhabited parts of the globe in the twinkling of an eye by shifting quantities of water to safer places. Can he not accomplish what our hydraulic engineers can accomplish after years of planning and toil?

Similarly can he not control and regulate the temperatures and pressures in the interior of the earth without tampering with laws of nature? So far as moral evil is concerned the discussion is far more complex. The theist insists on the supreme value of free will both in itself and as the foundation of our moral and spiritual life. I have a great deal of sympathy for him on this point. But his main thesis here is that since some of the greatest goods in human life lie in the cultivation of virtues like courage, patience and heroic self-sacrifice, suffering is a logical *precondition* of the development and exercise of these virtues. And for our benefit it is added that God may not be a hedonist like shallow atheists and agnostics. This argument has two faces depending on which end we apply it at. From the human end there is much to be said for taking the evil in the world as a challenge and stimulus. Fretting and fuming about it or indulging in lamentation is both unproductive and undignified. Even a non-believer – given that he possesses uncommon goodness – may adopt a quasi-religious attitude to such situations. But apply it at the Divine end, and it sounds preposterous to believe that God wills or permits unimaginable suffering so that a few heroic souls may scale the highest peaks of virtue and nobility is simply unbelievable. We would all think a lot less highly of Mother Teresa and her sisters of charity if they first went about creating destitution and suffering and then applied themselves to its alleviation with almost superhuman heroism. If it is said that every human soul has the potentiality of rising to great spiritual height, I can only say that God is persisting in an experiment which has turned out to be futile. Above all this type of theodicy is basically an exercise in book-keeping. Whether or not it explicitly uses quantitative terms the evil in the world generates good which is far greater so that we end up on the credit side. This may very well be so but it is not sufficient to show that 'all is well and all will be made well'. For that there must be an assurance that no soul is beyond the redemptive power of God. This is insisted on in *bhakti* religion, in Sufism, Mahāyāna and in the teaching of Jesus himself. Popular or even philosophical religion may be rather crude in describing heaven and hell and the details of the spiritual journey. But at their best they must express an element of truth: and if God is to be worthy of our worship, they must hold out the hope of universal redemption.

Sri Aurobindo[4] echoes the Mahāyāna ideal of the *bodhisattva* when he writes:

> But even if our personal deliverance is complete, still there is suffering of others, the world travail, which the greatest of souls cannot regard with indifference. There is a unity with all-being which something within us feels, and the deliverance of others must be felt as intimate to its own deliverance.

Like all profound and sensitive thinkers, he notes that the problem of evil 'most poignantly preoccupies the mind of man when it is turned on the mystery of his own existence and of cosmic existence'. Suffering is 'a great stumbling-block to our understanding of the universe, and pain and suffering are a perverse and contrary term of the delight of existence'. His own solution is in terms of

---

[4] Sri Aurobindo, *Life Divine*, Sri Aurobindo Ashram Trust, 1990, 1st edn. (1939-40), 1st American edn., 1949, Book II, part I, chaps. IV and XIV.

his refashioned Vedānta. Perhaps it will be generally agreed that Sri Aurobindo added two very significant dimensions to classical Vedānta. (i) He attempted to free Advaita from Māyāvāda and the extravagances of illusionism (it is arguable however that Śaṅkara did not really maintain the unreality of *prapañca*). (ii) He took evolution seriously and incorporated the evolutionary process into the unfolding of the supreme. The Absolute first veils itself by plunging into the 'inconscience' and then unveils itself through graded stages till the original *All-being*, *All-knowledge* and *All-bliss* are manifested. In the process, error, pain and suffering will be transmuted into their opposites. In predicting the emergence of gnostic beings and the transformation of our earthly life he went beyond the Indian tradition of regarding life on earth as futile or at best of instrumental value in overcoming it. However this part of his philosophy may be seen as an active fulfilment of the Christian prayer, 'Thy will be done on earth as it is in heaven' (I owe this suggestion to J.N. Chubb though he is not responsible for my errors).

It is not possible to comment in a short space on a theory of such majestic sweep. But echoes of older theories and their familiar difficulties can be discerned here too. Evil and falsehood are the consequences of partial knowledge, which goes inevitably, with partial ignorance. Ultimately they are rooted in the self- limitation of the supreme. Sri Aurobindo insists that they are not imaginary and that our valuation of them cannot be rejected out of hand. And yet – this is a big yet – there is no absolute evil or falsehood while there is an absolute truth and goodness. The problem of evil and falsehood may be taken up from three points of view: (i) their relation to the Absolute, (ii) their origin and place in the cosmos, and (iii) their action and point of hold in the individual being. Sri Aurobindo declares that these 'contrary phenomena have no direct root in the supreme Reality itself, there is nothing there which has this character; they are creations of Ignorance and Inconscience'. The tension between denying substantiality to evil and affirming its reality at the same time cannot be more evident. Second, the process of evolution is not of any great significance for our problem. Our valuations of something as evil and its magnitude are independent of when it occurs and at what stage in a continuous process it is placed. Some may rule out the question – 'why does the Supreme choose the evolutionary path of expression?' as improper. But Sri Aurobindo seems to allow the question when he says that if the Infinite's right of various manifestations is granted, evil becomes intelligible or even necessary. (But then who are we to grant the right?) Once again what is important is not the achievement of greater good but the assurance that no creature is used as a means to the greater glory of another. Zarathustra brings this out very well when he prays: 'O living God bestow upon us that by which we may overcome the hatred of our oppressors'; and again when he declares that 'the might and majesty of God will be revealed to sinners who will deliver the lie into the hands of truth'.

My reflections are those of an agnostic who is a timid fence sitter by definition. If I had some faint glimmer of a spiritual awakening no doubt the whole world would take on a different colouring. But until then for the vast majority of the unenlightened, 'Beer can do more than Milton can to justify God's ways to Man'. And for hapless persons like me, not even that consolation.

IV. Indian Philosophy

Introduction

Shubhada Joshi

PROF. N.G. Kulkarni was equally interested in both problems as well as debates in the Indian philosophical tradition. The areas of the Indian philosophical tradition that interested him most were early Buddhism and Pātañjala Yoga. His writings assume that the reader has primary descriptive knowledge about the philosophical topic under discussion, therefore, he probably thought that his job was not so much to expound the descriptive details, but to present a critical, conceptual, and at times, comparative picture. For example, while writing on 'Buddha's Personality and Buddhist Culture', he brings out the significance of Buddha to Buddhist culture quite well and also compares it with Jainism, Hinduism and Semitic religions in a very cryptic way saying, 'Buddhism spread to different parts of the world for peace by avoiding the evils of persecution and religious warfare'. He further points to the family resemblances between Jainism and Buddhism despite philosophical differences.

The central focus of 'sorrow', as an inherent aspect of human existence, is discussed in the following chapter on 'Early Buddhism'. It appears to be pessimistic but at the end of this inherent suffering is the hope of final peace. This hope of peace (*nirvāṇa*) is deeply rooted in the practice of virtue. Prof. Kulkarni appreciates the universality of this hope of peace having its foundation in the practice of virtue and makes interesting references from *Milinda Pañho, Poṭṭhapāda-Sutta, Kūṭadanta-Sutta* and many other works of early Buddhism to establish his point. Prof. Kulkarni picks up for discussion a neglected text called the *Poṭṭhapāda-Sutta,* for a detailed analysis in the following chapter by the same name and examines the arguments running through the philosophical dialogue in detail. The topic of 'consciousness' is discussed in *Poṭṭhapāda-Sutta* where the argumentative Poṭṭhapāda gives various arguments and theories of consciousness and Buddha goes on rationally denying each one. The argumentative element in the dialogue is well brought out by Prof. Kulkarni. He very clearly supports the Buddha in that the metaphysical and the speculative are not at all logically connected with moral and spiritual endeavours.

The famous *avyākṛta* (indeterminate) questions are discussed in 'The Buddha's Approach to Metaphysics' which shows how one can dissociate 'higher morality or spirituality from conflicting world-views'. Prof. Kulkarni agrees with the Buddha in accepting the irrelevance of metaphysics and laying emphasis on the importance and significance of the ethico-spiritual path. Buddha's silence about the ontological or metaphysical questions, which are futile and inappropriate according to Buddha (and also probably according to Prof. Kulkarni) appears to him as non-dogmatic and open for interpretations. The concept of a 'self' is consequently analysed, bringing into debate the nature of causal relations, role of memory as well as the problematic belief in re-incarnation in the chapter titled 'A Subtlety in the Buddhist Theory of the Self'.

As a rationalist, Prof. Kulkarni supports an egalitarian, liberal position which is reflected in the next article titled, 'Was the Buddha a Rationalist?'. It is in Buddhist ethics that he finds a support for this position, which accommodates everyone without any discrimination and equally avoids any dogmatism. His writings on Buddhist ethics reveal his concern for reason as well as socio-ethical virtues and a value-based life. He finds that Buddhist ethics go far beyond conformity to rules of right behaviour. It is for this reason that Prof. Kulkarni discusses methods of meditation and transformation of personality in the article on 'The Mahāsatipaṭṭhāna-Sutta and Patañjala Yoga', where he critically interprets the state of 'mindfulness' (*satī*) and also steps of mindfulness in *Mahāsatipaṭṭhāna-Sutta*.

'The Ideal of the Sthitaprajña: Some Platitudes and Some

Paradoxes' is another example of Prof. Kulkarni's interest in understanding the ethical and social dimension of a human being. He discusses in the context of traditional theological writings of the East and the West, and observes that the problem of spiritual emancipation needs to be reconciled with personal and social responsibility.

Both Indian and Western epistemology was studied by him with zest and zeal, and he wrote critically on schools of Buddhism, the debate on the nature of perception as *savikalpa* and *nirvikalpa* in the Buddhist and Nyāya schools of philosophy. He also took interest in re-evaluating the Jainism theory of truth (Anekāntavāda) which is seen in the final article in this section titled, 'Anekāntavāda: Some Logical Issues'.

In his writings on Indian philosophy, we may gather reflections of Prof. Kulkarni's philosophical position. He supports an egalitarian, liberal, rational position that admits of differences with a hope that someday there will be an answer and reconciliation for the better. In Prof. Kulkarni we find a philosopher not only interested in the theoretical aspect of philosophical discourse, but also in praxis where one is concerned with the well-being of all humanity without any discrimination. His appeal for universal and secular ethico-spiritual practices, free from any metaphysical controversial theorization, is of tremendous significance, especially in the present technocrat-obsessed society.

In one of his articles, Prof. Kulkarni asks whether the Buddha was a rationalist. One could ask this question with respect to Prof. Kulkarni as well. His observations on the Buddha may well apply to his own philosophical position. In the aforementioned article, he says, 'If a rationalist must necessarily be a materialist and a crusading atheist then the Buddha was not a rationalist'. Instead of calling him a rationalist, Prof. Kulkarni calls the Buddha a man of reason who rests on analysis and 'description of facts of experience'. So was Prof. Kulkarni, a man of reason who valued both knowledge and wisdom together for the betterment of human culture.

1

The Buddha's Personality and Buddhist Culture[1]

EVERYONE who seeks guidance from Buddhism, as a monk or layman or a plain perplexed human being in search of peace of mind takes refuge in the three jewels – the Buddha, Dhamma and Saṁgha. Of these Dhamma by common consent is the most important. The Buddha is revered as the teacher of Dhamma. One of his names *tathāgata* indicates that he is one of a long line of teachers who traverses the ancient path to persuade others to follow him. Truths needful for man's salvation have to be propounded again and again in every age. In spite of important philosophical differences this view has a family resemblance to the Hindu doctrine of *avatāra*s and the Jaina doctrine of *tīrthaṁkara*s. This attitude implies a devaluation of historical details and a neglect of the course of history among Indic religions as compared to Semitic religions in which there is a strong tendency to read clues to the purpose of the creator in the stages in the development of his creation. This naturally leads to immersion in secular enterprises and finding God's will in our own parochial purposes. Bigotry and persecution and religious warfare are the inevitable results. Buddhism spread to different parts of the world while escaping these great evils. But, closely connected with this is a neglect of social and economic life to which Buddhists and

---

1 'The Buddha's Personality and Buddhist Culture', in *Contribution of Buddhism to World Culture,* vol. 1, Somaiya Publications, 2006. (Conference jointly organized by K.J. Somaiya Centre for Buddhist Studies, Dept. of Philosophy, University of Mumbai, Indian Nava Nalanda Mahavira, Nalanda, Bihar, India and Otani University, Kyoto, Japan held between 11-14 March 2004.)

like-minded persons should pay serious attention.

The *saṁgha*, even more than the Buddha, is instrument in value. Its sole purpose is to preserve and propagate *dhamma*. In so far as it fails to do so, as is inevitable in all human institutions because of decay, inherent in their course of evaluation, it has to be replaced or renewed. The Buddha clearly foresaw the decline in his *saṁgha* when he predicted, after admitting women to the monastic order at the intervention of Ananda that the order would now last 500 years instead of 1,000. Thus, shifting the focus away from institutions and personalities to moral and spiritual truths is integral to Buddhism. That is why though Śākyamuni was undoubtedly a historical person we know very little about the details of the Buddha as a person. There are indeed traditional biographies of the Buddha and scholars have edited and annotated them with great care. But they are interspersed with legend and allegory and supply very few details of human interest. A critical biography, in the Western sense, does not exist. Karen Armstrong in her *Buddha* the first non-legendary story of the Buddha's life says that there is something 'unBuddhist' in writing a biography of the Buddha.[2] This devaluation of personality is closely related to Buddhist philosophy.

Nirvāṇa can be attained only by the elimination of *nāma–rūpa* without remainder (*anupādhiśeṣa*), whether it is anything more, it is difficult to say. But if the Buddha's original authentic teaching can be gathered from the Pāli dialogues, then a total silence is the only way to answer futile and inappropriate questions. Instead of waxing eloquent on the ineffable the Buddha tried to show his interlocutor that his question does not arise. This silence about the final goal of our spiritual journey is matched by the a-metaphysical approach to its beginning. The Buddha does not begin with a vision of reality – ultimate reality if you like – assigning everything including man, its proper place in the universe and then make practical recommendations about the best life for man. He begins with an analytical–descriptive account of the nature of suffering inherent

---

[2] Karen Armstrong, *Buddha*, Introduction, p. XI, Penguin Books, 2004.

in human life and lays down an efficacious method of overcoming it. This 'existential' approach is apt to disappoint many who come to philosophy with great expectations of finding out all about God, Nature and Man. That many contemporaries felt 'let down' by this approach is evident from *Poṭṭhapāda-Sutta*.

But whatever may be one's reaction to this approach, a certain non-dogmatism is built into it. That there is a well thought-out view underlying his teaching cannot be denied. But this *weltanschauung* is communicated not so much by argument, as by persuasive dialogue and personal example. The starting point is recognition of the fact of suffering – suffering inseparable from all finite, sentient existence. When we are physically ill we react immediately and take remedial measures. But spiritual malaise may go unrecognized. Indeed the patient may feel that he is fine and ridicule those who try to awaken in him a sense of dissatisfaction and a groping towards a higher goal. In a well-known metaphor the Buddha compares such person to those who are busy singing and dancing in a hall in a palace whose outskirts are on fire saying: 'The fire is far away, it won't reach us for quite some time'. He himself felt profoundly dissatisfied with the kind of life he was leading though youth and life seemed to stretch out like a long vista of pleasure and power. There are many stories of how he reminded his listeners of the urgency of seeking something that will bring us permanent peace. To be mindful of the misery inherent in our lives is the first step in our spiritual journey. The Buddha's teaching is not the 'opium of the people'. This pessimism, as it may be called, is more characteristic of Buddhism than of any other great religions of the world with the possible exception of Jainism. It is not born of any particularly unfavourable historical circumstances but is the result of unwavering concentration on the primordial patterns of human life – birth, ageing and death, ignorance, confusion of purpose, being subject to a cycle of desires and satisfactions followed by fresh desires and satisfactions apparently endlessly. And yet the final note is one of hope of deliverance held out to every one. *Nirvāṇa* is open to anyone who is alert and steadfast in the practice of virtue and mindfulness. It is not restricted to any particular race or nationality or an elite determined either by birth or status. A particularly eloquent expression of universality of outlook is to be found in *Milinda Pañho* [*Paññha*].[3] After disabusing the mind of the king that there is some region where *nirvāṇa* is stored (*sannihita*), Nāgasena proceeds to tell him that there is no special place particularly suitable for its realization. Just as a man with eyes can see the sky wherever he may be standing, so also, anyone with resolution established in virtue can realize *nirvāṇa* whether in the country of Greeks or China, Kashmir or Gāndhāra, Benares or Kosala or even *Brahmaloka*. Total freedom from racial and national prejudice cannot go further. In spite of occasional lapses Buddhists have preserved this legacy.

I have already pointed out that the metaphysical approach of the Buddha leads to freedom from dogmatism. But his temperament and personality were totally alien to any form of coercion, even the mental and verbal violence, involved in doctrinal disputes. All polemical passions were discouraged by him as a hindrance to enlightenment. He never threatens his opponents with dire consequences nor lures them with prospects of earthly or celestial pleasures. But this gentleness is combined with great earnestness and a readiness to speak out against evils. He accepts criticisms of himself in good humour. The purpose is not to humiliate one's opponent but to guide him to a better way of life. In *Kūṭadanta-Sutta* the Buddha tells Kūṭadanta, a brāhmin about to officiate at a sacrifice, that the right kind of sacrifice eschews forced labour and slaughter of animals and uses only cereals, ghee, etc. At the beginning of the *Buddhist Book of Genesis* while conversing with Vāsettha and Bhāradvāja the Buddha quietly punctures the brāhmin claim that they have directly descended from the mouth of Brahmā by appealing to simple and universally observed facts of biology. His gentleness of manner does not exclude forthrightness in criticizing and exposing what he considered to be wrong. Unfailingly he followed the maxim: 'The only way to speak the

---

3 *Milinda Pañho* (from the Sacred Books of the Buddhists Series, tr. I.B. Horner, Oxford: Pali Text Society), VII, pp. 92-94.

truth is to speak lovingly'.[4]

Buddhist ethics is through and through, egalitarian and liberal in spirit. This comes out in many ways and on many occasions. The Buddha discussed *dhamma* with persons from all strata of society – kings, rich merchants, learned brāhmins and wandering monks of different persuasions and people from humbler walks of life like Citta, the son of an elephant trainer.[5] He was accused by some contemporaries of forsaking his noble rank and persuading many others to do so, when he established his *saṁgha* and consorted with the shave-headed ascetics, the dark-skinned and the low born. For the orthodox this was confusion of castes (*varṇa-saṁkara*) and an invitation to social disorder. The Buddha did accept the broad division of society into nobles (warriors), brāhmins, traders and workers. He regarded the caste system predominantly as a functional social arrangement; this is particularly true of the distinction between a brāhmin and a *cāṇḍāla* (out caste). In *Sonadaṇḍa-Sutta*, Sonadaṇḍa lays down six qualifications of a brāhmin which can be telescoped into three, viz., noble birth, Vedic learning and virtuous conduct. The Buddha leads him step by step to drop all of them except virtuous conduct which is pronounced to be the only qualification of a true brāhmin. The complementary view that a *cāṇḍāla* is a person of evil conduct is set forth in a brief discourse in the *Sutta Nipāta*. Another brief discourse emphasizes that if a man is virtuous and self-restrained he is a brāhmin regardless of his birth. The theme of social stratification, its true basis and proper functioning, is a recurrent theme in the Pāli canon. In *Majjhima-Nikāya* we have the story of Assalāyana who is sent by some recluses and brāhmins to argue him out of his view that anyone belonging to any of the four castes is worthy of respect if he is pure of heart. The Buddha argues with him with his usual patience appealing to universally accepted moral rules and commonly accepted facts of experience. Assalāyana is compelled to admit that if a noble man or a brāhmin kills, steals and misbehaves in other ways he will,

---

4 I owe this quotation to my friend Dr S.V. Bokil.

5 See *Poṭṭapāda-Sutta, Dīgha-Nikāya*.

after his death, have a miserable rebirth in a lower world or lower order. Equally a member of the fourth caste will be reborn in a happy and noble state if he has been virtuous. In this context the Buddha gives the interesting metaphor of four different persons producing fires by rubbing sticks of different types of wood – *sāl*, sandalwood, castor, etc. The flames so produced will be the same in brilliance, hue and other relevant characteristics of a fire. Their being generated by different types of wood does not matter in the least in this context. The Buddha sums up the dissussion thus 'First, you Assalāyana, set off about birth: you went on to *mantra*s, from there you have come round to the purity of the four castes, which is what I am laying down.'

Śīla is the foundation of the threefold training necessary to attain *nirvāṇa*. The rules for the guidance of monks and nuns (*pātimokkha*) are well known and have been elaborately discussed. But *Sigālavāda-Sutta* is interesting as the only full-fledged discourse by the Buddha about ethics for laymen. In the Indian tradition rule by elders is accepted routinely and the young, especially women, have the supreme duty of obedience. The Buddha emphasizes the reciprocal nature of moral obligations. Sigāla, a young-house holder of Rājagr̥ha is found by the Buddha, early in the morning, doing obeisance to the various directions in the conventionally prescribed manner. After ascertaining from the young man why he was going through rather strange gestures and motions, the Buddha tells him that the true Aryan way of worshipping the quarters was to abstain from vice and discharge one's social obligations. I quote, as typical of the Buddha's humane and liberal spirit from the passages concerning the relation between husband and wife and master and servant. The husband should minister to his wife by faithfulness, by respect, by courtesy, by handing over authority to her, by providing adornments. The wife ministered to (in this way) by her husband should be hospitable to the kin of both, be watchful over the goods he brings and exercise skill and industry in discharging her functions. The noble master should minister to his servants, as the nadir, thus: by assigning work according to their strength, by supplying them with food and wages, by tending them in sickness, by granting them leave at appropriate times. The employees and servants should do their work well and spread their master's fame. They should be content with what is given and rise before him and retire after him. The dialogue also brings out that righteousness should not be confused with ritual piety, which orthodoxy tended to overvalue.

Buddha's non-authoritarian spirit comes out in many ways particularly in his last days. The *saṁgha* established by him, functioned democratically, at any rate when he was living. Revision of rules, imposing penalties for offences, and all important decisions were taken by a vote in a general assembly of the members of the order. When he was on his deathbed, Ānanda asked him to issue final instructions. He refused to do so and exhorted him and other monks to seek refuge in truth as their guide and their self as their saviour. There is again his well-known advice to his followers not to accept anything because he the Buddha had said it. They were to test it, like a goldsmith a piece of metal, in the light of their experience and make their choice according to their judgement. This invitation to think for oneself and strive after perfection has few parallels in the history of religion.

In the course of its historical development and dissemination Buddhism has assumed many forms and given rise to many sects (eighteen Hīnayāna sects were recognized in ancient India, i.e. about 300 BCE). Doctrinal disputes and bickering and mutual recriminations have punctuated this history. But with all the aberrations, nothing like the religious warfare and persecution that have characterized the West and the Middle East are to be found in its history. As Edward Conze,[6] warns us,

> we should not paint Buddhism too white: but something of the legacy of Buddha and the impress of his personality have been kept alive. Our problem is to preserve it and extend it. It is sometimes said that 'Buddhism is Hinduism for export'.

---

6 Edward Conze, *Buddhism: Its Essence and Development*, Dover Publications, 2003.

If so, it is a matter for satisfaction that we have exported the best in us without the evils that have marred our social history. And yet we must remind ourselves, in these days of growing bigotry and violence, that the overall picture in India, in spite of occasional aberrations, has been one of tolerance and letting a hundred thousand flowers bloom. The very fact that the Buddha and his older contemporary Mahāvīra were allowed to live to the ripe age of eighty and spread their teachings is unique in the history of the world though they denied Vedic authority and by-passed the question of the existence of God. Buddhsim is the best expression of this synergetic culture of peaceful coexistence. To me, the Buddha is the greatest 'Jagadguru', though it is possible to have different perspectives in different contexts. 'You pays your money, you has your choice.'

2

Early Buddhism[1]

THE purpose of this modest essay is to give an outline of the original teaching of the Buddha in so far as this can be ascertained. In the course of its long history Buddhism has developed a luxuriance of philosophical schools and religious sects. Our task is to extract the common basis – the highest common factor which makes them all, in spite of their striking divergences, expressions of a common faith. This is not an easy task in view of the fact that the Buddha like Socrates and Jesus did not write any books, and his teachings as we understand them today, have come down to us through his disciples and followers. Originally they were transmitted orally and were reduced to writing for the first time nearly half a millennium after the death of the Buddha, about the beginning of Christian era, under the reign of the Sinhalese king Vattagāmni. Traditionally, Buddhist scriptures have been divided into three 'baskets' (*tripiṭaka*) or divisions. The first called Sūtras, comprises the dialogues and discourses of the Buddha. The Vinaya – the second division – deals with the conduct of monks and matters of ecclesiastical discipline. The last and third division, called Abhidharma (literally, 'further *dharma*' or 'supreme *dharma*'), consists of commentaries and explanations by later writers on the philosophical and moral doctrines contained in the Sūtras. These learned treatises are heavy and dull and add very little to the main teachings of the Sūtras while lacking in their freshness and originality. There are three versions of the *tripiṭaka* – the Pāli version deriving from Ceylon and the Chinese

---

1 'Early Buddhism', in *Buddhist and Jaina Views in Indian Philosophy*, Raviwar Peth, Pune: P.D. Ghanekar, Managing Trustee, Datta Lakshmi Trust, 1992, p. 466.

and the Tibetan versions. There are significant divergences amongst them but the Pāli version is considered to be the most authoritative and nearest to the original teaching of the Buddha. The Theravādins (doctrine of elders) and the Hīnayāna schools accept the Pāli *tripiṭaka* as the only true scriptures. The Mahāyānists, in addition, recognize as canonical later-Sūtra works such as the Prajñā-Pāramitā group. In the Hīnayāna tradition 'Questions of King Milinda (*Milinda Pañho*)' of unknown authorship and composed in north-western India about the first century CE and *Viśuddhi-Magga* (Path of Purity) by Buddhaghoṣa, probably of the fourth century CE have almost canonical status.

II

The simplest and the best approach to basic Buddhism is through an exposition of the moral and practical teaching of the Buddha. There is no doubt whatever that the Buddha himself regarded the four noble truths (*ārya satya*s) as the core of his teaching. But the propounding and explanation of these truths involves philosophical and psychological analysis and a certain amount of doctrine though largely negative and non-committal in character.

When after years of struggle and search, reflection and meditation, the Buddha attained enlightenment, he formulated his wisdom in the four following truths:

1. All existence (life) is suffering (*duḥkham*)
2. This suffering has a cause, viz. craving or selfish desire (*tṛṣṇā*)
3. The suffering can be removed by removing the underlying cause
4. The way to remove suffering is the noble eightfold path (*ārya aṣṭāṅga mārga*)

It is immediately obvious that the teaching is expressed in the language of medical practice. The Buddha regarded himself and was regarded by his disciples as the great physician whose sole purpose was to cure suffering humanity of its ills. The first step is to recognize that you are ill. Part of human suffering is the liability to disease and pain. But if things are not going badly for us in the ordinary way we are contended. 'I am all right Jack', neatly sums up the attitude of the average sensual person if there is nothing obviously wrong. The Buddha's sensitiveness led him to perceive the misery built into the very texture of a temporal mode of existence – subject to never-ending desires, goaded by pleasure and pain and destined to end in old age and death. All conditioned existence (*dharmas*) is impermanent, miserable and lacking in essential selfhood (*anitya, duḥkha, anātma*). (This is emphasized in many dialogues and also in *The Dhammapada* 277-79.)

The cause of suffering is *tṛṣṇā* (selfish desire) rooted in ignorance (*avidyā*). The ignorance being the illusion, that there is a permanent soul within us, whereas there is nothing enduring anywhere in the phenomenal world, including the human personality. The Buddha would not have denied that external factors, notably the behaviour of others contributes to our suffering. But the primary source is the insatiable thirst for existence in us. By removing this cause we can remove the effect. Many have pointed out how very scientific and analytic the Buddha is in his approach to the world and human life. Our suffering is neither accidental nor is it the result of supernatural agencies beyond our control. It is the consequence of certain causes and by removing the causes the consequence too can be removed. This is the doctrine of *pratītya-samutpāda* commonly translated as 'dependent origination'. It represents the middle position between the view that chance governs the world and its opposite, that the world is governed by absolute, unchangeable necessity. Literally the phrase means 'given this (that) arises'. If *A* and *B* are cause and effect, the doctrine is that given *A*, *B* follows always and in the absence of *A*, *B* never follows. In modern terminology the cause is regarded as both the necessary and sufficient condition of the existence of the effect. The rule of law is not restricted to human experience and human life. It characterizes the entire universe embracing within its scope the physical elements as also the celestial realms of being. In the dialogues as well as later-Buddhist writings, the term *dharma* in addition to referring to phenomenal conditioned existence also symbolizes the law especially the law of righteousness whose observance leads to *nirvāṇa*.

III

The eightfold Āryan path is the means to deliverance from suffering. It consists of (1) right belief, (2) right aspiration or resolve, (3) right speech, (4) right conduct, (5) right living, (6) right effort, (7) right recollection, and (8) right concentration. The whole scheme is sometimes reduced to the threefold discipline (*triśikṣā*) of *śīla*, *samādhi* and *prajñā*. As in the case of Upaniṣadic philosophy and Jainism the way of life that leads to salvation comprises integrally related elements of (a) adoption of right outlook, (b) practice of virtue and self purification, and (c) mental and spiritual exercises which lead to the direct discernment of truth and hence to liberation. In the eightfold scheme the first two may be called philosophical and involve the committed acceptance of the four noble truths. The next four are moral and the last two psychological and spiritual. The moral discipline includes and imperceptibly passes into meditational exercises. Buddhist ethics is based on psychology and apart from its role in preparing the mind for the perception of the highest truth, meditation strengthens virtue and helps in eradicating evil tendencies. The moral steps do not require elaboration. Right conduct consists in the five observances (*pañcaśīla*), viz. abstaining from killing, theft, falsehood, unchaste behaviour and consumption of intoxicants. The Buddha advocated the middle path (*madhyama mārga*) between self indulgence and asceticism to the point of self torture. In *Dharmacakra Pravartana-Sūtra*, the Buddha is represented as saying in his first sermon:

> These are two extremes, O monks from which he who leads religious life must abstain. One is a life of pleasure devoted to desire and enjoyment that is base ignoble, unworthy unreal. The other is a life of mortification; it is gloomy, unworthy, unreal. The perfect one O monks is removed from both these extremes and has discovered the way which lies between them, the middle way which enlightens the eyes, enlightens the mind, which leads to

rest, to knowledge, to enlightenment, to *nirvāṇa*.

The ethical teaching of the Buddha like that of other great teachers of mankind goes far beyond conformity to rules of right behaviour. It involves culture of mind and the transfiguration of our whole personality which make evil deeds inconceivable. It is impossible to read *Dharmapada* without being moved by the sublimity, the grandeur and universality of its message. It asks us to liken others to oneself and refrain from doing anything to others which we dislike when done to us to. From several gems of spiritual wisdom I quote the following well-known verse:

akrodhena jayet krodhan asādhum sādhunā jayet ।
jayet kadaryam dānena satyenālīkavādinam ॥
– *Dharmapada* 223

One should conquer anger by gentleness, evil by good: One should win over a miser by liberality and a liar by truth.

In *Maitrī-Sūtra* the Buddha enjoins the practice of four *brahmavihāras*, viz. *maitrī* (friendliness), *karuṇā* (compassion), *muditā* (sympathetic joy) and *upekṣā* (equanimity). Later Mahāyāna writers mention the cultivation of six perfections, viz. *dāna*, *śīla*, *kṣānti*, *vīrya*, *dhyāna* and *prajñā* (giving, morality, patience, vigour, meditation and wisdom, respectively). The practice of *brahmavihāra*s brings together *śīla* and *dhyāna* for they consist in cultivating states of consciousness in which the mind is pervaded by universal love, compassion, sympathetic joy and serene detachment. The following quotation from *Maitrī-Sūtra* gives us a particularly apt theme of such meditations:

May all beings be happy and at their ease. . . . All beings whether weak or strong – omitting none in high, middle or low realms of existence – small or great, visible or invisible, near or far away, born or to be born – may all beings be at their ease. Let none deceive another, or despise any being in any state: let none by anger or ill-will wish harm to another. Even as a mother watches over and protects her only child, so with a boundless mind should one cherish all living beings, radiating friendliness over the entire world.

Methods of meditation have always been central to the Buddhist tradition. These are brought under the seventh step in the noble path, called *samyak-smṛti* (*satī* is the Pāli word). The expression is translated as right recollection or mindfulness. In *Mahā-Smṛti Prasthāna-Sūtra* the Buddha expounds the technique of mindfulness at great length. The essence of it is to be fully aware of what one is doing or undergoing, to pay attention to the goings on in the mind–body complex instead of being immersed in them. This is the reversal of the practical attitude, as stepping out of what we normally consider our self and the adoption of what Advaita would term *sākṣibhāva* the attitude of a witness. Four applications of mindfulness are mentioned (i) in relation to the body, (ii) in relation to sensations and feelings, (iii) in relation to emotions, and (iv) in relation to thoughts and mental objects. The first two prevent the mind from 'woolgathering' and concentrate it on the present condition of the body as a whole or some part of it, without effort. The other two are more complex and involve discursive meditation in the context of Buddhist philosophy. When directed on negative thoughts and emotions, mindfulness arrests their normal development and strengthens self-restraint. Unlike the common forms of meditation including Pātañjala Yoga, mindfulness does not involve concentration on a selected object. But Buddhism also employs the usual method of narrowing down consciousness to a selected object. Theravādins recognize eight forms of *dhyāna*. The first four employ some sensory object and the latter four dispense with all sensory aid. In the sermon (this is so important that it is reproduced with minor variation in practically all Sūtra collections) on mindfulness the Buddha himself mentions the four higher forms of meditations (*samādhi*). In the first stage all appetites, unwholesome thoughts and impulse are banished and there is experience of happiness and serenity. But at this stage there is discursive awareness of a selected idea – such as infinite space, infinite consciousness, etc. In the next stage there is no thought or deliberation; the mind is one-pointed (*ekāgra*) calm and happy. In the next stage there is no pleasure or pain and one experiences a sense of well-being in one's body. In the final stage even this sense of well-being is transcended and there is 'utter purity of equanimity and mindfulness'. At this stage one has direct insight into truth (*prajñā*) and this wisdom leads one into *nirvāṇa*. According to Buddhaghoṣa we see the path of purity which is the same as *nirvāṇa,* as we glimpse the bright full moon through a parting in the clouds.

IV

This brief account of the way to salvation has to be supplemented by an analysis of the cause and course of bondage which tells us in detail how the fetters are forged which chain us to the wheel of becoming. We are told that when Śākyamuni attained enlightenment the entire sequence of the links (*nidānas*) of the chain of bondage (*bhāva-cakra*) burst upon him in a flash and he exclaimed:

> *Gṛhakāraka dṛṣṭo 'sipunargeham na kariṣyasi.*
>
> Maker of houses (prisons) I have seen you. You will not build another habitation for me.

These words are the first line of a verse said to be the first utterance of the Buddha after attaining enlightment. It is reproduced from *Bhahmajāla-Sūtra* in verse 154 of *Dharmapada*. The elaboration of the chain is a detailed application of the doctrine of *pratītya-samutpāda*. Each link in the chain follows necessarily from the previous and equally necessarily it is removed of its predecessor is removed. The following are the twelve links in the chain.

1. *Avidyā* (ignorance)
2. *Saṁskāra* (active dispositions)
3. *Vijñāna* (consciousness)
4. *Nāma–rūpa* (mind–body)
5. *Ṣaḍāyatana* (field of six)
6. *Sparśa* (contact)
7. *Vedanā* (sensation)
8. *Tṛṣṇā* (craving)

9. *Upādāna* (clinging to life)
10. *Bhāva* (being)
11. *Jāti* (rebirth)
12. *Jarāmaraṇa* (age-death)

The precise interpretation of some of these steps is a matter of considerable controversy. Also, there is a certain amount of overlap between the different stages and the connections; between them are sometimes not so much causal but of logical mutual involvement. However the general pattern is clear enough. The twelve links are arranged under three heads because it is generally accepted that the chain extends over the immediately preceding and the immediately following life as well as the present. The first two, ignorance and the active dispositions rooted in it, carry us over to the next embodiment. They are as it were, the credit card with which we start a new life. The resultant *vijñāna* or (individual) consciousness is the most basic factor which begins the process of present embodiment by entering a womb and attracting the physical elements, thus setting up a new mind–body complex. From the evolution of the senses and their contact with their objects follow pleasant painful and neutral feelings, and from sensations spring up craving, clinging to life and accumulation of fresh *karma*. (Dasgupta takes *bhāva* to be *karma*, in which case it is *saṁskāra*s but this time with a prospective reference.) Birth, age and death follow from them and clearly refer to the life to come. The chain repeats itself indefinitely in the same order, and hence constitutes a cycle. The Buddha accepted without argument, the cyclical character of phenomenal existence and the doctrine of *karma* and rebirth. The only way to break the chain and effect and escape from the suffering of *saṁsāra* is to cut at the roots of *tṛṣṇā* in *avidyā* and attain to purity and peace by following the noble eightfold path.

V

If Buddhism were merely or even primarily a rational moral way of life it is needless to go any further than we have done. There are those who believe that it is just that, and other elements associated with it are religious, metaphysical, mythological accretions which can be eliminated without affecting its essence. The Buddha himself discouraged metaphysical speculation and directed his disciples to strive diligently for salvation. But, for a thoughtful person especially for a great visionary like the Buddha, it is impossible to avoid ultimate questions about the nature of the world and the destiny of man. As I have remarked earlier the very exposition of the four Āryan truths involves certain analytical and explanatory commitments. One of these is the nature of causality on which we have touched briefly. Another even more fundamental doctrine is the Buddha's teaching on the impermanence and soullessness (*nairātmya*) of all phenomena including human beings. Indeed all conditioned existence is sorrowful precisely because of *anitya* and hence incapable of providing any rest and abiding peace for us. Again and again Buddhist scriptures insist on the transitory character of all *dharma*s. Of the three characteristics of all conditioned existents (*saṁskāra*s), their impermanence is the basis for their lacking in selfhood.[2] The Buddha was perhaps the first person in human history to look up on the world as a process, a continuous flux with no enduring entities underlying it. The common sense view is to consider the world, for the most part, to be composed of substances, things or persons persisting through varying periods of time and undergoing changes of state. For the Buddha things are merely aggregates of changing elements. This is true as much of the human personality as of physical objects.

A human being is analysed into five *skandha*s (strands, branches) referred to as *nāma–rūpa*. *Rūpa* stands for the bodily frame and under *nāma* we have mental elements. These are distinguished into *vedanā, saṁjñā, saṁskāra* and *vijñāna*. The exact interpretation of these terms is a matter of controversy and varies in the scriptures as well as among the commentators. (And the uncertainty is made

---

[2] This is the seed of the later Mādhyamika doctrine, that all phenomena are *niḥsvabhāva* (and therefore *śūnya*) *and source of their sorrowfulness*) (italics by editor).

worse because *saṁskāra* mentioned above is frequently used to refer to all compound entities or constrictions, i.e. to all *dharmas*.) But broadly speaking *vedanā* refers to sensations and feelings, *saṁjñā* to perception or recognition *saṁskāra* to various reactive dispositions or conative tendencies and *vijñāna* to self-consciousness involving conceptual understanding. Man is simply as aggregate (*saṁghāta*) of these elements and his history, the history of the arising and passing away of these elements. To suppose that there is a soul, ego, or experiences over and above the *skandhas* is to be guilty of a delusion. Part of the difficulty in accepting or even understanding this view is its radical, un-commonsensical character. But there are genuine problems to be resolved before it can be made acceptable even to the pious and the faithful. This is clearly shown by the fact that some of the later-day realist philosophers (*sarvāstivādins*) were compelled to introduce an element called *pudgal*, neither different nor indifferent from the *skandhas*, which persists through all the lives of a person until *nirvāṇa* is attained. This is heresy and the philosophers concerned were careful to avoid the words *ātman* or *attā* in view of the Buddha's emphatic declaration that everything is *anātma*. The *ālaya-vijñāna* of the idealists serves a similar purpose.

But the orthodox Hīnayāna view is set forth clearly and vigorously in *Questions of King Milinda*. Milinda puts the difficulty pointedly, after Nāgasena's declaration that there is no individuality or permanent self. He asks:

> If, most reverend Nāgasena, there be no permanent individuality involved in the matter, who is it, pray, who gives you members of the order your robes and food and lodging? Who is it who enjoys such things when given? Who is it who lives a life of righteousness? Who is it who attains to the goal of *nirvāṇa* or arhatship? Who is it who lives a life of worldly lusts . . . which work out their better fruit even in this life? If that be so there is neither merit nor demerit, there is neither doer nor causer of good or evil deeds: there is neither fruit nor result of good or evil *karma*. – Book II, chap. II

This is a difficulty which has pursued Buddhism throughout its history and many thinkers take it to be a fatal one. Whether or not one accepts the solution offered by Nāgasena it cannot be said that his task is made easy by Milinda. The objection could not have been stated more forcefully. Nāgasena's response is to ask Milinda after ascertaining that he has come to the monastery in a chariot what the word 'chariot' stands for. It does not stand for any of its parts such as the wheels, the frame, the ropes or the yoke. Nor is it identical with all these parts, nor with anything outside of them all. And yet the word is not an empty sound. It is on account of the co-semblage of its various parts – their arrangement in a certain manner – that it comes under the common name 'chariot'. Similarly 'Nāgasena', Milinda, etc. are only generally understood terms, designations in common use. So it is, 'Nāgasena concludes, quoting from the *Saṁyukta-Nikāya* – that when the *skandhas* are there we talk of a "being"'. The only thing that may cause some puzzlement in this explanation is the refusal to identify the chariot with all its parts taken together. It is in fact quite common to say that for Buddhism, the 'self' is only a label for the aggregate of certain physical and psychical factors. Nāgasena here may have wished to make one of two points. The self is not a mere collection of elements. The elements and their succession are characterized by a pattern, a manner of arrangement. It is only when this characteristic arrangement is present that we can speak of a 'self'. Second the 'self' does not really name anything. It is a word we tend to use when and only when certain conditions are fulfilled. The two points are not exclusive of one another.

But this is not the end of the story. Nāgasena has yet to deal with the problems connected with moral agency and responsibility and the notions of wrong-doing and punishment. Even a Buddhist cannot deny that a person remains the same in some sense: throughout his life, and without some secret of unity our moral and spiritual life would be unintelligible. The answer, put very badly, is that the psycho-physical states which constitute one person are unified by causal relations. The later members are descendants of earlier ones and can therefore be properly ascribed to one person. Referring specially to the problem of crime and punishment, Nāgasena considers the plea of a clever thief that he cannot be punished because in taking mangoes from his neighbour's garden he has not stolen the fruits belonging to this neighbour, i.e. the very fruits planted by him. But different fruits produced by the tree. It is not very difficult to agree as the king does, that this plea cannot be entertained, and that the thief is punishable precisely because he has stolen the mangoes resulting from those planted by his neighbour. It is a little surprising that Nāgasena does not apply the analogy at the crucial end – to show that though evil actions lead to later suffering and that though the two do not belong to a common subject, the suffering is justified because it belongs to the same series as the evil intentions and actions. Nevertheless the conclusion what we are supposed to draw is fairly obvious.

It is not easy to evaluate such a phenomenalistic theory of personal identity. For Buddhism the difficulties are compounded by its acceptance of reincarnation. Popularly the doctrine is interpreted in terms of a persistent entity which leaves one body and lodges itself in another. There must be some element of truth in this picture if the doctrine is taken seriously. There are those who give an interpretation of the doctrine consistent with materialism. Others again are of the view that the Buddha did not really accept reincarnation but was making a concession to popular imagination in adopting the language of the doctrine. In my opinion neither view is justified. The Buddha did take seriously the doctrine of an indefinite succession of embodiments for a person. He rejects annihilationism (Ucchedavāda) as clearly as he rejects eternalism (Śāśvatavāda). It is one thing to say that there is something attractive and valid in the Buddhist scheme of life even for a materialist but quite another to excise large chunks of canonical Buddhist literature and try to demonstrate that the Buddha was a rationalist and materialist in the modern sense. In *Saṁyukta-Nikāya* the Buddha refuses to identify the self with either the mind or the body but declares that it would be better for the ordinary man to identify himself with his body. This is not because the body is more important or composed of permanent elements but because it is obviously subject to dissolution whereas the mind seems to have the potentiality of wandering on restlessly for ever. Identification with the mind therefore fosters the illusion that there can be something permanent within the world of becoming.

As regards the adequacy of a serial theory of the self the following points may be made:

1. If the Buddhist theory is adequate to explain personal identity in our present life, it can, with suitable extensions and modifications, be made to cover the alleged previous and forthcoming lives. (The admission of moral agents does not negate the doctrine of *anattā* as Mrs. Rhys Davids alleges.)
2. It is sometimes said that such a theory substitutes continuity for identity. This may be granted. But it is then added that what transmigrates in Buddhism is not a soul entity but character. But this is to turn a man's moral character into a subsistent entity which can exist by itself. Generalizing the difficulty we may say that dispositions of all kinds can be ascribed, according to our ordinary ways of speaking, only to continuants and not momentary particulars or series of them. The Buddhist doesn't do enough to meet the difficulty.
3. A standard objection against the serial theory is that it cannot account for facts of memory and self-conciousness.

Regarding the latter it is said that a momentary state cannot be aware of itself or other equally momentary states. There is a real difficulty here but the eternalists – for example, Śaṅkara – do not realize that a transcendent *ātman* is not of any help in accounting for empirical phenomena like memory and reflexive awareness. Philosophers who postulate eternal or subsistent entities do not realize how little such entities really explain. On the other hand, the Buddhists and their counterparts in the West do not realize that they have a great deal of explaining to do. If they set themselves to this task and succeed in their efforts, they would probably realize that they will have to return to the common man a great deal of what their philosophy seems to take away. After all, our ordinary notions of personal identity and moral responsibility must have some 'cash value'.

VI

The difficulty concerning the existence of the self the 'true self' of man if we like – is closely linked to an understanding of the nature of *nirvāṇa*. In early Buddhist literature it is largely – though not entirely – described in negative terms. It is a state in which the fires of greed and desire, delusion and suffering are put out. We may even say that individuality in the ordinary sense is extinguished. But if *nirvāṇa* is perfect peace and freedom, there must be a higher self to experience this peace and freedom. Otherwise the highest goal of Buddhist endeavour would be self-annihilation. In attaining *nirvāṇa* we would be signing and executing our own death-warrant. Considerations such as these have led thinkers like Radhakrishnan, Ananda K. Coomaraswamy and R.C. Zaehner to argue that the Buddha never denied and even that he affirmed, if only by implication that there is a higher self whose realization is the goal of human life. There is some support for this view especially in the following passage from 'Udāna' from *Kṣudraka-Nikāya*:

> There is an unborn, unbecome, unmade, incomposite, and were it not for this unborn incomposite, unbecome, unmade, no escape could be shown here from birth, becoming, making composition.

But this is balanced by the fact that both in *Aṅguttara* and *Saṁyukta*, when the Buddha describes the nature of the incomposite he does it in negative terms saying it is the destruction of passion, delusion and hatred, and the absence of origin, alteration and destruction. Coomarswamy and I.B. Horner seem to go too far when they write:

> In the whole of the Buddhist canonical literature it is nowhere stated that 'there is no self' though they take care to give a capital 'S' to the word self. In their anthology of the thoughts of the Buddha they alternate between the capital and the small-case 'S' where the texts give no hint of a change in meaning. It is of course possible that the Buddha's teaching implies, without explicitly stating, the reality of a higher self. Later, Mahāyāna identified *nirvāṇa* with the *dharmakāya* of the Buddha which again is the Absolute Reality. If this is the right interpretation of the Buddha, then he comes very close to some form of Advaita.

However, the Buddha's own procedure, when confronted with such ultimate questions, is to maintain silence and if pressed further to deny the affirmation and also the negation.[3] He adopts this technique not only an answer to the question 'Does the *tathāgata* or an *arhat* continue to exist after his death?' (see his handing of Vatsagotra on this question in *Madhyama-Nikāya*) but also in relation to other questions such as: 'Is the world finite or infinite?', 'Is the soul distinct from the body or not?', 'Is consciousness the same as a man's soul or different?'. In *Poṭṭhapāda-Sūtra*, after expounding his 'no-soul' theory, the Buddha refuses to answer these questions put by his brāhmin interlocutor of that name. He justifies his silence by saying that these are indeterminate (*avyākṛta*) questions which it is profitless for a man to pursue. 'The question is not calculated to profit, it is not concerned with *dharma* – it does not lead to detachment, nor to purification from lusts, nor to supra-normal knowledge nor to *nirvāṇa*.' He compares persons who raise and pursue such questions to a man who is deeply in love with a lady but is unable to say who she is or what she looks like or to a man who builds a staircase in the middle of a thoroughfare without the least idea of where it would lead to.

But is the practical irrelevance of these questions the only thing that is wrong with them? If this were so the Buddha himself must have known the answers being omniscient and must have held back the answer from his disciples on the ground that it was not conducive to their salvation to pursue such matters. In *Saṁyukta-Nikāya* the Buddha, holding a few *śiṁśapā* leaves in his hands and standing under a *śiṁśapā* tree, addresses the disciples after they declare that there are many more leaves in the tree than the Lord is holding in his hand, thus:

> In the same way, monks, many more are those things which

---

[3] If pressed further we should reject as inappropriate both affirmation and denial; also joint affirmation and joint denial. If P is theory and $\sim P$ its denial, we reject P, $\sim P$, $(P \cdot \sim P)$, and $(\sim P \cdot \sim\sim P)$. (Here we see the origin of the *catuṣkoṭi* of the Mādhyamikas.)

> through my super-knowledge I do not make known to you: a few are those things which I make known to you.

But against this is to be set his most emphatic declaration to Ananda in *Mahāparinirvāṇa-Sūtra* that the *tathāgata* has no such thing as the closed fist, that he has imparted the truth as he knew it, without making any distinction between esoteric and exoteric doctrines. I shall not pursue this matter any further, except to remark that the question cannot be settled by the number of quotations that can be mustered on either side.

There is, however, a very contemporary answer which would remove all the difficulties connected with any of the possible answers considered above. It is to treat these questions not as vague, unanswerable and practically irrelevant questions, but as improper or illegitimate questions. They rest on false assumptions or are inapplicable to the situation in relation to which they are raised. A good, ordinary example of such a question would be asking a bachelor whether his wife is interested in music. Both 'yes' and 'no' would be equally misleading and wrong. If metaphysical questions of the type that have exercised men's minds through centuries are of this kind, then they cannot be answered. They cannot be answered because they are not genuine questions at all. The Buddha's silence which was only re-emphasized dramatically by fourfold negation was intended to bring out the essential unanswerability of such questions. Perhaps this is the point made by the following passage from *Madhyama-Nikāya*:

> Vatsagotra asks: 'But has Gotama any theory of his own?'
>
> The Lord replies: 'The Tathāgata, O Vatsa, is free from all theories'.

[***Editor's Note***: In this paper N.G.K. has used Sanskritized forms of Pāli expressions wherever possible. For example: *Dharmapada* (*Dhammapada*), *Madhyama-Nikāya* (*Majjhima-Nikāya*), *Kṣudraka* (*Khuddaka*), *Smṛti-prasthāna* (*Satipaṭṭāna*).]

3

Poṭṭhapāda-Sutta A Conspectus and Analysis[1]

POṬṬHAPĀDA-*Sutta* is part of *Dīgha-Nikāya* and, arguably, the most intellectual dialogue in the Buddhist canon. Yet, it is a strangely neglected piece. It contains fairly long and sustained discussions of themes of the greatest importance. It lacks the focused character of *Satipaṭṭhāna, Sonadaṇḍa, Kūṭadanta,* etc. But it is full of great human interest and is constructed dramatically. The setting is the Anāthapiṇḍika park in Jetavan on the outskirts of Śrāvastī. The park included an *ārāma* (shelter) where Poṭṭhapāda was staying. Buddhaghoṣa says that he was a wealthy brāhmin, and his name is supposed by scholars to be derived from his birth in autumn. Throughout the dialogue he is referred to as *paribbajaka* (a homeless wanderer). He is eager for philosophical debate and courteously persistent in presenting his views. When the dialogue is about to begin he, together with 300 others, was in the shelter regularly used as an assembly for philosophical discussion. The Buddha, who had dressesd himself in his robes, early in the morning went to Śrāvastī with his begging bowl. Then he thought, 'It is too early now to enter Śrāvastī for alms. Let me go to the shelter in Mallika park, where Poṭṭhapāda is staying.' When the master reached the

---

1 'Poṭṭhapāda-Sutta: A Conspectus and Analysis', in *Buddhist Culture in Asia: Unity in Diversity,* vol. 1, Editor: Supriya Rai, Somaiya Publications, 2010-11. Proceedings of a conference jointly organized by K.J. Somaiya Centre for Buddhist Studies, Department of Philosophy, University of Mumbai, Indian Nava Nalanda Mahavira, Nalanda, Bihar, India, and Jade Buddha Temple, Shanghai, China, held in January 2008.

place 'there was a lot of talking and shouting on all kinds of wordly affairs, . . . legends about creation of land and sea and speculation about existence and non-existence.' When Poṭṭhapāda caught sight of the master approaching, he called the assembly to order, saying:

> Be quiet, venerable sirs! No more noise please! Samana Gotama is coming. He likes quietness and speaks in praise of quietude. It would be nice if, seeing how quiet our assembly is, he were to join us.

The assembly fell silent and the Buddha joined it. Poṭṭhapāda welcomed him and offered him a seat and seated himself on a low stool. He is asked what subject they were discussing. Poṭṭhapāda dismissed whatever they were discussing as of little consequence, compared to the views of the Buddha on certain topics or themes. He opened the discussion by raising, first of all, the question of:

> *abhisaññā nirodho hoti.*
>
> How the cessation of consciousness is brought about?

From this there is an easy transition to the question posed by Poṭṭhapāda:

> *sañña nu kho bhante purisassa attā udāhu, anna sañña annyo attā ti.*
>
> Is consciousness identical with a man's soul, or is consciousness one thing and a man's soul, another?

The Buddha's response leads to a discussion of his famous silence – his refusal to answer certain questions. Certain questions are listed as indeterminate (*avyākata*), and the practical and theoretical reasons for leaving them unanswered are given. The problem of personal identity is taken up again, a little later in the dialogue by Citta, the son of the elephant trainer. He asks: 'At the time a man is in possession of any one of the three modes of personality (past, present and future) are the other two unreal to him then?' The problem, as the Buddha points out, is that when one of the modes of personality is operating, then, it does not come under the category of either of the other two. Personality is identified according to the mode which is operating. It seems to follow, especially on the Buddhist view, that the other two modes which are not operating are unreal.

In introducing the first topic of conversation Poṭṭhapāda recalls that on several occasions, a number of brāhmins, ascetics and teachers assembled at the shelter had debated the question: How is the cessation of consciousness brought about? Different views were canvassed. One view was that ideas came to a man without reason and without cause (*ahetukam, apaccayā*). And in the same way, they pass away. Another was that consciousness is the soul of man (*saññā hi bho purisassa attā*); when the soul enters or leaves a man (*upeti, apeti*) he becomes conscious or unconscious, and hence it is implied, he has ideas or ceases to have them. The third view, which is in a way parasitic on the second, is that there are sāmaṇas and brāhmins of great influence and power who infuse consciousness into a man or draw it away from him (*upakaddhanti, apakaddhanti*), and accordingly he becomes conscious or unconscious. A sub-class of 'infusionists' ascribe this power to *devatā*'s (gods). I must confess that the problem is not entirely clear to me. It is one of those cases in philosophy, where the question posed is not clear until we consider the alternative answers.

The Buddha most emphatically rejects the views of those who are of the opinion that ideas come to a man and pass away without a reason and without a cause. They are wrong from the beginning (*āditah*). By training (*śikkhā*) some ideas arise, and by training other ideas pass away. The course of training for directing our mind and cultivating desirable ideas is the usual Buddhist prescription. *Śīla* is the foundation but the *bhikkhu* who alone can reach the summit of consciousness, must go far beyond the common commands and prohibitions applicable to householders, and adopt the life of a homeless wanderer. He must avoid all forms of dogmatism and practise mindfulness constantly. The entire course of training laid down at this point is taken from *Sāmañña Phala Sutta* and reproduced by our dialogue. There follows a description of the fruits of this method of training in reaching summits of consciousness. There are the four stages of rapture or meditation which run paralled to the four stages described towards the conclusion of *Mahāsatipaṭṭhān*. The highest stage is reached when the *bhikkhu* refuses to think and reason and, therefore, has no ideas at all. Thus the cessation of consciousness turns out to be the utter purity and equanimity of mindfulness (*upekkhā sati parisuddhi*). The Buddha claims that he lays down a method, here and now, by following which, any one can directly realize this purity and peace and thus bring about, step by step, the cessation of consciousness.

Poṭṭhapāda then moves to the next stage in the discussion and asks: 'Is Sir, consciousness identical with a man's soul, or is consciousness one thing and the soul another?' The Buddha gently twits Poṭṭhapāda for reverting to the idea of the soul. Poṭṭhapāda says, 'What I revert to, Sir, is material soul, having form, built up of the four elements, nourished by solid food.' Well. The Buddha says, 'if there were such a soul, Poṭṭhapāda, even so your consciousness would be one thing and your soul another'. Since ideas would arise in a man and pass away, consciousness which presumably includes the consciousness of the alleged material soul with form would be one thing and the soul another. Poṭṭhapāda then reverts to the notion of a soul 'made up of mind (*manomaya*) complete with all parts, not deficient in any organ'. The Buddha says that the same consideration applies. Such a soul is one thing and awareness of it (*saññā*) another. I think this argument is made plausible by the fact that in Indian philosophy the mind is regarded as an entity intermediate between the soul on the one hand, and gross matter on the other. In Sāṁkhya, which must have influenced the Buddha through Alāra Kālāma his first teacher, the various modifications of this 'mind-stuff' are regarded as various states of consciousness (at any rate, they would be so regarded, when the pure 'light' of *Puruṣa*'s consciousness is 'reflected' in them. There is trouble here, but not for us now!) On such a view it would be quite intelligible to say that this mind, a quasi-material entity, is one thing and awareness of it another.

As a last resort, Poṭṭhapāda takes his stand on a soul which is formless (*arūpī*) and full of consciousness (*saññāmaya*). The Budhha applies the same kind of argument. But here, a difficulty presents itself which was not present in the other two cases. So long as the self was construed as an entity which itself was not awareness, one could say that awareness was one thing and the alleged soul another. But when the self is identified with awareness, to say that awareness is one thing and the alleged self another, becomes highly paradoxical if not inconsistent. This matter involves many problems but I want to mention, without discussion, the following points:

(i) So far as the material and quasi-material self are concerned, their relegation to the fringe, if not dismissal, presupposes that the element of awareness is fundamental in the human person and that postulation of a further soul serves no purpose.

(ii) So far as awareness of awareness is concerned, one possible interpretation is that we are aware of various forms of consciousness that arise and pass away. The latter, being 'objectified', when we are aware of them, cannot be the true self of man.

(iii) And if this line of reflection is carried to its logical conclusion, we arrive at pure awareness which cannot be objectified; and this may be the 'cessation of consciousness', formless, free from all cognition. If so, this cessation of consciousness is, from another point of view, the *ātman* of Advaita. Anyway, consciousness has this quality of reflexiveness, like a nest of Chinese boxes, each within the next, until we arrive at the limiting, paradoxical concept of awareness which cannot be objectified. This can be regarded as the strength of Advaita. I am far from suggesting that I have discovered the hidden Vedānta of the Buddha. But not being sensitive enough to Pali usage, I do not know what interpretation should be placed on the argument.

(iv) Finally, a linguistic consideration. I find it curious that *saññā* which is a particular constituent of human personality and is generally taken to signify perception, should be used here, in an extended sense, to refer to consciousness in general. We may note that this generalized usage is present in English too, where words like 'perceive' and 'see' are used to refer to cognitive processes far removed from sense-perception in any form.

This discussion on Poṭṭhapāda's search for the soul of man is followed by a brief interlude on *avyākata* questions and an explanation of why the Buddha expressed no opinions on them. I shall skip this portion for the time being, and come to Citta's question of whether, when a man is in possession of one mode of personality, the other two are unreal. As I pointed out, at the beginning quoting the Buddha, when one of the modes of personality is operating (past, present or future) it does not come under either of the other two. Essentially the problem is one of the continuity of the self through time. The Buddha has to provide for it, without appealing to a persistent entity, that remains, numerically, the same throughout a given period. The explanation is provided by causal continuity, or in terms of a series of psycho-physical states bound together by the relation of cause and effect. The clearest expression occurs in this passage:

> Just as Citta, from a cow comes milk and from the milk curd, and from the curd butter, from the butter ghee, and from the ghee junket; and when it is curd it is not called either milk, or butter or ghee or junket, and when it is milk it is not called by any of the other names, and so on, so also Citta, when any one of the modes of personality is operating it is not called by the names of the others. For these, Citta, are merely names, expressions, figures of speech, designations in common use in the world. A *tathāgata* makes use of these words but is not misled by them. *Lokasañña, lokaniyuttiyo, lokabohara, lokapannattiyo* are the key expressions used. It will be recalled that almost identical expressions are used in *Milinda Pañho* with the declaration by Nāgasena that, philosophically speaking, there is no underlying entity (*paramatthto puggalo nūpalabbhati*).

We come now to the discussion of indeterminate (*avyākata*) questions, left unanswered by the Buddha. He insists that the one all-important overriding purpose was to put an end to suffering; the *tathāgata* had taught only those truths and imparted only those skills which subserve this central, spiritual mission. This is a large, recurrent theme in Buddhist canon. I have dealt with it elsewhere, at some length. The question has a theoretical as well as a practical aspect, though the latter has received the greatest attention and the former is either ignored or discussed in passing. The Sutta has some eloquent expressions of the Buddha's approach. Poṭṭhapāda is reduced to despair when all his suggestions about an enduring self are seen to be idle speculations. He asks:

> But it is possible for me, Sir, to understand whether consciousness is the same thing as a man's soul, or whether consciousness is one thing and a man's soul another.

The answer is:

> It is hard for you Poṭṭhapāda, holding, as you do, different views, other things approving themselves to you, and setting different aims before yourself, striving after a different perfection and trained in a different system of doctrine (*anyaditthikena, annyakhantikena, anyarucikena, anyatrayogena anyatra-acariyakena*) to understand either of these two – 'Consciousness is a man's soul' or 'Consciousness is one thing and the soul another'.

Then, like a child who is denied a visit to the circus and settles for icecream, Poṭṭhapāda says, 'Then, Sir, tell me at least, is the world eternal, is this alone the truth and any other view mere folly?' 'That', Poṭṭhapāda, 'is an undetermined question'. There follows a list of ten questions, all of which are declared to be indeterminate. (The list is rather unsystematic; the first three questions concerning the eternity of the world, its finitude or infinitude in space and the identity of the soul with the body are stated in terms of two alternatives, viz. affirmation or a positive answer, and denial or a negative answer. But the problem concerning the continued existence of the *tathāgata* after *mahā-parinibbāna* gets four alternatives, joint affirmation and joint denial being added to simple affirmation and simple denial.) To each of them, the Buddha's answer is the same – being *avyākata* they are not to be answered. Nāgasena later said that they were to be set aside (*ṭhapanīya*). Explaining why he had not expressed an opinion on any of them the Buddha says:

> The question is not calculated to profit, it is not concerned with *dhamma* (*na attha-saṁhitam, na dhamma-saṁhitam*), it does not lead to elements of right conduct, nor to detachment, nor to purification from lusts, not to cessation of passion, nor to supernormal knowledge (*na abhiññāya*), nor to *nibbāna*.

Therefore is it that I express no opinion on it positively. Poṭṭhapāda is told, in words reminiscent of a famous statement in *Majjhima-Nikāya*, that the Buddha had expounded the nature of suffering, its cause, its prevention and the path leading to its prevention. Poṭṭhapāda is won over and expresses approval of Buddha's procedure wholeheartedly: 'That is so master, that is so well-destined one' (*evametaṁ bhagavā, evametaṁ sugatā*). Soon after this the Buddha leaves the assembly.

No sooner had the master gone away than those mendicants bore down upon Poṭṭhapāda, with a torrent of jeering and taunting words saying 'so that is how it is!' Poṭṭhapāda approves anything that this Gotama says with his 'That is so master, that is so well destined one'. We, on the other hand, fail to see that this Gotama has put forward any doctrine that is distinct with regard to any of the ten points raised. Obviously they had come to listen to grand theories about the universe, and went away disappointed. It was like offering a glass of milk to a tiger. Their disappointment has echoed through the ages but Poṭṭhapāda and Citta were happy enough to return to the Buddha two or three days later. When told of the reactions of the mendicants, the Buddha says that they were blind. Some mendicants and Brahmins taught that the soul was perfectly happy and healthy after death, when they had no means of ascertaining the truth of the matter. They did not know a way or a method by which one can realize a perfectly happy state. On being questioned, they admitted that they had themselves not experienced perfect happiness for even half a day. Such peddlers of eternal bliss are compared to a man who says 'How I long for, how I love the most beautiful woman in the land'. On being questioned, our lover confesses that he knows neither her features, nor her name, nor her lineage, nor her whereabouts. Changing the metaphor the

Buddha compares such teachers to a man who puts up a staircase where four corssroads meet, as the way up to the upper storey of a mansion, when he is ignorant of the location, dimensions and style of construction of this mansion. His enterprise is futile or even worse, it is unintelligible.

The reasons against metaphysical speculations about the world are predominantly practical. But there is a theoretical point which is formulated clearly and explicitly, elsewhere. I cannot do better than quote a passage from *Majjhima-Nikāya*:

> *Brahmacariya* could not depend on the view that the world is eternal; nor upon the view that the world is not eternal. Although there is the view (*ditthi*) that the world is eternal and the view that world is not eternal, there is (*atthi eva*), ageing there is dying, there are grief, lamentation and sorrow. I lay down the destroying of these here and now. And I say the same with regard to other views.

The logical independence of moral evaluations and moral and spiritual endeavour in relation to contending metaphysical views could not have been set forth more clearly. The philosophical theories themselves are non-empirical and contentious. This peculiar character is discussed with Vaccagotta in the context of the problem whether the *tathāgata* ceases or continues to exit after *mahāparinibbāna*. Both *Samyutta* and *Majjhima* contain these discussions. But excuse because our Sutta contains discussion of related to consider them would to be go far beyond the exposition of our Sutta. I have already strayed a little with good matters of central importance in Buddhist philosophy. I have tried to give a concise account of these discussions. The dialogue ends happily, with Poṭṭhapāda declaring himself to be a lay follower of the Buddha and Citta joining the *saṁgha*.

4

The Buddha's Approach to Metaphysics*

> Vaccagotta asks: 'Has Gotama any theories of his own?' The Lord replies: 'The Tathāgata, O Vācca, is free from all theories'.
>
> –*Majjhima Nikāya*

> Buddha's coat left one side bare,
>
> But it hid the Absolute from the World's dust.
>
> Its ten thousand threads and thousand stitches fulfilled – the fruit of meditation.[1]

EXPLAINING why he expressed no view on the eternity of the world and other such 'indeterminate' (*avyākṛta*) questions, the Buddha says:

> The question is not calculated to profit, it is not concerned with the *dhamma*, it does not lead to the elements of right conduct, nor to detachment, nor to purification from lusts, nor to cessation of passing, nor to calmness, nor to super normal knowledge, nor to the highest wisdom, nor to *nibbāna*. Therefore is it that I express no opinion on it.
>
> –*Poṭṭhapāda-Sutta*

> I am at a loss Gotama, I am bewildered.
>
> You ought to be at a loss and bewildered Vacca for this Dhamma is hard to see and understand. . . .
>
> . . . If you were asked in what direction a put-out fire had gone,

---

* Published in *Buddhism in India and Abroad*, Bombay: Somaiya Publications, 1996.

[1] Lines from a poem quoted by the monk Tripiṭaka in 'Monkey' by Wu Ch'êng-ên, tr. Arther Waley, Penguin Classics, 1942.

> to the east or west, north or south, could you give me an answer?
>
> That does not apply. . . .
>
> In the same way Vacca (all things) by which a *tathāgata* might be made known have been destroyed by him, cut off at the root. . . . A *tathāgata* is freed of all denotations; he is profound, measureless, unfathomable even like the great ocean.
>
> –*Majjhima-Nikāya*[2]

The Buddha claimed that the four noble truths constituted the essence of his practical, moral and spiritual teaching. This is acceptable to all including the divergent sects and schools of Buddhism in its chequered history. It would also be acceptable to all that this practical teaching is not presented as a corollary to a metaphysical view of the world, as is the case with Upaniṣadic philosophy and Jainism. But it can be claimed and has been claimed that this eminently pragmatic, no-nonsense approach does have metaphysical presuppositions and implications. No reflective and sensitive person, it has been argued, can totally avoid commitments of a wider character. A way of life presupposes a world-view and the Buddha did have such a view though he presented it largely negatively, and in analytic terms. Whatever one's reaction to this way of reasoning, it cannot be denied that when confronted with 'ultimate problems', the Buddha maintained silence and, if pressed further, pointed out or made the questioner point out the inapplicability of all the possible answers. But this silence in the face of what appear to be urgent problems of human destiny, itself creates a difficulty for the faithful and not for them alone.

Milinda Pañho states the difficulty in the form of a dilemma. The Buddha declared emphatically in *Mahāparinibbāna-Sutta* 'that he did not have the closed fist of teacher'[3] and that he had taught *dhamma* to everyone without any distinction or discrimination. The Buddha was responding to Ānanda who had approached him, now

---

2 Quotation highly abridged and slightly modified.

3 T.W. David Rhys, *Sacred Books of the East*, ed. Max Müller, vol. 11, p. 36.

on his deathbed, for his final instruction. On the other hand, when questioned by Māluṅkyāputta[4] on certain 'Ultimates', he gave no answer (there are many cases of similar silence). The dilemma can be posed in this way. If the silence was the result of ignorance the Buddha was not omniscient and if he held back certain answers knowingly he was secretive. Nāgasena responds by saying that the Buddha was neither secretive nor ignorant. He escapes between the horns of the dilemma by suggesting that the type of question posed has to be just set aside (*thapanīya*). Four types of questions are distinguished. First, there are question which are to be answered with a simple 'yes' or 'no'. There are questions to be answered analytically by going into detail. Then there are questions to be answered with counter questions (perhaps to bring out precisely what the question means). Finally, there are questions about the eternity of the world, its infinity in space, etc. which have to be laid aside. The suggestion is that silence is the only possible response to them and attempt to answer them can only land us in difficulties, whatever the answer. King Milinda was by no means an easy, pliant, questioner, but in this case he was satisfied, when perhaps he should not have been.

What is the root of dissatisfaction felt by some with this solution? First of all there are the questions themselves. Some of them at least appear to be meaningful. Take the question of the eternity of the world. Surely either the world has a beginning and end in time or it is eternal. Both the alternatives cannot be correct. Indeed Buddhist cosmology, like Hindu and Jaina, presupposes that the world has no beginning and end in time and that its history is divided into great *kalpas* (aeons), each one of which has a beginning, a development and an end.

Other questions such as the existence of the soul or self and its identity with the body, or with consciousness, appear to be more difficult. But even here, we feel, when certain key terms are clarified, and a framework within which the sense of the question to be answered is agreed upon, then either a positive or a negative

---

[4] *Milinda Pañho*, ibid., vol. 35, p. 204.

answer is the correct one and both cannot be true. Second, there is a long Indo-European tradition in which the final goal of human life is linked to a metaphysical view of the world. As the latter varies, so does the former, and differences about the former are reflected in those about the latter. St. Thomas Aquinas, for example, persuasively argues that the final good of man is related to the specific nature of man and also to the relation between man and God or ultimate reality. Both these questions are important and controversial. There is a voluminous material about them. I shall discuss them only in passing, in so far as they have a bearing upon my central theme.

But in some ways the second question about Man's final good and its relation to the nature of the world appears to be more important. If indeed some questions are to be set aside, as Nāgasena claims, why are they unanswerable in the usual way? Why are they to be left hanging in the air, as it were? That the queries have been raised repeatedly in the history of philosophy shows that they occur naturally to the thinking mind. They are all trans-empirical, certainly, and answers to them, highly contentious.

In the Buddhist tradition they can be grouped around the notions of self, space and time. In *Poṭṭhapāda-Sutta* they are characterized as indeterminate (*avyākata*) and rather confusingly listed to be ten. Are they theoretically unanswerable so that even omniscience cannot answer them, or did the Buddha, an omniscient being, know the answers but refused to answer them on pragmatic considerations? And in the second case, can he escape the charge of secretiveness, unless indeed he was guilty of lack of omniscience, which appears to be even worse. That the practical grounds for remaining silent on them are overwhelming may be granted readily. That the prime motive of the Buddha in remaining silent was to prevent his followers from wasting their time and talent on metaphysical questions is undeniable too. In the quotation from *Poṭṭhapāda-Sutta* given above, both these points are amply clear. On any view – that of Hīnayāna or Mahāyāna, or that of the uncommitted observer – this must be an important component of the final answer.

But the extent of the Buddha's hostility of idle speculation is to be read to be believed. In *Sutta Nipāta* he declares: 'O monks, I do not dispute with the world, but the world disputes with me.' In the same 'Sutta' he advises his followers: 'Say thou, when a dispute has arisen, 'Here is no opponent for thee . . . . For the truth is one and there is not a second about which one intelligent man may dispute with another.' He compares teachers of different doctrines (*ditthi*s, *dhamma*s) and their disciples to monkeys who 'do not break asunder their fists, but following their desires, they grasp letting go of one branch to catch hold another'. But the most detailed condemnation of such quarrels about dogma and doctrine occurs in *Tevijja Sutta*. The Buddha says:

> Whereas some sāmaṇa's and bhāhmaṇa's, who live on the food given by the faithful, continue addicted to wrangling, that is to say,
>
> You are ignorant of the doctrine and discipline whereas I understand them.
>
> What do you know of the doctrine or discipline? You are heterodox but I am orthodox.
>
> My discourse is profitable, but yours is worthless.
>
> That which you should speak first you speak last and which you should speak last, you speak first.
>
> What you have long studied I have completely upturned.
>
> Your errors are made quite plain. You are disgraced.
>
> Go away and escape from this disputation, or else extricate yourself from your difficulties. He, on the other hand, refrains from such wrangling.[5]

Each of the doctrines[6] is compared in *Majjhima-Nikāya*,

> to a thicket, a wilderness, a tangle, a bondage, a fetter of views, attended by ill, perturbation and fever, and does not conduce to . . . tranquillity to super knowledge to awakening to *nibbāna*.

---

5 *Tevijja Sutta*, chap. II.118.

6 Parallel passages occur in *Samaññaphala-Sutta* and *Brahmajala-Sutta*, both in *Dīgha-Nikāya*.

Having gauged the Buddha's depth of hostility to metaphysics one can ask: But is that all? Are we ourselves to remain silent after ascribing the Buddha's silence to practical, spiritual, considerations?

As I have pointed out above, there is an easy way out if we give up the Buddha's omniscience, or at any rate restrict it to *dhamma* and the key to transmigratory existence. The Buddha's own words often lay claim to no more than insight into *dhamma* that will lead to the end of all sorrow, and *avidyā* and *tr̥ṣṇā* as the motive force of phenomenal existence. But the whole weight of Buddhist tradition and some of the words of the Buddha involve a more colourful, if more obscure, conception of omniscience. Even the charge of secrecy can be formally rebutted if we pay attention to the precise words of the Buddha. In *Mahāparinibbāna-Sutta* the Buddha says that *tathāgata* has no closed fist in the matter of *dhamma* (*na ānanda tathāgatasya dhammesu ācariya mutthi*). In general, the Buddha is very careful to say that he has taught the *dhamma* to all without any distinction and that *dhamma* is all that a man needs for attaining peace and purity of mind. Part of the solution by Mahāyāna is to adopt the charge of secrecy and render it harmless. However open the Buddha may have been like Jesus, like the latter he must have adapted his teaching to the needs and abilities of the persons whom he taught. A professor of mathematics cannot be accused of secrecy if he does not teach the integral calculus to a child. The beginner must learn numbers and the multiplication table before he goes on, gradually, to higher levels of mathematics. This is the essence of the Mahāyāna argument that their Sutta's and their teaching supplement and not confute the Pāli dialogues accepted by Hīnayāna as the sole source of the Buddha's original teaching. Even if we ignore the legendary story of Nāgārjuna going to the nether world to fetch the 'new' but authentic discourses of the Buddha, we must grant that the absolutist–mystical view of the Buddha is consistent with the Pāli dialogues. As is well known this view is also supported by Anand K. Coomaraswamy, Radhakrishnan and others. But we cannot go beyond admitting its consistency with the original teaching of the Buddha. We can hardly claim to discover in the original discourses clear suggestions of an ineffable Absolute which can be realized in mystical experience.

The arguments in support of this ineffability thesis overreach themselves. First of all, even the minimum of secrecy involved in the Advaitic–Mahāyānist view of the Buddha seems to be incongruous with the atmosphere of the Pāli dialogues. Moreover, if the Buddha wanted to say that the moral and psychological practices recommended by him brought you to the verge of the ineffable, why does he not say so as the Upaniṣadic thinkers do again and again? Indeed in the whole of Pāli literature it is hard to find a word which correctly or approximately translates as 'hard to express' or 'inexpressible'. As one who directed men to the realization of *nibbāna*, as much by example as by precept, the Buddha can be called a mystic but he refrained from all talk to avoid creating misunderstanding instead of speaking about the unspeakable. He is not open to Johnson's jeering words about Jacob Boheme the German mystic: 'If Jacob really saw the ineffable why does he talk about it?'

Radhakrishnan goes so far as to remark that in the *tevijja* the experience of *nibbāna* is interpreted in terms of union with *Brahman*. This seems to have little justification. In the first place, the Buddha speaks of Brahmā, the Creator of the world – the Vedic God Prajāpati – rather than the *Brahman* of Upaniṣads. He addresses Vāsettha and Bhāradvāja to convince them, and brāhmins in general, that if their goal was union with Brahmā free from all human limitations, they too must rid themselves of attachment, passion and selfish desire. Ritual piety is not enough. And ritual piety combined with Vedic learning seems to be valued most by the many brāhmins who appear in the dialogues. There is a general and important lesson taught by implication, and that is that proficiency in ceremonies suffices only for the more or less crude forms of pleasure-seeking. And this the Buddha considered as an unworthy goal for the earnest seeker.

There are indeed some positive descriptions of *nibbāna*. In *Udāna* and *Itivvuttaka* the Buddha declares that unless there were something unborn, uncompound, undying, escape from the miseries of the world would be impossible. But both in the above works and elsewhere, this sort of declaration is followed by description of *nibbāna* as the end of all attachment, hatred and grief. The following from *Sutta Nipāta*[7] are representative.

> I say that *nibbāna* is destruction of old age and death.
>
> The stopping of all becoming is *nibbāna*.

The question is not simply one of the number of quotations one can muster on either side – though even here the radical, antimetaphysical view is better than the conservative, absolutist view – but the temper and spirit of an entire philosophy. There are dialogues where the opposition to speculation seems to be wholly practical. But some of the illustrative examples bear and justify a far more radical interpretation.

The Buddha makes an extremely important point in the following passage from *Majjhima-Nikāya*[8] whose thrust is to separate the ethical life from world-views. The Buddha says:

> *Brahmacariya* could not depend on the view that the world is eternal. Nor could it depend on the view that the world is not eternal. Although there is the view that the world is eternal, and the view that the world is not eternal, there is (*atthi eva*) birth, there is ageing, there is dying, there are grief, lamentation and sorrow. I lay down the destroying of these here and now. And I say the same with regard to other views.

This passage is extremely important for the clear suggestion that high moral endeavour is logically independent of theories concerning the world.[9] The question of the objectivity of moral values – debated keenly by contemporary philosophers – was not present in the mind of the Buddha when he said the above. He took for granted – like many others – the validity of the purified intuitions of mankind concerning the right and the good. But if pressed on the

---

[7] *Sutta Nipāta* – *kappamānavapucchā*, 65, v.1094.

[8] *Majjhima-Nikāya* I.77.

[9] It is also psychologically independent in so far as spiritual exertion need not be motivated by prior metaphysical assurance.

point, I think he would have admitted, even advocated, the mutual, logical independence of moral and metaphysical judgements. I would agree that the wrongness of lying and thieving does not depend on the oneness or many-ness, the eternity or non-eternity of the world. To that extent ethics and metaphysics are independent. There is a minimum of bread and butter morality which is necessary to preserve society and make harmonious social life possible and which must be independent of diverse philosophies. But there is a way of life which includes elements like fasting not required by considerations of health, solitude, cultivation of humility and self-examination, self-control beyond the need of social harmony, which are justified only on a theistic or absolutist view. At any rate, they would be proper or with a purely secular goal as the final human end. The Buddha feels that the needs of higher morality or spirituality can be divorced from conflicting world-view, *śīla* from *diṭṭhi*'s. The Buddha never seems to have come across an out and out materialist who would question the need for many of his practices. He countered materialists in practice – which includes most men whatever their creed – by trying to raise the threshold of their sensitiveness. The way – *magga* – laid down by him is the only way to end sorrow, and this cannot be done so long as a trace of individuality remains. Spiritual practices are needed to put an end to the last trace of egotism. Hence so long as it is rational to endeavour to end sorrow, so long the adoption of his way would also be rational.

Added to this clear-cut divorce between *śīla* and *diṭṭhi*'s are certain mertaphors used to bring out the nature of metaphysical statements. The first part of *Poṭṭhapāda-Sutta* is arguably the most theoretical and intellectual to be found in any Buddhist Sutta. But the second part is eminently practical. The Buddha explains therein why he has answered only certain queries and left others unanswered. He naturally ridicules gently those who teach things beyond their experience. His own way, by contract, is discoverably efficacious in achieving peace and purity of mind. The man, for example, who believes in a permanent soul that can be made forever happy is compared to someone who is busy building at the cross-roads a staircase to no specifiable palace; or a person in love with a lady whom he cannot describe further by specifying her complexion, height, birth, etc. Now both the persons, mentioned in the examples, are attempting something not only practically futile, but puzzling to the intellect. How can you build a staircase unless you know the location of that to which you are building a staircase? How can you be in love except with a specifiable object of your love? We would fail to 'understand' such a person, to put it rather fashionably and smartly.

But the clearest indication of what may be called meaninglessness of metaphysical propositions comes in *Majjhima-Nikāya*. *Nibbāna* is compared to the putting out of a fire and the consequent coolness. When a fire goes out it would be pointless to ask whether it has gone north or south, east or west. Every possible answer of this kind is meaningless. All we can say is that the fire is extinguished because the sources of it have died out. Vaccagotta admits this and the Buddha points out a moral that should be obvious, viz. that when a *tathāgata* passes away we can say neither that he continues to be, nor that he does not continue to be. Equally, we can neither affirm the two jointly nor jointly deny them. None of them would apply and therefore all are unacceptable. Similar is the case with other metaphysical propositions.

But acceptance of this purely 'existential' account of Buddhism – particularly the justification of the *magga* – seems to leave us with a purely negative account of *nibbāna*. On the other hand, those who give a more positive account will have to accept, perhaps, something like the Vedāntic *ātman* which seems to saddle us with the old metaphysical views. The strength of the absolutist mystical view is that it makes for a more positive account of *nibbāna*. Hence the attraction of a more positive view for a person like R.C. Zaehner, who is by no means an absolutist. Without the underpinning of an all-embracing metaphysics we are inclined to feel the labour spread over millennia, recommended by the Buddha, would be like cutting off one's head to get rid of one's headache. There is, of course, the experience of *jīvanmukti*, which is supremely worthwhile. But it is only open to a handful. To believe that it is possible for all entails belief in rebirth which again brings back metaphysics. The Buddha took for granted reincarnation and rejected 'Ucchedavāda' as clearly and explicitly as he rejected 'Śāśvatavāda'. This, apart from contradictions on the surface, is in a way the central difficulty which may reintroduce metaphysics. It will be seen that though I am certain that the Buddha rejected all metaphysics, I remain uncertain as to the rationality of such a rejection. I am one of those monkeys whose antics are described vividly by the Buddha. But the leaps and somersaults of a monkey are a source of satisfaction to itself and also instructive to the onlooker. That is the halting justification of this article.

5

A Subtlety in the Buddhist Theory of the Self and Some (Further) Elaborations*

It is well known that Buddhism denies the existence of all substance whether in the physical world or in the case of human persons. The latter are analysed in terms of aggregation (*saṁghāta*) of five *khaṇḍa*s (strands). The first of these is the body (*rūpa*) and there are the four mental strands (*nāma*) of sensation, perception, understanding and disposition (*vedanā, saññа, viññāna* and *saṁkhara* respectively). The psycho-physical complex is known as *nāma-rūpa*. There is no ego or self (*jīva, attā, puggala*) over and above them and underlying them. *Na me so attā* is the standard formulation[1]: 'That is not myself'. It is repeatedly declared in the case of the body, sensation, etc. and with reference to every constituent with tiresome repetition, in the best or the worst Indian tradition. Proper names do not indicate any central entity acting as a kingpin to the constituents, nor any particular constituent. Buddhaghoṣa writes in *Viśuddhi-Magga*:

> Just as the word 'chariot' is but a mode of expression for axle, wheels and other constituent members placed in a certain relation to each other, but when we come to examine the members one by one we discover that, in an absolute sense, there is no chariot, just as the word, 'house', 'first', 'lute', 'army', 'city', 'tree', etc. are only modes of expression for collections of things disposed in a certain manner, in exactly the same way the words 'living being',

---

* Published in *Buddhism in Global Perspectives,* vol. 1, ed. by Kalpakam Sankarnarayan, Ravindra Panth, Ichijo Ogawa, Mumbai: Somaiya Publications, 2003.

1 There are numerous occurrences, but see e.g. *Samyutta* iii.44-45, 103; *Majjhima* iii.19.

'ego' are modes of expression for a complex of bodily and non-bodily constituents.[2]

This makes out that personal names and corresponding general names indicate complexes.

But in *Questions of King Milinda* there is a subtler view, viz. that they are not names at all, but that it is proper and convenient, practically, to use them when a complex with parts disposed in a definite manner is given. Nāgasena tells Milinda that the term 'chariot' does not denote any part of it such as an axle and wheel, nor anything in addition to them, nor to a collection of the various parts. This last point calls for some explanation (on the 'collective name' interpretation; this is the alternative favoured by the Buddha). The obvious point emphasized may be that the chariot is not a mere collection of parts. The various parts have to be arranged in a certain order and have to function in a certain manner. But even when the parts are disposed in the desired manner the term 'chariot' is only an expression with a useful role. It is not a denotative expression, or rather it is a denotative expression that fails to denote. 'Nāgasena', it is said, 'is a commonly understood expression, a designation in use.'[3] Strictly speaking there is no ego or self here.

This may seem an unnecessary and unprofitable complication. But there is a point being made. If proper names were names of complexes, whatever can be predicated of things or persons can be predicated of complexes of states and vice versa. This, however, is not the case. To think in this way is to commit the fallacy contained in the following reasoning:

1. I am sitting on this table.
2. This table is a logical construction.
3. I am sitting on a logical construction.

If an entity of the type *A* is a logical construction of entities of

---

[2] H.C. Warren's edition revised by Dharmananda Kosambi, see chap. XVIII, para 28.

[3] Rhys David (tr.), *Milinda Pañho*, ii I.I (SBE).

the type *B*, whatever can be said of *A* can be suitably restated into statements about *B's*. But we cannot simply predicate of complexes of *B's* what is ordinarily predicated of *A* and vice versa. And if *a* is a name of *A* and *b* of a complex of *B* we cannot simply substitute *a* and *b* mutually. Proper names have a legitimate practical use whenever a complex fulfilling certain conditions is present. But to turn them into collective names is to encourage the sort of fallacy illustrated above. There is a clear suggestion of the theory of 'incomplete symbols', i.e. denotative expressions that do not denote and which can be suitably translated out; but not by giving mutually substitutable expressions. It is not likely that (Mrs.) Rhys Davids was acquainted with Russell's logical theories but 'designations in use' comes very near 'definitions in use'.

As regards the identity of a human being, Nāgasena regards a person as a series of psycho-physical states united by causality. The earlier members give rise to the later, and the later ones in their turn gives rise to still later. We may add that casual continuity is the basis of continuity of memory which, in turn, is essential to teleological unity or the broad unity of character exhibited by a person throughout his life and in varying degrees. This should suffice for practical, moral and even spiritual purpose, provided the complexes of psycho-physical states are relatively isolated and stable. Continuity of memory particularly should be an insulating feature of our bundles.

Such a serial theory of the self is open to some common objections. Many thinkers – not just Westerners and Christians – hold that without an enduring self or soul, belief in reincarnation cannot be accepted. I do not see, however, why the Buddhist theory, if it is adequate in the ordinary way, cannot be extended to cover many alleged embodiments. All we require is a series persisting after the dissolution of the present organism, and reassociating itself with a new organism. The interval will be occupied by certain members of the series, particularly psychical members. These latter may be attenuated, but should be sufficient to transmit causal influence through them. Such a persistence of psychical elements seems highly improbable to many of us today but that is not to say that it is logically impossible. There will be no doubt, be a big disruption caused by death; but together with causal influence some continuity of character will have to be transmitted. This continuity obviously falls short of conscious recollection (most of the time, I should add, in view of alleged memories of past lives). This is a tall order, but the Buddhist does not need to bring back a persistent entity to account for the process.

Independently of belief in reincarnation, a theory like Nāgasena's faces certain difficulties. The common thread running through different criticisms is that it cannot satisfactorily analyse or account for certain features of our mental life accepted by all independently of their philosophical affiliations. In any serial theory the successive states of what is regarded as a single self must be unified by some relation or relations. Nāgasena chooses causality as the binding relation. But this is not enough. My perception of a tiger at large causes not only fear and flight in me but similar behaviour is caused in all who perceive my panic. We have to distinguish between direct and indirect causality and make the former the basis of personal identity. This distinction cannot be made very precise and care must be taken that in making it strict enough for our purpose we do not reintroduce the notion of self-identity. But an even more troublesome difficulty is that in providing for at least the possibility of telepathy. We may have to make some additional stipulation. This consideration, incidentally, rules out defining personal identity in terms of causation of a series of states by the 'same' recognizable body or brain (we assume that the unity of a thing is already defined). The Buddhist belief in reincarnation – unless it is interpreted very metaphorically – closes this route. A.J. Ayer, who discusses this problem very elaborately, ultimately arrives at a criterion of self identity which is negative in character. This is unsatisfactory – more unsatisfactory than Ayer seems to realize.[4] Spatio-temporal continuity added to direct causation may give us

[4] See A.J. Ayer's *Concept of a Person* and relevant sections of *Origins of Pragmatism.*

what we want, provided we rule out some weird coincidences.

Being united by causal relations gives us relatively isolated, stable, series of psycho-physical states. But this supplies a basis for continuity of memory and the resultant stability of character. Nāgasena does not make this point. Perhaps like most of us, he took this for granted. But for moral and social purposes these consequences of causal continuity are of great importance. What is more, they insulate our self-series more effectively than causal continuity by itself. And if we interpret memory broadly to include habit formation, feeling of familiarity, ease of action, strengthening and weakening of dispositions, in addition to conscious recollection we shall probably have a very effective criterion. But in our analytical elaboration we have to make use of conative and emotive dispositions to gather together distinct series of psycho-physical states. *Saṁkhāras* play an essential part in the Buddhist analysis of human personality. But dispositions are ascribed to continuants, and not occurents which are all that we are allowed on our theory. Where a disposition or causal property is based on, or is identical with, an actual state of a thing like the molecular arrangement of a metal in relation to its electrical or thermal behaviour, there is no difficulty. But psychical dispositions, unless they are reduced to 'brain-structures', cannot be so handled. What then is a mental structure which is independent, if not of all material organizations, at least of the present organism? To say that our entire past is gathered into our experience now, and that the present state 'appropriates' all past states, may not help much, if the goal is to explain the mechanism of this process. It is often said that in Buddhism what transmigrates is not an entity called 'the soul' but a man's character. But unless we treat a person's moral character as an entity which can 'subsist' in the interval between death and the next embodiment, some explanation is needed and there is homework to be done.[5]

An extremely common objection against our theory is that it cannot account for facts of memory and self-consciousness.

---

[5] See Note II at the end of this paper.

The discussion of the difficulty is, naturally, closely bound up with the criticisms of the doctrine of universal momentariness, so much so that it is the general doctrine that is under attack in a specific sphere. Śaṅkara argues in *Tarkapada* that the proponent of Kṣaṇikavāda cannot extend the doctrine to himself because of the facts of memory and recognition. When I recognize something now presented to be the same as what I perceived on some past occasion, I clearly imply that the present recognition and the past perception both belong to me as a single subject. We do not say there was an earlier act of perception and now there is an act of recognition. A correct description of the experience would be that I, who perceived something once, am now recognizing it. So far from our being able to define self-identity in terms of memory, memory itself presupposes personal identity.[6]

There are a number of issues involved here. Undoubtedly accepting a memory claim (of the kind under discussion) involves accepting that the identity of a person spanning a time interval. But where an underlying subject is not assumed we shall have to say the present memory and the recollected past experience belong to the same series united by mnemic causation (the term was first used by Russell to dispense with 'traces'). It assumes the direct influence of a past experience on a present one. This is the situation when the memory claim is veridical. However, the term 'memory' and related terms are sometime used phenomenologically to describe the 'feel' of an experience which is often accompanied by imagery with feelings of familiarity, pastness, etc. When the memory claim is not admitted the relevant past experience did not occur, or its occurrence is doubtful. So to say that memory presupposes personal identity is to grant the memory claim and not to endorse any particular analysis of personal identity. However, when the claim is rejected, the serial theory has this difficulty – that my present experience may correspond to or represent an experience in some other personal series. Once, again, we have to rule out weird coincidences or grant the possibility that two different personal series may have common

6 See Adhyāya 2, Pāda 2, Sūtra 25 (most likely the *Brahma-Sūtra Bhāṣya*).

members. We shall also have to round up stragglers – experience which apparently has no subsequent influence. Either we postulate modification not consciously felt in our experience or make them 'loose' members of a larger whole.

The difficulty about self-consciousness runs parallel to the one about memory and is, in a way, a continuation of it with no specific reference to the past. The self, it is said, particularly by the Vedāntins, is not exhausted by its successive states. It is the subject which can rise above its particular experiences. It can review its past, project itself into the future and even reflectively analyse ongoing experiences. If the self were a series of momentary experiences this would not be possible. No member of the series can become aware of another, nor can the series as a whole become aware of any member, or any stretch of the series. We may add that the series is temporal, and not present as a whole to be either subject or object.[7] This argument relies on certain features of a self that are undeniable, and are described fairly, though metaphorically. Perhaps the use of metaphor is unavoidable both for the advocates and opponents of a subject of experience. First, an *ad hominem* argument: What does a variety of Śāśvatavāda like Vedānta (particularly Advaita) gain by postulating an eternal *ātman*? An ego in the temporal world, presumably, can carry traces and undergo changes in some part of its being. But a transcendental *ātman* is no help in accounting for recognition or reflexive awareness. It is difficult to see why Śaṅkara, for example, thinks that he is in a better position than the Buddhist here. Vedāntins seem to think that the very presence of *ātman* unifies the series and 'the eternal appears as the persistent' (Chubb's words). The self here is like a fabulous fixed deposit which can never be 'broken' (*ātman* is pure unchanging, unstained, etc.). The Vedāntin however hopes to raise a loan against the security of a treasure that cannot be used in the nitty-gritty of transactions in the empirical world.

---

[7] This criticism is often made. For a particularly lucid and terse ciricism, see Hiriyanna's *Outlines of Indian Philosophy*, chap. 5, p. 146.

Moreover, if we analyse self-awareness, along the lines suggested by Śāśvatavāda, it should reveal itself as a subject aware of a present or recollected experience. That does not seem to be how reflexive awareness is structured. The argument is not so much that introspection does not reveal an experiencer apart from experiences, as Hume maintained. But when we reflect on self-awareness we require 'a self-aware of self-aware of experience'. Clearly we are launched on an infinite regress. It may be retorted that we are looking at the situation misleadingly. The subject is not to be looked at as an object but is revealed as the experiencer in every experience. There is something important in this contention whether it proves the *ātman* of Vedānta or something more humdrum.

There is however another way of looking at the situation without stepping behind or beyond experiences. We can say that we have a series which grows in complexity as we progress in time. Memory is a present experience referring to a past experience and modified as a result of the past experience. Self-consciousness, in simple cases, is the simultaneous awareness of a presentation such as a pain or a feeling. When introspection is directed to 'objective' experiences it is mostly retrospection or a rapid shifting between introspection and normal development of introspected experience. In the more complicated cases of reviewing one's life or resolving upon a new way of life there is still a succession of experiences each more complex than the preceding one, referring to the past or projected future. There is no limit to the complexity of this process, especially when not all the modifications may be consciously felt, but are present as an unanalysed total impression. That is how the self grows in time and weaves itself as a unity. That is, the series unifies itself as time progresses – it can, ofcourse, disintegrate, unfortunately. This incidentally answers Śaṅkara's objection that 'an aggregate requires an aggregator'.

Note I: The most common and natural interpretation of this formula is to construct it as a denial of the self – either as an entity identical with any of the *khaṇḍa*'s or as something central to them all. In the world of phenomena there is no such entity. Since the Buddha was resolutely silent about the transcendental, Anattavāda seems to be the inevitable conclusion. But A.K. Coomaraswamy and I.B. Horner, in their introduction to *The Teaching of Gotama – The Buddha in His Own Words*, put a different gloss altogether on these words. They declare that nowhere in Buddhist scriptures is the existence of a higher self denied. 'That is not myself' accordingly to them, distinguishes the transcendental self – whose existence is not denied – from the various constituents of *nāma-rūpa*.[8] A very apt analogue would be the declaration by a key witness, with reference to everyone presented in an identification parade. 'That is not the person seen by me'. Except for criticism of Śāśvatavāda, I have left the higher self severely alone. The lower self is troublesome enough!

Note II: It has been suggested – by M.P. Rege in discussion – that we could ascribe dispositions to occurents. This can be done without any formal contradiction. But the result would not be an extension of a familiar concept, unusual but justified by certain requirements. The notion of a disposition is so bound up with the notion of a continuant that to ascribe it to an occurrent would be to turn it upside down. The better course would allow that occurrences have minimal durations and overlap temporally. And further that events, and pairs and sequences of them, exemplify laws of patterns. These later would be eternal. It is of course true that Buddhism, especially in its later developments, is as hostile to universals as to persistent or subsistent entitles. But between the two, if it becomes necessary to accept one of them, the former is to be preferred. After all, *dhamma* is eternal, so is Buddhahood. Even the most self-denying Therāvādin admits that *nirvāṇa* is non-composite, unborn, undying. It is not a nonentity though describable only in negative language.

---

[8] I.B. Horner and A.K. Coomaraswamy, *The Living Thoughts of Gotama – The Buddha in His Own Words*, Dover Publications, 2000, see particularly pp. 18-21.

6

Was the Buddha a Rationalist?[1]

He was, I think, the tallest figure in man's spiritual history not merely in the content of his ethical teaching but in the way he presented and propagated it. There is a hallowed Indo-European tradition which treats ethical and social conduct as a corollary to a general, all embracing view of the world. 'What shall we do? How shall we live?' To answer question such as these finally we must know all about God, Nature and Man. This view is shared by religious persons of differenced persuasions, which is not surprising. But it is equally the view of anti-religious, materialistic, rationalists. Secularists from Democritus and Epicurus to Charles Bradlaugh and Julian Huxley, from the Cārvākas to M.N. Roy are just as zealous in placing man among the totality of things, and then making their recommendation about a life worthy of a man of reason. The Buddha alone stands out of this mainstream.

If you place his teachings in the context of his contemporaries, we have materialism, Jainism and Upaniṣadic philosophy. The first is rejected clearly but implicitly. Both Jainism and Vedānta, though diametrically opposed in some ways, first present a synoptic view of the world, and ethical and spiritual recommendations harmonizing with their respective visions. The Buddha, on the other hand, begins with an analysis and description of human life in the world marked by well-known stages. The Four Noble Truths are not simple, empirical statements to be marked off as correct or incorrect. They are evaluative descriptions. One may dispute them. Their acceptability will depend upon one's maturity and sensitiveness. But it is important to note that the point of departure is provided by

---

1 Published in *Radical Humanism*, June 2000.

the fact of suffering, the diagnosis of its causes and a prescription for overcoming it completely.

The novelty of this approach is apt to go unnoticed and when noticed, to cause disappointment. In *Poṭṭhapāda-Sutta* the Buddha discusses with Poṭṭhapāda the latter's various attempts to identify the soul and a little later, speculations about whether the world is finite or infinite are dismissed as attempts to answer indeterminate (*avyakta*) questions. The Buddha convinces Poṭṭhapāda of the futility of metaphysical speculation and the primacy of his own practical teaching. But as soon as the Buddha leaves Anantapiṇḍika Park, the venue of the debate, Poṭṭhapāda is verbally assaulted by the mendicants present. Now no sooner had the master gone away than the mendicants present bore down upon Poṭṭhapāda from all sides with a torrent of jeering and taunting words saying:

> So that is how it is! Poṭṭhapāda approves of anything that this Gotama says with his, 'That is so master, that is so well-destined one'. We, on the other hand fail to see that this Gotama has put forward any doctrine that is distinct with regard to any of the ten points raised.[2]

Well over two and a half millennia later, in a missionary book, *The Buddha and His Teachings*,[3] we read thus:

> The Buddha did not expound revolutionary philosophical theories nor did he attempt to create a new material science. In plain terms he explained both what is within and what is without, so far as it concerns emancipation from the ills of life and revealed the unique path of deliverance.

This is correct as far as it goes but is does not go far enough.

If the Buddha were merely a pragmatic moral teacher, with a

---

2 The ten points raised pertain to the notions of space, time and self, and are characterized as *avyakta* questions by the Buddha. The main reason for setting them aside is that they are matters of speculative opinion which cannot provide a secure basis for spiritual life.

3 Narada Mahathera (Ven), *The Buddha and His Teachings*, Jaico Publishing House, 2006.

programme for spiritual living, he would still be of great interest. But he is more than that. It is undoubtedly true that he did not put forward any metaphysical construction. The reason for this abstinence is the resolve not to go beyond experimental terms, a resolve which seems eminently rational. But his teaching, as placed against a philosophical setting, is part of a philosophical outlook: *sammā diṭṭhi* or the noble eightfold path. The world is understood in terms of processes with no enduring substances underlying them. Everything is momentary (*anitya*), therefore soulless (*anatta*) and therefore the nature of misery (*dukkha*). But there is order provided by causation in the psycho-physical world and the moral law governing men's action and their consequences. He latter takes the form of belief in the law of *karma* and rebirth to which I will return later.

The most important aspect of the Buddha's teachings is to free spiritual endeavour from dependence on conflicting creed (*diṭṭhi*). An extremely important page in *Majjhima-Nikāya* runs:

> *Brahmacariya* could not depend upon the view that the world is eternal. Nor could it depend upon the view that the world is not eternal. Although there is the view that the world is eternal and there is the view that the world is not eternal, there is (*atthi eva*) birth, there is ageing, there is dying, there are grief, lamentation and sorrow. I lay down the destroying of these here and now. And I say the same with regard to other views.

There is very little meta-ethical debate in the Indian tradition and the Buddha was certainly not engaging in one when he expressed the above view. But there is a very clear suggestion that the judgement that it is desirable to reach a goal which is beyond birth and death, sorrow and lamentation is certain. On the other hand, whether the world is eternal or non-eternal is a matter of speculative opinion. The former, i.e. the judgement that *brahmacariya* is desirable, therefore cannot depend on the acceptance or rejection of either view. It is but a small step to generalize and say that moral judgements are logically independent of alternative metaphysical theories of the world. The example considered here is particularly favourable to the Buddha but he is emphatic that the same is true with regard to other views. Some may be inclined to murmur that the existence of a Deity who is ruler of the world has a direct bearing on our moral life.

But with some patience and clarity of thought, I think, it can be shown that even for a believer, the objectivity of moral principles or standards, cannot be logically founded on the existence and commandments of a supreme deity. In any case the existence of God is peripheral to the concerns of Indian philosophy except for theistic systems of Vedānta. In the Western world a large part of rationalism is devoted to combating belief in the existence of a personal God, particularly the Christian form of it. Benn, for example, in his *History of English Rationalism in the Nineteenth Century* defines rationalism as 'the habit of using reason for the destruction of religious beliefs'. But this is to take a very narrow view of rationalism and a poor ground for denying that the Buddha was a rationalist. His consistent endeavour was to keep the acceptance of moral rules and their practice independent of the acceptance of particular view of the world. He in fact went a step further and made spiritual life (we may call it higher morality or something higher than morality) independent of the acceptance of any creed. This is very important.

The general tendency among philosophers is to provide secure foundations for morality, if not theological or metaphysical, then biological and sociological. Many an earnest student takes up philosophy in the hope that it may provide guidance to him and help him find some meaning in his life. The Buddha attempts to teach us to live with metaphysical uncertainty or rather to bypass it as something not vital to our lives. There are two components to this problem. One is the logical relation between the acceptance of certain moral judgements, standards or rules on the one hand, and the acceptance of certain views about reality on the other. It seems to me that moral judgements do not imply or presuppose metaphysical judgements. When some people feel vaguely that the objectivity of values requires that they proceed from some Supreme Being or that they be rooted in the structure of reality in some way, they are probably confusing objectivity of values with their supremacy.

The second, and in some ways the harder question, is of moral persuasion, of inducing people to conform to certain standards which you consider desirable, which indeed they may themselves profess. Here the Buddha relied on personal example more than on discourses. A life of simple unaffected goodness is better than volumes of moral exhortation. A great teacher like him raises the threshold of moral sensitiveness of the persons with whom he interacts. If moral judgements are primarily practical, then achieving and sustaining moral consensus and purifying it through constant criticism and reflection are more important than adoption and propagation of any cognitive or non-cognitive meta-ethical theory.

Two difficulties, however, remain. The first is that the Buddha observed and recommended certain practices, moral and psychological, which go beyond a purely secular view of humane life. I have no doubt that the distinction between right and wrong and the acceptance of certain moral rules do not necessitate the acceptance of any metaphysics or theology. A degree of self-denial and even self-sacrifice is needed to maintain any decent social order. But even with the adoption of the middle path (*madhyama mārga*) and the avoidance of ascetic self-torture, the noble eightfold path includes the cultivation of *vairāgya* (detachment) which must appear quaint and eccentric from the viewpoint of a this-worldly rational morality. For the Buddha and his followers the spiritual practices are justified by being necessary to *nirvāṇa*, the final goal of all sentient beings. To make it attainable for all and for other considerations the devout Buddhist, like the devout Hindu and Jaina, accepts the law of *karma* and rebirth. And this brings me to the second problem. The belief in rebirth was accepted by the Buddha, though the crudities of the popular view were avoided by him. It is encapsulated in the world-view which provides the setting for the enunciation of the noble truths and the eightfold path and is especially embodied in the setting forth of *bhāvacakra* – the chain of becoming with its sequential links. To many of us the whole doctrine seems to be a grim fairytale and it has its difficulties even when purified of superstitious accretions. We can reject it and, in the Indian context, rationalists in a rather restricted sense, may make such a rejection an important ingredient in their world-view.

But it is one thing to reject this cosmological background which is part of Buddhism no less than Hinduism and Jainism, and quite another to maintain that the Buddha did not accept it. He did, unless we reject the authority of the earliest Pāli dialogues which record his teachings including his first sermon. If we do this what sources do we have to believe anything about his life and teachings? We can, however, do one of the two things. We can maintain that the references to the doctrine in the teachings are metaphorical and are meant to emphasize certain elements in the teaching, especially ethical earnestness. This is a possible view though I do not at all find it plausible. Second, we can reject the doctrine or refrain from accepting it and find that a great deal of the ethical teaching still survives. This is analogous to some Christians and even non-Christians who reject Christian theology but accept Christ's ethical teaching, at any rate what they consider to be central to it. I suppose this exercise can be carried out much more easily in the case of Theravāda Buddhism, because of its a-metaphysical, analytical character.

All rationalists, who consider any 'transcendental' element in a philosophy, irrational and ultimately inimical to human well-being, will have to do this. Theravāda, shorn of the law of *karma* with the *saṁgha* turned into an intellectual and moral elite, functioning in an open, liberal and humane society which would be their ideal. It is not an unworthy ideal. When Amartya Sen came to India after winning the Nobel Prize, he paid a tribute to the Buddha placing him above Gandhi and Tagore. He noted that the Buddha was stimulated to philosophical reflection by the spectacle of age, sickness and death. Sen said that he himself was inspired by the thought of Buddha to do whatever he could as an economist and devise methods of fighting these old enemies of mankind. Service to mankind is entirely in the spirit of the Buddha.

There is a well-established story of the Buddha personally nursing a monk who had fallen ill with dysentery, exhorting other monks to take care of one another since they had no father or mother to look after them. But to emphasize 'works' at the expenses of 'faith' or even to make it the whole of religion is to miss out an important element in the Buddha's teaching or for that matter in any spiritual religion. This is the element of 'other-worldliness' or 'self-transcendence'. Though the words are misleading no others are available. In early Buddhism which is non-theistic, non-speculative, this element is provided by *nirvāṇa* as the supreme goal. Though described almost entirely in negative terms it is declared that but for its reality and its unborn, undying and incomposite character, no escape from the sorrows of this life is possible. In *Saṁyukta-Nikāya,* the Buddha repudiates the charge of teaching some form of Nihilism. It is not necessary to discuss this matter any further but the difficulties here have a family resemblance to those that arise when we try to describe the realization of the final truth in Advaita, Sāṁkhya and even in Jainism and theism, except in its popular forms. I have said enough to show that it is not plausible to reduce the Buddha's teaching to an ethical code of life based on reflection and presented non-dogmatically for acceptance by reasonable men. It is certainly that, but it is something more.

This something more we may choose to treat as a figure of speech, an attractive packing for selling ethical goods. We may wonder why we have saddled ourselves with notions that lead to endless debate and paradoxes verging on contradictions. If so, we can regard *nirvāṇa* as an imaginary ideal, a mathematical limit that is approached asymptotically but is never reached nor is even meant to be reached. With this reinterpretation, the need to believe in transmigration also disappears. As an interpretation of the Buddha this may not be acceptable but as an account of what we accept and adopt from his teachings it is unobjectionable. His teaching is best suited for such an exercise.

As regards the answer to the question which forms the title of this paper, it must depend partly upon definition of the term 'rationalist'. If a rationalist must necessarily be a materialist and a crusading atheist then the Buddha was not a rationalist. He also believed in the possibility of acquiring certain uncommon powers of cognition – what we would nowadays call ESP – though not of miraculous action. The agenda of the rationalists the world over includes not only the wholly admirable goal of fighting quacks and miracle-mongering godmen but also discounting accounts of paranormal phenomena and disproving their possibility. They may succeed in this aim also. But I see no a priori reason why such phenomena cannot occur and the genuineness of some of them should not be established by empirical investigation.

It is well known that in the course of its development and spread all over the world Buddhism gathered rituals and practices (some magical) far removed from the teaching of its founder. The deification of the Buddha began with his death. *Mahāparinirvāṇa-Sūtra* mentions the miraculous crossing of the Gaṅgā by the Buddha and some prophesies are ascribed to him. But the Buddha's own teaching, it is needless to say, does not in any way depend on any miracle or mystery and it must be said to the credit of Buddhism that the master's teaching is not recommended on the strength of alleged miracles.

I think that rationalism should not be defined in terms of the opinions one holds or does not hold but in terms of the spirit in which one advocates and recommends any view. The Buddha always recommended his views on the ground that they rest on an analysis and description of facts of experience. We may not always agree with him. But it is remarkable he *never* lost his temper or denounced his opponents. He recognized that everyone cannot be convinced by his arguments and he was content to let disagreement stand, without affecting his concern for the well-being and happiness of all. Anyone who reads the Pāli dialogues will be convinced that many conversions effected by him were through the power of his personality rather than by eloquence or brilliance. There are methods of non-rational persuasion which are not against reason, and whose operation requires exploration. In this context it is better to use terms like 'reasonable person' or 'man of reason', rather than 'rationalist', which has acquired a rather narrow connotation for historical reasons. The Buddha's greatest contribution to the life of reason is to make the good life independent of conflicting world-views. He may seem like an empiric-treating human suffering symptomatically whereas metaphysical purveyors of salvation have a method backed by insight into the nature of the ultimate reality. But this is to overlook the fact that alternative metaphysical constructions will always be open in philosophy. In the words of C.D. Broad, 'These are matters on which equally intelligent and equally virtuous people can differ'.

How the Buddha would have tackled a serious-minded rationalist who finds any 'transcendental' element in philosophy a source of mischief and superstition, it is difficult to visualize in detail. He rejected Ucchedavāda as clear as he dismissed Śāśvatavāda. The materialists he encountered were either wild, lawless persons or thoughtless persons bent upon immediate enjoyment who he converted, often, by the power of his presence. But what about those who find the few commitments involved in his *sammā diṭṭhi* unacceptable? What about those who find the tone of his teaching too sombre, austere, if not downright pessimistic? What is wrong with sensible enjoyment combined with interest in science, art and philosophy? What is wrong with fun and games, so long as we do not harm others?

> It's no go the Buddha; It's no go Blavatsky
>
> All we want is a mug of beer; And a bit of skirt in a taxi.[4]

I do not think the Buddha would have denounced such persons and condemmed them to half-fire or the darkness of limbo.[5] But he would have regarded them as tying themselves down to a recurrent pattern of life which is ultimately unsatisfactory. He would have left the choice to their maturity and understanding. For him, we must live with dispassion today for tomorrow we die.

---

4 Quotation from memory.

5 They may condemn themselves to a temporary stay in a home-made hell.

7

Mahāsatipaṭṭhāna-Sutta and Pātañjala Yoga*

My attention was first drawn to the above Sutta by a talk given by Chubb in Wilson College. With his usual clarity and forthrightness he set forth practice of mindfulness and its place in the spiritual life. The essence of the method is to see things as they are, he told us, without interpretation or any other kind of interference, the contents that keep bobbing up to the surface of consciousness. This is indeed the most important and distinctive technique in the practice of *satī* but the dialogue contains much more and is a veritable compendium of Buddhist yoga. *Mahāsatipaṭṭhāna-Sutta* occurs in the *Dīgha-Nikāya* but its great importance is indicated by the fact that it has four other occurrences. In *Majjhima, Saṁyutta* and *Aṅguttara-Nikāya*'s and also in *Sutta Vibhaṅga* which is part of *Vinaya Piṭaka*. Malasekera points out that 'in Sri Lanka the mere recital of the Sutta is said to ward off dangers and bring happiness' and that 'it is the desire of every Buddhist that he shall die with *Satipaṭṭhāna-Sutta* on his lips or, at least, with the sound of it in his ears'. The text of the Sutta is in the form of discourse by the Buddha to the mendicants and thus lacks the drama and human interest of some of the other dialogues.

At the outset the Buddha declares that 'the only way, *bhikkhus*, to purity living beings and to transcend sorrow and lamentation, to extinguish suffering and dejection, to acquire the right mode of life and to reach the realization of *nibbāna* is that of the four applications of mindfulness'. The four applications are

---

* Published in *J. Krishnamurti and Early Buddhism*, Pune: Datta Lakshmi Trust, 1996.

1. to observe the body qua body (*kāyekāyānuppassi*),
2. to observe sensations qua sensations (*vedanāsu vedanānupassi*),
3. to observe thoughts as thoughts (*citte cittānupassi*), and
4. to observe mental objects as mental objects (*dhammesu dhammānupassi*).

To observe bodily processes as bodily processes, it is explained, one retires to the forest or seeks the shelter of a tree or an empty room, sits cross-legged with an erect body and directs attention to the goings on in the psycho-physical complex. Inhalation and exhalation are performed mindfully. One is aware whether the breath is long or short. Just as a skilful turner, when turning his lathe a long way or only a little, is aware of what he is doing so is one aware of the modalities of one's breathing; when one is walking one is aware 'I am walking' and similarily with other postures. One contemplates the body 'from the soles of the feet to the crown of the head' or one fixes one's attention on some part that stands out of the total organic field, that is the felt body. If some bodily limb and its movements clamour for attention one may direct observation towards it, substituting the attitude of the doctor for that of the patient. The technique apparently precludes practical action but if something has to be done, one must do it, I suppose, with the awareness of what one is doing. Massaging, in the course of meditation, an itching or aching part readily springs to mind. The general attitude of the Buddhist is to maintain a healthy body free from ailments so that no action is needed during such sessions. A well-known saying in this regard is that the 6 ft and odd that constitute the length of the body are extremely important for they contain the key to salvation as well as damnation in the form of suffering.

The purpose of this as also of that of observing the arising and passing away of sensations is to cultivate disinterestedness or *sākṣibhāva*. Our normal tendency is to go along with the body, to be merged in it and to act in ways considered practically appropriate. The first two applications of mindfulness aim at alienating the psycho-physical complex and turning oneself into a detached observer. Sensations are to be observed in respect of their hedonic tone. We are told that they are to be observed 'internally or externally or both together'. This last I take to be noticing the intrinsic nature of sensations – the 'raw feels' as the Americans would put it, as also the causes of their origin and cessation. In fact, the first two forms of mindfulness can be taken together under the general heading of observing sensation both internal and external. For, though the body can be observed as one object among others, the most natural and dominant observation of it is through bodily or organic sensations. These two forms are intuitive in character as they involve presentations which can be attended to without altering their character or doing so only minimally. Even here reflection about the contents of consciousness can be combined with direct awareness of them.

One of the salient forms of meditation in the Buddhist tradition is on the general theme of change and decay. The dialogue explains at some length and recommends to the mendicant the superimposition of images of decay and ugliness on pleasant and attractive impressions of the body, which we are exhorted to regard as a bag closed at both ends containing impurities and filth. I shall not weary you by quoting details of the discourse on this point, but the images and thoughts recommended will tend to cause revulsion towards the most beautiful and vigorous body. This is a kind of repulsion therapy and may be regarded in William James' language as 'religion of the sick soul' as constrasted with 'religion of healthy mindedness'. But this is only one element in Buddhism which is on the whole, religion of the latter type. The Buddha apparently felt that strong methods are sometimes needed to create *vairāgya* and turn us away from frivolous, worldly pursuits. But analytically the important point is the combination of intuitive and discursive elements in meditation. The next two, involving representative consciousness are obviously discursive in character.

An example of observing thoughts qua thoughts is this:

> In our community, *bhikkhus*, if one's thought is lustful, one is aware that it is so, similarly if one's thought is free from lust.

> Or if it is full of hate; deluded or without delusion; attentive or inattentive; elevated or not elevated; higher or lower; concentrated or wandering; emancipated or unimancipated; in each case one is aware of the nature of the thought reflecting; 'my thought is lustful' and so on.

I suppose the distinguishing mark of this level as constrasted with the second, is that feeling tones and pleasure and pains centre round an idea or thought, i.e. an awareness of an object when it is absent and not acting on one's senses. But the mental embroidery of emotive accompaniments may as well be set off by a sensation as by a thought, and the second may easily turn into the third if the mind goes wool gathering. But in the case of emotive thinking, the inhibition of associations and natural impulses arrests the normal growth of the thought process. This is the aim of our technique as much as the cultivation of beneficial and desirable thoughts, which is obviously performed by mindfulness about *dhamma*. As the dialogue amply brings out, this consists in sustained reflection on *dhamma*. Mrs. Rhys Davids calls this level of mindfulness, observing mental objects, maybe because such observation as exists here is carried out in the context of Buddhist *dhamma* and the various analytical and classificatory doctrines included in it. This part of the dialogue is very enumerative. Apart from the Four Noble Truths and the five constituents of human personality, there are the five hindrances, seven factors of enlightenment and twelve bases of mental process. It is not necessary to go into the details, but it is obvious that elaborate, discursive meditation is needed to strengthen one's faith in the *dhamma*. An element of observation may be there when one notices, for example, the presence or absence of some factor of enlightenment. Even this takes the form of critical self-examination rather than simple observation. Moreover, there is the assertion that when one continually engages in observing objects in the context of *dhamma*, doctrinal truths become directly evident. When one hears the truth 'this is suffering' one understands the truth as it really is (*yathābhūtam pajānāti*). Perhaps the suggestion is that instead of being a formulae to which we give intellectual assent, they sink into the very bones of our being and condition our responses beneficially and effortlessly.

There is nothing surprising in a method of meditation that includes both intuitive and discursive elements, observation as well as reflection. On one view of intuition, it is the crystallization of prolonged thinking and reasoning. Both types of practices are found in different contemplative cultures. Whatever may be the mix of intuitive and discursive elements in mindfulness, the final goal is immediate insight or direct illumination. The crowning stage of mindfulness is *samādhi* (concentration). As a result of the steady practice of *satī* 'one remains energetic, conscious and mindful, having disciplined both the desire and the dejection which are common in the world. And one remains independent not grasping at anything in the world'. *Samādhi,* which is the unpredictable but inevitable culmination, is described as follows:

> In our community *bhikkhus* having separated oneself from sensuous appetites and unwholesome ideas, one enters into and dwells in the first stage of meditation which is born of seclusion and is accompanied with delight and happiness and in which there is thought and deliberation. Then allaying thought and deliberation one enters into and dwells in the second stage of meditation which leads to inner serenity and one-pointedness, accompanied with delight and happiness and born of concentration, unaccompanied by thought and deliberation. Then indifferent to joy and dispassion, one continues, mindful and conscious and experiences in one's body that well-being which the pure describe: one who has equanimity and is mindful continues in well-being. Thus one enters into and dwells in the third stage of meditation. Then putting away both well-being and suffering and having extinguished former feelings and elation and dejection, one enters into the fourth stage of meditation where there is no well-being or suffering and where there is utter purity of equanimity and mindfulness (*upekkhā sati pari suddhim*). This *bhikkhu*'s, is what is called right concentration (*samma samādhi*). This *bhikkhu*'s, is the noble truth concerning the path that leads to the cessations of suffering.

It is obviously futile for a person like me to comment upon the details and internal differences of the four stages of *samādhi* outlined above. But the first stage where thought and deliberation are present and the mind plays around and through a chosen theme corresponds to Patañjali's *dhyāna*. The second where reasoning and thinking are suppressed and the mind is *ekāgra* (the Buddhist expression is *cetaso ekādhibhāvam avitakkam avicāram*) would be *dhāraṇā*. The third stage where there is experience of well-being in one's body corresponds to *samprajñāta samādhi*. The fourth stage where suffering and well-being, elation and dejection are put away and only utter equanimity and purity remain may be likened to *asamprajñāta samādhi*. Bhikkhu Saṅgharakṣita in his contribution on Buddhism to Basham's volume on *Outlines of Indian Culture* writes that at this stage there is serenity and utter purity, but no experiencer of these. I find this puzzling to the point of incomprehension. The difficulties of this form of spiritual experience, where the sense of self is lost, are common to all the great mystical teachers and not exclusive to the Buddha. Philosophically it is significant that the Buddha's account of *samādhi* is phenomenological and free from metaphysical interpretation.

No purpose can be served by an extended and mechanical comparison of *Satipaṭṭhāna* with Pātañjala Yoga. For both, renunciation or *vairāgya* is the key to spiritual life. *Yama* and *niyama* are covered much more thoroughly by the earlier stages in the *ārya aṣṭāṅga mārga*. The Buddha exhorts the monks to seek solitude and assume firm posture before practising *satī*, which takes care of *pratyāhāra* and *āsana*, which are essential but relatively unimportant preliminaries. *Prāṇāyāma* (breath control) is not separately considered by the Buddha. It is part of the exercise of mindfulness on bodily processes. Moreover, it must be the experience of anyone who has tried meditation in any form, that breathing becomes regular and slow as a by-product of contemplative exercises. Any emotional disturbance immediately upsets the rhythm of breathing and affects other bodily processes. The entire process of preparing oneself for reaching the summits of human consciousness is summed up in the well-known formula of *triśikṣā* (threefold training) comprising *śīla*, *samādhi* and *prajñā*. A notable absence in our dialogue in the matter of techniques of meditation is that of *japa*, the attempt to focus the mind on a selected object through incantations and other repetitive methods. Patañjali's techniques, on the other hand, do not include anything like *vipassanā* which seems to be the Buddha's distinctive contribution to the contemplative culture of India.

A minor curiosity is the way the dialogue ends. Nobody has emphasized more than the Buddha the arduous nature of the spiritual journey extending over several epochs. And yet we find him promising that whoever practises the four applications of mindfulness for seven years will obtain either the highest knowledge in the present life or else the state of the non-returner, if there is reminder of individuality. Then salvation is offered at a discount and the period of practice is reduced through decreasing number of years and months to seven days! The paradox is not peculiar to the Buddha and is the result of an attempt to entice the common man to begin the spiritual journey, hoping that the early rewards will inspire him to persist in his undertaking. It is the same in the theistic tradition, where instant religion alternates with calls to unremitting labour. *Gītā,* which promises divine help to the dovotee, declares that only one of several thousands tries for *siddhi* and of the thousands who attempt it, only a few reach their goal. Nothing is easier to find than God and at the same time nothing more difficult. 'Ask and it shall be given'. But equally you must give up everything for the pearl of infinite price. Many are called but few are chosen and the kingdom of heaven does not suffer to be taken by storm.

8

The Ideal of the Sthitaprajña
Some Platitudes and Some Paradoxes[1]

VERSES 55-72 of the second *adhyāya* of *Bhagavad-Gītā* contain a description of the *sthitaprajña* (the sage of stable intelligence). Answering a query from Arjuna, Kr̥ṣṇa outlines a picture of the ideal man. The following is the gist of Kr̥ṣṇa's account. The *sthitaprajña* puts away all cravings and his soul is content in itself. His mind is untroubled in the midst of sorrows and is free from eagerness for pleasures. Passion, fear and anger have passed away from him. Freed from all attachment, he neither rejoices in good fortune nor does he indulge in lamentation when misfortune befalls him. He draws away the senses from their objects as the tortoise draws in its limbs. He abstains from enjoyment of sensual pleasures when the desire for them arises in his mind. Even the taste for such enjoyment falls away when he realizes the Supreme. Kr̥ṣṇa admits that this kind of mastery over self is difficult, for the powerful senses will carry off a man's mind by force. But the sage restrains them and turns his mind firmly towards God. It is necessary to give up brooding over objects of sense. If the mind dwells on objects of sense, attachment to them is born. From attachment springs desire and from desire when frustrated, comes anger. From anger arises confusion, from confusion, loss of memory or balance of mind and from loss of memory, destruction or discrimination. When a man loses his discrimination, he is destroyed. Therefore to save himself from destruction the wise man disciplines himself and moves about in the

---

[1] 'The Ideal of the Sthitaprajña: Some Platitudes and Some Paradoxes' in *The Concept of Sthitaprajña: A Stable-minded Person*, Dutta Lakshmi Trust, Pune, 1993.

world with his senses firmly under his control. From self-control he obtains purity of heart, overcomes sorrow and attains lasting peace. Kṛṣṇa declares that serenity of mind is the greatest bliss, for how can there be happiness for a restless person? The sage is compared to the deep, calm, ocean into which all rivers enter. The sage is awake to spiritual reality but is dead or indifferent to the world of senses. Whereas ordinary persons are dead to the spirit within them, and are preoccupied with the world of senses. This state of mental equilibrium when firmly established leads to lasting peace and liberation from all delusion and sorrow. It is called *brahma-nirvāṇa*.

The conceptual framework may be described very broadly but fairly accurately, as the superimposition of the theism of Bhāgavata religion on the absolutism of Upaniṣads. The practice of non-attachment, which is the essence of the ideal of the *sthitaprajña* is, for *Gītā*, a means to the final goal of human life, viz. self-realization. This self-realization is also God realization for *Gītā* postulates a supreme spiritual being which is the ground of the phenomenal world and also the indwelling and innermost self of man. The final purpose of human life is to realize the unity of all existence in the Godhead. Though *Gītā* wavers between an absolutistic and a theistic conception of this Supreme, infinite being, it finally seems to opt for theism and identifies the Supreme with Kṛṣṇa-Vāsudeva of the Bhāgavata tradition. The life recommended by it is theocentric and it is in such a life that man finds the highest knowledge, the greatest happiness and perfect peace and freedom. But I don't think the ideal necessitates logical commitment to certain specific and distinctive doctrine of Indian philosophy such as the law of *karma* and reincarnation. One may say that without some form of spiritual philosophy of the universe and human destiny, the rigorous self-mortification recommended would not be reasonable. But then the practice of inward and truly spiritual religion cuts across the historical and cultural traditions of the higher religions of the world, and contending metaphysical systems. In essence the 'non-attachment' of *Gītā* is the same as the 'holy indifference' recommended and practised by St. Francois de Sales. Even within the Indian tradition, this combination of moral discipline and mental training is the same basically and is to be found in early Buddhism, which bypasses along with other metaphysical riddles the question of existence of Īśvara, Jainism, which is explicitly atheistic, Advaita, which many theists regard as blasphemous and the various theistic schools of Vedānta.

Indeed the description of *sthitaprajña* in spite of a single reference to God (*tāni sarvāṇi saṁyamya yukta āsita matparaḥ* – *BG* II.61) is wholly Buddhist in character. The emphasis throughout is on freeing oneself from agitation of mind, confusion and suffering. Even the serenity of mind and peace – the fruits of non-attachment (*prasāda, śānti*) – are explained negatively. Radhakrishnan translates *brahma-nirvāṇa* into 'the bliss of God' but there is no justification for this in this portion of *Gītā*. Commenting on the penultimate verse of the *adhyāya* with reference to the word *śāntim*, Śaṅkara writes:

> *sarva-saṁsāra-duḥkha-uparāmatvalakṣaṇam nirvāṇākhyam* ।
>
> that peace which is designated *nirvāṇa* and which is characterized by the cessation of all miseries of worldly existence.

The term *nirvāṇa* in the concluding verse explains it simply as *mokṣa*. If we turn to the marks of a true devotee of God described in the 12th *adhyāya* (*BG* 13-20) the account of the higher life has much in common with the portrait of *sthitaprajña* though, reference to God is present naturally in every verse. But there are positive elements going beyond the universal indifference apparently recommended in the 2nd *adhyāya* (*BG*). The true devotee cultivates compassion and universal friendliness. But it is only in the 9th *adhyāya* and the concluding verses of the 18th *adhyāya* that the warmth of feeling and exaltation of spirit, characteristic of *bhakti* at its best, are foreshadowed. Otherwise *sthitaprajña* is not very different from the stoic philosopher of ancient Greece and the *samatva* or *sāmya* sought by him is essentially the same as the dispassion (ataraxia) of the stoic philosopher. Even an avowedly materialist like Lucretius, in his philosophical poem 'On the Nature of Things', writes:

> Religion does not consist in tuning ceaselessly to veiled stones,

> nor in approaching all the altars nor in prostrating oneself on the ground nor in uplifting ones hands before the habitations of gods, nor in flooding temples with the blood of beasts nor in heaping vows upon vows but in beholding all things with a peaceful mind.

I am not suggesting either that the ideal of *sthitaprajña* should be divorced from the metaphysical background of *Gītā* or that it should be considered apart from the concept of *lokasaṁgraha* – selfless action for social welfare – held up as an ideal and illustrated by reference to Janaka in the 3rd *adhyāya* (*BG* III.20). But the connections between metaphysical systems and recommendations concerning the ideal life for man are more tenuous than logical links. They are rooted partly in the temperament of the thinker and the circumstances of his life.

Gītā certainly made a valuable contribution to the religious and philosophic thought of ancient India. To appreciate the teaching of Gītākāra on the place of action in human life and its relation to the final goal of *mokṣa,* we must place it in its contemporary setting. In the epic period to which *Gītā* belongs, there were two sharply opposed views concerning action. The first was that of the followers of Vedic ritual (*karma-kāṇḍa*) who recommended action, particularly the performance of sacrifices, for enjoying happiness here and hereafter. Opposed to this ritualistic Brāhmanism was the heterodox view which recommended renunciation of all action, on the ground that all deeds, good as well as bad, have the effect of binding man to the wheel of becoming. On this view the right thing to do would be, to abandon all social activities and withdraw from the world. This latter standpoint though characterized as Buddhist by historians of Indian thought was also shared by certain Upaniṣadic and Jaina thinkers. *Gītā* itself shows the influence of this view when it is declared: 'The wise man renounces here both good and evil deeds' (II.50). Among those who advocated liberation as the final ideal and right knowledge as the indispensable means to it there was a unanimous condemnation of *karma* and exaltation of *jñāna*. *Gītā* rejects both these views and allows the path of action an equal, if not a superior, status with *jñāna* and *bhakti*. It upholds the ideal of *niṣkāma karma* which consists in the disinterested performance of one's duties and the renunciation not of action, but of the fruits of action (*karmaphala-tyāga*). *Gītā* is extremely forthright in its denunciation of Vedic ritualism.[2] This is remarkable when we consider that the Gītākāra belongs to the mainstream of orthodoxy and is a defender of the Sanātana Dharma. Those who turned away with revulsion and disapproval from the cult of sacrifices and yet did not opt out of the Vedic way, allowed only a limited value to action. More specifically, the wise man refrains from wrong action and unless he is *saṁnyāsin*, performs only those actions whose non-performance would lead to incurring sin. Beyond this he performs good deeds for cultivating purity of mind (*sattva-saṁśuddhi*) without which spiritual wisdom cannot be attained. This was a well-established part of orthodoxy which *Gītā* endorses repeatedly. (*Yogī*s engage in action without attachment and for self-purification, *BG* V.2.) But it goes far beyond this with its ideal of *lokasaṁgraha* and insists that even liberated persons should engage in action. While admitting that such persons have no obligations in the narrow sense or any personal ends to attain, *Gītā* insists that they should be active in promoting common welfare. This is a truly radical shift in the ethical thought of ancient India. So unusual is this point of view that even Śaṅkara commenting on verse 20 of 3rd *adhyāya* (*BG*) says that Janaka and other sages like him engaged in work lest people at large go astray and slide into inaction and indolence.

However to be fair to him, we must note that in his popular writings he presents a more human and emotional standpoint. A verse ascribed to him reads,

> *santo mahānto nivasanti śāntāḥ vasantavat lokahitaṁ carantaḥ* ।
> *tīrṇāḥ svayam bhīmabhavārṇavaṁ janān ahetunā anyānapi tārayanti* ॥

Rendered freely it means:

---

2 Refer particularly to verses 41-54 of the 2nd *adhyāya* of *Bhagavad-Gītā* (*BG*).

> There are (in this world) saints who are serene and great souled. Like the spring they do good to the world. Having themselves crossed the mighty ocean of becoming they help others to cross it without any selfish motive.

Kṛṣṇa himself, in the course of his description of how the world-wheel is set in motion and kept going, declares that he sustains the three worlds to set an example to others, certainly, in so far as a *sthitaprajña* is engaged in action, he works for the common good (*sarva-bhūta-hite rataḥ*). But the idea that such selfless activity is an expression, even a natural overflowing of love of God, is absent from *Gītā* – though certain statement in the 9th and 12th *adhyāyas* (*BG*) can be regarded as presaging an ideal whose full flowering is to be found in the lives and teaching of the great figures of the Bhakti movement. The reason for this, apart from the continuing influence of the traditional devalutation of action, could be the overriding concern with social order. And though the Gītākāra gives a new twist to the concept of *yajña* by linking it with the efficient discharge of one's social obligations, he is also an upholder of *varṇāśrama dharma* which keeps popping up now and then in spite of the reformist formulations of *Gītā*. Some of the greatest historical evils of Hindu social organization – which cannot be condemned too strongly – have arisen from subordinating *sādhāraṇa dharma* to *varṇāśrama dharma* and neglecting *lokasaṁgraha*.

So, I am afraid no social activism of 'liberation theology' can be extracted from the concept of *sthitaprajña* per se. But there is nothing in it which is incompatible with programmes of social reforms and taken together with other teachings of *Gītā* it can even provide an inspiration to disinterested social action. It may be that there is an element of other worldliness in it which normally leads to the neglect of our social life; but such other worldliness is a part, and an essential part, of every great religion. In India at any rate the very presence of saints – though on the fringes of society is supposed to have beneficial effects on others. Their life is their message more than in the case of an ordinary person. And not all of them have been content to sit back and enjoy their ecstacy or serenity of mind.

The Buddha devoted four decades to tireless missionary activity after attaining enlightenment and similar examples of saintly figures from all the different religious traditions of the world, can be quoted. So to the question in moral psychology whether totally selfless action is possible the answer seems to be 'yes; at any rate some persons have realized the ideal and the rest of us can approach it, asymptotically'. Even if there is an admixture of a higher form of egoism in the most saintly actions, even if the God sought by the saints is an imaginary focus of the highest human aspirations, there is a beauty in their lives whose appeal is difficult to resist. But there is a price to be paid. The saint's sacrifice not only the undesirable elements in human nature but also the desirable and admirable. 'You must give up every thing for the pearl of infinite price', Christ tells us. The best is the enemy of the good; and we may wonder whether we are wise to give up so much for so elusive a goal, especially when we are unable to accept the metaphysical underpinnings of the mystical search, for the highest. Second, there is another paradox in combining the systematic emasculation of our emotional and vital tendencies with the ideal of universal compassion. The love of our neighbour is not an intellectual love and we are all expected to cultivate sympathetic imagination which enables us to feel with our fellowmen and not merely for them. The saint sets no limits to his compassion so that his nervous system extends to all sentient beings. Janaka's declaration 'when Mithila burns nothing of me burns' (*mithilāyāṁpradīptāyāṁ na me kiñcitpradahyate*) is held up as a perfect example of non-attachment. But a similar attitude to the misfortunes of others would be disturbing even if accompanied by dispassionate helpfulness. If Narsi Mehta is an authority on matters spiritual, then you are not a true Vaiṣṇava unless you feel you are hurt when any man is hurt. And when compassion takes the form of charitable action any such action will involve ministering to human needs and attending to human wants such as feeding the hungry or relieving suffering. If man's true self-transcends all worldly events which are only shadows cast on its primal purity, then why should we worry so much about what happens to others, while totally ignoring and rising superior to similar happenings in our own case? This is not the old question of self vs. others. Rather it is a curious adoption of double standards in higher morality or in a way of life that transcends 'the morality of claims and counter-claims'.

9

Anekāntavāda : Some Logical Issues

ANEKĀNTAVĀDA, complete with the sevenfold scheme of propositions and the doctrine of *nayas*, is not present in the teaching of Mahāvīra as it has come down to us. It is a later development when Jaina philosophers vigorously defended their views against rival philosophers in Sanskrit, which was the language of learning and philosophical debate in ancient India. But it is a natural elaboration of Mahāvīra's method of answering philosophical questions concerning the eternity of the world and the soul, the finitude or infinitude of the world, etc. The essence of his approach is to reconcile alternative and apparently opposed answers by relating them to their respective standpoints. Matilal argues, persuasively, that Anekāntavāda is a development of the Vibhajjyavāda[1] of the Buddha. The crucial difference seems to be that the Buddha rejected the extremes before adopting the middle course whereas Mahāvīra accepts them after proper qualifications have been made. The first middle course depends upon rejection and exclusion, the second on acceptance and inclusion. This is, broadly speaking, a correct account. But I do not agree with Matilal's interpretation of the Buddha's handling of *avyākata* or indeterminate questions. This is a large issue and the relation between *mādhyamika catuṣkoṭi* which grew out of the silence of the Buddha and Syādvāda which is the core of Anekāntavāda is worthy of independent discussion. I shall only remark that the Buddha's silence was practical largely but had also a theoretical component. He thought it logically unnecessary to

---

[1] *Vibhajjya* in Sanskrit means having divided. It is said that the Buddha used to answer some questions by dividing it into parts and so was called Vibhajjyavādin.

discuss alternative world-views – *diṭṭhis* – to establish the desirability of the kind of life he advocated. The following passage is from *Majjhima-Nikāya*:

> *Brahmacariya* could not depend on the view that the world is eternal. Nor could it depend on the view that the world is not eternal. Although there is the view that the world is eternal and the view that the world is not eternal, there is (*atthi eva*) birth, there is dying, there are grief, lamentation and sorrow. I lay down the destroying of these, here and now. And I say the same regarding other views.

The autonomy of ethics and its logical independence from contending metaphysical views could not have been set forth more clearly. This is a very important element in the Buddha's teaching which has no parallel in any other Indian system or, for that matter, in any other philosophical system. But I shall not discuss it any further, and turn to some basic logical issues in Anekāntavāda.

Anekāntavāda is an emphatic assertion of the manifold character of reality. Since the world has many different facets, no single assertion can bring out its nature fully. We have to look at it from different points of view and thus get a synoptic picture of it. Any categorical statement, that reality is only this and nothing else is false in the sense of being partial or incomplete. The proper form of predication is not 'is' or 'is not' (*asti, nāsti*), but *syāt*. The word *syāt* can be given different shades or nuances of meaning. Being derived from the Sanskrit root for the verb 'to be' with an optative suffix, it means 'may be' or 'perhaps is', and indicates possibility or probability. In this context it is best taken, as Matilal argues, as provisional or conditional acceptance. But even this is not completely satisfactory. Provisional acceptance implies lack of sufficient evidence to justify certainty, and hence some unspecified degree of probability. Conditional suggests, particularly to persons like me brought up on a diet of Absolute Idealism, that conditions are attached to the truth of an assertion which, when followed up properly embrace the whole of reality. As Bradley says '*S* is *P*', is always implicitly 'Reality is such that "*S* is *P*"'. There are echoes of this in Anekāntavāda, but the inspiration and general outlook are totally different. For one thing, there is no attempt to dismiss anything as mere appearance. Every experienced or given feature of reality characterizes it and the corresponding statement is true from a certain standpoint or perspective called *naya*. What may appear false in a given perspective will be perfectly in order and valid from another standpoint which is equally legitimate.

Nayavāda is an integral part of Anekāntavāda and the necessary complement of Syādvāda. Seven *naya*s are distinguished commonly, four *arthanaya*s concerned with things and three *śabdanaya*s concerned with our use of language. The latter aim at sharpening our linguistic tools and have no great philosophical significance, so far as I can see. The four *arthanaya*s are (1) *naigama,* (2) *saṁgraha,* (3) *vyavahāra,* and (4) *ṛjusūtra*. *Naigama* is the point of view which describes a thing in relation to the general purpose it serves. Alternatively it is the standpoint where the generic and specific features are not distinguished. *Saṁgraha* looks at things from the standpoint of generality and subsumes things under a universal. The universals themselves may be subsumed under higher universal until we reach the highest of universals (*mahāsāmānya*), namely, Being. Advaita does this and when it insists that this is the only proper viewpoint it commits *saṁgrahanayābhāsa*. At the other end of the spectrum, Buddhism looks at things from *ṛjusūtra* standpoint and insists that a thing is what is revealed in a particular state here and now. The result is the view that only the succession of momentary events is real. Nyāya-Vaiśeṣika and materialism are taken to result from *vyavahāranaya* or the standpoint of practical empirical knowledge.

When we relate a statement to its standpoint, both of two apparently inconsistent statements are seen to be consistent and true when we say that the world is both eternal and non-eternal. It is eternal because it does not come into existence at any time nor does it cease to be at any particular time, it is non-eternal because it undergoes change or modifications (*paryāya*'s) endlessly. It is important to notice that once the explanatory background is provided the statements are asserted categorically. The sevenfold scheme – *saptabhaṅgī* – provides a schema of assertions. It does not make any concrete statements any more than the formal representation of an argument with variables propound a particular inference.

The *saptabhaṅgī* or the sevenfold formula is as follows:

1. *syād asti* – May be it is
2. *syād nāsti* – May be it is not
3. *syād asti nāsti* – May be it is and is not
4. *Syād avaktavyaḥ* – May be it is inexpressible
5. *syād asti ca avaktavyaḥ* – May be it is and is inexpressible
6. *syād nāsti ca avaktavyaḥ* – May be it is not and is inexpressible
7. *syādasti ca, nāsti ca, avaktavyaḥ* – May be it is, is not, and is inexpressible.

The scheme apparently includes inconsistent propositions. But the appearance of self-contradiction is removed by specifying the standpoint from which something is and the standpoint from which the same thing is not. The pot, for example, is or exists in its own form (*svarūpa*), own matter (*svadravya*), in its own place (*svakśetra*) and at its own time, and it is not, in an alien form (*pararūpa*), in another matter (*paradravya*), in another place (*parakṣetra*) and at another time (*parakāla*). This brings out the familiar truth that every finite object has a specific nature and therefore excludes other specific natures. If it has a certain attribute at a given time, it excludes other alternatives in the predicate range. So far as the first two steps are concerned, by relativizing our affirmation and denial to their respective standpoints, we can avoid inconsistency. But what about the third, where the two are combined in one statement? Samantabhadra quoted by Matilal in his monograph on Anekāntavāda[2] says there is joint but gradual and successive or non-simultaneous application (*kramārpaṇa*) of the positive and negative characters. As if to strengthen the Jaina position Matilal adds:

---

[2] B.K. Matilal, *Jaina Theory of Multiple Facets of Reality and Truth, (Anekāntavāda)*, ed. Nagin J. Shah, Motilal Banarsidass, 2000.

> But if the first and second are not contradictories, the third which is only truth-functional conjunction of the first and the second will not be self-contradictory.[3]

This is very curious. The contradiction arises from the manner of combining the affirmation and denial of the same predicate of the same subject. Neither p nor $\sim p$ is self-contradictory but their conjunction is. Similarly though neither is logically necessary their disjunction $p \vee \sim p$ is. Sometimes it is best to leave well alone and not paint the lily white.

When we come to the fourth *syād avaktavyaḥ*, there is apparently an insurmountable difficulty. For here we are told, following the same authorities, there is the combined and simultaneous application of both the positive and negative characters. Matilal writes:

> By simple application of contradictory predicates to a thing in the same breath or simultaneously, the speaker does not land himself in a self-contradiction. For example we can say of a man 'He is both over 6 ft tall and explain that he has a disease which makes him stoop, but that if he were cured and were able to stand upright, he would top the 6 ft mark'. Mahāvīra himself followed a similar line of explanation in order to elaborate upon the apparently contradictory assertions like 'the person is both eternal and non-eternal.'[4]

I think in his zeal the writer overshoots his mark in the example, given the man will be 6 ft or more when he is cured of his disease. But until this is done, he will be less than 6 ft tall. This in effect reduces the fourth step to the third. It has no tendency to show that the application of contradictory predicates to a thing in the same breath or simultaneously does not land the speaker in self-contradiction. As for the parallel drawn with Mahāvīrā's explanation of how a person is both eternal non-eternal, the two cases seem to me to be very different. In *Bhagavatī-Sūtra* Mahāvīra says:

> The soul is, Jamali, eternal for it does not cease to exist at any time.

---

3 B.K. Matilal, op. cit., p. 59 (most likely).

4 Motilal, op. cit. p. 60 (most likely).

> The soul is, Jamali, non-eternal for it becomes animal after being a hellish creature, becomes a man after being an animal and it becomes a god after being a man.

In general we may say that the soul as substance is uncreated, eternal; but it undergoes many *paryāya*'s (modes) which are of a passing nature until it attains liberation and becomes a *kevalin* and abides in its pure undefiled state. This is an instance of the Jaina insistence that both change and permanence are equally real features of reality.

How then is the contradiction to be resolved and the predicate *avaktavyaḥ* to be understood? When contradictory predicates are declared to characterize the same thing in one breath, the nature of the thing becomes incomprehensible and therefore, inexpressible. One half of what we say cancels the other half and the effect is, nothing intelligible has been said. Then why make such a statement? Apparently it is to expose the partial character of rival philosophies which are Ekāntavāda's. As we have seen Advaita insists on the sole reality of *Brahman* the *mahāsāmānya* of Pure Being which comprises everything that there is. At the other pole Buddhism takes its stand on a succession of momentary events – all talk of universals, self-natures and substances (*sāmānya, svarūpa* and *dravya*) – being ruled out of court. Against such uncompromising extremes we insist, so Jainism says, that reality is both 'eternal and non-eternal, permanent and changing, one and many'. When the first two steps of the *saptabhaṅgī* are properly explained either by making explicit our perspective or by explaining that a thing exists in its own form, at a particular place and a particular time and not as another in a different place, at a different time, the contradiction vanishes. Then these concrete statements, not the statement forms in our scheme, are truth-functional conjunctions of affirmation and denial. But the combination of steps 1 and 2 in 3 produces an impression of inexpressibility. Hence the fourth step. What about the remaining three steps? They seem to be superfluous. There were scholars who accepted only the first four steps. But Vidyānanda insists on seven types of statement. The motive is apparently logical completeness.

It is obvious that steps 5-7 arise by combining the fourth with 1, 2 and 3, respectively.

One explanation could be that inexpressibility is attached to every existential statement even after our best efforts at explanation. Against the insistence that experience reveals the world to be many-sided, the standard objection is that opposite characters cannot be combined in reality intelligibly. Dilecticians, from Zeno through Nāgārjuna to Bradley argue that unity and diversity cannot be combined logically. For example, if the changing qualities affect the one, underlying substance then it too changes. If on the other hand, they do not, they do not really belong to it. The two fall apart. This is a small sample of the kind of argument by which absolutists of all hues, prove that all common sense categories – thing, quality, change, cause, space, time, etc. – are riddled with contradictions and are, therefore, unintelligible. To all this the Jaina answer may be that somehow, contrary characters are combined in reality. This fact of experience cannot be denied though the how of it is inexpressible. We cannot explain it further. Once this many-sidedness of reality is found inexpressible, it is but one step more to the conclusion that when something is *A* in a perfectly ordinary way, then its being *A* at that time and place is also inexpressible. There may be, and generally is, a causal explanation of why it is *A* or alternatively why it is not *A*. But that does not affect the fact that there are moods when we find everything strange and mysterious. Our habitual ways of thinking and acting make the world a familiar dull place. But if we contemplate it philosophically the strangeness and mystery return. In that way everything is inexpressible even after, following *saptabhaṅgī* we have stated, exhaustively, every thing that can be stated. We must accept the world as we find it and not quarrel with it as Advaita and Mahāyāna do.

This is an attempt to find a place for inexpressibility without appealing to the ineffable character of an absolute reality for which there is no place in Jainism. *Avaktavyatā* is the less glamorous sister of *anirvacanīyatā* of Advaita. But the transcendental is not altogether absent in Jainism. *Kevala-jñāna*, to which the liberated soul attains, and the purity and peace that accompany it, must be unimaginable to us. It is formally defined as a state characterized by knowing everything as it is. But *kevala-jñāna* is intuitive and not mediate. Its character must therefore be incommunicable to us. That it is possible and that we should strive for it is an act of faith inspired by the example of great souls like Mahāvīra.

Bibliography

Aquinas Thomas (ed.), 1947-48, *Summa Theologica*, tr. Fathers of the English Dominican Province, New York: Benziger Bros.

Armstrong, D.M., 1968, *A Materialist Theory of the Mind*, London: Routledge and Kegan Paul.

Ayer, A.J., 1982, *Philosophy in the Twentieth Century*, London: Weidenfeld.

———, 1973, *Central Questions of Philosophy*, London: Weienfeld.

———, 1968, *The Origins of Pragmatism*, London: Macmillan.

———, 1963, *The Concept of a Person and Other Essays*, London: Macmillan.

——— (ed.), 1959, *Logical Positivism*, Free Press.

———, 1956, *The Problem of Knowledge*, London: Macmillan.

———, 1940, *The Foundations of Empirical Knowledge*, London: Macmillan.

Bonjour, L., 1985, *The Structure of Empirical Knowledge*, Harvard University Press.

Bradley, F.H., 1897, *Appearance and Reality*, 2nd edn., Oxford University Press.

Broad, C.D., 1978, *Kant: An Introduction*, Cambridge University Press.

———, 1952, *Ethics and the History of Philosophy*, London: Routledge.

Carnap, R., 1937, *Logical Syntax of Language* (English Translation), Routledge and Kegan Paul.

Church, A., 1954, "On Carnap's Analysis of Statements of Assertion and Belief", in *Philosophy and Analysis*, ed. M. Macdonald, Oxford: Blackwell.

Churchland, P., 1989, *A Neuro-Computational Perspective*, MIT Press.

Conze, Edward, 2003, *Buddhism: Its Essence and Development*, Dover Publications.

Coomaraswamy, A.K., 2003, *Buddha and the Gospel of Buddhism*, Kessinger Publishing.

Dasgupta, S., 2003, *Yoga as Philosophy and Religion* (Calcutta University Press, Kegan Paul, London, 1924, Dover 2002), Kessinger Publishing.

———, 1941, *Philosophical Essays*, University of Calcutta.

Davids, Mrs. Rhys, 1912, *Buddhism: A Study of the Buddhist Norm*, London: Williams and Norgate.

Davids, Rhys, (1879-1910), *The Dialogues of the Buddha* (in 3 parts, from the Sacred Books of the East (SBE) series, Oxford University Press as part of UNESCO project.

———, *Questions of King Milinda* (2 vols.) (SBE Series), Oxford University Press.

Davidson, D., 2001, *Essays on Actions and Events*, Oxford: Oxford University Press.

Dummett, M., 1978, *Truth and Other Enigmas*, Harvard University Press.

Feigl, H. and W. Sellars (eds.), 1949, *Readings in Philosophical Analysis*, NewYork: Appleton-Century Craft.

Flew, A.G.N. (ed.), 1964, *Body, Mind and Death*, New York: Macmillan.

Goodman, N., 1978, *Ways of Worldmaking*, Indianapolis: Hacket Publishing.

Guttenplan, Samuel (ed.), 1994, *Cambridge Companion to the Philosophy of Mind*, Blackwell.

Haack, S., 1978, *Philosophy of Logics*, Cambridge University Press.

Hiriyanna, M., 1993, *Outlines of Indian Philosophy*, Delhi: Motilal Banarsidass, 1st edn.

Hook, Sydney (ed.), 1960, *Dimensions of Mind: A Symposium*, New York University Press.

Horner, I. B. and A.K. Coomaraswamy, 2000, *The Living Thoughts of Gotama the Buddha*, Dover Publications.

Humphreys, Christmas, 1951, *Buddhism*, Penguin: Pelican Books.

Isherwood, Christopher (ed.), 1949, *Vedanta for the Western World*, Allen and Unwin.

Kant, 1991 (1972), *Critique of Pure Reason* (*CPR*), tr. J.M.D. Meiklejohn, Everyman's Library.

Kenny, Anthony, 1973, *Wittgenstein*, Cambridge, MA: Harvard University Press.

Kneale, W., 1963, 'Are Necessary Truths True by Convention?', in *Clarity Is not Enough,* ed. H.D. Lewis, Muirhead Library of Philosophy, Allen and Unwin.

Kneale, W.C. and M. Kneale, 1962, *Development of Logic,* Oxford University Press.

Leherer, K., 1990, *Theory of Knowledge,* West View Press, Routledge.

Lewis and Langford, 1958, *Symbolic Logic,* Dover Publications.

Marcel, A.J. and E. Bisiach (eds.), 1988, *Consciousness in Contemporary Society,* Oxford: Clarendon Press.

Matilal, B., 1998, *The Character of Logic in India,* ed. Jonardan Ganeri and Heeramn Tiwari, State University of New York Press.

Mitchell, D., 1972, *An Introduction to Logic,* London: Hutchinson.

Mitra, R.L. (tr.), 1883, *Yoga Aphorisms with Commentary of Bhoja,* Calcutta: Asiatic Society of Bengal.

Moore, G.E., 1903, *Principia Ethica,* first published by Cambridge University Press, Dover Philosophical Classics.

Moser, Paul K. and J.D. Trout (eds.), 1995, *Contemporary Materialism: A Reader,* London: Routledge.

Pitcher, George (ed.), 1966, *Wittgenstein: The Philosophical Investigations,* New York: Macmillan.

Price, H.H., 1962, *Thinking and Experience,* Harvard University Press.

Prior, A.N, 1962 (1955), *Formal Logic,* Oxford University Press.

Putnam, H., 1979 (1975), 'Is Logic Empirical?', in *Philosophical Papers I,* Cambridge University Press.

Quine, W.V.O., 1986 (1970), *Deviant Logics, Philosophy of Logic,* Harvard University Press.

———, 1986 (1970), *The Philosophy of Logic,* Harvard University Press.

———, 1976 (1966), 'Quantifiers and Propositional Attitudes', in *The Ways of Paradox,* Harvard University Press.

———, 1960, *Word and Object,* MIT Press.

———, 1949, 'Truth by Convention', in *Readings in Philosophical Analysis,* ed. Feigl and Sellars, Appleton-Century-Crofts, 1st edn.

Quinton, A., 1967, 'Analytic and Empirical', in *Philosophical Logic,* ed. P.F.

Strawson, Oxford University Press.

Radhakrishnan, S. (tr. and annot.), 1997 (1950), *The Dhammapada*, Oxford University Press.

———, 1971, *Indian Philosophy*, vol. II, chap. 5, London: Allen and Unwin.

Rorty, R., 1998, *Truth and Progress: Philosophical Papers*, vol. 3, Cambridge University Press.

Rosser, J.B. and A.R. Turquette, 1952, *Many Valued Logics*, Introduction, Amsterdam.

Russell, B., 1956, *Portraits from Memory and Other Essays*, George Allen and Unwin.

———, 1948, *Human Knowledge: Its Scope and Limits*, London: George Allen and Unwin.

———, 1940, *Inquiry into Meaning and Truth*, W.W. Norton and Co.

———, 1927, *Analysis of Matter*, London: Kegan and Paul.

———, 1921, *Analysis of Mind*, London: George Allen and Unwin; New York: Macmillan.

———, 1914, *Our Knowledge of the External World*, Open Court Publishing.

Searle, J., 1986, *Minds, Brains and Science: 1984 Reith Lectures*, Harvard University Press.

Strawson, P.F., 1974, *Freedom and Resentment and Other Essays*, London: Metheun.

———, 1952, *Introduction to Logical Theory*, Metheun.

Trevor, Ling (ed.), 1981, *The Buddha's Philosophy of Man*, Everyman.

Vesey, G.N., 1964, *Body and Mind: Readings in Philosophy*, Allen and Unwin.

Vivekananda, Swami, 2003, *Commentary on Raja Yoga*, Advaita Ashrama Calcutta.

Wilde, Oscar, 1990, *The Importance of Being Earnest* (Play), London: Dover Edition.

Winch, Peter, 1969, *Studies in the Philosophy of Wittgenstein*, Routledge and Kegan Paul.

Wittgenstein, L., 1969, *On Certainty*, eds. G.E.M. Anscombe and G.H. von Wright, trs. G.E.M. Anscombe and D. Paul, Oxford: Blackwell.

———, 1967, *Zettel*, ed. G.E.M. Anscombe and G.H. von Wright, tr. G.E.M.

Anscombe, Oxford: Blackwell.

———, 1958, *The Blue and Brown Books*, Oxford: Basil and Blackwell.

———, 1953, *Philosophical Investigations*, ed. G.E.M. Anscombe and R. Rhees, tr. G.E.M. Anscombe, Oxford: Blackwell.

Woods, J.H., 1914, *The Yoga System of Patañjali*, Harvard Oriental Series.

A Selection of Papers Presented and Published by Prof. N.G. Kulkarni

2010-11, 'Potthapāda Sutta: A Conspectus and Analysis', published in *Buddhist Culture in Asia: Unity in Diversity,* vol. 1, Editor: Supriya Rai, Somaiya Publications, 2010-11. (Conference jointly organized by K.J. Somaiya Centre for Buddhist Studies, Department of Philosophy, University of Mumbai, Indian Nava Nalanda Mahavira, Nalanda, Bihar, India, and Jade Buddha Temple, Shanghai, China, held in January 2008.)

2006, 'The Buddha's Personality and Buddhist Culture', in *Contribution of Buddhism to World Culture,* edited by Mrs. Kalpakam Sankarnarayan, Ravindra Panth, Ichijo Ogawa, vol. 1, Somaiya Publications (Conference jointly organized by K.J. Somaiya Centre for Buddhist Studies, Department of Philosophy, University of Mumbai, Indian Nava Nalanda Mahavira, Nalanda, Bihar, India, and Otani University, Kyoto, Japan held during 11-14 March 2004.)

2004-05, 'The Return of Coherence', in *Philosophy and the Life World, Journal of Philosophy,* vol. 7, Vidyasagar University, Midnapore, West Bengal, India.

2004, 'Kant's Critique of Metaphysics', *Indian Philosophical Quarterly,* Special Number (200 Years of Kant), Vol. XXXI, Nos. 1-4, Journal of the Department of Philosophy, University of Pune.

2003, 'A Subtlety in the Buddhist Theory of the Self', in *Buddhism in Global Perspective,* edited by Mrs. Kalpakam Sankarnarayan, Ravindra Panth, Ichijo Ogawa, vol. 1, Somaiya Publications (Conference jointly organized by K.J. Somaiya Centre for Buddhist Studies, Indian Nava Nalanda Mahavira, Nalanda, Bihar, India, and Otani University, Kyoto, Japan held during 13-25 March 2002.)

2002, 'Dualism and Duality', *Jadavpur Journal of Philosophy,* vol. 14 nos. 1-2, pp. 5-24.

2002, 'Putnam's Proposal for Logical Reform', *Indian Philosophical Quarterly,* vol. XXIV, nos. 2-3.

2000, 'Are There Alternative Logics', in *Realism: Response and Reactions – Essays in Honour of P.K. Sen,* eds. Sandhya Basu and D.P. Chattopadhyaya, Madhabendra Nath Misra, Ranjan Mukhopadhyay, New Delhi: ICPR.

2000, 'Was the Buddha a Rationalist?', in *The Radical Humanist,* June, written on the occasion of Buddha Purnima.

1996, 'Descartes Philosophy of Mind: Its Contemporary Understanding', *Indian Philosophical Quarterly,* vol. XXIII, nos. 1-2.

1996, 'Māhasattipatthāna Sutta and Pātañjala Yoga', in *J. Krishnamurti and Early Buddhism,* Pune: Datta Lakshmi Trust.

1996, 'The Buddha's Approach to Metaphysics', in *Buddhism in India and Abroad,* Somaiya Publications.

1993, 'The Ideal of the Sthitaprajña: Some Platitudes and Some Paradoxes', in *The Concept of Sthitaprajña: A Stable-Minded Person,* Pune: Datta Lakshmi Trust.

1992, 'Early Buddhism', in *Buddhist and Jaina Views in Indian Philosophy,* Pune: Datta Lakshmi Trust.

1973, 'Are There Sense-Data? (II)', *Journal of the Philosophical Association,* vol. XIV, nos. 45-46.

1968, 'Strawson on Persons', *The Journal of the Indian Academy of Philosophy,* vol.VII, no. 2.

1957, 'Bradley's Anti Relational Argument', *The Philosophical Quarterly,* Edinburgh University Press, April.

Index